MILITARY AND VETERAN ISSUES

THE ENEMY WITHIN

PREVENTING SUICIDES BY VETERANS AND MEMBERS OF THE ARMED FORCES

MILITARY AND VETERAN ISSUES

Additional books in this series can be found on Nova's website under the Series tab.

Additional E-books in this series can be found on Nova's website under the E-book tab.

MILITARY AND VETERAN ISSUES

THE ENEMY WITHIN

PREVENTING SUICIDES BY VETERANS AND MEMBERS OF THE ARMED FORCES

JACK M. WRIGHT
AND
GABRIEL E. LEWIS
EDITORS

Nova Science Publishers, Inc.
New York

For permission to use material from this book please contact us:
Telephone 631-231-7269; Fax 631-231-8175
Web Site: http://www.novapublishers.com

Library of Congress Cataloging-in-Publication Data

ISBN 978-1-62081-316-4

Published by Nova Science Publishers, Inc. †New York

CONTENTS

PREFACE

More than 1.9 million warriors have deployed for Operation Iraq Freedom and Operation Enduring Freedom, two of our Nation's longest conflicts. The physical and psychological demands on both the deployed and non-deployed warriors are enormous. In the 5 years from 2005-2009, more than 1,100 members of the Armed Forces took their own lives, an average of 1 suicide every 36 hours. This book examines suicide prevention efforts of the Veterans Health Administration (VHA) with a focus on suicide surveillance; suicide risk and protective factors; and suicide prevention interventions.

Chapter 1 - As directed by Section 733 of the National Defense Authorization Act (NDAA) for fiscal year 2009, the Secretary of Defense established a Task Force "to examine matters relating to prevention of suicide by members of the Armed Forces."

The Department of Defense (DoD) Task Force on the Prevention of Suicide by Members of the Armed Forces (hereafter referred to as the Task Force) was created and comprised of seven DoD and seven non-DoD professionals with expertise in national suicide prevention policy, military personnel policy, research in the field of suicide prevention, clinical care in mental health, military chaplaincy and pastoral care, and military families.

The Task Force, established in August 2009, has prepared the following report for the Secretary of Defense, detailing the research, results, and recommendations from a year-long review of data, studies, programs, and discussions with Service Members, their families, and their caregivers.

The intent of this report is to provide the Secretary of Defense and DoD leadership with actionable and measurable recommendations for policy and programs designed to prevent suicide by members of the Armed Forces.

The Task Force used five main data sources in the creation of the report (a compilation of each is located in the appendices):

- Review of existing scientific literature
- Presentations from subject matter experts
- Public information (including participation from family members of suicide victims)
- Panel discussions (including suicide attempt survivors)
- Information gathered from eyes-on field visits to military installations.

The report explains the evolution of suicide prevention programs within each of the Services and at the enterprise level within DoD. Also included are a series of powerful personal vignettes of Service Members and their families who are living with the loss of a loved one to suicide.

The Task Force arrived at 49 findings and 76 associated recommendations which are discussed in Section 7 of the body of the full report. A complete list of the recommendations can also be found at the end of the Executive Summary.

The findings fall into four primary Focus Areas: Organization and Leadership; Wellness Enhancement and Training; Access to, and Delivery of, Quality Care; and Surveillance, Investigations, and Research.

The findings in each Focus Area drive a set of Strategic Initiatives, and for each Strategic Initiative, there are a set of targeted, actionable recommendations.

The Task Force also provided a set of Foundational Recommendations that aggregate several of the targeted recommendations, of which the Task Force believes are critical to a successful DoD strategy. The Foundational Recommendations are listed on page ES-9 and can be found in Section 7 of the full report.

Chapter 2 - Responsibility for prevention of veteran suicide lies primarily with the Veterans Health Administration (VHA), within the Department of Veterans Affairs (VA). The VHA Strategic Plan for Suicide Prevention is based on a public health framework, which has three major components: (1) surveillance, (2) risk and protective factors, and (3) prevention interventions.

No nationwide surveillance system exists for suicide among all veterans; therefore, the actual incidence of suicide among veterans is not known. Surveillance, or systematic collection of data on completed (i.e., fatal) suicides, is essential to define the scope of the problem (i.e., the suicide rate among veterans), identify characteristics associated with higher or lower risk of suicide, and track changes in the suicide rate over time to evaluate suicide prevention interventions. In the absence of a nationwide surveillance system for veteran suicide, the VHA is attempting to determine the rate of suicide among veterans in two ways, both in collaboration with the Centers for Disease Control and Prevention (CDC).

Information collected in surveillance is used to identify suicide risk factors (i.e., characteristics associated with higher rates of suicide) and protective factors (i.e., characteristics associated with lower rates of suicide). This is essential in order to design interventions that reduce risk factors and/or increase protective factors, thus lowering overall risk of suicide. Risk factors are also helpful in identifying at-risk groups or individuals so that interventions can be delivered to the people who need them most. Within the VHA, this research is supported by the Office of Research and Development; a Center of Excellence in suicide prevention; and a Mental Illness Research, Education, and Clinical Center on suicide prevention.

The intervention cycle includes three stages: design and test interventions, implement interventions, and evaluate interventions. The research components mentioned above have roles in small-scale pilot testing and large-scale evaluations of interventions. This report discusses seven areas of VHA suicide prevention interventions: (1) easy access to care, (2) education, (3) screening and treatment, (4) limited access to lethal means, (5) suicide hotline, (6) media restrictions, and (7) suicide prevention coordinators.

This report identifies challenges the VHA faces in each component of suicide prevention and discusses potential issues for Congress. A recurring theme is the need for the VHA to work in concert with other federal, state, and local government agencies; private for-profit and not-forprofit health care providers; veterans, their families, and their communities; and other individuals or organizations that might be able to help. Specific challenges in surveillance include timeliness of data, accurate identification of decedents as veterans, and consistent classification of deaths as suicides. Challenges in risk and protective factors research include a need for more collaboration and dialogue among agencies involved in suicide prevention and across other areas of public health (because suicide has some of the same risk and protective factors as other public health problems). Challenges in VHA suicide prevention interventions also include the need for more collaboration and dialogue, as well as an apparent gap between policy and practice, and misperceptions about mental illness and mental health care.

Chapter 3 – This is opening statement of Ann Marie Buerkle, Chairwoman House Committee on Veterans Affairs, Subcommittee on Health Hearing on: Understanding and Preventing Veteran Suicide.

Chapter 4 – Testimony of Commander René A. Campos, USN (Ret.), Deputy Director, Government Relations.

Chapter 5 – Testimony of Tom Tarantino, Senior Legislative Associate, Iraq and Afghanistan Veterans of America House Committee on Veterans Affairs.

Chapter 6 – Testimony of Joy J. Ilem, Deputy National Legislative Director, Disabled American Veterans.

Chapter 7 – Testimony of Margaret C. Harrell, Ph.D., Senior Fellow and Director, Joining Forces Initiative Center for a New American Security.

Chapter 8 – Testimony of Katherine E. Watkins, M.D., Senior Natural Scientist, The RAND Corporation.

Chapter 9 – Testimony of Jan E. Kemp, RN, Ph.D., National Mental Health Director for Suicide Prevention, Veterans Heath Administration, U.S. Department of Veterans Affairs.

In: The Enemy Within
Editors: Jack M. Wright and Gabriel E. Lewis

ISBN: 978-1-62081-316-4

Chapter 1

THE CHALLENGE AND THE PROMISE: STRENGTHENING THE FORCE, PREVENTING SUICIDE AND SAVING LIVES*

The Department of Defense

EXECUTIVE ABSTRACT

As directed by Section 733 of the National Defense Authorization Act (NDAA) for fiscal year 2009, the Secretary of Defense established a Task Force "to examine matters relating to prevention of suicide by members of the Armed Forces."

The Department of Defense (DoD) Task Force on the Prevention of Suicide by Members of the Armed Forces (hereafter referred to as the Task Force) was created and comprised of seven DoD and seven non-DoD professionals with expertise in national suicide prevention policy, military personnel policy, research in the field of suicide prevention, clinical care in mental health, military chaplaincy and pastoral care, and military families.

The Task Force, established in August 2009, has prepared the following report for the Secretary of Defense, detailing the research, results, and recommendations from a year-long review of data, studies, programs, and discussions with Service Members, their families, and their caregivers.

The intent of this report is to provide the Secretary of Defense and DoD leadership with actionable and measurable recommendations for policy and programs designed to prevent suicide by members of the Armed Forces.

The Task Force used five main data sources in the creation of the report (a compilation of each is located in the appendices):

- Review of existing scientific literature
- Presentations from subject matter experts
- Public information (including participation from family members of suicide victims)

* This is an edited, reformatted and augmented version of a Final Report of the Department of Defense Task Force on the Prevention of Suicide by Members of the Armed Forces publication, dated August 2010.

- Panel discussions (including suicide attempt survivors)
- Information gathered from eyes-on field visits to military installations.

The report explains the evolution of suicide prevention programs within each of the Services and at the enterprise level within DoD. Also included are a series of powerful personal vignettes of Service Members and their families who are living with the loss of a loved one to suicide.

The Task Force arrived at 49 findings and 76 associated recommendations which are discussed in Section 7 of the body of the full report. A complete list of the recommendations can also be found at the end of the Executive Summary.

The findings fall into four primary Focus Areas: Organization and Leadership; Wellness Enhancement and Training; Access to, and Delivery of, Quality Care; and Surveillance, Investigations, and Research.

The findings in each Focus Area drive a set of Strategic Initiatives, and for each Strategic Initiative, there are a set of targeted, actionable recommendations.

The Task Force also provided a set of Foundational Recommendations that aggregate several of the targeted recommendations, of which the Task Force believes are critical to a successful DoD strategy. The Foundational Recommendations are listed on page ES-9 and can be found in Section 7 of the full report.

EXECUTIVE SUMMARY

Background

Task Force Vision Statement

A military force fit in mind, body, and spirit that wins the battle against suicide and stands ready to answer the Nation's call.

Section 733 of the National Defense Authorization Act (NDAA) for fiscal year 2009 directed the Secretary of Defense to "establish within the Department of Defense a Task Force to examine matters relating to prevention of suicide by members of the Armed Forces" and "submit to the Secretary (of Defense) a report containing recommendations regarding a comprehensive policy designed to prevent suicide by members of the Armed Forces." Thus, the Department of Defense (DoD) Task Force on the Prevention of Suicide by Members of the Armed Forces (hereafter referred to as the Task Force) was established, comprising seven DoD and seven nonDoD professionals with expertise in national suicide prevention policy, military personnel policy, research in the field of suicide prevention, clinical care in mental health, military chaplaincy and pastoral care, and military families. Task Force members were appointed in July 2009, with one military and one civilian member serving as co-chairs for the group. Major General Philip Volpe, initially the Deputy Commander of Joint Task Force, National Capital Region Medical (JTF CapMed), and later the Commanding General of the Army's Western Regional Medical Command, was appointed as the military co-chair of the

Task Force. Ms. Bonnie Carroll, Director of the Tragedy Assistance Program for Survivors (TAPS), was elected as the civilian co-chair.

The first step in reaching this vision is the production of this report, a culmination of reviews of data, studies, and programs; discussions with Service Members, families, and care providers; and analyses of site visits information, research, and expert opinion. In this report, the Task Force members have presented their findings and best consensus recommendations for effective suicide prevention for Service Members within the DoD. We are confident that the recommendations will make a difference by strengthening the force through total fitness, thereby helping to prevent suicide. Action must follow this report, and the recommendations must be implemented with a sense of urgency if we are to address the worrisome trend of increasing suicide by members of the Armed Forces. This report is a call for more effective action.

Introduction

More than 1.9 million warriors have deployed for Operation Iraqi Freedom (OIF) and Operation Enduring Freedom (OEF), two of our Nation's longest conflicts (IOM, 2010). The physical and psychological demands on both the deployed and non-deployed warriors are enormous. In the 5 years from 2005 to 2009, more than 1,100 members of the Armed Forces took their own lives, an average of 1 suicide every 36 hours. In that same period, the suicide rates among Marines and Soldiers sharply increased; the rate in the Army more than doubled. Numerous commissions, task forces, and research reports have documented the "hidden wounds of war"—the psychological and emotional injuries that have so affected our military members and their families. The years since 2002 have placed unprecedented demands on our Armed Forces and military families. Military operational requirements have risen significantly, and manning levels across the Services remain too low to meet the ever-increasing demand. This current imbalance places strain not only on those deploying, but equally on those who remain in garrison. In the judgment of the Task Force, the cumulative effects of all these factors are contributing significantly to the increase in the incidence of suicide and without effective action will persist well beyond the duration of the current operations and deployments. Heightened concern regarding this increase in suicides has led to development of scores of initiatives across the DoD to reduce risk.

The Task Force acknowledges the significant efforts made by the military Services. The Services have substantially increased their focus and investments in suicide prevention over the years to meet current requirements. This is evident at the highest levels of leadership in the military Departments. This Task Force has witnessed commitment, creativity, and compassion by uniformed and civilian employees across the Services in attempting to address this looming crisis. While lauding the level of this extraordinary effort, the Task Force concluded that the urgency to respond to the challenge of suicide may have driven the Services to deploy many of these initiatives without the benefit of strategic planning, evaluation, standardization, or plans for sustainment. The Task Force also found other unintended consequences of this rush to deploy critical programs. For instance, the Task Force discovered wide variations in the implementation of many initiatives, many programs that overlapped, creating unnecessary inefficiencies, and prevention opportunities that were missed because of gaps between programs. Furthermore, many programs were misunderstood by Service Members, their families, and commanders in the field. Finally, the Task Force concluded that the remarkable efforts of the Services seemed to lack the consistency and power that could have been achieved had the policies directing the programs been centrally developed by the Office of the Secretary of Defense (OSD). The Task Force concluded that current Service efforts would benefit from a comprehensive suicide prevention strategy, coordinated throughout DoD. This strategy should include additional leader accountability to foster a command climate promoting Service Member well-being and fitness. Command climates must continue to evolve to ensure the positive and engaged support of every Service Member in distress and view this support as a vital part of mission readiness and mission success.

Throughout history, the United States military has often led the Nation in addressing emerging concerns. Specifically, the Defense Advanced Research Projects Agency's (DARPA) BioRevolution programs develop and leverage advances in all areas of biological and medical sciences to improve DoD capabilities (Beard, 2008). In the past 15 years, in a similar fashion, the military Services have taken a leading role in the Nation's suicide prevention efforts and more recently have coordinated with other federal agencies to advance this work.

Suicide prevention presents a significant challenge to the country at large. Unfortunately, those who could provide the most help in understanding why people die by suicide are those who have taken their own lives and are no longer with us. However, those who have made near-lethal suicide attempts can provide important insights as well. They describe myriad factors that contributed to their inability to find another strategy to cope with their seemingly hopeless situation. After decades of research, there is still much that is not understood about the causes of suicide and effective approaches to prevent it. What we do know is that there is no single common cause, but rather dozens of known factors that increase one's risk for suicide. These risk factors interact in complex ways with other factors that are protective against suicidal behaviors. Therefore, solutions to the suicide problem must be, by definition, multifaceted and designed to reduce risk and increase protective factors. These solutions should be directed toward achieving the Task Force's vision of enhancing wellness, promoting total fitness, and sustaining a military force fit in mind, body and spirit. There must be a renewed focus at the troop level and a sense of urgency at all levels, especially in strategic planning, to interrupt the trend and save lives by preventing suicide.

Findings and Recommended Strategic Initiatives

The Task Force commends the Armed Forces for the suicide prevention initiatives it has undertaken and knows of no other employer that has focused as much attention and resources on suicide prevention. However, the Task Force found that the current vast expansion of suicide prevention initiatives across the Services was developed rapidly and separately by each Service for immediate execution. These initiatives could benefit from reengineering to improve suicide prevention efforts. The rapid establishment of these initiatives resulted in a lack of the cohesion and coordination that normally would have come through a focused strategic planning process. Furthermore, the Department's organization and structure for suicide prevention is not optimized. It lacks a designated policy office in OSD, essential for policy standardization and centralized surveillance. The Task Force also found that multiple deployments and long deployments have taken a toll on the force and its families, eroding the well-being (fitness) and resilience of the force. This assessment is based on a review of each Service's suicide prevention programs as well as Service and DoD policies, research data, additional data sought specifically by the Task Force, public testimony from experts and advocates, and site visits to 19 military installations throughout the continental United States. The Task Force heard from well over 2,000 individuals. Service Members (junior enlisted, non-commissioned officers [NCO], and officers), family members, commanders, behavioral health professionals, clergy, and military community support services personnel were given the opportunity to provide their input.

The Task Force arrived at 49 findings and 76 targeted recommendations which are discussed in Section 7 of the body of this report. A list of these recommendations can also be found at the end of the Executive Summary. The findings fall into four primary Focus Areas: Organization and Leadership; Wellness Enhancement and Training; Access to, and Delivery of, Quality Care; and Surveillance, Investigations, and Research.

The findings in each Focus Area drive a set of Strategic Initiatives, and for each Strategic Initiative, there are a set of actionable recommendations. We have also provided a set of Foundational Recommendations that generally aggregate several of the more targeted recommendations and which are critical to the success of the broader set of recommendations.

Focus Area 1: Organization and Leadership

Overview: The Task Force believes that suicide prevention begins with a comprehensive strategy that has the support of leaders at every level. The strategy will assist the office of the Undersecretary of Defense for Personal and Readiness (USD(P&R)) develop a coherent policy. Effective organizational structure is essential to develop enterprise-wide policy as well as procedural standardization and oversight. To enhance suicide prevention efforts, and maintain a lasting impact, DoD must organize appropriately, in conjunction with the Services. Suicide prevention is a leadership responsibility from the most senior leaders down to front-line supervisors (first-line leaders). Distressed Service Members must be led to the best available "helping agent" through a positive and supportive command climate. A culture of total fitness, should allow early identification and intervention opportunities before a member becomes suicidal. This focus area addresses the need for a functional organization with an engaged and informed leadership to ensure unity and clarity of effort in preventing suicide within the Services.

Summary of Findings: Although the Services are adapting to changing suicide prevention demands, the absence of an adequately staffed and resourced OSD policy office on suicide prevention leads to significant challenges to unity of effort. Similarly, the Service suicide prevention program offices are not sufficiently staffed and resourced to meet the demand. The Services provide numerous morale, quality of life, counseling, intervention, health and community services on installations and within units. Despite their availability, community support services, medical treatment facilities and unit leadership are often "stovepiped" on installations, leading to poorly integrated approaches for effective suicide prevention, particularly for those Service Members at high risk. Command climate surveys, which are utilized by commanders (although inconsistently) are not well designed to assess behavioral health risk in the unit. In general, commanders are not provided the tools they need to: detect, measure, and track unit-level suicide risk factors; identify individuals who are high risk; and inform local prevention activities. Military cultural norms, while beneficial for survival and mission accomplishment on a battlefield, can sometimes stifle responsible help-seeking behavior; the effect is a less fit force more vulnerable to suicide. Messages from some leaders regarding suicide, suicide prevention, resilience, health and Warrior readiness frequently do not sufficiently support suicide prevention efforts: Strategic communications are often not focused on positive prevention messages and thus there are missed opportunities to encourage help seeking and overcome stigma. The Task Force also found that occasionally leadership environments (usually at the junior supervisory and sometimes at the mid-grade level) resulted in discriminatory and humiliating treatment of Service Members who responsibly sought professional services for emotional, psychological, moral, ethical, or spiritual matters, which not only deters help seeking but also reinforces the stigma.

Detailed findings and discussion can be found in Section 7 of the report beginning on page 45.

Strategic Initiatives

A. Create, restructure, and resource suicide prevention offices at OSD, the Services, installations, and unit level to achieve unity of effort.
B. Equip and empower leaders (provide them tools) to establish a culture that fosters prevention as well as early recognition and intervention.
C. Develop strategic communications that promote life, normalize "help-seeking behaviors," and support DoD suicide prevention strategies.
D. Reduce stigma and overcome military cultural and leadership barriers to seeking help.
E. Standardize suicide prevention policies and procedures.

These Strategic Initiatives drive 25 targeted recommendations that can be found in Section 7 of the full report and are listed at the end of this Executive Summary.

Focus Area 2: Wellness Enhancement and Training

Overview: Military life, particularly in wartime, is inherently stressful on individuals and presents a unique challenge to maintaining wellness. Efforts to enhance well-being, mental fitness, resiliency, and the development of life skills in Service Members will have significant impact on preventing suicide. These efforts must include all areas of fitness: physical, psychological, family, social, spiritual, financial, vocational, and emotional. DoD and the Services must continue to expend substantial effort to mitigate stressors by supporting programs that strengthen protective factors in these domains. Stress on the force *must* be reduced. In addition, skills-based training is imperative to preventing suicide. When individuals exhibit signs of distress, peers, leaders, and family members must be able to recognize the danger and respond with appropriate support, including referral to intervention services. This focus area addresses the need to meet the issue of overall well-being and resiliency, not just by reducing stress, but also by providing the programs and training necessary to maintain and enhance both mental and physical health of Service Members and their families.

Summary of Findings: Heightened operational tempo, repeated deployments and insufficient quantity and quality of dwell time have had a cumulative fatiguing effect on Service Members, and a degradation of the overall fitness and readiness of the force. Service Members have been incredibly resilient and have met the challenges of functioning at maximum throttle year after year, but they need more than an occasional pit stop; they need an "off season" period to recover, restore and renew their well-being. Furthermore, suicide prevention training programs throughout the force have had less than optimal effectiveness because they lack a strategic approach and do not provide enough skills-based training. The Task Force found evidence that the Services have recently strengthened their emphasis on prevention and early intervention through such efforts as resiliency training, comprehensive fitness and operational stress control, but there is still insufficient time devoted to enhancing critical life skills as well as comprehensive fitness. In addition, family members generally do not receive adequate education and training in suicide prevention and they, above all, are the best "detectors" of subtle behavioral changes associated with suicidal risk. When training *is* offered to family members and friends, many obstacles prevent wider attendance. There is positive acceptance by Service Members of embedding behavioral health providers in operational units, which needs to be further exploited.

Detailed findings and discussion can be found in Section 7 of the report beginning on page 45.

Strategic Initiatives

A. Enhance well-being, mental fitness, life skills, and resiliency.
B. Reduce stress on the force and on military families.
C. Transform suicide prevention training of Service Members, leaders, and families to enhance skills.

These Strategic Initiatives drive 10 targeted recommendations that can be found in Section 7 of the full report and are listed at the end of this Executive Summary.

Focus Area 3: Access to, and Delivery of, Quality Care

Overview: An effective, multifaceted suicide prevention program must provide access to high-quality professional services across the entire health and wellness continuum. These services include assessment, diagnosis, counseling, and treatment. Services must be synchronized, and where appropriate, standardized. Because of the complex dynamics of suicidal individuals' behavior, strong lines of communication between service providers are essential and will be aided by quality electronic medical records and by electronic communications. A strongly linked chain of care depends on engaged leaders as well as highly competent first responders, crisis hotline workers, and emergency department personnel, as well as chaplains, primary care clinicians and behavioral health clinicians. Skill-based training programs that build essential competencies must be tailored for the various professional groups. A degree alone does not imply proper training to prevent suicide or to properly address suicidal behaviors. Continuity of care, particularly at times of transition, is absolutely critical. This focus area addresses the need to provide care that is both accessible and of high quality to Service Members and their dependents.

Summary of Findings: Although there has been some expansion in the number of behavioral health providers in all of the Services, timely access to quality behavioral healthcare for Service Members continues to be a challenge. Much of the challenge can be attributed to the fact that DoD medical treatment facilities suffer from the same wholesale shortage of behavioral health care providers as found across America in the civilian sector. In addition, despite the expansion of non-clinical support services, adequate coordination is inconsistent among both the support services and among the providers. Furthermore, Service Members in the Reserve Components face additional challenges when they lose easy access to myriad installation-based support and healthcare services because the Service Members are generally not physically collocated with military installations. Service Members and their families are often unaware of the available resources for suicide-related problems. There is insufficient communication among clinical providers, support services personnel, and commanders, which impedes the delivery of effective care, continuity, and management of transitions. The Health Insurance Portability and Accountability Act (HIPAA) is often misunderstood and over-interpreted, thus creating additional, self-induced obstacles to sharing information that may prevent suicide, especially for at-risk Service Members. In addition, the current DoD electronic medical documentation platforms do not allow easy and systematic tracking of the care provided to high-risk suicidal Service Members. "Suicide watch" is ungoverned, not standardized, and largely ineffective, and those conducting suicide watch are not trained. Furthermore, there is insufficient training of behavioral health, primary care and emergency medical personnel, as well as chaplains, on evidence-based assessment, management, and treatment services for Service Members with suicide-related behaviors. Due to the variety of numerous hotline services for crisis intervention, there is confusion as to which to utilize in what circumstances. Additionally, the quality of many hotline services is suspect because there does not appear to be universal standards, oversight and accountability. Integration of behavioral health services into primary care settings, which could potentially produce benefits in overcoming stigma and providing necessary services, is underutilized. Across DoD, after a tragedy or significant personal loss, postvention is underutilized to assist family members, fellow Service Members and unit leaders through the aftermath of emotions and psychological impact, thus missing a key opportunity to intervene early, to teach life skills and build resiliency, and to prevent potential suicidal behaviors as well as other destructive behaviors. Additionally, family members noted that they became highly distressed when suicide investigations were conducted by officers with little or no family liaison training.

Detailed findings and discussion can be found in Section 7 of the report beginning on page 45.

Strategic Initiatives

A. Ensure available and reliable access to high-quality behavioral healthcare.
B. Leverage and coordinate military community-based services, as well as local civilian community services (especially with respect to the Reserve Component).

C. Ensure continuity of behavioral healthcare, especially during times of transition, to ensure seamlessness of healthcare delivery and care management.
D. Standardize effective crisis intervention services and hotlines.
E. Ensure all "helping professionals" are trained in the competencies to deliver evidence-based care for the assessment, management, and treatment of suicidal behaviors.
F. Develop effective postvention programs to support families, Service Members, and unit leaders after a suicide.

These Strategic Initiatives drive 31 targeted recommendations that can be found in Section 7 of the full report and are listed at the end of this Executive Summary.

Focus Area 4: Surveillance, Investigations, and Research

Overview: The Task Force strongly believes that well-constructed surveillance is necessary to inform and shape future suicide prevention programs. For surveillance to be effective, it must be standardized, centrally driven, and reported from the Service-level to DoD in a timely, consistent, and reliable manner. Surveillance should be continuous and sustained.

Investigations into individual suicides and suicidal behaviors in a standardized manner will significantly contribute to knowledge and understanding of causal factors and trends. Program evaluation is sorely needed for every initiative and program implemented by the Services to determine the effectiveness of that program in improving outcomes.. Research must continue to advance the science of suicidology to learn more about suicide and effective prevention techniques.

Summary of Findings: DoD does not have an effective standardized approach to suicide surveillance with the current configuration of the Department of Defense Suicide Event Report (DoDSER), and it is suboptimized for informing the improvement of Service suicide prevention programs. The inability of the DoDSER to access the current Defense Medical Surveillance System (DMSS) further degrades its potential as a real-time, effective, surveillance tool. Moreover, the investigation of both suicide attempts and completed suicides is not standardized, hindering the ability to modify surveillance tools (i.e., DoDSER). Furthermore, investigations are usually completed to either determine the cause of death (in difficult cases) or to determine if criminal activity was involved in the death: Investigations are generally not done to improve suicide prevention programs or prevent future suicides. Program evaluation is not uniformly incorporated, thus the effectiveness of many programs cannot be determined.

Because a gold standard has not been established for evaluation, the Task Force was unable to "grade" Service suicide programs. In addition, given currently available data, the Task Force could not establish an association between suicide risk and specific military role or occupation. Finally, because of a historical lack of research investment in suicidology, there is a gap in knowledge, specifically evidence-based knowledge, with respect to suicidal behaviors and suicide prevention practices.

Detailed findings and discussion can be found in Section 7 of the report beginning on page 45.

Strategic Initiatives

A. Conduct comprehensive surveillance aimed at identifying individuals at-risk and informing prevention efforts.
B. Standardize investigations of suicides and suicide attempts to identify target areas for improving prevention policies, procedures, and programs.
C. Ensure all initiatives and programs have a program evaluation component.
D. Support and incorporate ongoing research to inform evidence-based suicide prevention practices.

These Strategic Initiatives drive 10 targeted recommendations that can be found in Section 7 of the full report and are listed at the end of this Executive Summary.

Foundational Recommendations

These Foundational Recommendations are derived from the 76 targeted recommendations developed by the Task Force. They are considered critically important to the success of developing a comprehensive DoD suicide prevention model.

1. Create a "Suicide Prevention Policy Division" at OSD within USD(P&R) to standardize policies and procedures with respect to resiliency, mental fitness, life skills, and suicide prevention. The office will provide standardization, integration of best practices, and general oversight, serve as a change agent, and establish an ongoing external review group of non-DoD experts to assess progress. Furthermore, this office will provide guidance from which the Services can design and implement their suicide prevention programs.
2. Keep suicide prevention programs in the leadership lane and hold leaders accountable at all levels for ensuring a positive command climate that promotes the well-being, total fitness, and "help seeking" of their Service Members. A significant focus on developing better tools to assist commanders in suicide prevention must be undertaken.
3. Reduce stress on the force. The pace of operations in today's military exceeds the ability of Service Members to be restored to their optimal state of readiness. There is a supply and demand mismatch that creates a cumulative negative impact on the force. Reduce stress by ensuring the quantity and quality of dwell time allows for individual restoration as the force is reconstituted over and over again. This will allow Service Members to reestablish relationships and connectedness. If necessary, either grow the size of the force to ensure additional uniformed end-strength to meet the demand or reduce the mission demand.
4. Focus efforts on Service Member well-being, total fitness (of the mind, body, and spirit), and development of life skills and resiliency to increase protective factors and decrease risk factors. This is the pinnacle of primary prevention.
5. Develop a Comprehensive Stigma Reduction Campaign Plan that attacks the issue on multiple fronts to encourage help-seeking behavior and normalizes the care of the "hidden wounds" incurred by Service Members.

6. Strengthen strategic messaging to enhance positive communications that generate the behaviors and outcomes desired rather than highlighting the negative messaging about today's challenges. The focus of messaging must migrate from speaking solely about the "tragedy" of suicide and the "actions" being taken to messages that reduce stigma, encourage help-seeking, portray concerned leadership, and inspire hope by showing that help really works.
7. Develop skills-based training in all aspects of training regarding suicide prevention. The current awareness and education efforts about suicide prevention are adequate, but skills-based training is deficient, especially among buddies, family members, first-line supervisors, clergy, and behavioral health personnel.
8. Incorporate program evaluation in all suicide prevention programs to determine the effectiveness of each program in obtaining its intended outcome.
9. Coordinate and leverage the strengths of installation and local community support services for both Active and Reserve Component Service Members. Community health and access to quality, competent services are essential to suicide prevention.
10. Ensure continuity and the management of quality behavioral healthcare, especially while in transition periods, to facilitate a seamless transfer of awareness, management, and treatment as Service Members change locations. Transitions need to be actively managed and tools must be developed to actively manage them.
11. Mature and expand the DoDSER to serve as the main surveillance method to inform future suicide prevention efforts. Further standardize data collection processes. Robust surveillance will produce data that allow us to anticipate and avoid future occurrences of that event before the individual or population (or unit) reaches a crisis point.
12. Standardize suicide investigations and expand their focus to learn about the last hours, days, and weeks preceding a suicide or attempted suicide. Pattern suicide investigations on aviation accident safety investigation procedures and use the safety investigation process as a model to develop a standardized suicide investigation process.
13. Support and fund ongoing DoD suicide prevention research to enhance knowledge and inform future suicide prevention efforts, and to incorporate evidenced-based solutions. Focused research in suicide prevention for Service Members is essential to identifying best practices, decreasing variation in prevention practices, and in achieving desired outcomes.

Concluding Remarks

Considerable effort has been expended by DoD, the Services, and innumerable caring and dedicated individuals across the world in support of Service Members and their families. The findings and recommendations herein are intended to guide DoD in its efforts to enhance the work already being done while ensuring a more fit and ready force for meeting the demands of serving in the military.

It is our belief that implementation of the Task Force recommendations and strategic initiatives will save lives and will further propel DoD as a national leader in suicide prevention.

ALL RECOMMENDATIONS LISTED BY FOCUS AREA AND STRATEGIC INITIATIVE

RECOMMENDATIONS Focus Area 1: Organization and Leadership (25 Recommendations)	
Strategic Initiative 1A:	*Create, restructure, and resource suicide prevention offices at OSD, the Services, installations, and unit level to achieve unity of effort (Section 7.1.1).*
Recommendation 1	Build, staff and resource a central OSD Suicide Prevention Office that can effectively develop, implement, integrate, and evaluate suicide prevention policies, procedures, and surveillance activities. This office should reside within the Office of the Under Secretary of Defense for Personnel and Readiness and be granted the coordinating authority that enables strategic suicide prevention oversight from OSD, through the Services, and down to the unit level.
Recommendation 2	Prioritize resources to adequately staff, fund, and organize the headquarters-level suicide prevention offices, within each Service, to successfully meet all current requirements.
Recommendation 3	Services should require full-time civilian suicide prevention coordinators at all installations identified by major commands. Major commands must facilitate the consistent implementation of Service suicide prevention strategy down to the small unit level and installations must ensure appropriate resourcing of this position in order to fully support both DoD suicide prevention policy, and Service policy and programs.
Recommendation 4	Sufficiently resource suicide prevention coalitions that strategically integrate installation and major command suicide prevention efforts and informs the Service-level program office. This coalition should also function to coordinate support services through collaboration on overarching social/behavioral risk problems on the installation.
Recommendation 5	Require full-time suicide prevention program coordinators at each MTF (or regionalized when covering several non-hospital MTFs) to facilitate the standardized implementation of Service suicide prevention strategy on behalf of the MTF commander and ensure the adherence to standardized policies and practices.
Recommendation 6	Direct unit-level suicide prevention program officers to facilitate the implementation of Service policies.
Strategic Initiative 1B:	*Equip and empower leaders (provide them tools) to establish a culture that fosters prevention as well as early recognition and*
Recommendation 7	Strengthen and reinvigorate the fundamentals of military garrison leadership at the unit level with a focus on supervisor-subordinate interactions and mentoring. Ensure that front-line supervisor training is mandatory, occurs prior to assuming a supervisory role, and includes critical skills building in interpersonal relationships.

Recommendation 8	Ensure that professional military education, ranging from basic training to Senior Service Schools, develops leaders with the interpersonal and leadership skills required to fulfill their leadership and mentoring responsibilities, as well as promotes the well-being and total fitness of the Service Members under their charge.
Recommendation 9	Maintain a sufficiently small front-line supervisor-to-subordinate ratio to ensure the person-centered leadership functions can occur.
Recommendation 10	Add validated behavioral risk questions to unit climate surveys to help commanders detect relative elevations in behavioral risk across their military units and respond with appropriate preventive measures. Mandate the use of unit climate and risk surveys annually and upon accepting and relinquishing command.
Recommendation 11	Develop monthly risk reports from a multitude of sources and services to create a snapshot of the unit and the ability to compare a commander's unit with like units across the Service and at the installation, while also allowing for the identification of positive and negative trends with reference to risk behaviors by members in that unit.
Recommendation 12	Disseminate and enforce "zero tolerance" policies that prohibit prejudice, discrimination, and public humiliation towards individuals who are responsibly addressing emotional, psychological, relational, spiritual, and behavioral issues; as well as towards those seeking help to increase their psychological fitness and operational readiness. Support these policies by holding leaders and supervisors accountable and by sustained communications campaigns.
Strategic Initiative 1C:	*Develop strategic communications that promote life, normalize "help-seeking behaviors," and support DoD suicide prevention strategies (Section 7.1.3).*
Recommendation 13	Develop and implement sustainable training programs for PAOs serving Service leaders, senior leaders, and installation commanders in crafting health-promoting messages that support the goals and objectives of the Services' suicide prevention and health promotion programs; avoid counterproductive or dangerous messages whenever making statements or discussing suicide-related information or statistics.
Recommendation 14	Instruct PAOs to disseminate nationally recognized recommendations for reporting on suicide as they interact with news media on the subject of suicide.
Recommendation 15	Develop and disseminate communication guidelines to commanders for use in the wake of a local suicide event.
Strategic Initiative 1D:	*Reduce stigma and overcome military cultural and leadership barriers to seeking help (Section 7.1.4).*
Recommendation 16	Develop an aggressive Stigma Reduction Campaign Plan, communications effort, and implement policies to root out stigma and discrimination. Follow scientifically based health communications principles in these campaigns.

Table (continued)

Recommendation 17	Promote values that encourage seeking the assistance of chaplains, healthcare, and behavioral healthcare professionals to enhance spiritual, physical, and psychological fitness.
Recommendation 18	Develop and implement campaigns to inculcate values and norms aligned with promoting the well-being, connectedness, and psychological and spiritual fitness of Service Members. Use well-planned, multi-year communications campaigns at the DoD and Service levels, employing the best of health communications science as part of that effort.
Recommendation 19	Target a specific component of the communications campaign to ensure that Service Members who hold security clearances and the mental health providers who see them are aware of policies that exclude reporting certain instances of mental health care on the SF-86.
Recommendation 20	Adjust manning levels, especially in elite units and certain military occupational specialties, to support developing and maintaining comprehensive fitness by all members.
Recommendation 21	Infuse curricula for all levels of military specialty training with expectations that even the most effective Service Members will occasionally experience difficulties that require temporary interruptions in their qualifications for full duty. Teach that the responsibility of others in the unit is to support them during those times.
Recommendation 22	Discourage and refrain from use of the term "malingering" in association with suicide-related behaviors. Ensure DoD and Service suicide prevention policies and guidelines eliminate using the word "malingering".
Strategic Initiative 1E:	Standardize Suicide Prevention Policies and Procedures (Section 7.1.5).
Recommendation 23	Implement DoD and Service guidance for commanders and military recruit instructors that addresses the management of suicide-related behaviors during basic training.
Recommendation 24	Develop and implement a DoD-wide policy requiring immediate command notification and chain of care (or chain of custody) for individuals who become aware they are being investigated for a criminal or other serious offense, immediately after they confess to a crime, and/or soon after they are arrested and taken into custody.
Recommendation 25	Establish clear DoD, Joint and Service guidance for removal and subsequent re-issue of military weapon and ammunition for Service Members recognized to be at risk for suicide. The guidance should emphasize a collaborative, team approach to the decision-making process and specify documentation requirements.
Focus Area 2: Wellness Enhancement and Training (10 Recommendations)	
Strategic Initiative 2A:	*Enhance well-being, mental fitness, life skills, and resiliency (Section 7.2.1).*

Recommendation 26	Improve access to, and promote utilization of, state-of-the-art training in critical life skills (e.g., financial management, communication, marriage and family relationships, anger management, and conflict resolution).
Recommendation 27	Expand the practice of embedding behavioral health providers in operational units. Conduct studies to determine the range of effective staffing ratios for embedded providers.
Strategic Initiative 2B:	*Reduce stress on the force and on military families (Section 7.2.2).*
Recommendation 28	Balance uniformed end-strength with operational requirements by either increasing military end-strength or decreasing operational commitments.
Recommendation 29	Provide sufficient, high-quality dwell time for redeploying Service Members in keeping with the most current military health research. Initial post-deployment dwell time should ensure an initial period (of at least several months) in which Service Members can restore their well-being, and should not include extended temporary duty (TDY) or extended "gear-up" training for the next deployment.
Recommendation 30	Reduce operations tempo and day-to-day work requirements on individuals and units to sustainable levels that support the wellness of Service Members and their families. Create white space in training schedules, especially in post-deployment periods.
Recommendation 31	Review in-garrison military training requirements with the goal of eliminating and/or combining training, thereby reducing the time burden on units and Service Members.
Strategic Initiative 2C:	Transform suicide prevention training of Service Members, leaders, and families to enhance skills (Section 7.2.3).
Recommendation 32	Develop DoD and Service-level comprehensive suicide prevention training strategies. Develop and disseminate state-of-the-art training curricula addressing the specific knowledge, skills, and attitudes required of each sub-population in the military community. Incorporate industry-standard evaluation practices throughout the development and dissemination phases. Focus efforts on skills-based training.
Recommendation 33	Target and train families (including parents, siblings, significant others, and next of kin) as a suicide prevention training strategy, and consider it an important part of the chain of care for Service Members. Family members should be educated and trained to recognize the signs of stress and distress, to know whom to call for advice, and to understand how to respond in emergencies.
Recommendation 34	Develop strategies to locate and remain in contact with families during every phase of the deployment cycle. Develop and disseminate pre-deployment and reintegration education and training programs germane to suicide prevention for family members.
Recommendation 35	Proactively seek opportunities to collaborate with other federal agencies in their efforts to support military families.

Table (continued)

Focus Area 3: Access to, and Delivery of, Quality Care (31 Recommendations)	
Strategic Initiative A:	*Ensure available and reliable access to high-quality behavioral healthcare (Section 7.3.1).*
Recommendation 36	Implement policies that optimize access to care for all Service Members which are specifically designed for behavioral health care, and monitor access standards closely for compliance.
Recommendation 37	Train all caregivers in the governing rules applicable to appropriate and necessary information sharing among providers, outside agencies, and with Service Members' commands.
Recommendation 38	Develop interdisciplinary treatment plans for Service Members at risk for suicidal behavior.
Recommendation 39	Implement coordination of care plans across longitudinal lines (e.g., permanent change of station, temporary change of station, deployment and redeployment transitions, temporary duty with other units, release from active duty, demobilization, confinement, hospitalization, and extended leave periods).
Recommendation 40	Establish multidisciplinary case management teams to ensure the highest quality of coordinated care by the team of commander, clinical provider, and non-clinical care provider.
Strategic Initiative 3B:	*Leverage and coordinate military community-based services, as well as local civilian community services (especially with respect to the Reserve Component) (Section 7.3.2).*
Recommendation 41	Optimize and coordinate community-based services to leverage their capabilities to enhance protective factors for Service Members.
Recommendation 42	Promote and utilize coordinated community outreach and awareness activities provided by clinicians and other installation-based care providers to improve access to care and reduce stigma.
Recommendation 43	Encourage Service Members to have annual face-to-face "conferences" with chaplains for the purpose of resolving questions of guilt and to obtain referrals to appropriate caregivers for other concerns beyond the chaplain's scope of expertise and experience.
Recommendation 44	Develop a comprehensive policy to promote systematic and regular communication among clinical and non-clinical providers.
Strategic Initiative 3C:	Ensure continuity of behavioral healthcare, especially during times of transition, to ensure seamlessness of healthcare delivery and care management (Section 7.3.3).
Recommendation 45	Manage care across transition points and monitor Service Members identified as being at risk for suicide.
Recommendation 46	Assess Military OneSource capabilities to ensure a seamless transition of care system is established for suicidal or at-risk Service Members who utilize their services. This transitional care system needs to take into account challenges involving medical documentation, timeline of transition, and maximizing Service Member compliance with the transition plan.

Recommendation 47	Develop, evaluate, and more widely disseminate peer-to-peer and other programs that intentionally promote not only connectedness but also risk identification and response among Reserve Component Service Members.
Recommendation 48	Promote easy access to evidence-based treatments and community support services for post-deployment Reserve Component Service Members.
Recommendation 49	Ensure all Reserve Component Service Members receive face-to-face behavioral health checks post-deployment/post-demobilization and before being remobilized, with an emphasis on connecting them with professional services during the post-deployment phase.
Recommendation 50	Provide guidance on how behavioral health providers and commanders should best communicate with each other to promote effective suicide prevention practices for Service Members.
Recommendation 51	Establish and use interdisciplinary "human factors" type boards (emphasizing topics like physical, social, behavioral, psychological, nutritional, environmental, spiritual, and medical health) on all installations to coordinate suicide prevention care for at-risk Service Members.
Recommendation 52	Take steps to make "mental fitness" commensurate with "physical fitness" within military culture as a core value of military life. Ensure every Service Member receives a mental fitness assessment and appropriate wellness education as part of his or her periodic heath assessment.
Recommendation 53	Integrate behavioral health treatment teams into DoD primary care settings to overcome stigma and increase the likelihood of access to care; as well as to establish an early intervention approach to suicide prevention. Where this is not possible, train primary care providers and their staff in the assessment and management (and triage) of acute suicide risk patients.
Recommendation 54	Develop a standard and systematic medical documentation system to identify high-risk patients and track the care provided. Continually review and update the record (documentation).
Recommendation 55	Suicide watch should be used only as a last resort and only until appropriate mental healthcare becomes available. Provide consistent guidance to units for these exceptional instances, as well as "just in time" training (e.g., online training). If units have a suicide prevention coordinator, the management of these rare instances could fall to that individual's responsibility. A suicide watch training program should be developed and similarly instituted.
Strategic Initiative 3D:	Standardize effective crisis intervention services and hotlines (Section 7.3.4).
Recommendation 56	Provide clear direction and consistent messaging regarding the promotion and usage of the National Suicide Prevention Lifeline 1-800-273-TALK (8255) as a national suicide prevention hotline resource available to all Service Members and their families, as well as the use of local crisis hotlines (or information lines) focusing on specific populations.

Table (continued)

Recommendation 57	Formalize existing interconnectedness of the DCoE Outreach Call Center, National Suicide Prevention Lifeline, and Military OneSource to enable each agency to quickly and effectively route calls to appropriate responders. Ensure ongoing quality review and quality improvement efforts focused on emergency rescue situations, follow-up referrals for callers at-risk, and linkages with community providers of crisis services (e.g., mobile outreach teams).
Recommendation 58	Optimize the availability of suicide hotline services to deployed Service Members using the same National Suicide Prevention Lifeline number to ensure best response capabilities.
Strategic Initiative 3E:	Ensure all "helping professionals" are trained in the competencies to deliver evidence-based care for the assessment, management, and treatment of suicide-related behaviors (Section 7.3.5).
Recommendation 59	Develop clinical practice guidelines to promote the utilization of evidence-based practices for the assessment, management, and treatment of suicide-related behaviors.
Recommendation 60	Dedicate sufficient mental health resources to military health facilities to allow for timely mental health assessment and treatment.
Recommendation 61	Train all military healthcare providers (including behavioral health providers) and chaplains on evidence-informed suicide risk assessment, management, and treatment planning. Create and provide continuing education tailored to their specialty and area of expertise.
Strategic Initiative 3F:	Develop effective postvention programs to support families, Service Members, and unit leaders after a suicide (Section 7.3.6).
Recommendation 62	Incorporate postvention programs targeted at the decedent's military unit, family and community after a tragedy or loss to reduce the risk of suicide. Postvention efforts must address Service Members affected by a significant loss, especially after a fallen comrade's death in combat or in garrison when the unit is impacted. Unit-level postvention efforts must focus on effective debriefing and prevention when they are impacted by a significant tragedy or loss.
Recommendation 63	Train first responders, chaplains, casualty notification officers, and family interviewers on how to best respond to suicide and suicide-related events when working with families or next of kin.
Recommendation 64	Provide families with comprehensive emotional support following the death of a loved one by suicide. All those affected, including significant others and battle buddies, should have access to resources that will help them cope with traumatic grief, such as the peer-based support organization Tragedy Assistance Program for Survivors (TAPS) and the Department of Veterans Affairs (VA) Vet Centers. These organizations offer free services to all who are grieving, with focused support for suicide loss.
Recommendation 65	Ensure that Service criminal investigation agencies are staffed appropriately with family advocates trained in communicating with family members whose loved ones might have died by suicide. Maintain

	effective communication with surviving family members during the investigative process.
Recommendation 66	Develop a consistent DoD policy on memorials that encourages remembrance based on how the Service Member lived, rather than the manner of death. Use WHO/IASP guidelines to avoid increasing risk through glamorizing death, and SPRC recommendations for conducting memorial services.
Focus Area 4: Surveillance, Investigations, and Research (10 Recommendations)	
Strategic Initiative 4A:	*Conduct comprehensive surveillance aimed at identifying individuals at-risk and informing prevention efforts (Section 7.4.1).*
Recommendation 67	Structure DoD to implement surveillance efforts in a standardized manner, with a core focus on informing and improving suicide prevention activities. The DoDSER must be matured, expanded, and refocused to fulfill this surveillance role.
Recommendation 68	Standardize DoDSER surveillance throughout the DoD, including specification of qualifications of surveyor and required training.
Recommendation 69	Facilitate consistent and fluid access to DMSS by DoDSER for appropriate surveillance purposes that also allows for automatic filling of select data fields as appropriate. Aggregation of surveillance data reported using the DoDSER is intended to inform suicide prevention efforts across DoD and the Services through centralized offices at both levels, thus access to DMSS is essential.
Strategic Initiative 4B:	*Standardize investigations of suicides and suicide attempts to identify target areas for prevention policies, procedures, and programs (Section 7.4.2).*
Recommendation 70	Standardize the suicide investigation process across DoD with the sole focus being suicide prevention. The investigation process should be non-attributional, all-inclusive of the days and weeks preceding a suicide or suicide attempt, and be reported in a redacted form, from the Services to OSD, to maintain confidentiality.
Recommendation 71	Institute a modified psychological autopsy and root cause analysis protocol with a standardized process of reporting to a centralized office at the Service and OSD-level. The results of modified standardized investigative procedures can be used to refine and modify the DoDSER and improve surveillance methods. A modified investigatory protocol must include a focus on last days of life; development of a pathway to death that enables identification of potential points of intervention; interaction between person and environment; and access to all currently collected surveillance, as well as medical and personnel records.
Recommendation 72	Place investigative responsibilities in the Safety Division offices of each Service to leverage the expertise, external party team management experience, protected (confidential) approach, and effectiveness of aviation mishap investigations.
Recommendation 73	Review legal protections and make recommendations to Congress, as necessary, to ensure protected status of investigations.

Table (continued)

Recommendation 74	Recommend legislation to create procedures that facilitate the timely transfer and sharing of civilian autopsy findings on Service Members (Active Duty, Reserve Component, National Guard) with the Armed Forces Medical Examiner's Office. Evaluate the appropriateness and necessity of access to other civilian findings to improve the tracking of members of the Armed Forces at-risk.
Strategic Initiative 4C:	Ensure that all initiatives and programs have a program evaluation component (Section 7.4.3).
Recommendation 75	Every suicide prevention program initiated by DoD or the Services must contain a program evaluation component.
Strategic Initiative 4D:	Support and incorporate ongoing research to inform evidence-based suicide prevention practices (Section 7.4.4).
Recommendation 76	Create a unified, strategic, and comprehensive DoD plan for research in military suicide prevention: (1) ensuring that the DoD's military suicide prevention research portfolio is thoughtfully planned to cover topics in prevention, intervention, and postvention; and (2) assisting investigators by creating a DoD regulatory and human protections consultation board that is responsible primarily for moving suicide-related research forward in an expedited manner.

Detailed Findings, Discussions and Recommendations can be found in Section 7 of the full report.

Dedication

The Task Force would like to dedicate this report to all Service Members who died by suicide and to the grieving loved ones left behind who will forever feel the pain of the loss of their son, daughter, husband, wife, father, mother, relative, or friend. The world was a better place while they were with us. Their family, friends, fellow Service Members, and our Nation mourn their loss.

We, the members of the Task Force, express our sincere appreciation to the countless people who provided invaluable information and assistance throughout our data-gathering phase.

Without their dedication and commitment, this report would not have been possible.

Personal Stories of Suicide

Every life is valuable. The following vignettes, although a small sampling, provide valuable insight to understanding the depth of our loss through suicide.

The vignettes were prepared to highlight the faithful and honorable service of men and women who served their Nation in uniform but who also tragically succumbed to suicide. All of the following vignettes and the photographs contained in this report are used with the full express written permission of surviving families. The Task Force was inspired by and learned much from understanding the conditions and circumstances surrounding those who lost their lives to suicide.

Age: 22
Rank/Occupation: Specialist/Aviation
Mechanic Service Branch: Army

As one of six siblings, this Soldier proudly joined the Army as part of a long standing family legacy of service including his father's current duty as an ROTC instructor. He was an Army helicopter mechanic. He and his oldest brother were deployed to different parts of Iraq within days of each other.

When he returned from his deployment, he was significantly troubled. He needed help but did not seek it. Others did not recognize that he was troubled and needed professional assistance.

He spiraled downward and took his own life. "He felt that he could not get the psychological help he needed from the military for fear it would jeopardize his future career in the Army," his father said.

"The [Army] wants its Soldiers to be mentally healthy but it's very hard for the Soldiers to get the help they need," he added.

Age: 22
Rank/Occupation: Private First Class/Infantry
Branch of Service: Marine Corps

This Marine was a very talented musician and had turned down a record deal with Atlantic Records in order to join the Marine Corps. He was incredibly proud to be a Marine, and wanted nothing more than to faithfully serve his country. In July, 2009, he was diagnosed with Bipolar Disorder and went to his Sergeant for help because he was concerned about how this diagnosis was going to affect his service. According to witnesses, his Sergeant berated him openly and called him "weak." The Marine went back to his barracks and, within two hours, hung himself. When he was found in his barracks, a well-worn suicide hotline card was found lying on his bed.

Age: 27
Rank/Occupation: Electronics Technician First Class
Branch of Service: Navy

This Sailor was challenged by juggling his career with the Navy and care for his wife who had been diagnosed with a debilitating illness. He became overwhelmed, withdrawn and depressed.

Eventually, he was reprimanded at work for an unkempt appearance. On January 31, 2007, he was ordered to report to his superiors in his dress blues for an inspection. Instead, he returned home and shot himself in his vehicle outside the home that he shared with his wife and teenage stepdaughter.

Age: 23
Rank/Occupation: Specialist/Special Electronics
Service Branch: Army National Guard

This Soldier was a decorated member of the Army National Guard. He served some very personally challenging months in Iraq where he witnessed the death of several of his buddies as well as others he did not know. When he returned home after his deployment, he had a very brief demobilization and was rapidly released from active duty. He returned to his hometown with some emotional scars.

According to his family and friends, he was a fun loving, life-of-theparty type of person when he left for Iraq; when he returned he was alone and became depressed.

His depression was so severe that he chose to end his own life with a handgun on Thanksgiving Day.

His father said, "He returned with absolutely no support systems and struggled because he was separated from the only people who knew what he had been through, and we as parents had no idea how to help him."

Age: 32
Rank/Occupation: Staff Sergeant/Security Forces
Branch of Service: Air Force

This Airman served honorably in the Air Force for 14 years and received numerous accolades throughout his career. His friends and fellow Airmen described him as "someone selfless" who was always looking out for his fellow Airmen and acted as "a friend, big brother, mentor and a leader."

His family reported that he suffered from Post-Traumatic Stress Disorder and was overwhelmed by his impending deployment, his fourth to Iraq. He died by suicide in the basement of his own home with his family upstairs.

Age: 19
Rank/Occupation: Private First Class/Combat Support Battalion
Branch of Service: Army

This female Soldier and her sister joined the Army in hopes of building a rewarding career. Their father was an active duty Army Chaplain. During her initial advanced individual training, she was raped by a fellow soldier. She told her father that she was afraid to tell anyone about the sexual assault for fear that she would be "judged". She graduated from training and was transferred to another installation for her first duty assignment. A month after arriving, she was deployed to Iraq.

Although the policy in Iraq was that female Soldiers would always have a buddy, she was alone most of the time because her "buddy" had been diagnosed with cancer. Seven days before she died, a female friend (also a sexual assault victim) died by suicide in Iraq. The Private did not leave a suicide note, but her journal was discovered lying open to an entry describing the torment, pain and impact of her rape. She died by gunshot wound in Baghdad, Iraq.

Age: 40
Rank/Occupation: Major/Pilot
Service Branch: Marine Corps Reserve

This Marine was a Cobra pilot. He was fit, a model Marine, and the one that everyone else would rely on; the one that others wanted to be like. He was highly respected by his Marines and feared letting any of them down.

He had a very successful tour in Iraq where he flew 75 missions. With exposure to numerous traumatic events during his 15-year military career, he suffered from both depression and anxiety.

When his depression worsened following Iraq, he felt that he was no longer valuable to his unit and that everyone would be better off without him. His feelings of isolation deepened. He hid the pain and torment that he was experiencing from his family. He refused to seek help because he felt "it would be the end of his career because everyone would see him differently."

He died by hanging and is survived by his wife and two young sons. At the funeral, a fellow Marine said, "Superman finally hit some Kryptonite."

Additional vignettes can be found in Section 7 of the Report.

1. Background, Organization, and Activities of the Task Force

1.1. Congressional Charter and Task Force Membership

Charter

Section 733 of the National Defense Authorizatrion Act for fiscal year 2009 (FY09 NDAA) directed the Secretary of Defense to "establish within the Department of Defense a task force to examine matters relating to prevention of suicide by Members of the Armed Forces." In response to this directive, the Department of Defense Task Force on the Prevention of Suicide by Members of the Armed Forces (Task Force) was established on 7 August 2009. The Task Force was constituted as a subcommittee of the Defense Health Board (DHB), a standing Federal Advisory Committee. Section 733 also stated that the Task Force was required to submit to the Secretary of Defense a report containing "recommendations regarding a comprehensive policy designed to prevent suicide by members of the Armed Forces."

NDAA Requirements Matrix	Section(s) where Addressed
1. Not later than 12 months after the date on which all members of the task force have been appointed, the task force shall submit to the Secretary a report containing recommendations regarding a comprehensive policy designed to prevent suicide by members of the Armed Forces.	Section 7; App B
2. Task force shall take into consideration completed and ongoing efforts by the military departments to improve the efficacy of suicide prevention programs.	1.3; 1.4; Section 3; App B; D-F
3. The recommendations (including recommendations for legislative or administrative action) shall include measures to address the following:	App B

(Continued)

A. Methods to identify trends and common causal factors in suicides by members of the Armed Forces.	7.4.1; 7.4.2; App B
B. Methods to establish or update suicide education and prevention programs conducted by each military department based on identified trends and causal factors.	7.1; 7.2.3; 7.4; App B
C. An assessment of current suicide education and prevention programs of each military department.	6.1;7.2.1; 7.2.3; 7.4.3; App B
D. An assessment of suicide incidence by military occupation to include identification of military occupations with a high incidence of suicide.	6.2, App B; App G
E The appropriate type and method of investigation to determine the causes and factors surrounding each suicide by a member of the Armed Forces.	7.4.2; App B
F. The qualifications of the individual appointed to conduct an investigation of a suicide by a member of the Armed Forces.	7.4.2; App B
G. The required information to be determined by an investigation in order to determine the causes and factors surrounding suicides by members of the Armed Forces.	7.4.1; 7.4.2; App B
H. The appropriate reporting requirements following an investigation conducted on a suicide by a member of the Armed Forces.	7.1.1; 7.4.2; App B
I. The appropriate official or executive agent within the military department and Department of Defense to receive and analyze reports on investigations of suicides by members of the Armed Forces.	7.1.1; 7.4.2; App B
J. The appropriate use of the information gathered during investigations of suicides by members of the Armed Forces.	7.4.1; 7.4.2; App B
K. Methods for protecting confidentiality of information contained in reports of investigations of suicides by members of the Armed Forces.	7.4.2; App B

Legislative language of Section 733 of the FY2009 NDAA can be found in Appendix A. The full set of requirements for the report, as well as the section(s) in which they are addressed, is listed below.

Summarized responses to each question can be found in Appendix B.

Membership

The Task Force is composed of seven DoD and seven non-DoD professionals, with specific expertise in national suicide prevention policy, military personnel policy, research in the field of suicide prevention, clinical care in mental health, and military pastoral care, as well as a family member representative and representation from each Service. Major General Philip Volpe was appointed as the military co-chair, and Ms. Bonnie Carroll was elected as the civilian co-chair. The full list of Task Force members is shown below:

Alan Berman, PhD, ABPP Executive Director American Association of Suicidology President, International Association for Suicide Prevention	*David Jobes, PhD, ABPP* Board Certified Clinical Psychologist Professor of Psychology The Catholic University of America
COL John Bradley, MD, MC, USA Chairman, Department of Psychiatry Walter Reed Army Medical Center and National Naval Medical Center	*Janet Kemp, RN, PhD* National Suicide Prevention Coordinator VA, Office of Mental Health Service Canandaigua, NY

Bonnie Carroll, Major, USAFR (ret) National Director Tragedy Assistance Programs for Survivors (TAPS)	*David Litts, OD, Colonel, USAF* (ret) Director, Science and Policy National Suicide Prevention Resource Center (SPRC)
Robert Glenn Certain, DMin Colonel, USAFR (ret) Rector St. Peter-St. Paul Episcopal Church	*Richard McKeon, PhD, MPH* Acting Branch Chief, Suicide Prevention Substance Abuse and Mental Health Services Administration (SAMHSA)
CMSgt Jeffory C. Gabrelcik, USAF Chief, Air Force Review Boards Deputy Secretary AF Manpower & Reserve Affairs (M&RA)	*MGySgt Peter Proietto, USMC* Senior Enlisted Advisor Safety Division Headquarters, US Marine Corps
SgtMaj Ronald Green, USMC Senior Enlisted Advisor Headquarters and Service Battalion Headquarters, US Marine Corps	*MG Philip Volpe, DO, MC, USA* Fellow, American Academy of Family Physicians Commanding General Western Regional Medical Command
Marjan Ghahramounlou Holloway, PhD Assistant Professor Department of Medical and Clinical Psychology, Psychiatry Uniformed Services University of the Health Sciences	*CDR Aaron Werbel, PhD, USN* Suicide Prevention Program Manager for the US Marine Corps Headquarters, US Marine Corps

Appendix C contains biographies for Task Force members. The Task Force would also like to thank CMSgt Troy McIntosh for his service on the Task Force from August 2009 to October 2009.

Initial Task Force operations beginning 7 August 2009 were supported by the DHB Executive Secretary, CDR Edmond Feeks, USN, and then with a full-time Task Force Executive Secretary, Col Joanne McPherson, USAF, effective 12 November 2009. Program management support to the Task Force was provided by Booz Allen Hamilton beginning on 24 September 2009.

1.2. Methodology

The Task Force used five main data sources in the compilation of this report:

- Review of existing scientific literature
- Presentations from subject-matter experts
- Public information (including participation from family members of suicide victims)
- Panel discussions (including suicide attempt survivors)
- Information gathered from eyes-on field visits to military installations.

Following a general orientation to existing data on Service Member suicide and on the Services' suicide prevention programs through formal meetings and briefings, the Task Force focused on gathering information from experts in the field, a review of "best practices," and from public participation. After considerable collaboration, discussion, analysis, and validation of the data, the Task Force formed its initial impressions and deduced general conclusions. Eyes-on field visits, i.e., site visits, allowed the Task Force to confirm or reject initial conclusions and to determine additional areas of strengths and weaknesses regarding suicide prevention. Once briefings and site visits concluded, Task Force members began to methodically deliberate regarding the findings and recommendations, and the report was constructed and finalized.

1.3. Task Force Meetings

The Task Force held its first preparatory meeting on 7 August 2009. From 1 October 2009 to 6 August 2010, the Task Force held monthly and twice-monthly face-to-face meetings both open (for public information) and preparatory (for administration). Appendix D contains a complete list of the Task Force meetings with dates and locations. Appendix E contains a complete list of speakers for each Task Force public meeting. During Task Force meetings, members received informational briefings from the Services and from military and civilian subject matter experts. Topics included, but were not limited to, DoD/Service suicide data and prevention programs, ongoing research in suicidology, surviving family member input, epidemiology, testimony from those who had previously attempted suicide, suicide and other serious incident investigations, and Reserve and National Guard programs. The Task Force also received briefings regarding the Department of Veterans Affairs (VA) and the United States Coast Guard (USCG).

Panel discussions held at several of the public Task Force meetings facilitated discussion between speakers and Task Force members. Time was also allocated during each of these open meetings for preparatory sessions so that Task Force members could focus on both current and future efforts. In addition, the Task Force held several preparatory working sessions, during which members synthesized the captured information and discussed related findings and recommendations. All open meetings were transcribed, and the transcriptions and meeting minutes are posted on the DHB website.

In October 2009, several Task Force members participated in the TAPS Suicide Survivors Seminar, attended by 360 family survivors of Service Members who died by suicide, including parents, spouses, children, and siblings from across the DoD. In January 2010, most Task Force members attended the DoD/VA Annual Suicide Prevention Conference, ensuring coverage of the maximum number of sessions possible.

1.4. Sites Visited

Delegations of the Task Force formally visited 19 military installations over the course of the year. Each site visit was typically two days long. The delegations met and spoke with a variety of groups separately, including junior enlisted members (including recruits and trainees), noncommissioned officers (NCOs), commissioned officers of varying ranks (including installation and unit leaders at all levels); behavioral health clinicians, emergency room clinicians, and primary care clinicians; installation support services personnel, first responders, and chaplains; and family members. Appendix F contains a complete list of site visit locations and dates. Furthermore, information from informal site visits and experiences by individual members about suicide and suicide prevention efforts were included during deliberations.

1.5. Writing Groups

The Task Force divided itself into three writing groups. Task Force members were assigned to work on multiple groups and had either a primary or a secondary responsibility for the content material in that portion of the report. This division of subject matter expertise allowed sharing of ideas within and between the writing groups. Training and policy issues were addressed by all of the writing groups.

1.6. Guiding Principles

The Task Force is an independent body created by Congressional mandate as established within the FY09 NDAA. It operated separately from the Services but sought to obtain information related to the Services' current suicide prevention programs, policies, procedures, and regulations. However, Task Force members were careful to avoid Service influence so that they could openly consider all possible findings and recommendations. Task Force meetings were held in open and transparent sessions and afforded the public the opportunity to provide comments and gain access to Task Force members. The public could also submit comments to the Task Force via e-mail.

Eliminating suicide by members of the Armed Forces is a noble and worthy effort. To create a set of strategies and recommendations that are useful and attainable, the Task Force developed the following six guiding principles:

1. Suicide and suicidal behaviors are preventable.
2. Suicide prevention begins with leadership and requires engagement from all facets of the military community.
3. Suicide prevention requires long-term, sustained commitment using a comprehensive public health approach.
4. Service Member wellness and fitness (mind, body, and spirit) is essential to mission accomplishment (and suicide prevention).
5. Recommendations of the Task Force should reflect the best available practices and scientific evidence, as well as expert consensus.
6. The recommendations should be consistent with the culture of the Armed Forces and capitalize on the strengths of the Armed Forces.

2. Introduction

2.1. Overview

This Nation's Service men and women constitute the most resilient fighting force in the world. They benefit from the Services' suicide prevention efforts, which have few peers for comparison throughout the United States. DoD is one of the only employers in the United States that tracks suicide-related behaviors, mandates suicide awareness, education and training programs and attempts to comprehensively benefit from a multidimensional approach using line leadership, healthcare capabilities, religious personnel, and community services. The US Armed Forces have now been engaged in one of the longest continuous armed conflicts in our Nation's history—a daunting commitment highlighted by frequent interruptions of lifelong goals and frequent separations from loved ones—yet our Service Members continue to meet their mission with passion, commitment, devotion to duty, and success.

This Task Force recognizes that DoD leads the Nation in many ways in suicide prevention efforts. The Task Force's recommendations are designed to facilitate a refinement from the strong effort made today into one that also effectively responds to new requirements that have resulted from a long, sustained, high operational tempo environment.

2.2. Nature of the Challenge of Preventing Suicide

Suicide is a complex human behavior that has occurred throughout the history of civilization. Examples of suicidal behaviors have occurred in all cultures, races, and religions across the world. Suicidal behavior occurs in all demographic, socio-cultural, or economic groups. Because the impact of suicide is so profound in terms of its social costs, as well as the impact on individual survivors and social systems, there has been a long-term interest in preventing its occurrence.

The "TIP" of the iceberg (above the surface) represents the suicide -related behaviors and the act of suicide. The enormous mass below the surface represents the much larger set of complex psychological, physical, spiritual, emotional, relationship, environmental, occupational and social stressors. The impact of the stressors **are influenced by the individual's resiliency, and stigma** within the environment. To prevent suicide and sustain suicide prevention efforts, we must also address the stressors which lurk beneath the surface, as well as build resiliency and decrease stigma.

Diagram 2-1. The Challenge of Preventing Suicide.

However, despite our efforts to prevent tragic losses by suicide and the desire to preserve life, our ability to actually understand and effectively prevent suicide has been a challenge throughout history and continues to plague us in modern times. Several aspects make understanding and preventing suicide particularly challenging, but one of the most challenging aspects is the multitude of factors that underlie and precede the event. Just as the proverbial tip of the iceberg belies the enormous mass beneath the surface, suicide is the visible manifestation of a much larger set of physical, mental, and spiritual stressors. To prevent suicide, we must address the part of the iceberg that lurks beneath the surface.

Other challenges in understanding suicide-related behaviors include, but are not limited to:

- Those from whom we can best learn about suicide are those who have died by suicide, hence are unavailable for study.
- Those who survive a suicide attempt may have some characteristics that differ from those who have died by suicide, making generalizations from one to the other difficult.
- Uniformly agreed upon language and nomenclature for various forms of suicidal behavior have been elusive, hampering efforts to aggregate study findings and coordinate communications about persons needing care.
- Suicide is a statistically low base rate event, which makes its reliable prediction difficult; program evaluation efforts often focused on proxy measures.
- Given the scope and impact of suicidal behavior, sophisticated empirical research on understanding and ultimately preventing suicide has been remarkably limited.
- Although there are some data about what may prevent suicide, we have yet to develop a broad array of evidence-based public health and clinical prevention approaches.
- Suicide is a very controversial topic, with moral, religious, civil liberty, and political implications that may directly or indirectly affect prevention efforts.

2.3. International Perspective on Suicide and Suicide Prevention

Statistics on suicide rates for various countries indicate that each year there are an estimated 900,000 deaths by suicide across the globe, 1 suicide every 40 seconds. The World Health Organization (WHO) ranks suicide as the 10th leading cause of death, accounting for 1.5 percent of all deaths annually. More people die by suicide across the world than die in war, terrorist activities, and homicides, combined.

The rate of suicide in the United States tends to be in the mid-range when considering rates in all countries; however, international comparisons are notoriously unreliable because of great differences in death registration systems among nations. Some of the least developed countries do not even have vital statistics registration systems because they have little or no means to collect and process mortality data. The suicide rate in the United States in 2007, the latest year for which there are national statistics, was 11.5 per 100,000, compared with a worldwide average rate of 14 per 100,000 (18 per 100,00 for males; 11 per 100,000 for females).

Worldwide rates have increased 60 percent in the last 45 years. Annually, suicide rates tend to be highest among the countries of Eastern Europe, notably the old Soviet Socialist Republics (i.e., Belarus, Lithuania, and Russian Federation) (World Health Organization, 2010). Research on the causes of these high rates has been limited in these countries. It is suspected that the high rates are associated with the psychological instability caused by political, social, and economic crises in combination with the elevated rates of unemployment. The high prevalence of alcohol dependence also seems to be a significant factor (Krasnov & Voitsekh, 2009).

The World Health Organization (WHO) and the International Association for Suicide Prevention (IASP) are actively engaged in promoting suicide prevention activities around the world, each noting that there is compelling evidence to indicate that various strategies can reduce rates. In 1993, the United Nations (UN) and WHO convened a meeting of international experts that culminated in a report published in 1996 that included a comprehensive set of guidelines for developing national strategies for the prevention of suicide around the world. That said, at latest count, only 16 countries have a national suicide prevention strategy in place, accounting for about 8 percent of the countries of the world. Where these strategies exist, they share a number of approaches in common as follows:

- Promoting awareness of suicide as a preventable public health problem
- Enhancing access to behavioral health and substance abuse services
- Reducing stigma associated with behavioral health problems
- Improving detection and treatment of mental disorders associated with risk of suicide
- Reducing access to lethal means
- Implementing training to improve caregivers' **recognition** and clinical treatment of those with risk for suicide
- Improving and enhancing the reach of crisis intervention services
- Improving media portrayals of, and public commentary about, suicidal behaviors
- Improving surveillance
- Improving continuity of care
- Enhancing sensitivity toward and care for those bereaved by suicide. Suicide, and thus its prevention, knows no geographic boundary and is an issue for a number of countries other than the United States.

2.4. National Perspective on Suicide and Suicide Prevention

In 2007, more than 34,000 Americans died by suicide, outnumbering homicide deaths by almost 2 to 1 (CDC, 2010). In 2008, an estimated 8.3 million adults aged 18 or older had serious suicidal thoughts, 2.3 million made a suicide plan, and 1.1 million attempted suicide (SAMHSA, 2009). Each year in the United States, hundreds of thousands of people require emergency department treatment as a result of attempted suicide. While there has been a recent decrease in suicide among youth, [traditionally one of the highest-rate demographic groups], suicide among the ages of 25 to 64 has actually been increasing. In addition to the profound personal and emotional impact of suicide, the sheer economic impact in terms of services and years of life lost are staggering.

Until recently, despite the tragic toll in lives lost and families bereaved, and the enormous impact on the healthcare system, there has been a minimal national focus on suicide and suicide prevention. Responding to the anguished pleas of family members who had lost a loved one to suicide, members of US Congress, in both the Senate and House of Representatives, passed resolutions in 1997 declaring that suicide was a national problem and that suicide prevention should be a national priority. Congress called for the development of a comprehensive national strategy for suicide prevention to guide a national effort to reduce suicidal behaviors.

US Surgeon General Dr. David Satcher led the Nation through a series of steps to respond to this new national mandate. A groundbreaking conference in Reno, Nevada, in fall 1998, assembled researchers, clinicians, government officials, survivors of suicide loss, public health leaders, and other experts to develop recommendations for action. These recommendations were used to frame the "Surgeon General's Call to Action to Prevent Suicide," released in summer 1999, the first time a Surgeon General had issued a report on suicide. About this same time, the Air Force's pioneering suicide prevention program was producing the first empirical evidence that a comprehensive, public health approach could, in fact, reduce suicide across a population. This evidence added an additional measure of optimism to a series of regional public hearings that followed for the purpose of shaping the Reno recommendations into 11 goals and 68 objectives, framed as the 2001 National Strategy for Suicide Prevention: Goals and Objectives for Action (NSSP). The NSSP articulated an extremely ambitious, comprehensive, public health strategy to prevent suicide and suicidal behaviors in the United States. It required a variety of organizations and sectors, both public and private, to become involved in suicide prevention. The NSSP represented the first attempt in the United States to prevent suicide through a coordinated approach by both the public and private sectors.

Since the publication of the NSSP, activities in the field of suicide prevention have increased exponentially. Government agencies at all levels, schools, not-for-profit organizations, and others have initiated programs and campaigns to address suicide risks. Every State now has coordinated suicide prevention plans and initiatives that are implemented at the state level. DoD and each Service branch of the military (along with the VA) are to be commended for being among the first organizations in the United States to make "reducing suicide" a core priority. Beyond embracing this focus, these organizations have made considerable and sustained efforts to reduce suicide and suicidal behaviors for their respective populations.

Despite the recent concerted efforts in the field of suicide prevention, much more remains to be done. The Institute of Medicine confirmed in its 2002 analysis of the national suicide problem that significant empirical, clinical, and public health efforts were still needed to meaningfully affect the nation's suicide-related challenges. In 2002, the President's New Freedom Commission on Mental Health also noted considerable gaps in research, surveillance data, treatment, training, and service delivery.

2.5. Military Perspective on Suicide and Suicide Prevention

Suicide in the military has existed as long have there have been standing armies. In May 1996, Admiral Jeremy Boorda, the Chief of Naval Operations, took his own life in the wake of allegations regarding the legitimacy of two of his wartime medals. His suicide served as a "wakeup call" to the military that suicide can occur at any level within the organization. Media attention added a sense of urgency, and the Services began to develop formal suicide prevention programs in the mid to late 1990s, collaborating with military and civilian experts. Notably, the Air Force initiated development of a comprehensive suicide prevention program that is now considered one of a very few evidence-based suicide prevention programs. Suicide prevention had also become a focus at the national level, which fostered collaboration between military and civilian communities.

In recent years, suicide in the military has continued to receive attention both nationally and internationally. While many historically known risk factors, such as exposure to trauma and access to lethal means, continue to influence the level of military suicide and suicide-related behaviors, a number of additional layers of complexity require consideration.

Two current examples of military-specific factors include the impact of multiple deployments and the use of Internet-based communication with family while deployed.

Multiple efforts to enhance our understanding of military suicide have been launched. The IASP Task Force on Defense and Police Forces was organized in 2007, and the North Atlantic Treaty Organization (NATO) has tasked an Exploratory Team to look into the problem of international military suicide and is currently in the process of forming a Research Task Group. Nationally, the DoD Suicide Prevention and Risk Reduction Committee (SPARRC) has been formed to actively address military suicide related topics. The Department of Defense Suicide Event Reporting (DoDSER) system was initiated in 2008 to track suicide and suicide-related behaviors among all military Service Members.

3. Evolution of Service Suicide Prevention Programs

3.1. Department of Defense

As previously noted, the US Surgeon General in 1999 released the Surgeon General's "Call to Action to Prevent Suicide" report stating that suicide was a national public health issue that needed to be addressed. Simultaneously, the Pentagon was also addressing the issue across the whole of DoD. The DoD SPARRC was formally established in September 1999 as a result of a White House conference held in July 1999. The SPARRC is composed of both military and VA members and has been recognized throughout the DoD as a "model" for collaboration among the Services, DoD, and other agencies.

The SPARRC established several work groups to accomplish specific tasks and goals: a Suicide Rate Standardization Work Group in 2005; a Suicide Nomenclature Standardization Work Group in 2006; and a work group focused on a suicide data collection form and database in 2007 (later called the DoDSER Working Group). The SPARRC also expanded the annual suicide prevention conference, from approximately 50 attendees in 2002 to approximately 850 attendees by 2010 to include international attendees from foreign military organizations.

The Suicide Rate Standardization Work Group was established to standardize the analysis of Service suicide data (including attempts), and allow for direct comparison across the Services. By mid-2006, a policy memorandum was approved as formal DoD policy, standardizing suicide reporting methods and establishing the schedule for reporting suicide data to DoD leadership.

The Suicide Nomenclature Standardization Work Group was formed to establish common definitions for suicide nomenclature. Its input was included in the empirical article titled "Rebuilding the Tower of Babel: A Revised Nomenclature for the Study of Suicide and Suicidal Behaviors Part 2: Suicide-Related Ideations, Communications, and Behaviors" (Silverman, Berman, Sanddal, O'Carroll, & Joiner, 2007). A common nomenclature would further standardize suicide data across the Services, ensuring that common definitions for terms relating to suicide were being used. However, the Centers for Disease Control and Prevention (CDC) were already working on standardizing suicide nomenclature for the civilian sector, and there were indications that other federal agencies would very possibly adopt that work. With increasing collaboration among DoD, VA, and federal civilian agencies, it was important that everyone use the same terms and definitions to the greatest reasonable extent. Therefore, the SPARRC chose not to immediately implement a standardized suicide nomenclature policy for DoD so it could make an informed decision regarding the adoption of the CDC nomenclature, or another. Of particular importance was consideration of the nomenclature to be adopted by the VA because DoD and the VA need to ensure continuity of care for the same population at different stages in their lives. At the time that this report was published, DoD, VA, CDC, and SAMHSA had all agreed to adopt the same nomenclature for suicide-related behaviors.

On 1 January 2008, the DoDSER developed by the SPARRC and its collaborators over the course of 2007 was implemented in each of the Services and replaced separate Service-specific forms.

Each Service still collects data specific to its branch on some aspects of deaths (e.g., Navy collects data on personnel having died by going overboard on a ship, which is specific to its operational environment), but the DoDSER provides common data points for the majority of information gathered in suicide-related cases across the Services. The DoDSER form populates the DoDSER database, which houses the suicide data repository for the DoD at the National Center for Telehealth and Technology (T2). A tasking memorandum to the Services ensures that the control and release of Service-level suicide data remains with the Services and must be modified or released by the Service-appointed DoDSER Program Manager. The Defense Centers of Excellence for Psychological Health and Traumatic Brain Injury (DCoE) generates an annual report from this database for the Assistant Secretary of Defense for Health Affairs (ASD(HA)), with approval and input by each of the Services. The first year for which this report was generated from the DoDSER was 2008; prior years were generated with separate input from each of the Services.

In November 2007, DCoE was established, based on the recommendations of the 2006–2007 DoD Task Force on Mental Health and the Secretary of Defense to establish a tri-Service center of excellence with the goal of promoting resilience, recovery, and reintegration of warriors and their families. The SPARRC and all of its subsidiary work groups began operating under DCoE beginning with the new fiscal year in October 2008. The DoD/VA Annual Suicide Prevention Conference, beginning with the 2009 event, is now also under the umbrella of DCoE.

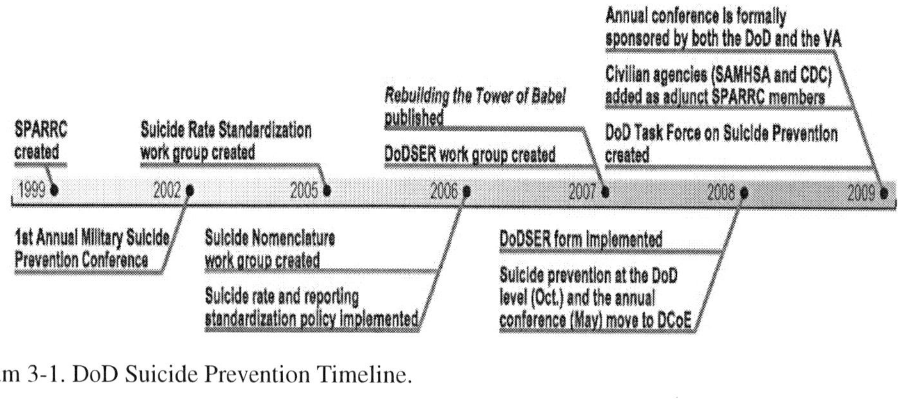

Diagram 3-1. DoD Suicide Prevention Timeline.

The following charts depict the total number and rates of suicide by Service Component for calendar years 2001-2009.

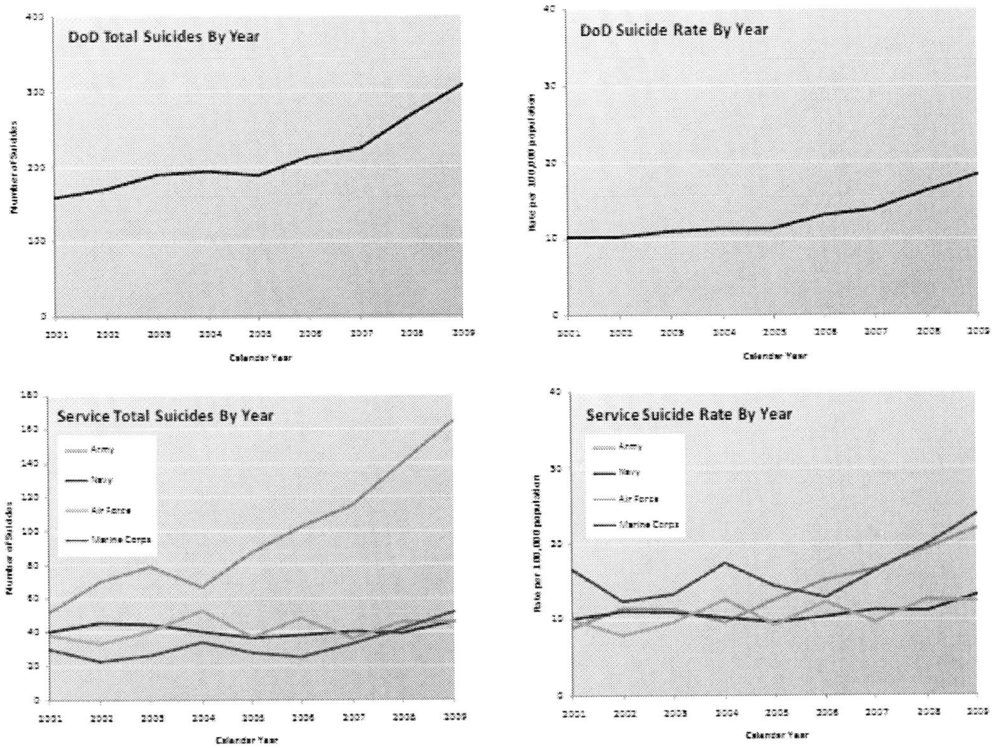

Source: Mortality Surveillance Division, Armed Forces Medical Examiner System, AFIP, 2010.

Diagram 3-2. All Services Suicides 2001–2009.

The Services have been actively involved in suicide prevention for many years. A brief summary of each program as provided by the Services follows.

3.2. United States Army

Army suicide statistics from the mid-1970s relied largely on line of duty (LOD) investigations, the Individual Patient Data System of the Army Medical Department, the Adjutant General's Office Casualty Information System, autopsy reports at the Armed Force's Institute of Pathology, and files from the Crimes Records Center of the Army Criminal Investigation Command, as well as the National Personnel Record Center (Datel, 1981). From 1977 to 1978, 228 Soldiers took their lives. Using mid-year strength data produced an annual crude suicide rate of 14.3 per 100,000 for 1977 and 15.4 per 100,000 for 1978 (Datel, 1981).

The Army's suicide prevention program began in 1984. The 1980s (FY 1980–89) saw 836 Soldiers lose their lives by suicide, with the most common means being from gunshot and hanging, 522 and 104, respectively (GAO, 1989). In 1999, the Army Chief of Staff called for a panel of experts to review the existing suicide prevention efforts of the Army and make recommendations for additional methods to reduce suicides.

In 2000, the Army G-1, the Army Office of the Surgeon General (OTSG), and the Office of Chief of Chaplains (OCCH) completed the review and stated that the program was basically sound, but the Army needed to increase emphasis on leadership involvement and offer more advanced training. From the beginning, leadership involvement and command policy and action were the cornerstones of suicide prevention in the Army, but efforts in these areas needed strengthening and renewed emphasis. Therefore, the Army refined its suicide prevention program to focus on five major strategies:

1. Developing life-coping skills
2. Encouraging help-seeking behaviors
3. Raising awareness and vigilance to suicide prevention
4. Integrating suicide prevention programs
5. Conducting suicide surveillance and analysis.

While there is a medical component to suicide prevention, the Army's program is grounded in leadership and fosters a community approach, involving chaplains, family support centers, the chain of command, and each individual Soldier to help identify someone who needs help.

In 2001, the Army implemented a Suicide Prevention Campaign Plan that focused on prevention and intervention methods, directed commanders to take ownership, and synchronized and integrated resources at the installation level.

Because there was a need for more advanced training, in 2002, the Army contracted with Living Works Education for Applied Suicide Intervention Skills Training (ASIST) workshops. In 2005, the Army also funded Question, Persuade, Refer (QPR) workshops Army-wide to provide an additional resource in suicide prevention awareness and intervention training.

With the involvement of the US military in combat operations in Afghanistan and Iraq, completed suicides in theater increased during the period of 2002 to the present. To assess the mental fitness of the force and look at its suicide prevention programs, OTSG sent Mental Health Assessment Teams (MHAT) from 2003 to 2009 to the OIF/OEF theaters. The MHAT II report in 2005 stated that suicide prevention training was being conducted at specific intervals during the deployment cycle and was conducted primarily by Unit Ministry Teams (UMT). Occasionally, behavioral health personnel would also be involved, but this was not consistent.

The report also showed Soldiers' confidence in the adequacy of the suicide prevention training they were receiving had declined.

Historically, suicide prevention training targeted junior enlisted Soldiers because this population was believed to be most at-risk. As demonstrated by Diagram 3-3, the Army demographic profile of suicide victims tend to be male (86%), age 18-24 years old (46%), Caucasian/white (74.6%) and married (53.4%). Diagram 3.4 shows that of all Army suicides from CY 2005 to CY 2009, 48.7% had received one or more behavioral health diagnoses, 21.6% had mood disorders, and 14.9% had an anxiety disorder (not PTSD). This illustrates the need to train all Soldiers in suicide prevention and for senior leaders to recognize the need to attend suicide awareness training.

Number of Suicide Cases		2005-2009 606 n (%)	Overall Army‡ %
Male		572 (94.4)	86.0
Female		34 (5.6)	14.0
Age (Years)	Mean	28	25
	18-24	271 (44.7)	46.0
	25-34	199 (32.8)	33.2
	35-60	136 (22.4)	20.8
Race-Ethnicity	Caucasian/White	450 (74.3)	74.6
	African-American	81 (13.4)	15.7
	Hispanic and Other	75 (12.4)	9.7
Marital Status	Single	263 (43.4)	39.1
	Married	316 (52.1)	53.4
	Divorced/Separated /Widowed	27 (4.5)	7.5

‡ Based on 2008 data.
Source: US Army Public Health Command (Provisional), Epidemiological Report No. 14-Hk-0BW9-10c, Analyses of Army Suicides, 2003-2009.

Diagram 3-3. Army Suicides, CY 2005-2009, Demographic Characteristics of Army Suicide Cases.

The Army's **suicide** rate has continued to climb despite increased efforts and programs for suicide prevention and intervention. In the past, being in the military was a protective factor for suicide, with the military rate being well below the civilian rate. Since 2005, the **Army's suicide rate has exceeded that of the US civilian population.**

Number of Suicide Cases	2005-2009 606 n (%)
Any BH Diagnosis	295 (48.7)
Adjustment Disorder	157 (25.9)
Mood Disorder	131 (21.6)
Substance Related	110 (18.2)
Any Anxiety Disorder (not PTSD)	90 (14.9)
PTSD	55 (9.1)
Personality Disorder	37 (6.1)
Acute Stress	19 (3.1)
Psychoses	19 (3.1)

Source: US Army Public Health Command (Provisional), Epidemiological Report No. 14-Hk-0BW9-10c, Analyses of Army Suicides, 2003-2009.

Diagram 3-4. Army Suicides, CY 2005-2009, Behavioral Health (BH) Conditions of Army Suicide Cases, Unadjusted.

In 2006 the Army implemented Battlemind training, which is now called Resilience Training. Battlemind is defined as "the Warrior's inner strength to face the realities of the environment with courage, confidence, and resilience. This means meeting the mental challenges of training, operations, combat, and transitioning home. Warriors with Battlemind take care of themselves, their buddies, and those they lead." In 2007 the Army mandated Battlemind training for the entire Service, and it continues to be developed and expanded to fill gaps in other training and include evidence-based skills. While the training stems from the Army, it is available to all members of the military. Training for military spouses is also part of the overall program. In 2008 the Army established a memorandum of agreement (MOA) with the National Institutes of Mental Health (NIMH) for the Army Study to Assess Risk and Resilience in Service Members (Army STARRS). The study will be conducted over 5 years and is the largest study of suicide and mental health in members of the military ever attempted. One of the early primary goals of the study is to identify risk and protective factors that can be modified. On 1 October 2008, the Army established the Comprehensive Soldier Fitness (CSF) directorate. The CSF program is geared to bolster the strengths of Soldiers and their families, thereby improving their resilience in certain important areas: emotional, social, spiritual, family, and physical. The program uses training, intervention, and treatment that have proven effective. CSF program personnel will assess the total fitness of all Soldiers. The results of each assessment will help in designing individualized training, intervention, or treatment programs, as needed. The CSF program begins at accession into the Army and includes reassessments at appropriate intervals. At the 2009 DoD/VA Annual Suicide Prevention Conference, the interactive video "Beyond the Front" was introduced. The video was developed via collaboration among the Army Research Laboratory, Lincoln University, and WILL Interactive. The video was rolled out Army-wide as a tool to help train Soldiers in suicide prevention. The Army had also developed another suicide prevention video prior to "Beyond the Front," entitled, "Shoulder-to-Shoulder, No Soldier Stands Alone." In March 2009 during a month-long "stand-down" for suicide prevention training, the Army established its own Suicide Prevention Task Force.

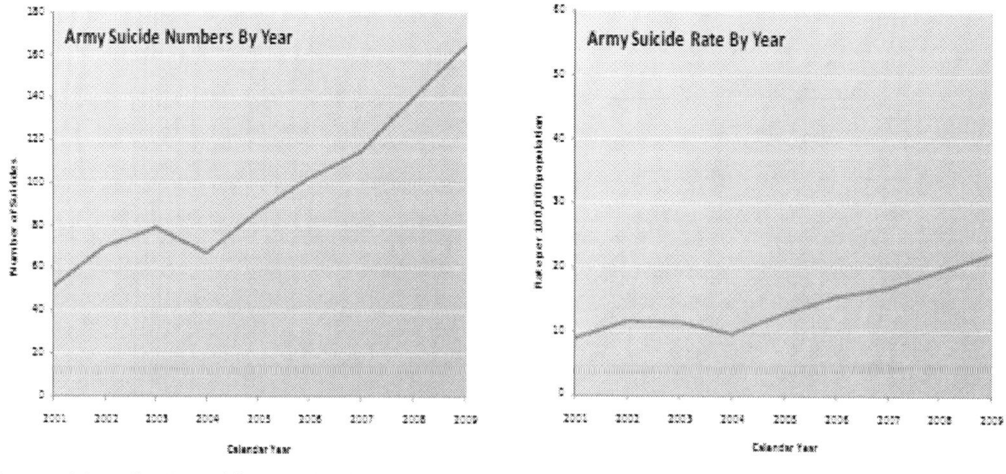

Source: Mortality Surveillance Division, Armed Forces Medical Examiner System, AFIP, 2010).

Diagram 3-5. Army Suicides 2001–2009.

The Task Force was created to address the rising suicide rate among Soldiers, and began by examining the most recent Army suicides, in an attempt to find commonalities and/or trends that could be addressed. One of the primary goals of the Army Task Force is to analyze and assess the Army's current suicide prevention programs and determine which are most effective. The findings of the Task Force will be used to inform future changes in Army regulations, policies, and programs. Diagram 3-5 depicts the total number and rate of Army suicides for calendar years 2001-2009.

3.3. United States Navy

Ad hoc and localized suicide prevention training and leadership communication have occurred in the US Navy (USN) for many decades. However, efforts were formalized in 1996 when all Services initiated suicide prevention programs following suicide rates that had reached record highs in 1995. ADM Boorda's suicide in May 1996 particularly brought the issue front and center in the USN. Viewed as a Sailor readiness concern, suicide prevention was placed at Navy Personnel Command, and the cornerstones of suicide prevention were identified as Leadership, Policy, and Education. Following reorganization, suicide prevention as a component of the Behavioral Health Program of Record has been part of OPNAV N135, Personal Readiness and Community Support. November 2009 marked the official start of Navy Operational Stress Control, an increasingly integrated structure of health promotion, family readiness, and prevention programs aimed at building resilience, addressing problems early, and creating a healthy climate. Operational Stress Control elements, including policy, an accession to flag training continuum, innovative and integrated strategic communications, and assessment and analysis to measure baseline state and progress in program effectiveness, are all critical to USN's early prevention strategy. In 2009, the Chief of Naval Operations (CNO) formed a cross-functional team with representation from the fleet, medical, family programs, religious ministries, safety, policy, public affairs, and budget expertise to conduct an analysis of Navy suicide prevention, factors and influences, and alignment of prevention efforts. In 2010 the CNO special projects team conducted a review of all 2008 and 2009 suicide cases to identify trends and lessons learned, and the Center for Naval Analyses (CNA) conducted an analysis of career factors associated with Navy suicides.

Policy

The USN's first overarching suicide prevention policy, published in 2005 as OPNAVINST 1720.4, articulates a 10-point action plan:

1) Annual training
2) A command Suicide Prevention Coordinator
3) Messages of concern
4) Command-level suicide prevention and crisis intervention plan
5) Local medical, religious, and family services, along with health promotion and substance abuse services to support leaders in their plans
6) Plans for identification, referral, access to treatment, and follow-up for at-risk personnel

7) Training that it is every member's duty to obtain assistance for other Service Members
8) Suicide prevention part of life skills/health promotion education
9) Families and units affected by suicide events provided sensitive support
10) Post-suicide data collection, surveillance, and analysis.

Policy revision published in August 2009 as OPNAVINST 1720.4A focused on the four key elements of the local command suicide prevention program: training, intervention, response, and reporting. OPNAVINST 1720.4a extended USN DoDSER surveillance to drilling Selected Reserve personnel and suicide attempts, and extended training to civilian employees with additional training requirements for first responders.

Training

Suicide prevention information has been a mainstay of required annual General Military Training for all Sailors with information on warning signs, risk factors, and protective factors provided in live briefings, videos, and computer-based training over the years. Recent changes have required live training with video and other support materials available to tailor training to the target audience. Materials include the USN General Military Training (GMT), the video "Suicide Prevention: A Message from Survivors" (April 2010), a USN peer-to-peer facilitated interactive PowerPoint brief with discussion and role play, and Front Line Supervisor Training— facilitated hands-on leader training. Workshop training for command Suicide Prevention Coordinators started in November 2008 and has been conducted at locations worldwide., The Navy conducted a 2.5-day training conference in June 2010 for more than 200 upper echelon and installation level suicide prevention coordinators, providing participants the tools to train and mentor Suicide Prevention Coordinators in their subordinate and tenant commands.

Communications

Year-round communications efforts through multiple media are a key strategy to increase awareness about suicide and resources to get help. Communications have included print and broadcast media and leader messages. In 2008 a series of four posters was distributed, along with tri-fold brochures. In 2009 a poster contest enabled Sailors to design entries and vote on the winners. The top 3 of more than 40 entries were printed and distributed. In 2009, the Navy formed a working group to focus on extending information to families. A family-focused tri-fold brochure was distributed in 2009; local commands were encouraged to include families in their communications efforts, and the initiative continues to move forward.

Surveillance and Data Analysis (Navy and USMC)

The Department of the Navy Suicide Incident Report (DONSIR) supported the first official suicide surveillance program within the Department of the Navy (DON). Between 1999 and 2007 inclusive, data on all completed suicides in the USN and Marine Corps (USMC) were systematically collected (Hourani & Hilton, 1999; Hourani, Hilton, Kennedy, & Jones, 2000; Hourani, Hilton, Kennedy, & Robbins, 2001; Jones, Kennedy, Hawkes, Hourani, Long, & Robbins, 2001; Stander, Hilton, Doran, Gaskin, & Thomsen, 2005; Stander, Hilton, Doran, Werbel, & Thomsen, 2006; Stander, Hilton, Kennedy, & Gaskin,

2004; Stander, Hilton, Kennedy, & Robbins, 2004). The long-term goals of this program were to (1) provide military leadership and public affairs personnel with accurate and detailed information regarding suicide trends within the DON, and (2) improve suicide prevention by identifying and modifying military-specific risk factors for suicide. The DONSIR provided the DON with longitudinal data that can be compared across the USN and the USMC. This report also conformed to 2006 guidelines established by the ASD(HA)regarding how active duty suicides should be counted and how suicide rates should be calculated so that statistics can be compared more meaningfully across all of the US military services.

The DONSIR established baselines for suicide rates and suicide event characteristics that can be used to track trends over time. It evaluated military-specific correlates of suicide that are not addressed in the civilian academic literature. The DONSIR's focus on military-specific risk factors is important because military personnel are not representative of the US population. Differences in gender, race, age, health, and employment may result in unique correlates of suicide for active-duty personnel. Also, US military governance, compared with civilian, may better facilitate the implementation and monitoring of policies and procedures to address risk factors and suicide prevention.

The DONSIR also served to inform the development of the DoDSER that replaced DONSIR in January 2008. In addition to completed-suicide events, DoDSER collects data on suicide attempts. And, in addition to active-duty DON personnel, DoDSER applies to Army, Air Force, and Coast Guard personnel. DoDSER represents the first standardized tri-Service suicide data registry and owes much to DONSIR development and use over the decade preceding DoDSER's 2008 launch.

Diagram 3-6 reflects Navy suicide demographics from 1999-2009 from both the DONSIR and DODSER reports.

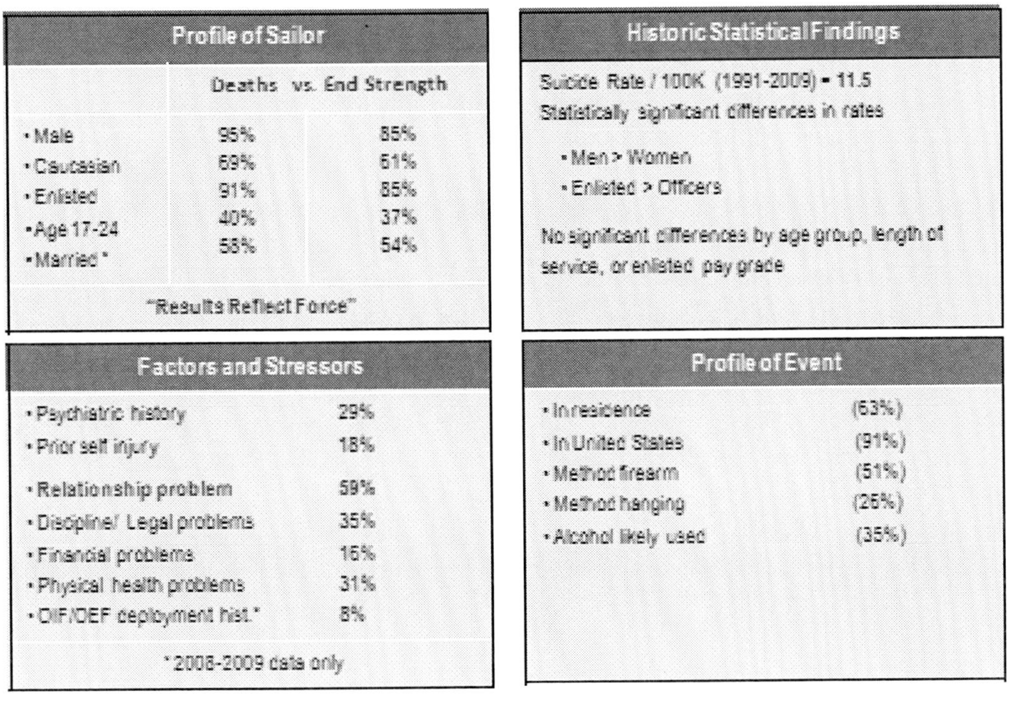

Diagram 3-6. Summary of 1999-2009 Navy Findings, 1999-2007 DONSIR / 2008-2009 DODSER.

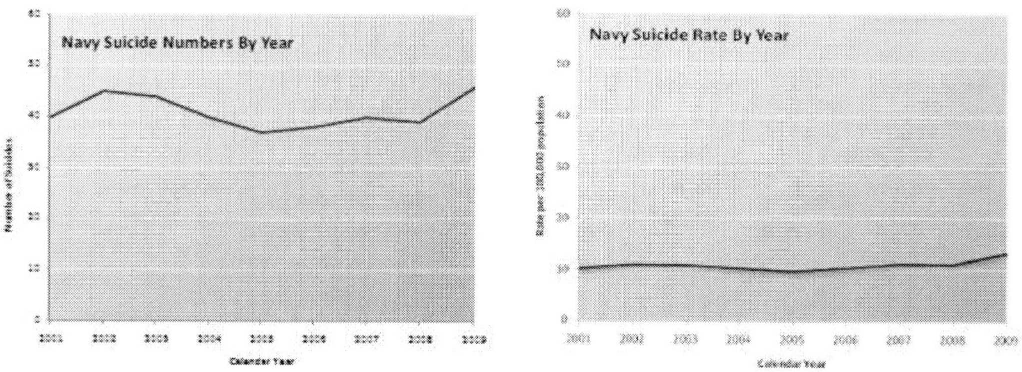

Source: Mortality Surveillance Division, Armed Forces Medical Examiner System, AFIP, 2010.

Diagram 3-7. Navy Suicides 2001–2009.

3.4. United States Air Force

The US Air Force has been tracking suicide rates within the force since the 1980s. In response to an identified increase in suicide rates in the mid 1990s, the Air Force established an integrated product team (IPT) in 1996 to address the Air Force suicide rate and subsequently created the Air Force Suicide Prevention Program. The basis of the program is a conceptual shift from suicide prevention as a medical issue to a commander's issue, encompassing all areas of an Airman's life.

Surveillance

At the time of the program's development, data revealed three primary risk factors associated with those who committed suicide: relationship, legal, and financial troubles. Data also demonstrated that two-thirds of suicide victims in the Air Force had no contact with the healthcare system. Protective factors were also identified: social support and interconnectedness, individual coping skills, and cultural norms that promote and protect responsible help-seeking behavior. A critical component of the new program was the creation of the Suicide Event Surveillance System (SESS), a central database for surveillance data on both fatal and nonfatal self-injuries (including suicide attempts and gestures). The intent was that this database would track injuries and fatalities, as well as provide data for analysis of potential risk factors for a suicide event. SESS was initially part of the Air Force public health tracking system, but became a separate system in 1999 to expand reporting beyond active duty members and to improve patient confidentiality. The SESS was established as a secure, web-based system. The Force Health Protection office of the Air Force would use the data to create monthly and yearly reports, and address requests from customers and leaders.

The Air Force began to transition from the SESS to the DoDSER in 2008, and in 2009 the DoDSER replaced SESS as the data collection system for all suicide deaths and attempts. The Air Force has also expanded its capability to track the suicides of Airmen assigned to the Guard and Reserve who are not in active status, and in 2008 began to track the suicide deaths of AF civilian personnel. Currently, as stated in Diagram 3-8, there were 273 ADAF suicides from CY 03-CY09 with 67% having experienced relationship problems, 39% having legal problems, and 25% had financial problems.

There were 273 ADAF suicides from CY03-CY09
67% had relationship problems
39% had legal problems
25% had financial problems
19% had deployed in previous year
26% were engaged in mental health care
55% of CY03-CY09 AF suicides involved Airmen who had never deployed

Actions/Services to address risk factors:
97 additional Mental Health (MH) providers hired
Targeted suicide prevention training for high risk career fields
Financial and personal counseling via Airmen and Family Readiness Centers and Military OneSource

Diagram 3-8. Air Force Suicide Risk Factors.

Program and Policy

The Air Force's comprehensive approach to suicide prevention began in 1996 with the IPT and subsequent development of 11 elements key to successful accomplishment of that program. The program was strongly supported by Chief of Staff of the Air Force and the Surgeon General of the Air Force. The Air Force Suicide Prevention program and its elements were subsequently codified in several Air Force-level publications. AFPAM 44-160, The Air Force Suicide Prevention Program, provides an overview of each of the 11 program elements:

1) Leadership Involvement: Air Force leaders actively support the entire spectrum of suicide prevention initiatives in the Air Force community. Regular messages from the Chief of Staff Air Force, other senior leaders, and base commanders motivate the community to fully engage in suicide prevention efforts.
2) Addressing Suicide Prevention Through Professional Military Education: Suicide prevention education is included in all formal military training.
3) Guidelines for Commanders: Use of Mental Health Services: Commanders receive training on how and when to use behavioral healthcare services and their role in encouraging early help-seeking behavior.
4) Community Preventive Services: Community prevention efforts carry more impact than treating individual patients one at a time.
5) Community Education and Training: Annual suicide prevention training is provided for all military and civilian employees in the Air Force.
6) Investigative Interview Policy: The period following an arrest or investigative interview is a high-risk time for suicide. Following any investigative interview, the investigator is required to "hand off" the individual directly to the commander, first sergeant, or supervisor.

7) Traumatic Stress Response (formerly Critical Incident Stress Management): Trauma Stress Response teams were established worldwide to respond to traumatic incidents such as terrorist attacks, serious accidents, or suicide. These teams help survivors deal with their reactions to traumatic incidents.
8) Integrated Delivery System (IDS) and Community Action Information Board (CAIB): At the Air Force, Major Command, and base levels, the CAIB and IDS provide a forum for the cross-organizational review and resolution of individual, family, installation, and community issues that affect the readiness of the force and the quality of life for Air Force members and their families.
9) Limited Privilege Suicide Prevention Program: Patients at risk for suicide are afforded increased confidentiality when seen by mental health providers (Limited Privilege Suicide Prevention Program). In addition, Limited Patient-Psychotherapist Privilege was established in 1999, limiting the release of patient information to legal authorities during Uniform Code of Military Justice proceedings (see AFI 44-109, Mental Health and Military Law, for additional details).
10) IDS Consultation Assessment Tool (formerly Behavioral Health Survey): The IDS Consultation Assessment Tool was released in December 2005. This tool, administered upon the request of the commander, allows commanders to assess unit strengths and identify areas of vulnerability. Commanders can use this tool in collaboration with IDS consultants to design interventions to support the health and welfare of their personnel.
11) DoD Suicide Event Report: Information on all Air Force active duty suicides and suicide attempts are entered into a central database that tracks suicide events and facilitates the analysis of potential risk factors for suicide in Air Force personnel.

Current Initiatives

The Air Force has actively enhanced its program since the development of the original 11 elements, using information revealed during suicide investigations to modify its policies as necessary. These enhancements have included the development of a Clinicians Guide to Managing Suicidal Behavior, and establishment of a training program to ensure that providers have access to evidence-based approaches to treating patients with suicidal ideation. The Air Force also developed a more advanced training program for supervisors designed to enhance their ability to foster a work environment in which they are engaged in their Airmen's lives and are postured to identify and respond appropriately to warning signs of suicide and other life problems. This Frontline Supervisor Training was first fielded in 2008, and in 2010 was made mandatory for supervisors in identified higher risk career fields as part of a tiered approach to suicide prevention in which those at greatest risk receive more intensive prevention or intervention services.

The Air Force has actively participated on the DoD SPARRC committee since its inception in 1999 and embraces the ideal of sharing best practices that each Service could then adapt to its unique culture. Examples of this sharing include the adoption of the Air Force's Leaders Guide for Managing Personnel in Distress, by the Marine Corps; and the Air Force building on the Army's "Beyond the Front" interactive video with its own "Message Home" interactive video which was used as the basis of a recent AF-wide stand-down training session focusing on suicide prevention.

In short, the Air Force Suicide Prevention Program involves leadership: removing stovepipes and streamlining helping agencies and programs to decrease stigma and increase help-seeking behaviors; establishing a program for limited access to information to protect those who might be at risk of suicide because of pending criminal investigation; and encouraging all Air Force members to care and watch out for one another. Air Force suicides did decrease in the years following the implementation of the program. An article on the impact of the program by Dr. Kerry Knox and colleagues was published in December 2003 in the *British Medical Journal*, and an evaluation of the program for its public health implications worldwide was published in the *American Journal of Public Health* in May 2010. Overall, the program has been lauded as very effective and successful, and other suicide prevention programs—both military and civilian— have incorporated some of its elements, and used it as a model.

Diagram 3-9 depicts the total number and rate of Air Force suicides for calendar years 2001- 2009.

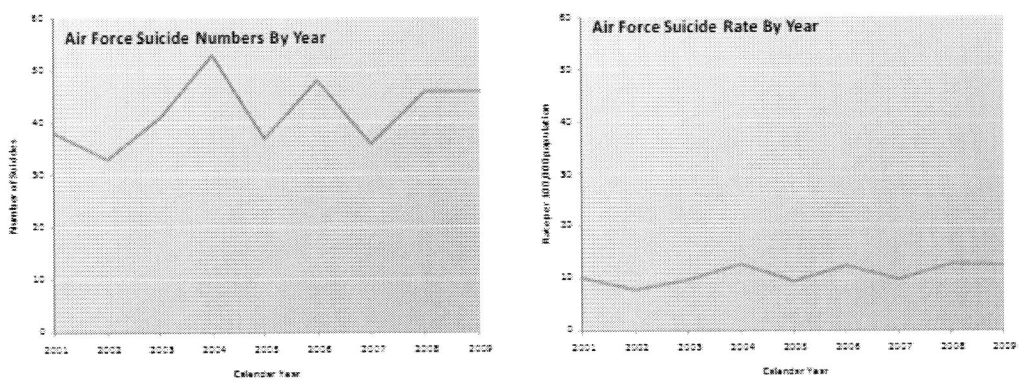

Source: Mortality Surveillance Division, Armed Forces Medical Examiner System, AFIP, 2010.

Diagram 3-9. Air Force Suicides 2001–2009.

3.5. United States Marine Corps Surveillance

USMC suicides have been recorded since the 1970s but studies analyzing suicides did not begin until 1980 (Helmkamp, 1995; Hourani, Warrack, & Coben, 1997). Early surveillance activities were sponsored by both the USN and USMC. DONSIR, the first official suicide surveillance program within the DON, systematically collected data on all completed suicides beginning in 1999 (Hourani & Hilton, 1999; Hourani, Hilton, Kennedy, & Jones, 2000; Hourani, Hilton, Kennedy, & Robbins, 2001; Jones et al., 2001; Stander, Hilton, Doran, Gaskin, & Thomsen, 2005; Stander, Hilton, Kennedy, & Gaskin, 2004; Stander, Hilton, Kennedy, & Robbins, 2004; Stander, Hilton, Doran, Werbel, & Thomsen, 2007; Hilton, Stander, Werbel, & Chavez, 2008). The DONSIR established baselines for suicide rates and suicide event characteristics that were used to track trends over time. For the first time it was also possible to assess military-specific characteristics that were not evaluated in the civilian literature such as deployments and rank. The DONSIR was used through calendar year 2007 at which time the USN and USMC worked with the other Services to adapt and endorse use of DoDSER. Diagram 3-10 displays the demographics of Marines who died by suicide in CY2009 as well as the current suspected suicides and the number of suspected suicides and suicidal attempts through July 2010.

2010 Month	Suspected Suicides	Suicide Attempts
January	7	23
February	2	21
March	3	15
April	2	19
May	7	19
June	1	12
July	6	7
August		
September		
October		
November		
December		

Gender	52 Male	0 Female
Race	41 Caucasion	4 African American
	5 Hispanic	1 Am. Indian/ Alaska Native
	1 Asian	
Age	40 (18-24)	5 (25-29)
	6 (30-39)	1 (40-50)
Marital Status	25 (Single)	24 (Married)
	3 (Divorced)	
Paygrade	27 (E1-E3)	20 (E4-E5)
	3 (E6-E9)	1 (WO-CW05)
	1 (01-010)	
Method	31 Gunshot	17 Hanging
	3 Laceration	1 Suffocation

Diagram 3-10. Marine Corps suspected suicides, suicide attempts, and demographic profile.

The USMC began to use the DoDSER for all suicide related deaths on 1 January 2008 and continues to lead the DoD in compliance with 100-percent completion rates for both 2008 and 2009. On 24 December 2009, the USMC directed that the DoDSER be completed for all behaviors diagnosed as suicide attempts by competent medical authorities. Although previously tracked through the Personnel Casualty Reporting system, this refinement provided a dual track reporting process to improve the reliability and validity of data collection on suicide attempts. It also allowed for more robust data collection on suicide attempts than was previously required.

Policy

Although suicide prevention as a leadership and medical activity certainly predated the first Marine Corps Order on the topic, the Marine Corps Health Promotion order of 8 May 1992 (MCO 6200.4) was the first to identify suicide prevention as an integral part of USMC guidance, with requirements for small unit suicide prevention and awareness training. Such efforts were quickly supported by the 1993 Marine Corps Quality of Life assessment (Kerce, 1995).

The Human Resources Division of the Headquarters, Marine Corps (HQMC) produced the first standardized lesson plan on "Suicide Awareness and Prevention" in August 1994.

The suicide of the CNO ADM Jeremy M. Boorda in May 1996 resulted in a full review of all DoD suicide prevention programs.

The DON conducted a comprehensive assessment of suicide prevention efforts in 1998 that resulted in new initiatives that included significant coordination among HQMC, Naval Personnel Command, the Bureau of Medicine and Surgery, Naval Criminal Investigative Service, the Naval Health Research Center, and the Navy Environmental Health Center. One of the initiatives that resulted directly from this effort was the previously mentioned DONSIR.

Suicide awareness and prevention policy was updated in MCO 6200.4A (7 April 1997), mandating annual training for all Marines with additional guidance to be found in the SECNAVINST 6320.24A (16 February 1999). These documents established a coherent direction for leaders at all levels in suicide prevention.

Numerous White Letters, All Marine Corps Activities (ALMARS), and Marine Administrative letters further clarified guidance. In 1998 the USMC reorganized its headquarters sections on suicide prevention, drug and alcohol abuse, and domestic violence to benefit from greater collaboration.

Today, guidance on the USMC suicide prevention program is found in numerous Marine Corps Orders (P1700.24B Marine Corps Personal Services Manual, P1700.27A Marine Corps Community Services Policy Manual, P1700.29 Marine Corps Semper Fi Program Manual, P3040.4E Marine Corps Casualty Procedures Manual, MCRP 6-11C Marine Corps Combat Stress Manual, 1510.89B Individual Training Standards (ITS) System for Marine Corps Common Skills (Volume 1)).

Program Elements

The Suicide Prevention Program involves a continuum of care with several elements:

- Awareness education and health promotion
- Life Skills Training to enhance coping skills and social support to reduce the incidence of problems that detract from personal and unit readiness
- Leadership Training to provide leaders at all levels with information and skills to enhance risk identification and early intervention with at-risk personnel
- Crisis Intervention and Risk Management to provide procedures for the referral and evaluation of Marines requiring emergency psychiatric care and/or Marines who have problems that increase risk for suicide, such as depression and/or alcohol abuse
- Counseling and Treatment to provide services and programs that support the resolution of personal, family, and mental health issues that underlie suicidal behavior
- Postvention Services to provide sensitive family support and debriefing services for units affected by the suicide of a member
- Casualty Reports and Trend Analysis to provide incident reports to higher authority to assist in improving institutional knowledge about suicide through research into risk and protective factors to improve future prevention efforts
- Regularly scheduled inspections to ensure the full implementation of the USMC suicide prevention program by Commanding Generals.

In the last few years the USMC has released numerous administrative messages to guide Marines through emerging requirements and new initiatives. The USMC continues to refine policy and is currently revising guidance on suicide prevention.

Diagram 3-11 identifies the top risk factors and stressors associated with USMC suicides for the years 1999-2007.

Top Risk Factors / Warning Signs	Identified in 1999-2007 Suicides
1. Negative Emotional State	51%
2. Mental Health History	40%
3. Changes in Mood or Behavior	34%
4. Self Destructive/ Aggressive Behavior	28%

Top Associated Stressors	Identified in 1999-2007 Suicides
1. Relationship Problems/Loss	53%
2. Work Related Problems	50%
3. Pending Disciplinary Action	43%
4. Physical Illness	33%
5. Financial Problems	13%

Diagram 3-11. Marine Corps Top Risk Factors and Associated Stressors, 1999 to 2007.

Current Initiatives

The USMC has actively participated on the DoD SPARRC since its inception and embraced the sharing of best practices for each Service's unique culture. One example of this sharing was the adoption of the Air Force's Leaders' Guide for Managing Personnel in Distress. The USMC developed the Leaders' Guide for Managing Marines in Distress and modified the format to more accurately reflect USMC culture and ethos. This resulted in a dynamic Web site that became, within just 3 months of its release, the second most visited site on the Marine Corps Community Services portal after employment opportunities. The USMC distributed 150,000 copies of a pocket guide across the Corps to give leaders quick access to critical information for helping Marines in distress.

In 2009 training evolution in the USMC led to evocative, targeted, peer-taught training developed specifically for Marine NCOs to offer additional tools. NCOs were selected for initial targeting because of their proximity and therefore influence on those Marines at greatest risk of suicide—privates to sergeants. Early success with this program and consistent positive feedback from NCOs led to the current development of targeted training for younger Marines, staff NCOs, and officers. The USMC is also developing more initiatives to reach family members.

Research is an ongoing concern, and the USMC is partnering with the Army and the National Institute for Mental Health (NIMH) to assess suicide and resilience in a 5-year longitudinal study.

The USMC established the Combat and Operational Stress Control Program and Operational Stress Control and Readiness (OSCAR) training as a primary prevention tool to help Marines identify and mitigate stress early and to encourage them to seek help within the unit setting whether deployed or in garrison.

The USMC recently broadened the scope of the former Executive Safety Board, a bi-annual meeting chaired by the Assistant Commandant of the Marine Corps and renamed it the Executive Force Preservation Board (EFPB). It is now focused on all behavioral health concerns such as combat and operational stress, suicide, domestic violence, substance abuse, and sexual assault. A current initiative of the EFPB is a Marine Crisis Hotline that is scheduled for a pilot release in 2010. This 24/7 behavioral health crisis hotline that individuals can call anonymously is specifically designed for the USMC culture and will employ former Marines to provide Marines (former and current, active, and reserve), family members, and significant others with access to behavioral healthcare.

Diagram 3-12 depicts the total number and rate of Marine Corps suicides for calendar years 2001-2009.

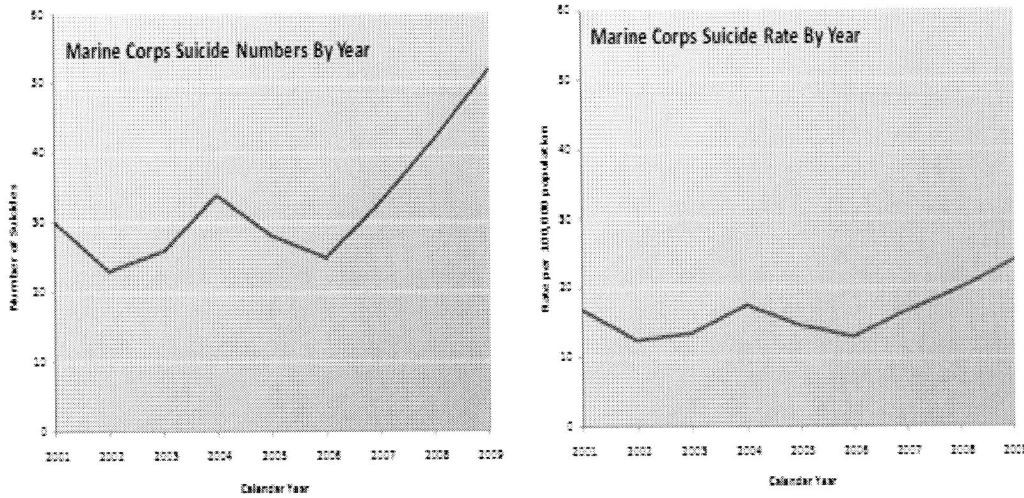

Source: Mortality Surveillance Division, Armed Forces Medical Examiner System, AFIP, 2010.

Diagram 3-12. Marine Corps Suicides 2001–2009.

3.6. United States Coast Guard

The US Coast Guard (USCG) is considered the fifth member of the Armed Forces and thus the Task Force has included it in this report. Members of the USCG receive their medical care from a variety of sources. Sixty-five percent of their care is provided through USCG clinics, which are staffed with US Public Health Service physicians and Coast Guard Physician Assistant officers.

The USCG also has about 780 enlisted members at its 42 clinics. The balance of care that USCG members receive is provided through DoD Military Treatment Facilities (MTF) (19 percent) and through the TRICARE network (17 percent).

Most USCG clinics are not staffed to see family members; therefore, most USCG families receive their care from DoD MTFs and the TRICARE network. Nearly all behavioral healthcare for USCG members and their families is received outside of Coast Guard clinics. The USCG relies heavily on Employee Assistance Program (EAP) providers to offer "short-term problem solving" or counseling services.

For the calendar years 2001 through 2009, there was an average of 4.8 active duty USCG suicides per year.

This translates into an average annual rate of 11.4 per 100,000 active duty members. Diagram 3-13 depicts the total number and rate of Coast Guard suicides for calendar years 2001-2009.

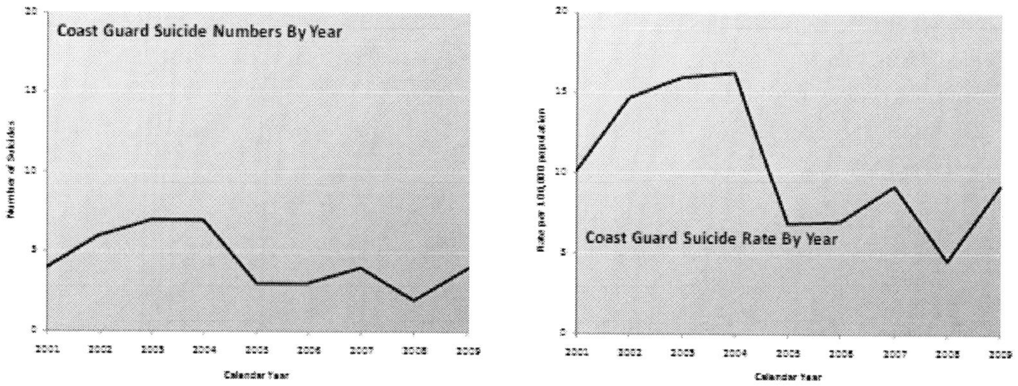

Diagram 3-13. USCG Suicides 2001–2009.

The USCG's Suicide Prevention Program was revised in December 2009. The goals of the program are to empower all members and civilian employees to recognize and react appropriately to the signs of suicidal behavior, reduce the stigma associated with getting psychological help, and protect those who responsibly seek behavioral healthcare. The USCG program has seven elements:

- Command Climate
- Crisis Response
- Limit on Command Access to Mental Healthcare Information
- Notification and Hands-off in Criminal Investigations
- Postvention
- Reporting
- Training.

Each of these elements is discussed in Commandant Instruction (COMDTINST) 1734.1A, Suicide Prevention Program.

COMDTINST 1734.1A clarifies that it is a command responsibility to provide a command climate in which members feel that it is okay to seek help. In addition, commands are now responsible for establishing a protocol for responding to persons considered at-risk. The new policy also attempts to implement the Air Force's 18 medical requirements for managing suicidal behavior. Providing quality assurance to ensure compliance with these 18 requirements will be particularly challenging because almost the USCG's entire behavioral healthcare is delivered outside the USCG. However, *ensuring* that the care provided to USCG members meets requirements is the responsibility of the USCG and is consistent with "medical home," a concept of operations that all USCG medical clinics are implementing to ensure proper care and follow-up for all USCG members.

Formal reporting of incidents to USCG Headquarters by medical personnel is required in all cases of suicide attempts involving physical injury. In cases of suicide, the Suicide Prevention Program Manager completes the form after all related investigations are completed. The form mirrors the DoDSER form. Eventually, it is the USCG's intent to participate in the DoDSER, if possible.

The USCG Suicide Prevention Program Manager also monitors all active duty hospitalizations related to suicidal communications and/or behaviors to ensure that the USCG medical chain of command is aware of the hospitalization. The Manager also tracks each case to ensure a report is received if the patient required medical treatment as a result of suicidal behavior.

Annual suicide prevention training is mandated for all USCG members and civilian employees. Although it is generally recognized that this training is most effective if delivered face to face, the training is now provided online. Online training, however, is considered a positive development because the training is now accessible to the estimated 30 percent of personnel who previously were not able to attend training. Commands still have the option to provide this training face to face.

For the first time in 2008, the USCG participated in the triennial DoD Survey of Health-Related Behaviors Among Active Duty Military Personnel. Below is a sampling of relevant USCG findings:

DoD Survey of Health-Related Behaviors: Coast Guard

- 18 percent of personnel met screening criteria suggesting the need for further depression evaluation.
- 10 percent met screening criteria suggesting the need for further evaluation for generalized anxiety disorder.
- 7 percent met screening criteria suggesting the need for further evaluation of PTSD.
- 18 percent reported heavy alcohol use (five or more drinks on the same occasion at least once a week in the past 30 days).
- 12 percent met criteria for "serious psychological distress" as determined by analysis of data collected for depression, anxiety, and PTSD.
- 2.8 percent answered positively when asked whether they had "seriously considered suicide within the past year."
- 1.7 percent answered positively when asked whether they had attempted suicide within the past year.
- 11 percent believed that their career would "definitely" be damaged if they sought mental health counseling through the military.

Diagram 3-14. Relevant USCG Findings.

The USCG Suicide Prevention Program Manager will monitor Health-Related Behavior findings in future surveys as measures of the effectiveness of the USCG's suicide prevention efforts.

The USCG's Critical Incident Stress Management (CISM) Program has provided interventions after critical incidents such as body recovery missions, mishaps, and major disasters since the mid-1990s. These interventions typically involve trained persons outside the affected unit coming in to assist the unit in responding to psychological needs of members.

The USCG is in the beginning stages of determining the courses of action needed to implement a leader-driven Operational Stress Control (OSC) Program, modeled after the USN's OSC Program, that will empower supervisors to practice "intrusive leadership" by not only recognizing the signs of stress but being vigilant in taking appropriate action to "keep personnel in the green" and mission-ready. An effective USCG OSC Program will further USCG suicide prevention efforts and decrease the need for CISM interventions.

4. VISION

Task Force Vision Statement

A military force fit in mind, body, and spirit that wins the battle against suicide and stands ready to answer the Nation's call.

5. STRATEGY

To prevent suicide by Service Members, it is absolutely essential to implement a comprehensive suicide prevention program. After considerable research and deliberation, the Task Force identified four major focus areas that constitute a sound suicide prevention program poised for success (see Diagram 5-1). All Service suicide prevention programs must consider initiatives and policies that align under each of these four focus areas in order to holistically organize their efforts for suicide prevention. In addition, based on current Service programs and identified gaps, the Task Force identified 18 strategies for DoD to adopt to enhance suicide prevention efforts. Each of the 18 strategies were placed in 1 of the 4 focus areas. The recommendations are based on findings. While some recommendations are specific to a particular strategy, others covered several strategies within a focus area; and some even covered strategies in several focus areas. The four major focus areas emerged not only as a model of a comprehensive suicide prevention program, but they also became a way for the Task Force to organize its strategies and recommendations in the report. It is important to note that each of the focus areas both informs and builds on one another.

Diagram 5-1. Developing a Comprehensive Suicide Prevention Strategy.

Diagram 5-2. Total Fitness.

Focus Area 1: Organization and Leadership

Institutions and entities must be organized structurally for suicide prevention, and leaders must be involved at every level. Consequently, the Task Force strongly believes that suicide prevention begins with coherent policy generated from OSD. Command attention and review at the highest level will ensure that every other level of supervision and care pays careful attention to the well-being of members of the Armed Forces, that suicidal thoughts and behaviors are reduced, and that suicide risks are minimized.

Organization: Effective organizational structure is essential to develop enterprise-wide policy as well as program standardization and oversight. To enhance suicide prevention efforts and maintain a lasting impact, DoD must organize appropriately, in conjunction with the Services, to more effectively obtain positive outcomes of their suicide prevention programs. This organizational structure would be responsible for DoD suicide prevention oversight, stigma reduction efforts, and strategic communication.

Leadership: Effective leadership involvement, from the most senior leaders to the most junior first-line/front-line/first-time supervisors (junior leaders) of our Service Members, remains critical to suicide prevention. Officers and NCOs are, in many ways, the primary agents with the ability to reduce the stressors that lead to suicide—through a positive and supportive command climate and by establishing a culture of intervention before a member becomes suicidal. Troubled Service Members must be led to the best available "helping agent" to prevent suicide or suicide-related behaviors free from stigmatization.

Effective DoD organization and leadership is a key line of defense in our fight to prevent suicide in members of the Armed Forces.

Focus Area 2: Wellness Enhancement and Training

Wellness and fitness are essential to maintaining a healthy outlook on life. Therefore, the Task Force strongly believes that any effort to enhance the well-being, resiliency, life skills, and mental fitness of Service Members will have significant impact on preventing suicide as a primary prevention effort. The Services should focus on all the domains of total fitness (i.e., total well being). In addition, if primary prevention fails, the community of people surrounding an individual who has become "un-well/un-fit" must be educated to recognize suicidal vulnerabilities, risks, and behaviors, and trained to ensure the Service Member gets timely access to intervention services.

Wellness: Maintaining wellness and mental fitness is vital to suicide prevention.

Military life, particularly in wartime, is inherently stressful on individuals and presents a unique challenge to maintaining wellness. Physical, psychological, spiritual, family, social, financial, vocational, and emotional well-being are protective factors against suicide (see Diagram 5-3).

A comprehensive suicide prevention strategy involves reducing and mitigating risk factors while at the same time enhancing protective factors. Therefore, DoD and the Services must continue to expend substantial effort to mitigate stressors by supporting programs that strengthen these protective factors. Fostering wellness is prevention in its purest form.

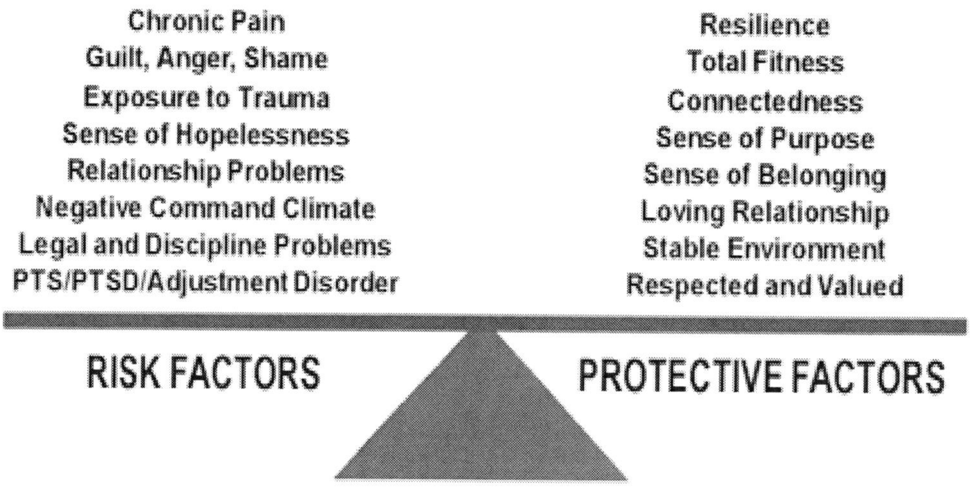

With the unique demands placed on service members, programs that eliminate and mitigate risk and enhance protective factors are important to preventing suicide.

Diagram 5-3. Risk Factors and Protective Factors in Suicide Prevention.

Training: Training is imperative to preventing suicide. When individuals exhibit signs of suicidal behaviors, everyone around them must be equipped to recognize their distress and ensure referral to appropriate intervention services. Peers, first-line supervisors, and especially family members must be trained to recognize suicidal behaviors and know how to get the person to intervention services.

Individual Service Member well-being, fitness and resiliency is another key line of defense in the fight against suicide.

Focus Area 3: Access to, and Delivery of, Quality Care

Any effective suicide prevention program must make quality professional intervention, counseling, diagnosis, and treatment accessible. The Task Force strongly believes that intervention services must be well-coordinated and standardized, and caregivers must be specifically trained in suicide assessment and risk reduction. Because of the complex dynamics of suicide prevention, all care services must share information. Ready access to high-quality care is essential to preventing suicide.

Access to Quality Care: Access to effective intervention services must be 24/7/365. Intervention services must be available at the right time and the right place. Availability of first responders, trained people on crisis hotlines, trained emergency room personnel, chaplains, primary care clinicians, and behavioral health clinicians is essential as a line of defense for preventing suicide. All existing barriers to accessing care must be removed.

Delivery of Quality Care: The delivery of quality care, both medical and non-medical, is an important aspect of all suicide prevention programs. Established training programs that build competencies in clinicians (such as behavioral health, primary care, and emergency medicine clinicians) and non-clinicians (such as first responders, hotline personnel, and chaplains) must be standardized for everyone involved in suicide prevention. Continuity of care, particularly during times of transition, is critical to suicide prevention. Electronic medical records that enhance information sharing will ensure greater effectiveness and are vital to preventing potential suicide victims from falling through the cracks.

A third line of defense in suicide prevention is ready access to high-quality care.

Focus Area 4: Surveillance, Investigations, and Research

Suicide prevention requires a public health approach, and effective surveillance is essential to public health benefits. The Task Force strongly believes that much can be learned from standardized data collection and analysis that addresses risk factors and trends, and assists in identifying decision points for targeted interventions. Well-constructed surveillance that ideally leads to a predictive model can inform and shape future suicide prevention programs and efforts as well as improve public health efforts. Investigations must be standardized in order inform surveillance efforts. Program evaluation must be incorporated to measure program effectiveness. Knowledge gaps must be closed with research.

Surveillance: For surveillance to be effective it must be standardized and centrally driven, and data must be reported in a timely, consistent, and reliable manner. Surveillance should be continuous and sustained. The information must be centrally analyzed so it can be acted on appropriately. Surveillance data can be used to modify and enhance policy, programs, and communications. It can identify commands that have Service Members at higher risk and can be used as an indicator for the possibility of a negative command climate (one not conducive to suicide prevention).

Investigations: Much can be learned by investigating suicide and suicide attempts in a standardized manner that contributes to knowledge and understanding of causal factors and trends. Because of the stigma and attribution associated with those surrounding a suicide victim, suicide investigations (once criminality is ruled out) should focus solely on identifying contributing and non-contributing factors important to suicide prevention.

Research: Research must continue to advance the science of suicidology in order to learn more about suicide-related behaviors and effective prevention techniques. Research must be accomplished to determine best practices as well as develop evidence based clinical practice guidelines in order to decrease variations in suicide prevention practices. Research efforts should be based on requirements identified by knowledge gaps. Research must be resourced and prioritized to focus efforts for maximal impact in achieving better outcomes.

Vigilant surveillance, thorough and informative investigations, program evaluation, and research form a fourth and final line of defense in a comprehensive suicide prevention program.

6. ASSESSMENT

6.1. Service Suicide Data and Statistics

The diagram below details the count and crude rate of suicides among Active Duty and Reserve Component Service Members per 100,000 population for calendar years 2001- 2009. The rates have not been calculated for cells with counts less than five. The counts include both confirmed and suspected suicides. The rates are based on yearly September end strength reports from the Defense Manpower Data Center (DMDC). Reserve Component rates include Active Duty Guard and Reserve Service Members.

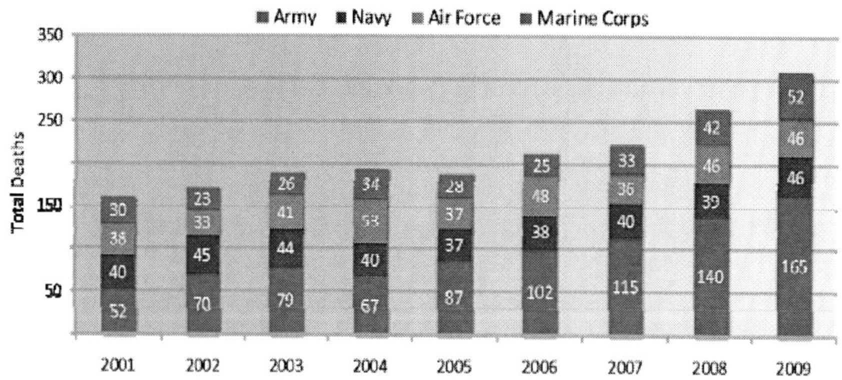

	2001		2002		2003		2004		2005		2006		2007		2008		2009		Year Total
	No.	Rate	No.	Rate	No.	Rate	No.	Rate	No.	Rate	No.	Rate	No.	Rate	No.	Rate	No.	Rate	
Total/Year	160	10.3	171	10.3	190	11	194	11.3	189	11.3	213	13.1	224	13.8	267	15.8	309	18.4	1917
Regular	145	10.5	146	10.3	158	11	171	12	148	10.7	187	13.5	197	14.3	234	16.9	285	20.3	1671
Reserve	15	9.3	25	10.6	32	11.1	23	8	41	14.8	26	10.7	27	10.8	33	10.5	24	8.6	246
OEF	1		3		4		2		4		3		5		7		10		39
OIF	0		0		27		20		25		31		41		35		33		212

Source: Mortality Surveillance Division, Armed Forces Medical Examiner System, AFIP, 2010.

Diagram 6-1. Count and Crude Suicide Rates Among Active Duty and Reserve Service Members.

Suicide in the US military has consistently been reported as a leading cause of mortality over the past decade (DMDC, 2010). A brief description of the 2008 DoDSER data (Gahm, Reger, Luxton, Skopp, & Lee, 2009; Reger, Luxton, Skopp, Lee & Gahm, 2009) presented at the November 2009 meeting of the Task Force is noted here to provide a perspective on the most recently documented US military suicides. As Diagram 6-2 demonstrates, a higher prevalence of military suicide is reported for males (18.2 per 100,000), Caucasians (17.4 per 100,000), divorced Service Members (27.6 per 100,000), those under age 25 (20.1 per 100,000), E1 through E4 ranks (20.1 per 100,000), and members with a GED (29.1 per 100,000). (Gahm, Reger, Luxton, Skopp, & Lee, 2009; Reger, Luxton, Skopp, Lee & Gahm, 2009.)

Additionally, across Services, the most frequent method of suicide was self-inflicted gun shot wounds using non-military firearms which accounted for 41 percent of all suicides. Military firearms were used in 21 percent of suicides, with higher incidence noted for the Army and the Marine Corps. Approximately 70 percent of 2008 DoD suicides indicated some evidence of intent to die by suicide. Communication of intent to die has been documented for 30 percent of 2008 suicides. One of every four (23 percent) Service Members left a suicide note. Up to 36 percent of suicides had a history of at least one documented mental disorder, and 49 percent had been seen in at least one DoD program or clinic within 30 days prior to death (Gahm, Reger, Luxton, Skopp, & Lee, 2009; Reger, Luxton, Skopp, Lee & Gahm, 2009).

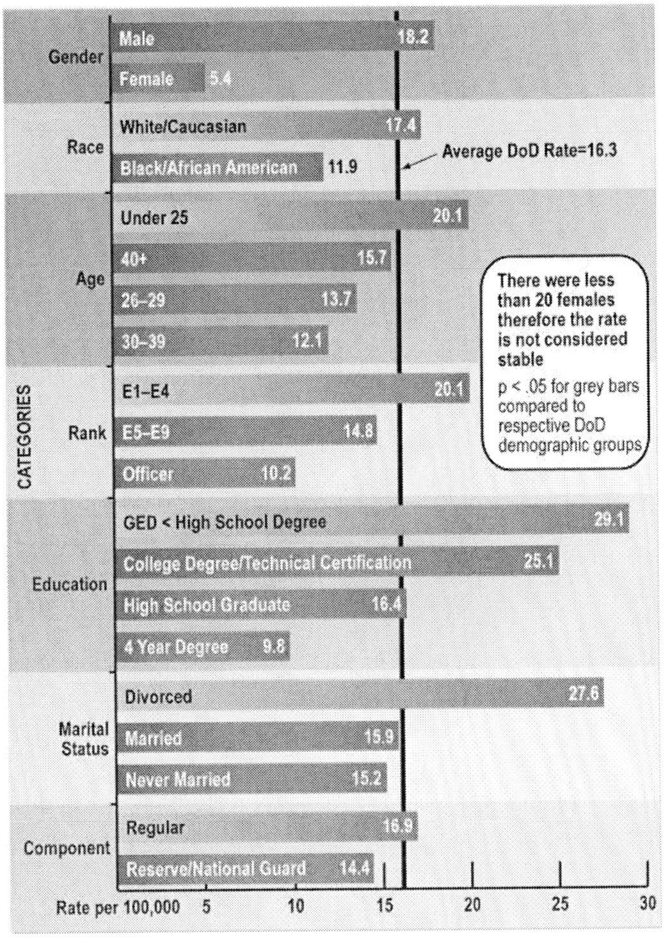

Source: Gahm, et al. 2009.

Diagram 6-2. Military Demographics.

6.2. An Assessment of Service Suicide Prevention Programs

The Services clearly have a long and committed history of recognizing the risk of suicide and implementing suicide prevention programs. Each is devoting enormous energy and resources to nearly 900 suicide prevention activities across the 407 military installations worldwide. The Task Force certainly commends the remarkable efforts of each Service, because they, along with the VA, are among the Nation's leaders in this important and noble endeavor. Individually, the Services have implemented programs that address each of the four focus areas identified by the Task Force as key to the success of a comprehensive suicide prevention program: Organization and Leadership; Wellness Enhancement and Training; Access to, and Delivery of, Quality Care; and Surveillance, Investigations, and Research. The four focus areas, when viewed and considered collectively, constitute the lines of defense in which the Task Force organized its recommendations for preventing suicides.

While the Services are addressing many areas in their individual efforts, these efforts need to be better coordinated within and across the Services. Many programs are stand-alone undertakings or only loosely tied into other similar programs on the installations.

Better coordination would enhance the lines of defense available to Service Members and their families. Service Member and family awareness of these programs and services is inconsistent. Even if the necessary services, programs, and skills training are available, moving between them or leveraging the strengths of each to form a cohesive whole is lacking.

If one imagines suicide prevention as a net, with ropes tied together at certain cross-points, the lack of coordinated efforts across and within military installations results in ropes that are too short to meet one another...a net with holes through which Service Members are falling.

The Services require a coordinated DoD approach to suicide prevention that employs the most effective skills-based training available to strengthen both individuals and families.

In addition, quality care should be accessible not only in the MTFs, but proactively offered in the workplace and in local communities. Finally, should a Service Member fall through the prevention net, DoD needs to ensure that the lessons learned from that fall are quickly gathered and put to good use in preventing future falls.

Program improvement must become a core priority in DoD through surveillance, investigation, program evaluation and research.

6.3. Occupational Risk and Military Suicides

The Task Force in unable to determine any suicide risk attributable specifically to occupation.

There are insufficient data at this time to support identification of military occupations with a high incidence of suicide owing to occupation alone. In addition, at the time of this writing, scientific evidence does not seem to support a relationship between suicide and military occupational specialty.

The Task Force did obtain information related to suicides by career field from each of the Services.

The individual Service statistics are provided in Appendix G. However, the Task Force strongly cautions readers against drawing any conclusions from the data provided for the following reasons:

- The low rate of suicide in any specific career field makes determining statistically valid rates of suicide in a career field challenging. Less than statistically valid data make comparisons between career fields almost impossible.
- The definition of career fields changes over the years—career fields come and go, or are merged into, or diverged from, existing career fields. Therefore, the denominator of the rate calculation (i.e., the total population in a career field) may vary from year to year, nullifying comparison data.
- Career fields among the Services also vary, so comparisons at that level are generally also not valid.
- Data on some high interest career fields such as recruiting and instructing reflect the duty being performed at the time of the suicide, not the underlying career field of the deceased.

Preliminary evidence provided to the Task Force examined the relationship between career field and suicide and did not find a significant relationship (Gahm, 2010). Consistent with previous studies, failed relationships and a mental health diagnosis were identified as primary stressors. In addition, Soldiers who view their leadership positively experienced a greater sense of unit cohesion and morale (MHAT VI, 2009). Numerous efforts are underway to continue to understand the role an individual's career field may have in relation to suicide and suicide prevention.

7. Findings and Recommendations

Opening Statement by the Task Force

The numbers and rates of Service Member suicides are unacceptable and continue to climb. A crisis situation continues to unfold and must be dealt with immediately. Action must proceed with a sense of urgency to reverse the current troublesome trend and to prevent future suicides. Suicide is preventable. Suicidal behaviors must be prevented and dealt with early. Having any one of our nation's warriors die by suicide is not acceptable--not now, not ever.

The Task Force acknowledges the significant efforts made by the military Services in the area of suicide prevention. The Services have substantially increased their focus and investments in suicide prevention over the years to meet current requirements. This is evident at the highest levels of leadership in the military Departments. This Task Force witnessed commitment, creativity, and compassion by uniformed and civilian employees across the Services in attempting to address this looming crisis.

The Task Force also believes the remarkable efforts made by the Services are not permeating consistently throughout the Services and are not reaching the levels necessary to prevent suicide in all cases. Furthermore, the Task Force believes that current Service efforts can benefit from a comprehensive suicide prevention strategy, coordinated throughout DoD with additional leader accountability, to foster a command climate that promotes Service Member wellness and fitness – in mind, in body and in spirit. Command climates must continue to evolve to ensure the positive and engaged support of every Service Member in distress; and view this support as a vital part of mission readiness and mission success.

General Observations

"The most important ingredient is leadership: aggressive, focused, listening leadership."
—Chairman, Joint Chiefs of Staff

1. Suicide is preventable.
2. The Services are heavily engaged in suicide prevention.
3. Leadership is involved at the senior levels universally.
4. No one can know for sure just how many suicides there would be if it were not for current Service suicide prevention efforts.
5. This Task Force is unable to "grade" Service suicide prevention programs.
6. There is a relationship between increased operations tempo, deployments and separations with overall stress on the force and increased suicide rates.
7. This Task Force is unable to determine any risk for suicide due specifically to occupation, although targeted suicide prevention in those occupations with higher rates owing to other risk factors makes perfectly good sense.
8. Suicide has multiple, complex risk factors: Suicide prevention must have multi-dimensional approaches and solutions.
9. There must be a renewed focus at the troop level and a sense of urgency at all levels, especially in strategic planning, to interrupt the trend and save lives by preventing suicide.

Overview Approach (Focus Areas and Strategies)

The Task Force arrived at 49 findings and 76 associated recommendations. They fall into four primary focus areas that emerged not only as a model of a comprehensive suicide prevention program, but also as a strategic framework to organize the findings and recommendations.

In addition, based on current Service programs and identified gaps, the Task Force identified 18 strategies for DoD to adopt to enhance suicide prevention efforts. These strategies are listed by focus area in Section 7.2.

Organization and Leadership (7.1)

- 7.1.1. Create, restructure and resource suicide prevention offices at OSD, the Services, installations, and unit level to achieve unity of effort.
- 7.1.2. Equip and empower leaders (provide them tools) to establish a culture that fosters prevention as well as early recognition and intervention
- 7.1.3. Develop strategic communications that promote life, normalize "help seeking behaviors," and support DoD suicide prevention strategies.
- 7.1.4. Reduce stigma and overcome military cultural and leadership barriers to seeking help.
- 7.1.5. Standardize suicide prevention policies and procedures.

Wellness Enhancement and Training (7.2)

- 7.2.1. Enhance well-being, mental fitness, life skills, and resiliency.
- 7.2.2. Reduce stress on the force and on military families.
- 7.2.3. Transform suicide prevention training of Service Members, leaders, and families to enhance skills.

Access to, and Delivery of, Quality Care (7.3)

- 7.3.1. Ensure available and reliable access to high-quality behavioral healthcare.
- 7.3.2. Leverage and coordinate military community-based services, as well as local civilian community services (especially with respect to the Reserve Component).
- 7.3.3. Ensure continuity of behavioral healthcare, especially during times of transition, to ensure seamlessness of healthcare and care management.
- 7.3.4. Standardize effective crisis intervention services and hotlines.
- 7.3.5. Ensure all "helping professionals" are trained in the competencies to deliver evidence-based care for the assessment, management, and treatment of suicide-related behaviors.
- 7.3.6. Develop effective postvention programs to support families, Service Members, and units leaders after a suicide.

Surveillance, Investigations, and Research (7.4)

- 7.4.1. Conduct comprehensive surveillance aimed at identifying individuals at-risk and informing prevention efforts.
- 7.4.2. Standardize investigations of suicides and suicide attempts to identify target areas for prevention policies, procedures, and programs.
- 7.4.3. Ensure that all initiatives and programs have a program evaluation component.
- 7.4.4. Support and incorporate ongoing research to inform evidence-based suicide prevention practices.

Foundational Recommendations

As the Task Force conducted its work, the members arrived at unanimous agreement that successful suicide prevention had to be structured using a public health model with defined focus areas, each containing strategies inherent to a comprehensive suicide prevention approach.

The Task Force considered 49 findings and 76 recommendations to be report worthy. In addition, the Task Force developed 13 foundational recommendations that aggregated several of the targeted recommendations. These 13 underscore success of all the recommendations. Without implementation of these critical actions, the other recommendations are destined for failure. The 13 foundational recommendations are:

1) Create a "Suicide Prevention Policy Division" at OSD within USD(P&R) to standardize policies and procedures with respect to resiliency, mental fitness, life skills, and suicide prevention. The office will provide standardization, integration of best practices, and general oversight, serve as a change agent, and establish an ongoing external review group of non-DoD experts to assess progress. Furthermore, this office will provide guidance from which the Services can design and implement their suicide prevention programs.
2) Keep suicide prevention programs in the leadership lane and hold leaders accountable at all levels for ensuring a positive command climate that promotes the well-being, total fitness, and "help seeking" of their Service Members. A significant focus on developing better tools to assist commanders in suicide prevention must be undertaken.
3) Reduce stress on the force. The pace of operations in today's military exceeds the ability of Service Members to be restored to their optimal state of readiness. There is a supply and demand mismatch that creates a cumulative negative impact on the force. Reduce stress by ensuring the quantity and quality of dwell time allows for individual restoration as the force is reconstituted over and over again. This will allow Service Members to reestablish relationships and connectedness. If necessary, either grow the size of the force to ensure additional uniformed end-strength to meet the demand or reduce the mission demand.
4) Focus efforts on Service Member well-being, total fitness (of the mind, body, and spirit), and development of life skills and resiliency to increase protective factors and decrease risk factors. This is the pinnacle of primary prevention.
5) Develop a Comprehensive Stigma Reduction Campaign Plan that attacks the issue on multiple fronts to encourage help-seeking behavior and normalizes the care of the "hidden wounds" incurred by Service Members.
6) Strengthen strategic messaging to enhance positive communications that generate the behaviors and outcomes desired rather than highlighting the negative messaging about today's challenges. The focus of messaging must migrate from speaking solely about the "tragedy" of suicide and the "actions" being taken to messages that reduces stigma, encourages help seeking, portrays concerned leadership, and inspires hope by showing that help really works.
7) Develop skills-based training in all aspects of training regarding suicide prevention. The current awareness and education efforts about suicide prevention are adequate, but skills-based training is deficient, especially among buddies, family members, first-line supervisors, clergy, and behavioral health personnel.
8) Incorporate program evaluation in all suicide prevention programs to determine the effectiveness of each program in obtaining its intended outcome.
9) Coordinate and leverage the strengths of installation and local community support services for both Active and Reserve Component Service Members. Community health and access to quality, competent services are essential to suicide prevention.
10) Ensure continuity and the management of quality behavioral healthcare, especially while in transition periods, to facilitate a seamless transfer of awareness, management, and treatment as Service Members change locations. Transitions must be actively managed; and tools must be developed to actively manage them.

11) Mature and expand the DoDSER to serve as the main surveillance method to inform future suicide prevention efforts. Further standardize data collection processes. Robust surveillance will produce data that allows us to anticipate and avoid future occurrences of that event before the individual or population (or unit) reaches a crisis point.
12) Standardize suicide investigations and expand their focus to learn about the last hours, days, and weeks preceding a suicide or attempted suicide. Pattern suicide investigations on aviation accident safety investigation procedures and use the safety investigation process as a model to develop a standardized suicide investigation process.
13) Support and fund ongoing DoD suicide prevention research to enhance our knowledge and inform future suicide prevention efforts, and to incorporate evidenced-based solutions. Focused research in suicide prevention for Service Members is essential to identifying best practices, decreasing variation in prevention practices, and in achieving desired outcomes.

Considerable effort has been expended by DoD, the Services, and innumerable caring and dedicated individuals across the world in support of Service Members and their families. The findings and recommendations herein are intended to guide DoD in its efforts to enhance the work already being done while ensuring a more fit and ready force for meeting the demands of serving in the military. It is the Task Force's belief that implementation of the recommendations and strategic initiatives in this report will save lives and will further propel DoD as a national leader in suicide prevention.

7.1. Organization and Leadership

7.1.1. Create, Restructure and Resource Suicide Prevention Offices at OSD, the Services, Installations, and Unit Level to Achieve Unity of Effort

Finding: The absence of an adequately staffed and resourced OSD policy office on suicide prevention leads to significant challenges to the unity of effort. Service programs are not benefiting from the guidance of a Department-wide strategic approach.

DoD-Level Suicide Prevention Program Office

DISCUSSION: Adaptive adjustments to new requirements have occurred at the Service, installation, and command levels, but have suffered at the DoD-level because of the lack of a suicide prevention policy office with full-time staffing. Strategic planning, one of the most critical aspects of program management, routinely occurs at the DoD level yet suicide prevention planning is notably deficient at this policy level. The Department has no military, civilian, or contract staff dedicated full time in the area of suicide prevention. The best example of coordination and collaboration of suicide prevention efforts within the DoD is the SPARRC. The SPARRC began in 1999 as a group chaired by the Program Director for

Mental Health Policy under the ASD(HA) and moved in 2008 to the DCoE. While this move was within ASD Health Affairs, it incongruously moved DoD-level suicide prevention efforts to a position further removed from the policymaking centers at a time when the Service programs were moving closer to them. In addition, structural inconsistency adds a level of challenge to unity of effort as exemplified by three of the four Service-level program offices residing within manpower and personnel staff directorates while the fourth remains in the Office of the Surgeon General. The SPARRC also remains within Health Affairs and medical community.

The SPARRC chair is a Public Health Service officer on assignment to DCoE, and four part-time contract staff members support the committee (J. Hawkins, personal communication, 18 June 2010). Membership on the SPARRC is a collateral duty for all members, who are task saturated by their full-time billets but are regularly tasked as action officers for the SPARRC because of the absence of full-time dedicated staff focused solely on suicide prevention.

The SPARRC has made tremendous progress given the limited resources supporting its charge. Despite the lack of staff and funding, the committee created a standardized rate calculation and reporting policy, and a standardized web-based reporting and surveillance tool, and is in the process of finalizing standardized nomenclature and developing the first-ever DoD-level suicide prevention website. In addition, the SPARRC sponsored eight annual suicide prevention conferences; the most recent conference, in collaboration with the VA, in January 2010 had more than 850 attendees (J. Hawkins, personal communication, 18 June 2010).

While the SPARRC has made significant headway, other notable initiatives have been significantly delayed and some opportunities were missed because of insufficient staff and resourcing. For example, the 2008 DoDSER Annual Report has yet to be publicly released despite its completion a year ago, in July 2009. The SPARRC drafted a new DoD Instruction on suicide prevention but it has not been approved and released. Currently, the only DoD guidance on suicide prevention is a 2006 memorandum on rate standardization. OSD lacks a strategic plan and therefore provides little to no guidance to the Services in suicide prevention. This paucity of policy guidance trickles down and affects unit-level suicide prevention. In the military, at the critical unit level, units are currently unable to determine whether their suicide prevention efforts are in line with OSD intent.

Each Service has at least one, and generally several, examples of remarkably well-conceptualized, theoretically sound suicide prevention efforts. The Department's method of sharing best practices and Service-level success is through the SPARRC. The Task Force found examples of successful sharing and adoption of tools (e.g., Leaders' Guides for Managing Service Members in Distress, front-line supervisor training, and awareness acronyms). Unfortunately, the current level of workload has inhibited this type of collaboration, and little has been seen in the last few years. The diminished collaboration of recent years has likely reduced efficiencies that could be gained from the effective adoption of programs across the Services. A staffed OSD office is necessary to analyze and recommend best practices and assist the Services in collaborative development and adoption of effective tools. OSD is also needed to obtain resources from which the Services can benefit.

DoD programs that employ a hierarchical and collaborative structure permeating the military system from OSD down, and with each Service involved, have substantial benefits in the areas of unity of effort, standardization (decreased variation), and sharing of best practices and resources. One example is the DoD Sexual Assault Prevention and Response Office (SAPRO) under the Deputy Undersecretary of Defense (Plans).

SAPRO "serves as the single point of accountability and oversight for sexual assault policy, provides guidance to the DoD components, and facilitates the resolution of issues common to all military Services and joint commands" (SAPRO, 2010). SAPRO objectives are to enhance and improve prevention through: 1) training and education programs; 2) treatment and support of victims; and 3) system accountability (SAPRO, 2010). The SAPRO program benefits from structural penetration throughout the Department and the Services, ensuring centralized guidance, full-time staff, and sufficient resourcing to meet its mission.

Another example is the VA's Center of Excellence in Suicide Prevention, which includes a central office of suicide prevention with a full-time staff that disseminates directives to standardize care strategies, event reporting, and community outreach with strategic and consistent national messaging. The central office full-time staff includes a director, a deputy director, a clinical trainer, a clinical psychologist, and several information management and support personnel.

The VA uses this structure to quickly disseminate lessons learned throughout the country. The VA provides specialized training and has published a manual to ensure standardization of the Suicide Prevention Coordinator (SPC) positions.

One possible staffing model for a DoD-level office resourced to effectively develop and manage a strategic suicide prevention effort would include the following full-time personnel: a policy director, deputy director, policy specialist, suicide research scientist, suicide training specialist, suicide prevention specialist, health communications specialist, and sufficient administrative and support staff.

Responsibilities would include coordinating the receipt, analysis, and reporting of DoD-level suicide surveillance data; using analysis of surveillance data to formulate suicide prevention program recommendations through policy changes; implementing standard program evaluation processes to produce outcome-oriented suicide prevention; and conducting collaborative risk reduction, resiliency analyses and making recommendations.

Organizationally, this office would be best placed within the Office of the Under Secretary of Defense for Personnel and Readiness to parallel the military and civilian leadership of suicide prevention in the Services, with medical, religious, personnel, and wellness/fitness programs, and other offices in support of primary prevention services.

"Usualy those that organize for success obtain it"

—military officer

Recommendation:

Build, staff and resource a central OSD Suicide Prevention Office that can effectively develop, implement, integrate, and evaluate suicide prevention policies, procedures, and surveillance activities.

This office should reside within the Office of the Under Secretary of Defense for Personnel and Readiness and be granted the coordinating authority that enables strategic suicide prevention oversight from OSD, through the Services, and down to the unit level.

Service-Level Suicide Prevention Program Office

Finding: The Service suicide prevention program offices are not staffed or resourced sufficiently to successfully manage the current level of requirements in response to suicidal behavior.

DISCUSSION: Over the last few years, the Services have each responded to increasing suicide rates by fortifying their suicide prevention program offices. Six years ago, each of the Services had one Suicide Prevention Program Manager (SPPM) and that was the sum total staffing. At that time, none of the SPPMs were resourced full time for suicide prevention but were required to divide their time between suicide prevention and other behavioral health-related prevention programs such as combat operational stress control, family advocacy, health promotions, and general psychological health issues.

Recently, all four Services have increased staffing levels within their suicide prevention offices. The Army has a full-time civilian SPPM and a full-time civilian senior analyst. The Army plans to expand its office within the next few months by adding five full-time civilians to support the Army Suicide Prevention Program and the Army Campaign Plan for Health Promotion (W. Morales, personal communication, 17 June 2010). In addition, the most significant staff increase within Army suicide prevention is related to the Army Suicide Prevention Task Force. The Army Task Force support staffing levels vary; peak staffing was 12 military and 8 civilian personnel (B. Shahbaz, personal communication, 18 June 2010). The USMC staff expanded from one SPPM (a Navy clinical psychologist) to include three full-time civilians, a senior enlisted leader, and a Marine Colonel who heads the suicide prevention office. The Air Force has one full-time SPPM (an Air Force psychiatrist) with one part-time executive assistant (M. Kindt, personal communication, 17 June 2010). Navy suicide prevention is led by the SPPM (a Navy clinical psychologist) with responsibility for both suicide prevention and operational stress control programs. Navy suicide prevention training and outreach were supported by one full-time mobilized reservist until the end of July 2010 (B. Chavez, personal communication, 18 June 2010).

Briefings from multiple Service representatives and site visits to installations suggested to the Task Force that while resourcing has increased over previous years, the resource levels of Service suicide prevention program offices remain insufficient to meet the increased requirements and demands resulting from the current level of suicide-related activities. The Task Force found that the Service-level offices have competing time demands—either focusing on unit-level needs or on responding to higher headquarters and DoD requests for information, but not both. Each Service-level office suffers from a lack of consistent and standard resourcing at both the installation and Service level.

Recommendation:

Prioritize resources to adequately staff, fund, and organize the headquarters-level suicide prevention offices, within each Service, to successfully meet all current requirements.

Age: 23
Rank/Occupation: Specialist/Infantry
Service Branch: US Army

This Soldier joined the Army in 2002 to serve his Nation and defend his country. He deployed to Iraq as part of the initial invasion in spring 2003. After deploying to Iraq for a second time in 2005, he became increasingly sullen and depressed while deployed. He wrote to his mother from Iraq, "Lately I have been thinking I don't even want to come back alive. Granted I would never kill myself, but I hate life. If I died here, I would be young and it would be an honorable way to go. Let's face it; I have no future when I get back." He completed his tour of duty and returned stateside. He was diagnosed with Post Traumatic Stress Disorder (PTSD) and attended counseling. In poetry written shortly before his death he wrote, "Physically I am home, mentally I will never be home." He then started drinking. "Time's finally up," he wrote, "I am not a good person, I have done bad things. I have taken lives, now it's time to take mine." He died by self-inflicted gunshot wound.

Installation and Major Command Level Suicide Prevention Programs

Finding: Installation and major command suicide prevention program coordinators are not present on a consistent basis, which has led to diminished effectiveness of local suicide prevention programs.

Discussion: Some of the Services currently require full-time civilian program coordinators at installations and major commands while other Services do not require these positions. The Task Force found motivated and dedicated installation-level coordinators engaged in proactive suicide prevention activities during site visits.

Because of the lack of standardized guidance from Service-level program management, however, the effectiveness of suicide prevention activities at those installations often depended on the creativity of the individual appointed, and these activities were not always consistent with the Service's overall program intent. Some coordinators were also marginalized because of a lack of consistent placement of their offices in relation to the installation or senior-level commander.

The DoD Task Force on Mental Health (2007) recommended implementation of Installation Directors for Psychological Health to serve as the installation commander's consultant for psychological health with the authority to convene meetings of all resources on the installation that support psychological health.

During site visits, the current Task Force found that most installations still lacked a unifying office to ensure that installation support services operate seamlessly to provide prevention services and facilitate access to care. The current Task Force validated the need for implementation of that recommendation and further suggests that every installation and major command have a full-time civilian suicide prevention program coordinator to act as the consultant for that commander to ensure that Service-level suicide prevention strategy is consistently conveyed and implemented within installations and major commands; and facilitates unit-level programs.

Recommendation

Services should require full-time civilian suicide prevention coordinators at all installations identified by major commands. Major commands must facilitate the consistent implementation of Service suicide prevention strategy down to the small unit level and installations must ensure appropriate resourcing of this position in order to fully support both DoD suicide prevention policy, and Service policy and programs.

Installation-Level Suicide Prevention Coalition

DISCUSSION: The Services are to be commended on the large number of support services that exist under the management of various agencies and organizations on any given installation. In addition to the services offered by clinical mental health providers at MTFs or deployment health centers, services are also provided by Service Member and family counseling centers, religious programs, family advocacy programs, substance abuse prevention and treatment programs, personal financial management offices, and numerous others.

The DoD Task Force on Mental Health noted "various degrees of segregation for these programs and no consistent plan for collaboration in promoting the psychological health of Service Members and their families" (Department of Defense Task Force on Mental Health, 2007, pg 53). During site visits, the current Task Force also noted this situation continues today and that support agencies remain largely independent and confusing in the eyes of the individual Service Member as well as family members.

The current Task Force found examples of wonderful attempts at cross-pollination and coordination of services by each of the Services and at installations that the Task Force visited. The USMC has Human Factors Councils that take a proactive look at behavioral issues that might minimize mission readiness.

The Air Force has years of experience with the IDSs and higher-level CAIBs, which function to bring together community service providers with line leadership to ensure behavioral health related issues are addressed in policy and practice.

The USN has been bringing together various professionals in community workshops at all its installations. The Army sends a Composite Risk Assessment Report to each unit commander on each installation on a regular basis, which covers behavioral health risks involving its Soldiers. Each installation has a Director of Health Services and a Public Health Emergency Officer.

These organizations and systems can facilitate the communication of systemic risk by having regular meetings of members that include leadership from commands, medical, chaplaincy, community services, etc. Visits to installations suggested that consistent utilization and optimization of these regulatory bodies was undisciplined and poorly utilized. The Air Force appeared to have the best standardized system in place that desegregates these services from each other with the local command leadership involved.

The Services would benefit from installation-based suicide prevention coalitions that can effectively address coordinated care for Service Members and problem high-risk behavior issues.

They can also inform higher headquarters suicide prevention program offices about issues that require Service-level policy revisions.

Recommendation

Sufficiently resource suicide prevention coalitions that strategically integrate installation and major command suicide prevention efforts and informs the Service-level program office. This coalition should also function to coordinate support services through collaboration on overarching social/behavioral risk problems on the installation.

Medical Treatment Facility Suicide Prevention

DISCUSSION: The Task Force found excellent examples of full-time suicide prevention program coordinators at some MTFs. However, they were not consistently employed across each Service or throughout DoD. Coordinators at an MTF function as both clinical case managers for those identified as at risk for suicide and as administrative coordinators of suicide prevention program requirements. The VA employs suicide prevention coordinators at all veterans' medical facilities and often has two different individuals, one focused on case management and the other on administrative procedures. The need to standardize the completion of the DoDSER by trained individuals may also be best accomplished by MTF-based suicide prevention program coordinators, who can also function as the medical representative to an installation-based coalition that removes the stovepipes in community services.

Recommendation

Require full-time suicide prevention program coordinators at each MTF (or regionalized when covering several non-hospital MTFs) to facilitate the standardized implementation of Service suicide prevention strategy on behalf of the MTF commander and ensure the adherence to standardized policies and practices.

Unit-Level Prevention Programs

Finding: Implementation of Service suicide prevention programs suffers at the unit level because of the lack of consistent requirements for assigned suicide prevention officers.

DISCUSSION: The Services inconsistently require unit-level collateral duty officers to lead suicide prevention. When the positions exist, they are often the result of local unit commander initiatives and the responsibilities may be vague. In addition, there is a lack of clarity regarding what type of individual is best suited to fill the position. The Task Force discovered a variety of personnel filling unit-level suicide prevention program officer positions—from personnel specialists, to medical officers and enlisted, to chaplain officers and enlisted, to senior enlisted and junior officers—all tasked with the same duties but with variable training, experiences, and approaches. This confusion is the result of the paucity of policy guidance from higher levels. The Task Force heard that several Services were implementing clearer and more consistent guidance but current policy is sparse in this area.

Recommendation

Direct unit-level suicide prevention program officers to facilitate the implementation of Service policies.

> Age: 23
> Rank/Occupation: Second Lieutenant/Adjuntant General
> Service Branch: US Army
>
> *This Soldier took his own life while stationed in Europe in his first assignment after being commissioned. All communications from him prior to his death indicate that the source of stress in his life was this new assignment and the transition it involved. According to his family, he had experienced a poor command climate with no strong leadership to respect or follow. He was the product of Army training yet was reprimanded for not knowing his job better. His mother said, "My son joined the Army after graduating from college. He scored at the top of his Officer Candidates School class and was an honor grad in the Adjutant General Basic Officer Leadership Course, receiving numerous awards during training. Despite this level of achievement, he expressed to his family that he felt unprepared for, and overwhelmed by, his work." His family said, "His death is, to us, an irreparable loss."*

> *Finding:* Competing priorities have degraded the fundamentals of unit-level leadership, resulting in lost opportunities for suicide prevention.

7.1.2. Equip and Empower Leaders (Provide Them Tools) to Establish a Culture That Fosters Prevention As Well As Early Recognition and Intervention

DISCUSSION: Small-unit leadership is critically important as it is here we see the direct effect of leadership throughout the supervisory structure via interaction and engagement with unit personnel. In a few commands and among some specialty groups interviewed by the Task Force, small-unit leadership, deck-plate leadership, and other similar terms were being used to refocus attention on the fundamentals of mentoring and caring for Service Members. This renewed emphasis was not found consistently across installations. Interviews at many installations indicated that supervisors up and down the chain were so focused on mission requirements and accomplishing "accountable" and "required" tasks that no time was left for attending to the "human" elements of leadership and management. Supervisors reported they did not have time to spend one-on-one with subordinates either because they supervised too many individuals to make such practical or because of an overwhelming load of administrative requirements. Subordinates told us their supervisors were either too busy to talk personally with them or that their supervisors did not care about, or appreciate, them. In far too many cases, interactions between supervisors and subordinates were essentially limited to those that were work related and required to get the job done. This situation stems directly from having insufficient staffing to meet operational requirements and adding more and more requirements to units without removing less important requirements or adding staff.

During site visits, the Task Force observed that formal mentoring tools were being disseminated throughout the ranks with strong command emphasis. Strong mentoring practices should be universal across the Services. Mentoring programs have been well evaluated and have a strong evidence base for influencing several important risk and protective factors for suicide. A return to the fundamentals of small-unit leadership should include incorporation of structured mentorship tools that closely follow the principles of evidence-based approaches. New social media should support more flexibility in matching mentors with protégés, allowing effective relationships over geographic barriers. Many suggested that Service Members should have input into selecting their mentor whenever possible, and that long-term relationships maintained through electronic communications media would be of substantial value.

Because so many Service Members are single and geographically separated from family and friends that are best able to detect signs of suicide risk and to provide the sense of social support and belongingness that protect one from suicidal behaviors, the role of an involved supervisor and chain of command is critical in providing these protective functions. During site visits, the Task Force was told over and over again that those in supervisory roles are overwhelmed with too many subordinates and are thus unable to support them at the levels necessary for personal involvement. There appears to be inadequate time for effective interaction between leaders and their subordinates. The same is true during deployment, as well.

> "Provide a structure where those who are seeking help remain valuable to the unit and continue to have a sense of purpose."
>
> —civilian psychologist

Recommendations

- *Strengthen and reinvigorate the fundamentals of military garrison leadership at the unit level with a focus on supervisor-subordinate interactions and mentoring. Ensure that frontline supervisor training is mandatory, occurs prior to assuming a supervisory role, and includes critical skills building in interpersonal relationships.*
- *Ensure that professional military education, ranging from basic training to Senior Service Schools, develops leaders with the interpersonal and leadership skills required to fulfill their leadership and mentoring responsibilities, as well as promotes the well-being and total fitness of the Service Members under their charge.*
- *Maintain a sufficiently small front-line supervisor-to-subordinate ratio to ensure the person-centered leadership functions can occur.*

Finding: Commanders either lack the necessary tools or do not effectively use existing tools to detect, measure, and track unit-level suicide risk factors and inform local prevention activities.

DISCUSSION: Command climate surveys are currently used across the Services to assess the effectiveness of leadership and the morale of a unit. At the present time, each Service has different requirements defining when a climate survey is completed. For instance, the USMC requires such a survey to be completed for every commander on his or her incoming assignment, whereas the Air Force requires use of the survey in response to Equal Employment Opportunity (EEO) or Inspector General (IG) complaints. The primary goal of a climate assessment is to provide the unit's leadership with an understanding of areas of concern as well as areas in which the unit is excelling. For the tool to be effective, it must use validated scales that are sensitive enough to detect meaningful changes over time. At this time, there is no formal evidence to support this tool's effectiveness but, in general, the approach is viewed positively. However, its use as a method to investigate possible failures of command has sometimes tainted its reputation.

Unit climate surveys have potential as a suicide prevention strategy from two perspectives: First, with evidence that positively viewed leadership decreases stress among combatants (OTSG, 2009) the judicious use of command climate surveys could strengthen the credibility of leaders in the Armed Forces; second, command climate surveys could be augmented with questions or scales regarding behavioral risk and protective factors associated with suicide to give commanders important information about their specific unit's relative risk.

The questions could address the frequency of binge or problem drinking, interpersonal violence, gambling, financial stress, anger outbursts, relationship difficulties, and other important risk factors for suicidal behaviors. Commanders could use the results of these surveys to tailor prevention efforts among their unit members before full-blown negative outcomes—e.g., police reports of family violence, alcohol-related incidents, and criminal activity, or financial crises—become evident. These prevention efforts could also include measures to enhance life skills and interpersonal relationships, and education geared towards prevent of alcohol and drug abuse, sexual assault, and harassment, gambling, and other risky behaviors.

Recommendations

- *Add validated behavioral risk questions to unit climate surveys to help commanders detect relative elevations in behavioral risk across their military units and respond with appropriate preventive measures. Mandate the use of unit climate and risk surveys annually and upon accepting and relinquishing command.*
- *Develop monthly risk reports from a multitude of sources and services to create a snapshot of the unit and the ability to compare a commander's unit with like units across the Service and at the installation, while also allowing for the identification of positive and negative trends with reference to risk behaviors by members in that unit.*

FINDING: Some leadership environments result in discriminatory and humiliating treatment of Service Members who responsibly seek professional services for emotional, psychological, moral, ethical, or spiritual matters.

DISCUSSION: Site visits revealed widespread reports in some military branches and specialties of discriminatory treatment of Service Members who had made appointments to see mental health professionals or chaplains for assistance with personal, psychological, emotional, or spiritual concerns.

These Service Members reported being singled out and publicly humiliated, often in front of their entire units. The Task Force heard that many had become so desperate for help that they were willing to endure certain humiliation in order to receive it.

This type of senseless discriminatory behavior is one of the worst manifestations of stigma. Although the Army has recently disseminated policy (AR 600-63, Army Health Promotion) prohibiting such behaviors, the Task Force did not find any instances of Soldiers in the field being aware of the policy.

In addition, the few headquarters-based Service Members who *were* aware of this policy pointed out that sanctions against the behaviors did not carry the same level of punishment as for those who committed sexual harassment or other offenses of similar magnitude, and were, therefore, largely ineffective.

"**We should never underestimate the impact of positive leadership** on suicide prevention."
—senior military leader

Recommendation

Disseminate and enforce "zero tolerance" policies that prohibit prejudice, discrimination, and public humiliation towards individuals who are responsibly addressing emotional, psychological, relational, spiritual, and behavioral issues; as well as towards those seeking help to increase their psychological fitness and operational readiness. Support these policies by holding leaders and supervisors accountable and by sustained communications campaigns.

7.1.3. Develop Strategic Communications That Promote Life, Normalize "Help-Seeking Behaviors," and Support DoD Suicide Prevention Strategies

Finding: Messages from senior leaders regarding suicide, suicide prevention, resilience, health, and readiness frequently do not sufficiently support—and sometimes significantly detract from—suicide prevention efforts. The news media commonly report on suicide in ways that contribute to suicide risk.

DISCUSSION: Health communications science strongly suggests that each strategy employed in a public health effort must be supported by a well-developed communications campaign using principles supported by health communication research (US Department of Health and Human Services, National Institute of Health, and National Cancer Institute, 2005).

Messages that leaders transmit, ranging from Service Chiefs to the unit commanders, should be aligned closely with and enhance communications campaign goals. Overall, the Task Force **found that the Services' communications about suicide**, including the messages that senior leaders transmit when they talk publicly about suicide and suicide prevention, are often not well aligned with, nor supportive of, the strategies and interventions being disseminated by the Services themselves. At times, they violate evidence-based best practices in suicide prevention communication (SPRC, 2010).

The Task Force observed that senior Service leaders and their public affairs offices often transmit public messages about the incidence of suicides, suicide rates, factors involved in suicide events, research initiatives, and suicide prevention that do not seem to be part of a coordinated communications campaign. Specifically, they frequently use talking points that may lead their audiences to believe that suicides are far more common among Service Members than they really are and that an "epidemic" of suicide exists, especially in combat veterans. These communications also unknowingly transmit the message that the Services know neither why suicides are occurring nor what to do about the problem. Statements without sufficient context may lead a distressed or vulnerable Service Member to conclude that the "normal" response to symptoms of deployment-related distress is to take one's own life. Research (Cialdini, 2001) has shown that people are highly motivated to behave in conformity with most of their peers. Therefore, messages that leaders transmit should make it clear that the *vast majority*—nearly 100 percent—of Service Members who feel distressed after a deployment find more effective ways to cope than by ending their lives. These messages should tout the huge numbers of Service Members (in the tens of thousands) who are responsibly seeking care and treatment for symptoms of PTSD (e.g., nightmares, sleep disturbances, irritability, anger, depression, hyper-vigilance, and anxiety), alcohol abuse, prescription drug abuse, relationship problems, guilt, and other existential problems, and that those who end their lives are a tiny minority. It should be made clear to the audience that *normal* reactions to deployment stress do not include suicidal behaviors; rather, suicidal behaviors are *never* normal. Furthermore, messages crafted for senior leaders should follow other principles of health communications (i.e., target specific messages to specific sub-populations with clear behaviorally-oriented messages). For instance, rather than a statement that "suicide prevention is a leadership issue," statements should tell leaders at specific levels exactly what behaviors are expected from them (e.g., being supportive and respectful of Service Members who seek help responsibly to manage psychological, emotional, and spiritual issues) and what behaviors will not be tolerated (e.g., discrimination and humiliation of responsible help seekers).

Although Public Affairs Officers (PAO) cannot control the way that the media will handle the messages and talking points they craft, Task Force experts have found that when individual reporters are informed of strong evidence that some approaches to reporting on suicide are linked to increases in suicides, the reporters are likely to craft stories that follow the recommendations cited above. It is critically important for military PAOs to have access to, and an understanding of, these reporting guidelines. It also is importantthat whenever military PAOs interact with reporters on the subject of suicide, they discuss these recommendations and the importance of considering them carefully in writing their stories.

The Task Force observed that when leaders personalize suicide prevention messages (i.e., speak about their own experiences with depression, PTSD symptoms, relationship problems, or other personal crises, and how they were able to access assistance from peers, supervisors, friends, or professionals to respond), the power of those messages increases immeasurably. The Task Force encourages those types of personalized messages, with the caveat that they do not violate evidence-informed principles of safe and effective suicide prevention messages as outlined in *Safe and Effective Messaging for Suicide Prevention* (SPRC, 2010).

At various levels of command, leaders are concerned that talking about suicide too much may have detrimental effects, and in the worst case scenario, contribute to suicidal behavior. This may indeed be the case. Reports of supervisors giving perfunctory warnings against killing oneself during a 3-day weekend or while on leave, and messages delivered without a sense of concern for the well being of the unit members, were common on site visits.

Focusing too much on suicide seems to be having a negative effect, resulting in a range of responses from hyper-vigilance for others who may be suicidal (so no one wants to divulge having any problems, lest they be accused of being suicidal) to indifference and joking about what should be considered a very serious subject. Instead, leaders should focus their comments on health, wellness, mental fitness, resiliency, performance enhancement, and peer-to-peer support and thereby contribute to a change in cultural values and norms that will indirectly promote suicide prevention. If communications about suicide and suicide prevention cannot be made reliably with appropriate sincerity and concern, no communication should occur at all.

> "The day soldiers stop bringing you their problems is the day you have stopped leading them. They have either lost confidence that you can help them or concluded that you do not care. Either case is a failure of leadership."
>
> —Colin Powell

Recommendations

- *Develop and implement sustainable training programs for PAOs serving Service leaders, senior leaders, and installation commanders in crafting health-promoting messages that support the goals and objectives of the Services' suicide prevention and health promotion programs; avoid counterproductive or dangerous messages whenever making statements or discussing suicide-related information or statistics.*
- *Instruct PAOs to disseminate nationally recognized recommendations for reporting on suicide as they interact with news media on the subject of suicide.*
- *Develop and disseminate communication guidelines to commanders for use in the wake of a local suicide event.*

Age: 19
Rank/Occupation: Airman First Class/Combat Communications
Service Branch: US Air Force

This Airman enlisted in the Air Force a month after he graduated high school where he was voted "Most Likely to Succeed."

After basic training, he volunteered for his first deployment. During the deployment he relayed to his family that he believed wholeheartedly in the good that the US military was doing in Afghanistan, but that the horrors of war were overwhelming to him personally. On May 3, 2010, this Airman shot himself in Khyber, Afghanistan... according to his family, "so he would never be responsible for the loss of another life."

7.1.4. Reduce Stigma and Overcome Military Cultural and Leadership Barriers to Seeking Help

> *Finding*: Those who seek or need behavioral healthcare are commonly stigmatized and discriminated against, reinforcing the pervasive belief in the military that receiving behavioral healthcare is career ending and that those who seek it are constitutionally weak. These prevalent behaviors in the military culture seriously undermine suicide prevention efforts. Some policies that have been disseminated to reduce stigma have not achieved their objectives.

DISCUSSION: Access to the highest quality behavioral healthcare is as fundamental to a fit force as are physical training and medical care. Furthermore, assessment and treatment for behavioral health concerns at the first signs of a problem may prevent that problem from escalating to a crisis, and in the worst case, leading to a suicide. Service Members commonly loathe the thought of entering a behavioral health clinic for care largely because of the stigma and discrimination they experience or expect to experience as a consequence. They told the Task Force that they would avoid behavioral healthcare to escape being labeled as "that guy"— a person who cannot be relied on in a pinch—or worse, one who uses the cloak of illness to malinger and avoid duty or deployment. Service Members repeatedly described seeking behavioral healthcare as a last resort—action they chose only when they deemed the consequences of not seeking care (e.g., their spouse leaving with the children or the fear of "going crazy") to be worse than the consequences they expected at work. Rather than entering a behavioral healthcare clinic, many expressed their preference for the chaplaincy because of the added confidentiality and/or the more acceptable primary care setting.

Research about stigma indicates that it manifests itself in many ways and through various constructs. The roots of stigma are anchored in stereotypes—generalizations that are perceived to be accepted by the population at large—such as, "people with mental health problems are crazy" and "Service Members who seek behavioral healthcare are weak." These stereotypes do their damage when individuals begin to agree with the stereotypes and develop prejudicial views toward a Service Member based on his or her current circumstance (e.g., seeking help for an emotional, relationship, psychological, or spiritual problem). In the military, as referenced above, these prejudicial thoughts might include, "he is not carrying or cannot carry his weight in the unit" or "I cannot trust him to have my back in battle." Stigma erodes unit cohesion, it erodes trust, it erodes fitness, and erodes readiness.

The Task Force recognizes that the military system is filled with discriminatory regulations—and for good reason. Certain physical or mental conditions have been determined to be incompatible with military service. Fortunately, a vast majority of emotional, psychological, spiritual, or relational problems that Service Members experience would not disqualify them from service, regardless of whether those problems are related to operational stressors.

This is especially true if they seek assistance early in the developmental trajectory of a problem.

Nonetheless, and contradictory to the experience of behavioral healthcare providers, most of the Service Members with whom the Task Force spoke during site visits believed that seeking behavioral healthcare is career ending. Although command-directed mental health evaluations *do* frequently lead to the end of a military career, the overwhelming majority of mental health providers interviewed reported that self-sought behavioral healthcare nearly always enhanced Service Members' interpersonal relationships, improved their job performance, and their career potential.

On only a small minority of "self-referrals" were the results detrimental to a Service Member's career.

"Stigma kills."

—surviving spouse

Stigma in any of its three prejudice, and discrimination) manifestations interferes with (stereotypes, "help-seeking" behavior" and can lead to a lethal outcome. Although stigma related to mental health and help-seeking for emotional, relational, and spiritual problems is a national and international problem, the significance of stigma in the military is substantially worsened by prevalent cultural beliefs and values that are distinctive to the military.

To date, the Services' attempts at reducing stigma associated with mental health have not been fruitful because of the pervasive belief—reinforced with personal experience—that having a mental, psychological, emotional, or relational problem leads to marginalization by peers, career setbacks, and alienation by leaders.

The Task Force noted one important DoD policy that has the potential of decreasing the negative perceptions of seeking mental health treatment—the exclusions in Question 21 on SF 86 (Questionnaire for National Security Positions). The Task Force agreed that these exclusions are critical to opening doors for responsible help-seeking, given the prevalence of occupational exposure to psychological, spiritual, moral, and ethical injuries from combat. Unfortunately, the Task Force found that very few Service Members were aware of the exclusions and those few who were did not have confidence that the policy would protect them in practice. It became clear to the Task Force that until most Service Members with security clearances are aware of the policy and have confidence that it will be enforced (i.e., they see examples of fellow Service Members protected by its provisions), it will have minimal effect in promoting access to behavioral healthcare services and the overall mental and psychological fitness of the force.

Strategic communication campaigns can be useful in changing cultural norms and values. Messages can be tailored to address specific cultural facets of the military population with the goal of eliminating false perceptions of the effects mental health treatment usually has on a Service Member's career and replace it with a more positive view (i.e., those Service Members who have voluntarily sought help not only did not experience negative effects but also found their careers and relationships benefited). SAMHSA has developed a Stigma Reduction Initiative kit (http://download.ncadi.samhsa.gov/ken/ pdf/SMA06-4176/DevelopingaStigmaReduction.pdf) that can provide guidance on developing such a campaign. Wright and colleagues (2009) examined organizational constructs, such as positive leadership and unit cohesion, and found they also have a role in reducing the perceptions of stigma as it relates to getting treatment.

The stigma associated with seeking help of any kind, including spiritual counseling, must be reduced in order for Service Members to maintain the high levels of personal health and readiness the military expects. The need for a stigma reduction campaign will have ended when leaders at all levels have "zero tolerance" for any behavior or activity that undermines the psychological, emotional, or spiritual fitness of Service Members.

Recommendations

- *Develop an aggressive Stigma Reduction Campaign Plan, communications effort, and implement policies to root out stigma and discrimination. Follow scientifically based health communications principles in these campaigns.*
- *Promote values that encourage seeking the assistance of chaplains, healthcare, and behavioral healthcare professionals to enhance spiritual, physical, and psychological fitness.*
- *Develop and implement campaigns to inculcate values and norms aligned with promoting the well-being, connectedness, and psychological and spiritual fitness of Service Members. Use well-planned, multi-year communications campaigns at the DoD and Service levels, employing the best of health communications science as part of that effort.*
- *Target a specific component of the communications campaign to ensure that Service Members who hold security clearances and the mental health providers who see them are aware of policies that exclude reporting certain instances of mental healthcare on the SF-86.*

> *Finding:* Some military cultural norms establish unachievable performance expectations for Service Members and stifle responsible help-seeking; the effect is a less fit force more vulnerable to suicide.

DISCUSSION: With many of the norms and values prevalent in military culture also comes a set of unrealistic, even unachievable, expectations for those wearing the uniform. For instance, physical, mental, psychological, and spiritual fitness and strength are highly valued. It follows that Service Members who develop and maintain a high level of overall fitness are themselves highly valued by their peers, their leaders, and the military community overall. The expectation is that a fully fit Service Member—sometimes referred to as a "full-up round"—will never need help dealing with problems in any of the "soft" dimensions: emotional, psychological, moral, ethical, mental, spiritual, or relational. The military culture has a very low tolerance for any perceived weakness (some call it a "zero deficit" mentality). Consequently, any weakness, even temporary, may result in the Service Member being viewed as less than adequate and marginalized from the remainder of the unit (OTSG, 2009). Psychological or emotional "weaknesses" are most apt to result in this marginalization (Hoge, Castro, Messer, McGurk, Cotting, & Koffman, 2004).

In some military specialties, the expectation of perfection is established very early in training. By the end of the first phase of specialty training, it is perfectly clear that members of these more elite career fields are expected to be sufficiently strong in mind, body, and spirit so as to complete their military careers (frequently decades of life) without any personal setbacks other than occasional physical ailments. Certainly, none would experience a single situation that would require outside professional help or require a temporary break from their high-demand military work environment resulting from a need in their "softer" side. This training and acculturation process produces a cadre of people with unrealistic life expectations who are very highly resistant to seeking help of any kind—especially behavioral healthcare—and that resistance is even more pronounced for men (Felker, Hawkins, Dobie, Gutierrez, & McFall).

The "zero deficit" mentality (zero tolerance for "weakness") permits Service Members to openly discriminate against fellow Service Members, a practice that undermines a fundamental military tenet-- watching out for one's buddies. A much better cultural norm, especially for high-performing military units, would be one that promotes optimizing fitness and thereby optimizing performance assistance of all kinds, including spiritual and psychological services, throughout one's life course. Professional athletes commonly use the services of psychologists to improve their mental,

psychological, and emotional functions, which in turn, contributes to improved performance in competition. Similarly, Service Members should be encouraged to seek and accept mental health professionals and clergy in this "coaching" role. This effort would be more likely to happen if such services were framed as an approach to enhancing performance rather than to remedying a deficit. Furthermore, access to and early use of these professional services could be expected to prevent the kinds of crises that render one unqualified to fulfill military duties, whether temporarily or permanently.

Taking steps that will eradicate non-productive norms and values, and overcome essential norms that may be counterproductive in suicide prevention, must be a central element of the Service's suicide prevention strategies. Efforts must specifically address military occupations requiring special duty qualifications such as, intelligence, communications, aviation, special operations, security forces, nuclear surety and others requiring requiring high-level clearances or personnal reliability.

Efforts to change these cultural norms must be backed up with policies and staffing to allow members to take temporary relief from duty without negative repercussions on others who must pick up the slack. This standard is currently established in Army Ranger units, which are manned at 110 percent of requirements.

This "overmanning" reduces the pressure on individuals who need time to address personal problems, knowing their unit will remain mission capable without an undue burden on others, even if they are sidelined temporarily.

> "Inside of a ring or out, ain't nothing wrong with going down. It's staying down that's wrong."
>
> —Muhammed Ali

Recommendations

- *Adjust manning levels, especially in elite units and certain military occupational specialties, to support developing and maintaining comprehensive fitness by all members.*
- *Infuse curricula for all levels of military specialty training with expectations that even the most effective Service Members will occasionally experience difficulties that require temporary interruptions in their qualifications for full duty. Teach that the responsibility of others in the unit is to support them during those times.*

Age: 40
Rank/Occupation: First Sergeant/Infantry
Service Branch: US Army

This Soldier served honorably for over two decades and deployed to Iraq as a First Sergeant. While out on a meet-and-greet patrol in Iraq, he suddenly stepped out of his vehicle and swore loudly. He then shot himself with his M4 and died. At first, his fellow Soldiers scrambled to find the sniper whom they believed must have fired the shot. When they realized the truth, they were bewildered.

"That's not First Sergeant," his driver, who witnessed his death, later told investigators; "Never!" His family also felt completely shocked as he had no history of mental health issues. However, as his parents and wife accumulated documentation from the investigation into his death, it became clear that the First Sergeant's leadership demands, his physical injuries, and his hidden psychological wounds all collided with the unrealistic stoicism of a very dedicated Soldier. He left behind his wife and two sons.

Finding: Frequent use of the term "malingering" within the DoD system to describe suicide-related behaviors that are judged to be related to one's desire to avoid service may adversely contribute to military cultural barriers to care and the overall stigma associated with suicide-related behaviors.

DISCUSSION: The term "malingering" has a long-standing history in psychological and military literature. Gerson and Fox (2006) defined malingering as the "intentional production of false or grossly exaggerated physical or psychological symptoms, motivated by external incentives such as avoiding military duty, avoiding work, evading criminal prosecution, or obtaining drugs.".

Language used in any culture has direct implications on social issues such as prejudice, discrimination, and stigma. Although use of "malingering" may be warranted in certain military situations, the Task Force views usage of the term in the context of describing suicide-related behaviors problematic and counterproductive to the broad mission of DoD suicide prevention.

Furthermore, to date, there is no empirical evidence to definitively indicate how to best differentiate between those who have suicide intention and those who may report suicide intention for external incentives. To judge a person's reports of suicide intent as a form of malingering is professionally insensitive, at times misinformed, and not based on any reliable scientific evidence.

Hypothetically, even if an individual's report of suicide intent is a form of malingering, the behavior may reflect ineffective coping skills and/or personality issues that need to be addressed appropriately in the context of behavioral healthcare.

The primary concern in continuing the military practice of using this term to describe the behavior of certain Service Members is related to the further promotion of stigma associated with suicide and seeking of care by distressed individuals.

Until the military scientific community has clearly established assessment procedures for reliably identifying malingering in the case of suicide intent, the Task Force's recommendation is to discourage all providers and military leadership from the using of this term in discourse about military suicide-related behaviors.

Recommendation

Discourage and refrain from use of the term "malingering" in association with suicide-related behaviors. Ensure DoD and Service suicide prevention policies and guidelines eliminate using the word "malingering".

7.1.5. Standardize Suicide Prevention Policies and Procedures

FINDING: Current DoD guidance on how to best manage and respond to suicidal behaviors during recruit training is insufficient relative to the need.

DISCUSSION: Even though the incidence of suicide during basic training is extremely rare, the prevalence of suicide-related behaviors appears to have increased in recent years based on the Task Force discussions with basic training instructors. The Task Force cannot directly comment on the prevalence of suicide attempts during basic training because such data have historically not been routinely collected and tracked for all Services. However, anecdotal reports indicate that some recruits may view suicide-related behaviors as a mechanism of escape, coping, and/or relief from the daily pressures of basic training. During installation site visits, the Task Force learned that some commanders have seen their recruits/trainees "play the S-card" (i.e., playing the suicide card) more frequently as a means of getting out of their military commitment. Several also mentioned that suicide appears now, more than ever before, as an option in some recruits' "drop-down menu."

Given the common occurrence of either verbalization of suicide intent and/or suicide-related behaviors during basic training, the Task Force believes that attention to this issue in the context of DoD's broader approach to suicide prevention is much needed. The problem of suicide and suicide-related behaviors is complex.

If suicide-related behaviors occurring in the context of basic training are either not addressed or inadequately addressed, this may result in a professional trajectory for the Service Member's use of similar coping behaviors (i.e., reliance on suicide-related behaviors as a method of dealing with perceived military stressors).

Furthermore, the verbalization and/or threat of suicide-related behaviors places a significant pressure and burden on military recruit instructors who are not trained behavioral healthcare providers and therefore cannot make informed decisions about the absence or presence of suicide risk and the severity of risk.

Although some instructors may decide to refer the recruit for a suicide risk assessment, others may decide to monitor the recruit for a period of time before formally making the referral to behavioral health.

The Services should address the problem of suicide-related behaviors in recruits by developing clear guidance for commanders and military recruit instructors. This guidance should specify how to best respond, track, and follow up with recruits who demonstrate suicide-related behaviors during basic training.

Formal guidance will not only help maximize the care provided to recruits during basic training, but also assist leadership and military instructors in the important job they perform in training our future military force. Individuals tasked with the creation of this guidance can monitor responses and manage strategies to prevent potential unintended reinforcement of suicide-related behaviors in our young recruits.

Recommendation

Implement DoD and Service guidance for commanders and military recruit instructors that addresses the management of suicide-related behaviors during basic training.

FINDING: A significant number of suicides among Service Members occur in the context of an investigation or allegation of a criminal or other serious offense.

DISCUSSION: Legal problems are an associated risk factor in many Service Member suicides as indicated in Diagram 7-1. In many instances, these deaths occur in the context of commanders, investigators, or defense counsels being aware of the individual's risk but not taking the next step to help build protective factors around him or her. For those notified they are under investigation but not yet arrested, command authorities must be notified immediately so they can ensure that the Service Member has the necessary support and resources to remain safe from self-harm. For those charged, a supervised, person-to-person custody transfer should occur, followed by a suicide risk assessment. If the individual confesses to a crime or other offense that brings humiliation or loss of financial or social status upon that individual, an intentional handoff of the individual should occur from authority to authority, essentially maintaining a suicide "watch" until a risk assessment can be made by a qualified professional. In the process of transferring responsibility for the individual, any statements or behaviors that the individual makes suggesting that suicide ideation might be a factor should be communicated at once throughout the chain of custody.

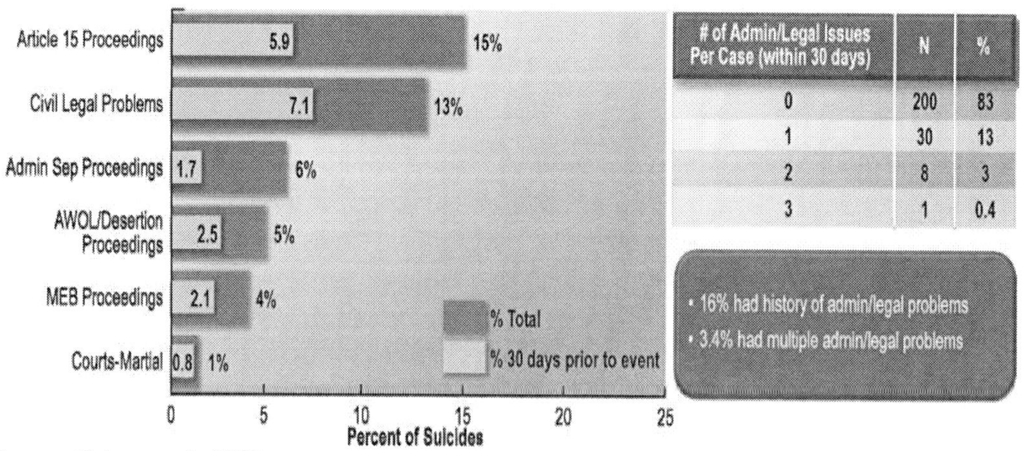

Source: Gahm, et. al., 2009.

Diagram 7-1. Legal, Disciplinary, and Administrative Issues.

Recommendation

Develop and implement a DoD-wide policy requiring immediate command notification and chain of care (or chain of custody) for individuals who become aware they are being investigated for a criminal or other serious offense, immediately after they confess to a crime, and/or soon after they are arrested and taken into custody.

Finding: Current DoD guidance regarding the removal and subsequent re issue of Weapons to Service Members who are recognized to be at risk of suicide is not sufficiently clear.

DISCUSSION: Empirical literature suggests that removal of access to lethal means for those deemed to be at acute risk may serve as a robust suicide prevention strategy. Guns are the primary method of suicide among Service Members. Most suicides that occur in theater are completed with the Service weapon and ammunition issued as part of the combat load.

Extra care must be given to identify Service Members at elevated risk for suicide so that their access to lethal means is controlled immediately, to the extent possible.

The removal of one's Service weapon and ammunition is a highly sensitive issue and each Service Member can be expected to have a different reaction.

For instance, although one Service Member might experience considerable distress and subsequent anger at losing one's weapon, another might feel an additional level of humiliation, embarrassment, and fear within his military unit.

Decisions made by providers and commanders about denial of access to lethal means (or removal of a weapon) for those recognized to be at imminent risk for suicide, and subsequent return of privileges to be armed, must be collaborative and thoughtfully executed.

Recommendation

Establish clear DoD, Joint and Service guidance for removal and subsequent re-issue of military weapon and ammunition for Service Members recognized to be at risk for suicide. The guidance should emphasize a collaborative, team approach to the decision-making process and specify documentation requirements.

Age: 40
Rank/Occupation: Gunnery Sergeant/Rifleman
Service Branch: US Marines

Just a month before he took his own life, this Marine helped stop one of his own Marines from committing suicide. He saved that Marine's life. After his return from Iraq where more than 12 people in his unit were killed, including the commanding officer, his wife shared that "he never spoke of anything." When she tried to talk about his behavioral changes—sleeping more, not showering—he insisted, "I'm a Gunny; I'm fine." He hung himself.

His wife believes that the stigma surrounding behavioral healthcare played a major role in keeping her husband from seeking the help he needed.

7.2. Wellness Enhancement and Training

7.2.1. Enhance Well-Being, Mental Fitness, Life Skills, and Resiliency

Finding: There is insufficient emphasis on training and other approaches to enhance critical life skills and build mental, emotional, and spiritual fitness.

DISCUSSION: Mastery of an array of life skills has been shown repeatedly to protect individuals from suicidal behaviors. The IOM report, *Reducing Suicide: A National Imperative* (2002), concluded that life skills can be taught and therefore teaching them constitutes an important and valuable suicide prevention strategy. Programs that build on the inherent resiliency in Service Members and increase personal financial management, anger management, decision making, and relationship skills across the force could significantly reduce suicide risk. Resiliency is the process by which positive adaptation occurs despite adverse or stressful environments; for the military, there is a strong emphasis on promoting positive, adaptive behaviors and preventing maladaptive responses (Luthar, Cicchetti, & Becker, 2000; Ritchie, Schneider, Bradley, & Forsten, 2008).

The Services have developed literally hundreds of programs and initiatives designed to reduce risk factors and strengthen protective factors for suicidal behaviors. However, there is no evidence of the effect, if any; these programs have had on the suicide rate in the military, partially because of a near absence of rigorous program evaluation.

Financial crisis and relationship problems are precipitating factors in large proportion of Service Member suicides. Diagram 7-2 shows that 65% of Service Members who completed a suicide had a failed relationship of some kind prior to their death (Gahm, et. al., 2009; Reger, *et.al.,* 2009). A strategically sound suicide prevention program should address suicide risk reduction issues (e.g., marital and relationship counseling, substance abuse programs, financial counseling) and strengthen protective factors (e.g., resilience, social connectedness, emotional regulation) with awareness and emergency intervention training modules.

For example, the Air Force program established in the mid-1990s was shown through rigorous evaluation to have been effective in substantially reducing suicide rates, as well as several other forms of violence and injury that share common risk and protective factors with suicide.

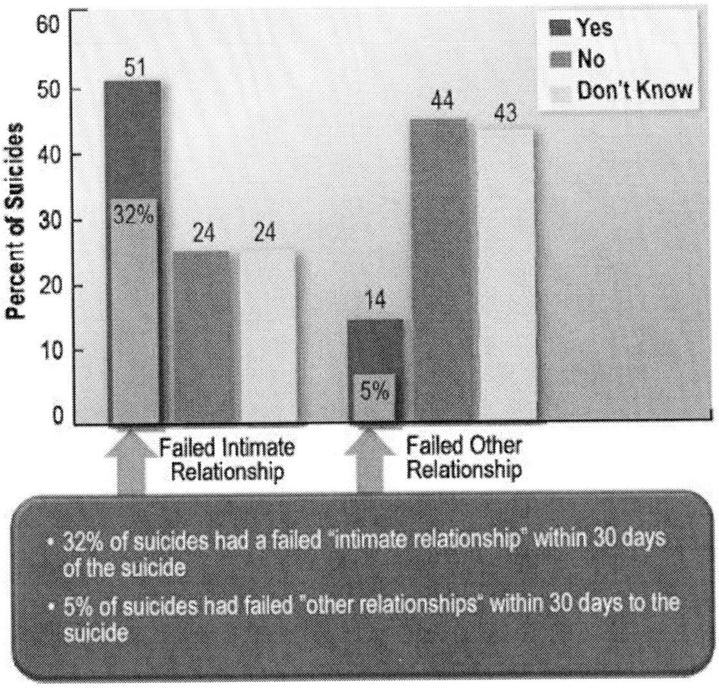

Source: Gahm, et. al., 2009.

Diagram 7-2. Relationship History.

The program had strong support from the very top Air Force leadership and emphasized interventions to reduce risk factors and strengthen protective factors long before Service Members' problems developed into crises. The vibrancy of this constellation of programs, however, seems to have waned over the years and was unable to achieve the early results over the longer term.

The Task Force did find evidence that the Services have recently strengthened their emphasis on early intervention programs through such efforts as resiliency training, comprehensive fitness, and operational stress control. Concentrating on the development and enhancement of Service Member strengths and life skills provides the Service Member with a set of skills she can leverage when faced with life stressors. These programs should help make Service Members relatively more "suicide resistant." However, at most installations visited, the skills training programs provided through various installation service providers were accessed by only a very small proportion of the base population. The Task Force was impressed, however, by one Army installation at which incoming personnel and spouses receive a full day of training using state-of-the-art curricula on financial management and relationship skills.

To increase participation, training is conducted off-post, with free childcare and meals provided. Additionally, the Air Force mandates a week of attendance at each installation's First Term Airman Center (FTAC), where airman arriving at their first permanent duty station receive all their mandatory base inprocessing (Right Start) briefings and where they also receive training in basic life skills such as financial management. They also receive information on other important opportunities and programs offered by the Airman and Family Readiness Center, base education center, and other support organizations. FTAC helps provides each new airman a standardized transition from their regimented training environment to life on an operational base and gives them training on a basic set of life skills and a myriad of information on how to obtain other assistance when needed. The Task Force believes that this type of "universal" training effort, using state-of-the-art training curricula, is an important component of building a resilient military force. Training such as this, targeting some of the known triggers for suicide, should be part of the Department's comprehensive suicide prevention strategy.

> "Resilience is the inner strength, that certain something that enables some people to thrive through hardship... the ability to turn loss into gain... to be strengthened by and even transformed by adversity."
>
> —Wounded Warrior Project

Recommendation

Improve access to, and promote utilization of, state-of-the-art training in critical life skills (e.g., financial management, communication, marriage and family relationships, anger management, and conflict resolution).

Finding: Service Members and behavioral health providers report overwhelmingly positive experiences with embedded mental health providers in operational units; however, the practice is underutilized.

DISCUSSION: Mental health professionals have been embedded successfully in Army combat units, including Ranger units and special operations units, for several years (for some, decades), with anecdotal evidence that they help Soldiers retain functionality in stressful environments. These embedded professionals act as consultants to commanders as well as coaches to Service Members in order to improve Service Member psychological and emotional fitness, and expedite their return to duty when exposed to traumatic events. They not only improve the psychological health of individuals and units but also help reduce stigma associated with behavioral healthcare. Embedded behavioral health professionals provide early intervention for Service Members through informal hallway chats, preventing early symptoms of psychological distress or interpersonal problems from becoming full-blown crises or illnesses. The Task Force found universal and eager acceptance of this approach among the representatives of a wide variety of units, but especially by members of "specially monitored" units with cultural and policy barriers to behavioral healthcare (e.g., security forces, units with large portions of members on PRP status, aviators and space operations controllers, submariners, military intelligence). Embedding professionals in operational units holds great promise, both as a means to reducing stigma and of increasing the psychological fitness, resiliency, and readiness of the force. The Services should further study this practice to determine the range of effective staffing ratios. Currently, no data exist to guide staffing ratios.

Recommendation

Expand the practice of embedding behavioral health providers in operational units. Conduct studies to determine the range of effective staffing ratios for embedded providers.

7.2.2. Reduce Stress on the Force and on Military Families

Finding: Heightened operations tempo, repeated deployments, and insufficient quantity and quality of dwell time since 2001 have had an adverse effect on the overall well-being of deploying and non-deploying Service Members and their families.

DISCUSSION: To meet current operational requirements with the existing end-strength, members of the military have faced repeated combat deployments with relatively short "dwell" times in between. This practice has added significant stress to the deploying forces. The Task Force also found that members of non-deploying units often have experienced significant stress associated with continuously heightened operations tempo at home. Based on all inputs, the Task Force concluded that the current end-strength is not sufficient to meet operational requirements *and* maintain the well-being of the force if DoD cannot find ways to internally reduce the stress on the force. Because of the strong connection between suicide risk and the various domains of physical, mental, psychological, emotional, and spiritual wellness, the Task Force strongly believes that resolving this supply-and-demand imbalance is foundational to any suicide prevention measure the Department considers.

> "Quality of dwell time is a myth. Can't build marital relationships or move them forward during 14 months of dwell time when my husband is a guest in my house."
>
> —military spouse

The current length of deployment varies by Service. At present, the average length of an Army unit's deployment in theater is 12 or more months; for the Marines, 7 to 12 months; for the Navy, 6 to 12 months; and for the Air Force, 4 to 12 months. Multiple deployments place considerable stress on the Service Member and are disruptive to the family as the Service Member regularly deploys and then re-integrates.

The latest Mental Health Advisory Team VI (USFOR-A & OTSG, 2009) reports Service Members on their third or fourth deployment experience a greater degree of psychological problems and acute stress.

Married Service Members in that same group report significantly more marital problems compared with those Service Members who are only on their first or second deployment.

Dwell time refers to the time Service Members spend in garrison between deployments. Dwell time provides a Service Member time away from the stress of a combat environment, ensures reset and training time, and provides an opportunity to reconnect with their family and community.

The quantity and quality of dwell time has been associated with levels of mental and emotional distress— specifically, the shorter and poorer the dwell time between deployments, the higher the levels of symptoms of depression and PTSD (USFOR-A & OTSG-Army, 2009).

Quality dwell time requires that Service Member have an adequate amount of in-garrison time (off time and personal time) to rebuild relationships, reconnect with family and friends, and recover from the psychological stress of deployment—to restore their physical, emotional, and spiritual well-being.

Competing military requirements often compromise the quality of dwell time. Services have added missions, training, and operational requirements that must be completed during dwell time without making adjustments to previously existing requirements.

There are two different types of dwell time: individual and unit. Individual dwell time refers to time Service Members have before they are required to deploy again. Unit dwell time is the time the entire unit has before it is required to deploy again.

Dwell time allows Service Members' time to re-connect with their families and friends as well as re-integrate into society following a lengthy deployment.

"Dwell time should be an off season, not a pit stop."

—Army soldier

However, upon returning from a deployment, Service Members are frequently transferred to another unit.

Dwell time schedule for a unit does not benefit a Service Member who changes units shortly after returning from a deployment, only to deploy again with the new unit after a very short individual dwell time.

MHAT VI found that 20 or more months of dwell time is required for symptoms of psychological distress to return to normal "in garrison" levels after a 12-month combat deployment.

"Changing leadership soon after returning from a deployment, especially the commander, is like putting a fresh rider on a tired horse."

—Non-Commissioned Officer

Recommendations

Balance uniformed end-strength with operational requirements by either increasing military end-strength or decreasing operational commitments.

Provide sufficient, high-quality dwell time for redeploying Service Members in keeping with the most current military health research. Initial post-deployment dwell time should ensure an initial period (of at least several months) in which Service Members can restore their well-being, and should not include extended temporary duty (TDY) or extended "gear-up" training for the next deployment.

Reduce operations tempo and day-to-day work requirements on individuals and units to sustainable levels that support the wellness of Service Members and their families. Create white space in training schedules, especially in post-deployment periods.

Review in-garrison military training requirements with the goal of eliminating and/or combining training, thereby reducing the time burden on units and Service Members.

7.2.3. Transform Suicide Prevention Training of Service Members, Leaders, and Families to Enhance Skills

Finding: Service suicide prevention training programs have limited effectiveness due to a lack of a strategic approach to skills-based suicide prevention training.

DISCUSSION: Enhancing suicide prevention education and training is universally considered a core strategy for a comprehensive public health suicide prevention campaign. The military Services clearly value the importance of both education and training. A vast array of training programs have been developed and disseminated to address suicide prevention at multiple levels across the Services. At the installation level, most suicide prevention training programs help Service Members identify individuals who are at acute risk of suicide, understand the variety of resources available, and get linked with a professional caregiver (usually a chaplain or mental health professional). These programs generally consist of a short awareness module that places the responsibility for prevention on fellow Services Members without ensuring they have the skills to do so. These training programs represent a gargantuan investment of time and money, yet the Task Force did not find any evidence that these programs had been evaluated for effectiveness The primary focus of most training programs has been to educate and inform the audience of the warning signs and risk factors associated with suicide.

At the vast majority of site visits, Service Members stated that suicide prevention training was ineffective and even detrimental. Many Service Members reported the training is too frequent and redundant and is delivered in the typical "death by PowerPoint" method with minimal, if any, positive effect. Nearly every Service Member who had more than a couple years in the Armed Forces stated that he or she was familiar with the warning signs of suicide. The Task Force heard of countless incidents in which evidence of warning signs resulted in at-risk Service Members being taken to chaplains or mental health professionals and receiving professional care services. This indicates to the Task Force that the amount of suicide prevention training being provided was sufficient in this one aspect. Unfortunately, the Task Force also heard of several incidents in which warning signs were not observed before a Service Member took his or her life, reinforcing the fact that education on warning signs alone is not a sufficient training strategy.

The manner in which training is frequently delivered is of concern. In many units in which computer-based training was conducted annually or mini-briefings were given before every 3- day weekend and prior to leave periods, the messages have become, in the words of some Service Members, "a joke." Based on research about health communications in similar fields, these practices may well lead Service Members to conclude that suicide is more common that it actually is, and may paradoxically add to suicide risk. Furthermore, by delivering the training in large classroom-style settings (thereby eliminating any possibility of interaction between the trainer and trainees and among the trainees themselves), the effectiveness of the training is further limited. The Task Force concluded that this narrow approach to teaching the warning signs of suicide in large group settings has heightened awareness of suicide risk and warning signs; however, opportunities have been missed for developing essential "help-seeking" and "asking" skills that are necessary for effective suicide prevention.

From another perspective, the Task Force was concerned that the education programs of the Services lacked a focus on skills and behaviors. Like other public health prevention campaigns, suicide prevention depends on changing behaviors. Although knowledge and attitudes are important components of a change strategy, many of the behaviors that are needed in suicide prevention require skill-based training; in other words, the behaviors needed (ranging from self-initiated help-seeking to asking others very intrusive, but caring, questions) are skills that most people do not have. For the Services' suicide prevention education and training efforts to be most effective, they must be based on an overarching strategy with a skill-based training program that supports each component of that strategy.

The strategy must first identify which knowledge, skills, and attitudes must be present in individuals fulfilling various roles in the military community and develop training tailored to these specific groups. Each training curriculum is then developed around defined objectives for each target audience, taking into consideration the organization's mission. Consideration must be given to the organization's mission.

Service Members consistently reported that training platforms involving small interactive groups were engaging, memorable, and had impact. Part of the success of this type of training was attributed to the incorporation of basic program evaluation tenets: (1) the program was designed for its audience; (2) the objectives and goals of the training were clearly defined; and (3) the training was measureable.

The Task Force also observed that the Services disseminate prevention-oriented training that shares many of the same components. These include training on preventing racial and gender discrimination, preventing sexual harassment, preventing alcohol abuse, and preventing family violence. Coordinating the content of these programs could potentially save many millions of man-hours without sacrificing effectiveness.

The curriculum development process must include rigorous and formal evaluation, and the dissemination phase must include procedures to further evaluate the effectiveness of training; and to ensure fidelity to the original curriculum design. Further evaluation should be conducted to inform the frequency required to keep knowledge, skills, and attitudes at desired levels across the force.

Only by taking a strategic approach of this kind of training can the Services expect to achieve the magnitude of behavior change they desire.

The Task Force noted two promising skill-based training programs in the USMC: a carefully developed, front-line NCO course delivered in interactive small groups and a curriculum for customer service staff entitled "*Are you listening?*" These curricula were developed through thorough evaluation and reflect the USMC culture.

Recommendation

Develop DoD and Service-level comprehensive suicide prevention training strategies. Develop and disseminate state-of-the-art training curricula addressing the specific knowledge, skills, and attitudes required of each sub-population in the military community. Incorporate industry-standard evaluation practices throughout the development and dissemination phases. Focus efforts on skills-based training.

> *Finding:* Family members of married and single Service Members do not generally receive service-sponsored education and training in suicide prevention. When training is offered to family members and friends, many obstacles prevent wider attendance.

DISCUSSION: A significant number of Service Member suicides occur in the context of friends and family members having recognized out-of-the-ordinary behaviors by their loved ones in the days and weeks before the suicide event. As Diagram 7-3 shows, 12% (28) of

Service Members who died by suicide in 2008 communicated to their spouses a potential to harm themselves.

Some family members who lost loved ones to suicide reported that they "knew something was not right" but were unaware of the significance of what they were "seeing," especially post-deployment changes and stress reactions. When family members did recognize the significance of distress, they often reported that they did not know whom to call for help.

Often family members feel as though they are left on their own to endure the personal pain and struggles of their loved one in the Armed Forces, with no one to turn to.

The importance of the military family's role is increasingly being recognized in Service suicide prevention programs. Service Members repeatedly stated that their health and well-being was intertwined with the health and well-being of their families. Furthermore, recent empirical literature has demonstrated a relationship between the effects of deployments on spouse's and children's mental health (Mansfield, et. al, 2010; Lester, et. al, 2010), making it clear that military families themselves need significant education, training, support, and services.

Developing strategies to locate and remain in contact with families during all phases of the deployment cycle is imperative. Friends and families are often made aware of a Service Member's growing distress and are in a unique position to help activate a chain of concern to prevent suicide.

All too often, these loved ones have no idea how to access vital support systems. They often do not know whom to call in the Service Member's chain of command, and they rarely have a mechanism for establishing contact with command.

Although the American Red Cross messaging system is a vital conduit for information, it is unlikely to be swift enough in a suicidal crisis.

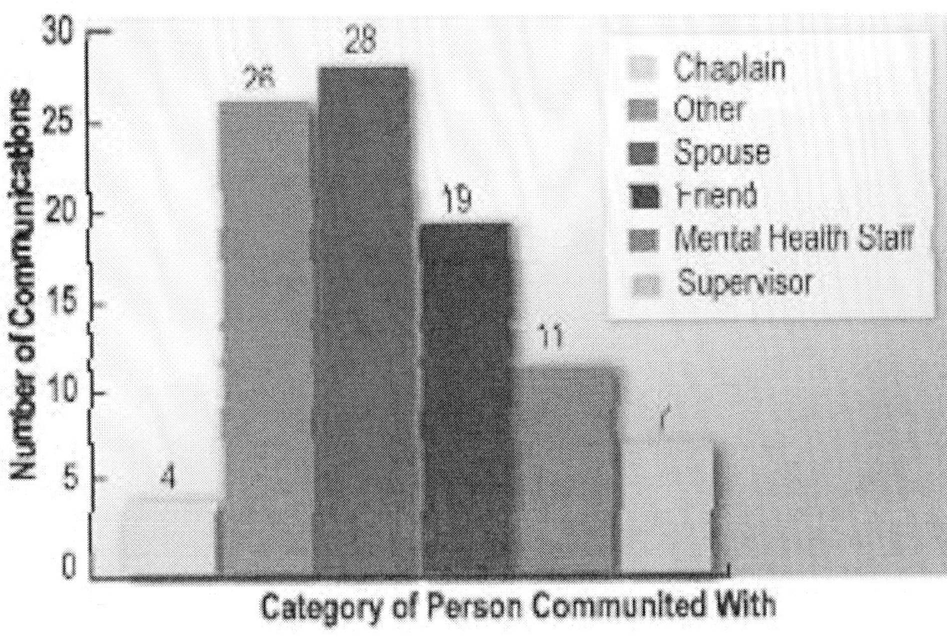

Diagram 7-3. Communication Prior to Suicide.

Generally, family members do not receive the Services' suicide awareness education and training and are usually unaware of resources available to support Service Members and their families.

This is especially true for non-local family members, such as parents and siblings of single Service Members who see their loved ones only when they are on leave. The Task Force believes that family members should receive training about suicide prevention, with a particular focus on raising awareness of warning signs, identifying risk, and gaining access to emergency support services (e.g., crisis response teams, emergency departments, and crisis phone numbers).

Programs to support military families are being implemented across the executive branch of the Federal Government; family members would benefit from strong collaboration on the efforts across the entire government.

Recommendations:

Target and train families (including parents, siblings, significant others, and next of kin) as a suicide prevention training strategy, and consider it an important part of the chain of care for Service Members. Family members should be educated and trained to recognize the signs of stress and distress, to know whom to call for advice, and to understand how to respond in emergencies.

Develop strategies to locate and remain in contact with families during every phase of the deployment cycle. Develop and disseminate pre-deployment and reintegration education and training programs germane to suicide prevention for family members.

Proactively seek opportunities to collaborate with other federal agencies in their efforts to support military families.

7.3. Access to, and Delivery of, Quality Care

7.3.1. Ensure Available and Reliable Access to High-Quality Behavioral Healthcare

FINDING: Access to care for Service Members with behavioral health disorders and/or suicide-related behaviors is not yet optimally and uniformly provided across the DoD healthcare system.

DISCUSSION: Access to quality behavioral healthcare has been expanded greatly through expansion of direct care and partnerships with civilian healthcare systems (e.g., TRICARE, VA, and private partnerships). Although these efforts should be commended, more needs to be done given the growing need.

Service Members with mental health disorders and/or suicide-related behaviors require easy access to care. Additionally, according to the 2008 DoDSER Annual Report (Gahm, et.al, 2009; Reger, et.al. 2009) 49% of Service Members who committed suicide had accessed at least one program or clinic within 30 days of their suicide. However, barriers that prevent easy access to care may interfere with a Service Member's ability to receive adequate and timely interventions.

Access-to-care problems include delays in obtaining a routine behavioral health appointment, lack of availability of evening and/or weekend hours at MTFs, and work-related demands that impede a Service Member's ability to access and use routine care.

While the Services have greatly expanded the availability of behavioral healthcare within the direct care system, this expansion has been highly variable across and within the Services. The DoD has funded the greatest expansion of initiatives in decades through its Psychological Health and Traumatic Brain Injury (PH/TBI) program. Through this program, the DoD has in recent years funded a significant expansion of behavioral health services within the direct care system, adding hundreds of behavioral health providers across all Services.

There remain, however, many locations with inadequate behavioral health staffing to meet the true demand, and providers at many locations visited described great difficulty in meeting the current access standard for new evaluations. Providers at more remote installations described considerable difficulty recruiting and retaining qualified practitioners to staff their clinics, and several are clearly working with skeleton crews.

In cases where MTFs have been more successful in hiring additional clinical staff, these providers are not necessarily well trained and familiar with the military healthcare model, including issues such as the need for close collaboration with unit commanders for effective systems-based practice. Their steep learning curve can often lead to provider frustration, burnout, and ultimately poorly coordinated care for the patient.

"I've been exhausted for a decade."
—military psychiatrist

It is clear that across every installation the Task Force visited, behavioral health providers as well as primary care and emergency providers, are strained by the demands placed upon them to manage large numbers of patients at risk for suicide. That said, the dedication and professionalism of these care providers is evident, as is their acknowledgement that they desire to provide more comprehensive and well-coordinated care.

Access to behavioral health practitioners who are fully qualified to perform comprehensive suicide risk assessments is also not uniformly available in crisis situations. Although many MTFs offer the capacity for 24/7 crisis coverage, many do not, and must instead rely on chaplains, behavioral health technicians, or clinicians (masters degree-prepared) to evaluate suicidal patients during or after normal duty hours. These providers do not uniformly have the support of a doctoral-level licensed provider to supervise the evaluation of the patient and are not generally clinically privileged (credentialed) to perform suicide risk assessments. In these cases, the general medical officer, primary care provider, or emergency physician may be neither trained nor familiar with current standards of clinical risk determination, treatment, and disposition.

"Having a single psychiatrist is not a concern, until that same psychiatrist is deployed."
—MTF mental health provider

Behavioral health providers demonstrated wide variability in the clinical competencies of suicide risk assessment and treatment. Contrary to conventional wisdom suicide risk management is not uniformly taught, nor is it a demonstrable core competency within training programs for mental health providers. Military internship and residency programs generally train this competency, but many civilian programs do not. The lack of a clearly defined and uniform standard in the community for suicide risk assessment makes conformity to a high-quality standard nearly impossible. Several good models are available, such as the Air Force's Managing Suicidal Behavior model (Oordt et al., 2005; Oordt, Jobes, Fonseca, & Schmidt, 2009), and several others which define optimal standards of care for suicide risk management.

Many smaller installations do not have any emergency medical capability and must rely on the local civilian facilities, particularly after duty hours. The standard of care in the civilian community is highly variable. Practitioners are largely unaware of military-specific considerations (e.g., the importance of command consultation and other collateral contacts) in completing a thorough risk assessment and treatment plan. Often, the default disposition is to hospitalize the patient in a local civilian psychiatric ward with little or no coordination with the Service Member's unit.

Most MTFs the Task Force visited did track and manage referrals to the civilian network very aggressively, and served as an effective conduit of information among the civilian hospital, the military MTF, and the Service Member's unit. Additionally, all nineteen sites visited reported strong community/managed-care-support contractor support for Service Members needing intervention services or inpatient psychiatric care.

Recommendations:

Implement policies that optimize access to care for all Service Members which are specifically designed for behavioral health care, and monitor access standards closely for compliance.

Train all caregivers in the governing rules applicable to appropriate and necessary information sharing among providers, outside agencies, and with Service Members' commands.

Develop interdisciplinary treatment plans for Service Members at risk for suicidal behavior.

Implement coordination of care plans across longitudinal lines (e.g., permanent change of station, temporary change of station, deployment and redeployment transitions, temporary duty with other units, release from active duty, demobilization, confinement, hospitalization, and extended leave periods).

Establish multidisciplinary case management teams to ensure the highest quality of coordinated care by the team of commander, clinical provider, and non-clinical care provider.

Age: 29
Rank/Occupation: Petty Officer Second Class/Helicopter Combat Support
Service Branch: US Navy

Following two tours in Iraq, this Petty Officer struggled with anxiety and depression. Six weeks after ending his 6-year enlistment and release from active duty, he decided to stop taking his medication for depression. He was subsequently checked into a hospital for treatment and then released. He went into a downward spiral that no one saw coming even after his inpatient stay. In a state of desperation, he ended his own life.

7.3.2. Leverage and Coordinate Military Community-Based Services, As Well As Local Civilian Community Services (Especially With Respect to the Reserve Component)

> *Finding:* While on-base non-clinical support services have been greatly expanded by the services, too often they are not well coordinated to best support/protect Service Members and their families, and they too rarely share information with each other.

DISCUSSION: The Task Force strongly asserts that suicide prevention and risk reduction are *not* solely clinical or mental health issues. There are various DoD-wide services that have multiple non-clinical opportunities to make an impact on, and reduce the risk of suicide. For example, military chaplains, family support activities, financial assistance agencies, and legal assistance services are pervasive across military installations. They serve a critical function to enhance the well-being and preparedness of individuals and families in military communities, which may directly and indirectly affect mental fitness and suicide behaviors therein. Staff at these support services frequently interact with Service Members who may be in crisis or are at an elevated risk for suicide. The Task Force observed that service providers do not consistently communicate with one another or the Service Member's command except when specifically mandated by regulation. Improving cross-communication, coordination, and cooperation between and among "helping agencies" and "helping people" would greatly enhance comprehensive suicide risk reduction and improve our ability to intervene effectively.

During the Task Force's site visits, members observed that Service behavioral health providers too often had little to no time in their current work schedules to engage in proactive outreach activities directed at increasing awareness related to psychological stressors and promoting positive attitudes about the value of pursuing mental fitness and the merits of seeking behavioral healthcare when indicated. Chaplains, social workers, community service agencies, public affairs, etc., across the DoD system devote a reasonable percentage of their work hours to outreach activities performed within military communities These activities are typically geared toward informing and educating military community members about various services available for risk reduction and suicide intervention. The Services might also consider using existing Reserve Centers, National Guard Centers, and Recruiting Stations, as conduits for information and availability of installation services especially with respect to the Reserve Component.

The Task Force believes that lives could be saved if DoD care providers, both medical and nonmedical, and commanders work together to establish close networks that facilitate effective communication and processing of information about suicidal Service Members. Based on the Task Force's site visits, the members observed that in the more effective settings, providers and commanders held frequent meetings with support services and personnel to discuss and further improve their process of optimal communications about high-risk Service Members. These discussions were held regularly and were thoughtful and systematic in addressing the needs of suicidal Service Members.

Recommendations

Optimize and coordinate community-based services to leverage their capabilities to enhance protective factors for Service Members.

Promote and utilize coordinated community outreach and awareness activities provided by clinicians and other installation-based care providers to improve access to care and reduce stigma.

> Finding: Current screening efforts are not effective in identifying Service Members who have significant moral and ethical problems resulting from their combat experience, resulting in a sense of guilt and loss of self-worth that places them at risk for suicide.

DISCUSSION: In the face of the considerable necessity of having a warrior culture across the Service to destroy property and to take human life (conduct combat), a fundamental need exists to address and resolve the sense of guilt that comes from violating normative peacetime moral codes. One way to fulfill this need is to further emphasize spiritual and moral fitness as a means for developing a more fit, successful, and resilient fighting force.

Various forms of guilt may adversely affect a Service Member's combat effectiveness, sense of self-worth, relationships with others, and ability to cope with stressful situations. Guilt can be associated with the commission of violence, having survived when others died, being absent from the battlefield, neglecting family duties while deployed, and a host of other circumstances out of the Service Member's control.

Guilt is fundamentally a spiritual and moral issue but currently there is no routine focus on spiritual/moral/ethical health as part of the annual physical health assessment. A "Spiritual Fitness Check" (SFC) could be embedded or linked to routine physical health assessments to normalize the importance of spiritual fitness as a shared priority for Service Members.

Although the Global Assessment Tool used as part of Comprehensive Soldier Fitness in the US Army self-assesses spirituality as a domain, further spiritual assessment and care needs to be accomplished in all the Services. Service Members returning from combat generally are insufficiently screened for spiritual, moral, or ethical health issues following their return from deployment. The reintegration period is an opportune time to properly screen and assess a Service member's "spiritual fitness" because it allows for early identification and potential resolution of problems associated with post-combat guilt and shame.

Recommendation

Encourage Service Members to have annual face-to-face "conferences" with chaplains for the purpose of resolving questions of guilt and to obtain referrals to appropriate caregivers for other concerns beyond the chaplain's scope of expertise and experience.

> *Finding*: Service providers do not consistently collaborate well within or across clinical and non-clinical disciplines.

DISCUSSION: Well-intended efforts to improve access to care too often result in fragmentation of that care. The recent enhancement of access to care through programs such as Military OneSource, Military Family Life Consultants (MFLC), community service agencies, and the TRICARE network have undoubtedly provided valuable benefits to our Service Members and families. Service Members who sought these services specifically noted that the attraction of these providers is rooted in the perception that such care will not have a negative impact on their career. The Task Force consistently found throughout its site visits, expert presentations, case reports, and discussions with leaders, that enhanced access to clinical and community programs have had some unintended consequences. While access to less stigmatizing care has improved, an unintended consequence has been the increased potential for poor communications between service providers, helping agencies, families, and command leadership.

Because these services function outside the MTF and do not share a common platform for documentation of care, coordination of interdisciplinary care suffers. Each program has its own charter and business rules, and each one benefits from the cloak of confidentiality, often citing Health Insurance Portability and Accountability Act (HIPAA) and their fiduciary relationship with the individual client to avoid sharing information with other care providers without written consent. Frankly, this situation is both a blessing and a curse. It is a"blessing"from the perspective of the Service Member patient, who perceives a benefit from the enhanced privacy gained, and a "curse" from the perspective of commanders, who naturally seek total situational awareness about the well-being of those in their charge and for whom they are responsible.

The inherent risk of reduced communication resulting from improved access must be balanced with a "need to know" about risk factors for suicide. This risk must either be accepted as a necessary byproduct of enhanced access or managed through more aggressive case management and coordination of care. The alternative would be to bring all care under the umbrella of the MTF and create a unified documentation platform that would inform clinicians and commanders about the risks experienced by their Service Members. However, improving visibility and communication may result in the reluctance of Service Members to seek care at all.

Recommendation

Develop a comprehensive policy to promote systematic and regular communication among clinical and non-clinical providers.

7.3.3. Ensure Continuity of Behavioral Healthcare, Especially During Times of Transition, to Ensure Seamlessness of Healthcare and Care Management

Finding: There is high potential for Service Members at risk for suicide to fall through the cracks in the continuum of care.

DISCUSSION: Currently, the military does not have a "chain of care" approach for those Service Members identified as being at risk for suicide. Although Military OneSource provides an important behavioral health option to distressed and suicidal Service Members who may otherwise refuse to seek mental health services, the Task Force is aware of problems in the transition period for Service Members from Military OneSource providers to military treatment facilities. Problems in the transition of care may exacerbate the distress experienced by a suicidal or at-risk Service Member. For example, the Task Force heard of cases in which the chain of care between Military OneSource and MTFs did not take into account issues involving medical documentation, timeline of transition, or a Service Member's compliance with the transition plan of care. Fifteen percent of Army suicides occur after discharge from an inpatient psychiatric unit (Schoenbaum, Heinssen, & Pearson, 2010).

As highlighted in the NIMH recommendations to the Vice Chief of the Army, a chain of care provides for close monitoring, follow-up, and appropriate services for those identified as being at risk for suicide (Schoenbaum, Heinssen, & Pearson, 2010). Transitions include transfers from installation to installation, between units of assignments, from civilian to military settings, and for deploying and redeploying Service Members, as well as when discharged from inpatient services.

Recommendations

Manage care across transition points and monitor Service Members identified as being at- risk for suicide.

Assess Military OneSource capabilities to ensure a seamless transition of care system is established for suicidal or at-risk Service Members who utilize their services. This transitional care system needs to take into account challenges involving medical documentation, timeline of transition, and maximizing Service Member compliance with the transition plan.

Age: 28
Rank/Occupation: Staff Sergeant/Infantry
Branch of Service: US Army

This Soldier was 28 years old and had completed multiple deployments. He suffered from post-traumatic stress disorder following his first tour where he had experienced close combat. When he left his unit because of transfer to another base, his post-traumatic stress and depressive symptoms worsened. Prior to his suicide, he made two unsuccessful attempts. His mother said the following about her son; "He felt most at home with his unit; he loved them and worked as hard as he could to be worthy of them. He gave his blood, sweat, and tears; he gave it all to them. I feel the Army let him down, and that when he needed them the most, they were not there for him."

Finding: Service Members in the Reserve Component lose important military-related protective factors during post-mobilization phases and lose access to myriad installation-based support and healthcare service.

DISCUSSION: Upon return from deployment or completion of annual or weekend duty, Reserve Component personnel return to civilian employment and to their home. These Reserve Component Service Members often live or work in areas hundreds of miles from their colleagues, their unit headquarters, and military installations. In peace time, this separation had minimal impact. But in wartime, with mobilization and demobilization, the isolation and separation may be deadly, especially in those experiencing post-traumatic stress. Social separation and lack of access to the many protective services provided to members of the Active Component likely contributes to Reserve Component suicide risk and may explain recent data showing increasing suicide rates among post-deployment National Guard and Reserve Soldiers. To this end, the Michigan National Guard has developed and tested a peer-support program ("Buddy 2 Buddy") designed to keep Soldiers connected with one another during the post-deployment phase. Moreover, the program also employs a network of trained, experienced veterans, not associated with the unit, to act as peer counselors and to connect Soldiers believed to be at-risk with veterans services (including behavioral health). Such an innovative program holds significant promise for suicide prevention among Reserve Component Service Members. The task force was also impressed with the New Jersey "Veteran to Veteran" helpline program which has significantly lowered suicide rates among veterans in that state.

Recommendations

Develop, evaluate, and more widely disseminate peer-to-peer and other programs that intentionally promote not only connectedness but also risk identification and response among Reserve Component Service Members.

Promote easy access to evidence-based treatments and community support services for post-deployment Reserve Component Service Members.

Ensure all Reserve Component Service Members receive face-to-face behavioral health checks post-deployment/post-demobilization and before being remobilized, with an emphasis on connecting them with professional services during the post-deployment phase.

> *Finding:* Many commanders express a genuine desire to know about the safety of Service Members under their command so that they can intervene effectively, as needed; however, they are often left in the dark or not effectively used as helpful resources by DoD behavioral health providers because of issues related to privacy and confidentiality.

DISCUSSION: Although the need to respect individual privacy and confidentiality rights is recognized, in cases where imminent suicide risk is determined, commanders may serve as a key ally in suicide prevention efforts. Therefore, behavioral health providers are strongly encouraged to disclose and discuss assessment and management strategies with the Service Member's commander to maximize the chances of keeping that individual alive. In cases in which imminent suicide risk is not noted, the behavioral health provider may share information with a multidisciplinary committee, including representation from behavioral health providers, chaplains, and commanders, to make a decision about the best course of action.

Recommendation

Provide guidance on how behavioral health providers and commanders should best communicate with each other to promote effective suicide prevention practices for Service Members.

> *Finding:* The general lack of communication between the DoD healthcare system providers, support services providers (e.g., chaplains, Family Advocacy Programs), and commanders is currently an impediment in the delivery of effective assessment, intervention, and aftercare services and support offered to suicidal Service Members.

DISCUSSION: Clinicians, installation support service providers, and commanders must network in order to establish effective communication and processing of information about Service Members recognized to be at risk for suicidal behaviors. To promote the establishment of such a network, providers and commanders could implement a structure for case conferences to formalize the process of communication about high-risk cases. These discussions should preferably be held regularly so that they are not reactive and are instead thoughtful and systematic in addressing the needs of suicidal Service Members. A Human Factors Board model used in the USMC may be a solid model of how this recommendation can be implemented appropriately.

Recommendation

***Establish and use interdisciplinary "human factors" type boards** (emphasizing topics like physical, social, behavioral, psychological, nutritional, environmental, spiritual, and medical health) on all installations to coordinate suicide prevention care for at-risk Service Members.*

> *Finding:* Current screening efforts are not effective in identifying Service Members at risk for suicide and tend to perpetuate negative feelings about mental healthcare, which leads to further stigma.

DISCUSSION: In the face of considerable obstacles to seeking mental health care, due to both stigma to seeking care and the military culture of self-sufficiency (both counterproductive to getting much-needed healthcare), there is a fundamental need to completely "re-brand" associations and perceptions related to mental health. One way to accomplish this effort would be a greater emphasis on psychological "resiliency" as a means to a mentally fit and more successful fighting force. Currently, there is no routine focus on behavioral health and wellness as part of the annual physical health assessment. A mental fitness assessment could be embedded or linked to routine physical health assessments to normalize the importance of mental fitness as a shared priority on par with the broad appreciation and acceptance of physical fitness as a core value of military life. This mental fitness assessment would provide a unique opportunity to provide appropriate education about strategies to increase protective factors and to enhance overall wellness.

Recommendation

Take steps to make "mental fitness" commensurate with "physical fitness" within military culture as a core value of military life. Ensure every Service Member receives a mental fitness assessment and appropriate wellness education as part of his or her periodic heath assessment.

Finding: The integration of behavioral health into military primary care settings is a viable and significant suicide prevention strategy that can potentially produce huge benefits in overcoming stigma and providing necessary services.

DISCUSSION: Although many Service Members do not readily seek behavioral health services, they are likely to have regular visits with their primary care physicians. The integration of behavioral health into primary care has shown promising results in various military settings. There are numerous advantages for such integration, including the following: (1) reduction of stigma-related effects in seeking care, (2) exposure to behavioral health providers, which may be associated with a decrease in perceived barriers to care and subsequent increase in help seeking behaviors, and (3) early detection of mental health problems to offer a targeted and timely behavioral health intervention.

MTFs are already moving in the direction of making behavioral health providers available within primary healthcare settings. Coincidentally, the integration of behavioral healthcare into primary care settings is increasingly seen in civilian and VA healthcare settings. Service Members (and providers) reported to the Task Force that they liked this integrative approach because it afforded ready access to care in a familiar setting with less fear of stigmatization. An excellent established example of this effective integration is the Air Force's Behavioral Health Optimization Program (BHOP).

Recommendation

Integrate behavioral health treatment teams into DoD primary care settings to overcome stigma and increase the likelihood of access to care; as well as to establish an early intervention approach to suicide prevention. Where this is not possible, train primary care providers and their staff in the assessment and management (and triage) of acute suicide risk patients.

Finding: The current DoD electronic medical documentation platforms do not allow for easy and systematic tracking of the care provided to high-risk suicidal Service Members.

DISCUSSION: Appropriate medical documentation is imperative for effective communication between DoD primary and specialty care providers for the delivery of effective and timely psychiatric care, especially for suicidal Service Members. Two primary medical documentation platforms exist within the DoD healthcare system: Essentris and the Armed Forces Health Longitudinal Technology Application (AHLTA). Currently Essentris is used by MTF inpatient units but is not connected to AHLTA or other inpatient units. Although some DoD providers may have access to both systems, others may lack access or rely solely on the AHLTA system, which does not contain inpatient psychiatric records.

Therefore a provider may not have knowledge of a Service Member's prior psychiatric hospitalizations and consequently lack a comprehensive understanding of the Service Member's health status. Furthermore, non-integrated medical records underscore efforts at coordinated care, a common difficulty within the DoD healthcare system.

Given the complexity of the issues associated with developing an electronic, user-friendly system, it may be helpful to form a designated expert group to address the stated objective. The newly developed documentation system should take into account the tracking of suicidal behaviors throughout various deployments as well. The VA healthcare system has implemented specific medical documentation procedures for suicidal veterans, and the DoD should carefully evaluate lessons they learned from this effort.

Recommendation

Develop a standard and systematic medical documentation system to identify high-risk patients and track the care provided. Continually review and update the record (documentation).

> *Finding*: Unit suicide watch practices are frequently inappropriate and harmful to Service Members.

DISCUSSION: Service Members deemed to be at risk for suicide are being placed on unit suicide watch in addition to, and sometimes in lieu of, treatment. The individual being watched views this practice as punitive and stigmatizing rather than therapeutic. Paradoxically, this practice may ultimately *increase* suicide risk. The Task Force found that suicide watch practices vary widely in the absence of specific Service policies.

Suicide watch, also referred to as unit watch, is a monitoring system for those Service Members considered at risk for suicide. At present, only the Army has provided guidance regarding suicide watches but has decentralized its implementation (US Army, 2009). While on suicide watch, the Service Member's unit peers are tasked with the responsibility of monitoring the Service Member 24 hours a day. There is no formalized suicide watch training and no individual consistently identified as responsible for managing suicide watches (Scoville, Gubata, Potter, White, & Pearse, 2007). Suicide watch is characterized by unrealistic expectations and has no therapeutic value. Those tasked with watching a Service Member are often identified at random and unexpectedly. When a Service Member is placed on suicide watch, the impact is significant on the entire unit. For the Service Member who is the subject of a suicide watch, it negates any confidentiality and ostracizes the Service Member from the unit, thereby identifying that individual as a social outcast within the one group in which he or she should feel safest. Suicide watch also creates a hostile environment because the unit becomes frustrated with the tasking for lengthy watches. As reported to the Task Force from Service Members, individuals on suicide watch reported being shunned by their fellow Soldiers, placed in isolation, and taunted by their peers and leaders.

Recommendation

Suicide watch should be used only as a last resort and only until appropriate mental healthcare becomes available. Provide consistent guidance to units for these exceptional instances, as well as "just in time" training (e.g., online training). If units have a suicide prevention coordinator, the management of these rare instances could fall to that individual's responsibility. A suicide watch training program should be developed and similarly instituted.

7.3.4. Standardize Effective Crisis Intervention Services and Hotlines

Finding: Service Members and their families do not know which of the multiple DoD publicized call centers to contact for suicide-related or emotional crisis calls. Suicide Hotline services are frequently unavailable for deployed Service Members

DISCUSSION: Evidence exists that competent crisis response lines are effective in reducing suicidal risk (Gould et al., 2007). Currently, DoD suicide prevention efforts, materials, and press announcements provide inconsistent information regarding whom to contact if a suicidal crisis occurs. Some identify Military OneSource; others, the DCoE Outreach Call Center; and still others, the National Suicide Prevention Lifeline (800-273-TALK). DoD must clearly distinguish between crisis hotlines that have a capacity to respond to acutely suicidal callers (e.g., Lifeline), and call centers that offer information and referral or counseling, but do not provide a 24-hour capacity to intervene in a suicidal crisis (e.g., OneSource and DCoE Outreach). The DCoE Outreach Call Center provides information and referrals, but it is not well known as an option among family members. Military OneSource provides information and counseling on a limited basis, but is neither a crisis response center nor available to all family members.

Service Members and their families need rapid access to a suicide hotline and crisis intervention services. In situations in which a suicide attempt may be in progress or imminent, rapid access to crisis intervention services, including the dispatching of emergency rescue, may be life saving. Widespread dissemination of accurate information to Service Members and their families regarding which service to call when a suicide attempt might be imminent is therefore vital, along with ongoing quality review of responses to these situations.

Given the significant national and VA infrastructure affiliated with 1-800-273-TALK (8255) as a 24/7 suicide prevention hotline number, the DoD's promotion of this crisis hotline would ensure that the best response and resources are provided to a Service Member and his/her family during a crisis.

Recommendations

Provide clear direction and consistent messaging regarding the promotion and usage of the National Suicide Prevention Lifeline 1-800-273-TALK (8255) as a national suicide prevention hotline resource available to all Service Members and their families, as well as the use of local crisis hotlines (or information lines) focusing on specific populations.

Formalize existing interconnectedness of the DCoE Outreach Call Center, National Suicide Prevention Lifeline, and Military OneSource to enable each agency to quickly and effectively route calls to appropriate responders. Ensure ongoing quality review and quality improvement efforts focused on emergency rescue situations, follow-up referrals for callers at-risk, and linkages with community providers of crisis services (e.g., mobile outreach teams).

Optimize the availability of suicide hotline services to deployed Service Members using the same National Suicide Prevention Lifeline number to ensure best response capabilities.

> Age: 45
> Rank/Occupation: Brigadier General/Flag Officer
> Service Branch: US Air Force
> Fellow senior officers said he "was a remarkable officer with a reputation for excellence and tremendous love for his Airmen and his family. One of the tragic aspects of this event is that we are unlikely to ever fully understand his actions that evening." The General is survived by his wife, a college-age daughter, and a teenage nephew he was helping to raise. The family felt they were unable to provide valuable input into the investigation and little was shared with them after the investigation, causing further secondary trauma to loved ones. A statement released by the family expressed both sadness and lingering bewilderment at his passing. "To lose him as a leader is immense; to lose him as a husband, father, brother, and son are immeasurable."

7.3.5. Ensure All "Helping Professionals" Are Trained in the Competencies to Deliver Evidence-Based Care for the Assessment, Management, and Treatment of Suicide-Related Behaviors

> *Finding:* No DoD clinical practice guidelines exist for evidence-based assessment, management, and treatment of suicide-related behaviors.

DISCUSSION: Based on discussions with "helping professionals" at various installations and an overall review of suicide prevention efforts within the DoD healthcare system, the Task Force, noted that current clinical practices for the assessment, management, and treatment of suicide-related behaviors are not often evidence-based. Although the field of suicidology continues to struggle with establishment of evidence-based practices for suicide prevention, there is solid expert consensus on assessment, management, and intervention strategies considered as best practices for the care of suicidal individuals. Given that the current DoD healthcare system shows much variability in the care of suicidal Service Members, a uniform, systematic, and scientifically informed approach is much needed. The development of clinical practice guidelines for evidence-based assessment, management, and treatment of suicide-related behaviors should address the currently observed system-wide gap.

Furthermore, a standard practice for documentation of care has not yet been developed. The Veteran's Health Administration (VHA) has already established a standard of care and developed the medical documentation infrastructure to document care, create comprehensive interdisciplinary treatment plans, and identify high-risk individuals across the continuum of healthcare. Within the DoD, multiple applications have been developed to complement AHLTA, but none have been proven to be functional, reliable, or are close to fruition.

A DoD suicide prevention practice guideline can establish a scientifically informed standard of care and documentation for suicidal Service Members. The practice guidelines may be established by the formation of an expert group of civilian, DoD, and VA suicidologists, researchers, practitioners, chaplains, and even consumers who can then consider the specific needs of suicidal Service Members.

Clinical issues, such as the management of suicide-related behaviors in deployed settings, determination of suicide risk, consultation versus second opinion practices, standardized assessment and documentation procedures, and treatment strategies, can be addressed comprehensively in the practice guideline.

The development and implementation of a DoD practice guide for suicide prevention, as described, can then be used as a solid foundation for the continuing education training provided to all DoD providers.

Recommendation

Develop clinical practice guidelines to promote the utilization of evidence-based practices for the assessment, management, and treatment of suicide-related behaviors.

> *Finding*: Timely access to behavioral healthcare is inconsistent across military installations.

DISCUSSION: Task Force site visits, as well as formal and informal conversations with DoD healthcare providers, indicated that providers appear to be under-resourced for the large amount of tasks they must complete. The Task Force received contradictory reports on the waiting times needed to receive services at installations, including outpatient treatment.

For military behavioral healthcare to play an effective role in suicide prevention, Service Members at-risk must be able to access care in a reasonable time frame.

Although waiting times for services at many DoD healthcare facilities may be reviewed routinely as part of continuous quality management, efforts to shorten these waiting times may be challenging given the current strain on the system.

Therefore, it is imperative that given the demand for behavioral healthcare services within the DoD, sufficient resources are allocated to ensure Service Members have timely access.

Recommendation

Dedicate sufficient behavioral health resources to military health facilities to allow for timely mental health assessment and treatment.

> *Finding:* Military healthcare providers (including behavioral health providers) and chaplains are insufficiently trained to deliver evidence-based assessment, management, and treatment services to Service Members with suicide-related behaviors.

DISCUSSION: Given that DoD healthcare providers and chaplains have a wide range of academic and professional backgrounds, there is concern that not all may have had focused training on the topics of suicide risk assessment, management, and treatment. Even if some providers and chaplains had received such training previously, continuing education on recently established evidence-based practices for suicide assessment, management, and treatment of suicidal Service Members is needed for all involved in the delivery of care. Although it might be assumed that all mental health professionals are routinely trained in suicide prevention skills as part of their education and training, research has shown that this is not the case.

Neither the Army nor the Navy has provided systematic training in suicide risk assessment, management, and treatment to its behavioral healthcare workforce. The Air Force and USMC provided one-time training on assessing and managing suicide risk, with no known plans to repeat this training, although both have manuals for their behavioral health providers regarding the assessment and management of suicidal patients. Service Members at risk for suicide deserve to receive optimal treatment.

By ensuring that all healthcare providers—especially primary care physicians, behavioral health specialists, and chaplains—are trained in the most advanced suicide prevention strategies, DoD can be more confident that all at-risk Service Members will be managed properly and therefore will be less likely to relapse. The training of chaplains cannot be emphasized enough. Frequently, these are the first professional caregivers that distressed military personnel consult; consequently, chaplains serve an instrumental role in the DoD suicide prevention effort. All chaplains should receive appropriate ongoing suicide prevention and care training.

Recommendation

Train all military healthcare providers (including behavioral health providers) and chaplains on evidence-informed suicide risk assessment, management, and treatment planning. Create and provide continuing education tailored to their specialty and area of expertise.

7.3.6. Develop Effective Postvention Programs to Support Families, Service Members, and Unit Leaders after a Suicide

Finding: Current DoD efforts in the area of suicide postvention are notably lacking.

DISCUSSION: Postvention is the provision of crisis intervention, support, and assistance for those affected by a suicide death or by any tragedy or loss. The focus on postvention is likely to contribute strongly to a comprehensive DoD suicide prevention strategy because postvention is commonly known as one form of prevention.

Currently, none of the Service-specific suicide prevention programs have targeted programs for postvention. The Task Force recognizes the importance and value of postvention, and the Task Force hopes that the recommendation provided here will address this observed gap.

The death or severe injury of a Service Member, in peacetime as well as wartime, is inherently traumatic and is often a source of guilt and anger for survivors in the unit and family. Although many survivors cope effectively, others struggle with the aftermath of the suicide event or tragic loss of a loved one, experiencing adjustment and/or grief-related responses. In worst-case circumstances, survivors (including military personnel exposed to a peer's suicide) may experience suicidal ideation and be at elevated risk for suicide themselves.

Unit leaders, chaplains, and behavioral health providers must be aware of this increased risk and foster group cohesion to support the healing process and minimize isolation. This awareness can be accomplished by Service-specific programs that address the issue of postvention. For example, informational pamphlets that include a listing of resources may be prepared to disseminate knowledge to the immediate family and military unit.

Recommendation

Incorporate postvention programs targeted at the decedent's military unit, family, and community after a tragedy or loss to reduce the risk of suicide. Postvention efforts must address Service Members affected by a significant loss, especially after a fallen comrade's death in combat or in garrison when the unit is impacted. Unit-level postvention efforts also must focus on effective debriefing and prevention when they are impacted by a significant tragedy or loss.

> *Finding:* No DoD suicide postvention training program exists that is targeted at first responders, chaplains, and casualty notification officers on how to best work with famiies and next of kin.

DISCUSSION: Following the death of a Service Member by suicide, first responders (the "medics"), chaplains, and casualty notification officers have an important and sensitive role in interacting with the survivor's family members.

Many surviving family members note the significance of such interaction in their grieving and healing process. In turn, many first responders, chaplains, and casualty notification officers who are exposed to suicide (and death cases, in general) face emotional consequences such as vicarious traumatization which may become a "hidden wound".

Although all first responders, chaplains, casualty notification officers, and investigators interviewing surviving family members receive training about handling cases of death, generally they do not receive targeted training for handling a suicide death event; nor do they receive training in dealing with their emotions, especially in regard to dealing with grieving families. During visits, Task Force members learned that these individuals expressed an interest in training and noted that they would benefit from it. Targeted postvention training for this group would focus on many factors that separate a death by natural causes from a death by suicide. For instance, first responders should learn about the types of concerns and immediate reactions that surviving family members might have following a suicide death of a loved one. Chaplains may benefit from increased sensitivity to issues pertaining to religion, spirituality, and death by suicide, and how, occasionally, well-intentioned but insensitive mention of such issues might cause harm to the surviving family member.

Casualty notification officers can learn about specific procedures for implementation in the cases of suicide and/or suspected suicide deaths. Overall, a DoD suicide postvention training program tailored to the needs of first responders, chaplains, casualty notification officers, and family interviewers would have significant value to all involved.

Recommendation

Train first responders, chaplains, casualty notification officers, and family interviewers on how to best respond to suicide and suicide-related events when working with families or next of kin.

> *Finding:* No DoD-sponsored postvention programs exist that directly meet the needs of surviving family members of Service Members who die by suicide.

DISCUSSION: During visits to 19 military installations, 8 public meetings, and discussions with military surviving family members at the TAPS National Military Suicide Survivor Seminar and Good Grief Camp, the Task Force learned that surviving family members have numerous questions following the deaths of their loved ones. Family members explained that from their perception, some commanders and others in the military community believe that discussing the death of a Service Member by suicide with their families would be harmful or damaging to them. Actually, families need information to fill the voids created by their questions in order for them to reach a sense of closure. In addition, many families reported that they had information to share with the military about the circumstances of their loved one's death and wanted to give input to the military so that important preventive lessons could be learned; however, they were not provided an opportunity to contribute. Recent research reveals that suicide survivors benefit from active involvement in the discovery process regarding the loss of their loved one, along with participation in a support group. Survivors also may benefit—if ready, willing, and trained to do so—from assisting others in their grief process. For instance, survivors who helped others at difficult times of discovery and notification reported healing from their own losses in ways they could not have imagined (Suicide Survivors as First Responders: The LOSS TEAM, http://www. lossteam. com/).

Recommendation

Provide families with comprehensive emotional support following the death of a loved one by suicide. All those affected, including significant others and battle buddies, should have access to resources that will help them cope with traumatic grief, such as the peer-based support organization Tragedy Assistance Program for Survivors (TAPS) and the Department of Veterans Affairs (VA) Vet Centers. These organizations offer free services to all who are grieving, with focused support for suicide loss.

> *Finding:* Services Investigative agencies benefit from a family advocate avaliable to support families through the investigative process, gain key information from family members and respond to inquiriesinvestigation when the investigation department is staffed with trained officers assigned to conduct family liaison.

DISCUSSION: Families, friends, and peers of Service Members who die by suicide are affected profoundly by the trauma of the suicide death and struggle to understand causal factors. As they search for information pertaining to the death, they often talk with loved ones' comrades in arms, read the suicide note, review incident reports, study the autopsy, and reflect on childhood experiences. When the surviving family members are at a point in their grief that they are able to focus on learning these factors, they become active investigators. In time, they often come to understand the larger picture of the death, beyond the "final straw" (e.g., a fight with their spouse or a drinking binge).

Throughout the criminal investigation process, many surviving families have contact with investigators assigned to review the death of their loved one. Communication between these two parties is important to not only the manner of death determination but also the overall suicide postvention efforts. However, many officers do not receive focused training regarding how to best interact and communicate with family members of Service Members who died by suicide.

To benefit from the wealth of information potentially available from surviving family members and to provide surviving family members with a respectful and efficient handling of their case, investigators could best interact with families through a trained "family advocate," preferably with some training in psychology, social work, behavioral health, or related field as part of the investigation team.

Key to this advocate's success is his/her training in sensitivity when dealing with suicide survivors.

Training should focus on how to effectively gather information from families, support them through their traumatic grief, filter this new information for evidentiary value, and submit relevant evidence and information to the appropriate investigators. Lacking this family advocate, families may turn to their Members of Congress or to the media to obtain important information about their loved ones' death. Meeting the needs of surviving family members during the investigative process is a significant endeavor to which DoD must pay close attention.

One Soldier wrote in his suicide note that the final trigger on the day of his death was "the snowflake that toppled the iceberg."

His family learned from reading his journals covering the previous years that it could have been the memory of the Iraqi child he crushed under his Bradley.

It could have been the unarmed man he shot point-blank in the forehead during a house-to-house raid, or the friend he tried madly to gather into a plastic bag after the friend had been blown to bits by a roadside bomb, or the doctor he killed at a checkpoint.

His family carefully sought out every bit of information, every clue to their son's suicide. They felt that "no matter the terrible things he might have done, their son was a good person, a sensitive young man who wanted to serve his country."

They were motivated to identify every factor leading to their son's death; in doing so, they became valuable investigators.

As is understandable, family members could benefit greatly from a trained, caring family advocate.

In addition to providing the family with a centralized point to provide additional information, the evidence and insight collected by the family and submitted to the family advocate will inform the investigation and offer insight into future suicide prevention activities.

Recommendation

Ensure that Service criminal investigation agencies are staffed appropriately with family advocates trained in communicating with family members whose loved ones might have died by suicide. Maintain effective communication with surviving family members during the investigative process.

Age: 19
Rank/Occupation: Army Private First Class/Infantry
Service Branch: US Army

This young Soldier became troubled by an e-mail message that he received from his fiancée at the airport while waiting to depart Iraq for mid-tour leave.

She told him that she was breaking off their engagement because she had found someone else. Once home during leave he was quiet and shared very little of his experiences about Iraq.

His mother said, "He couldn't sleep or eat and was withdrawn. We walked on eggshells, not knowing what to say or what not to say. There was no Army base nearby. I had no one to call. I didn't know what to do." The day before he was due to return to Iraq, the 19- year-old killed himself in their garage.

"If only he could have reached out to someone who understood his pain," his mother said. "He was sent home in a critical state without a support group. He had never been exposed to death before. I think he would've been OK if he hadn't come home on leave... if he had the support of his Army buddies."

Finding: Occasionally, Service Members who die by suicide are denied a military memorial service with military honors.

DISCUSSION: Suicide survivors expressed concern regarding the lack of consistency in memorial services provided for Service Members who died by suicide. At some installations, the death was not publicly acknowledged at all, whereas at others, full memorial services hosted by the unit and or installation were provided.

It is apparent that some leaders choose to differentiate which deceased Service Members were honored by military-sponsored memorial services based on the member's manner of death rather than their life, their service to the nation and their contributions.

In the words of Major General William Troy, "We should be memorializing his service to the nation, his service in combat. He's a volunteer, a member of a free nation who came and joined our ranks to defend this country, and that's what we should be memorializing—not passing judgment on the manner of his death" (Mauer, 2010).)

Recommendation

Develop a consistent DoD policy on memorials that encourages remembrance based on how the Service Member lived, rather than the manner of death. Use WHO/IASP guidelines to avoid increasing risk through glamorizing death, and SPRC recommendations for conducting memorial services.

7.4. Surveillance, Investigations, and Research

7.4.1. Conduct Comprehensive Surveillance Aimed at Identifying Individuals at-Risk and Informing Prevention Efforts

Finding: Currently, DoD does not have a standardized approach to suicide surveillance that informs suicide prevention efforts.

DISCUSSION: Surveillance, which is a critical part of public health practice, is defined as "the ongoing and systematic collection, analysis, and interpretation of outcome-specific data for use in the planning, implementation, and evaluation of public health practice" (Thacker & Berkelman, 1988). By definition, surveillance systems provide data collection and analyses. The timely dissemination of the analyses to persons or a group of persons responsible for the design and implementation of effective prevention and intervention related to suicide and suicidal behaviors among Service Members is critically important. The DoDSER is a good start in enhancing surveillance, and the Task Force recommends that it be refocused and matured as an effective suicide prevention surveillance tool.

Surveillance via the DoDSER, properly and systematically conducted, should consistently inform prevention activities and programs. This effort can be best accomplished by collecting data through epidemiological research that indicates subgroups at increased risk. A structural mechanism needs to be developed and implemented to analyze surveillance data, interpret its relevance, and translate findings into policy and program strategy to modify and adapt programs in a dynamic manner as often as appropriate to effectively prevent suicides.

Recommendation

Structure DoD to implement surveillance efforts in a standardized manner, with a core focus on informing and improving suicide prevention activities.

The DoDSER must be matured, expanded, and refocused to fulfill this surveillance role.

Finding: Standardization of the DoDSER is hindered by variable processes regarding who collects and enters data and a lack of training for the surveyor.

DISCUSSION: The only current surveillance tool used by all military Services is the DoDSER. The DoDSER is a significant improvement on previous methods of surveillance and reflects success at standardizing the data elements collected across the Services. However, the DoDSER in its current form is inadequate and insufficient to inform prevention efforts or aid in the reduction of suicide mortality and morbidity. The DoDSER represents an admirable effort to standardize reporting of suicide deaths across the four Services, but it has not yet been shown to be effective as a tool for suicide prevention. In its current format, the DoDSER does not provide valid and reliable data, and it often relies on data identified only if the command is aware. The DoDSER focuses on demographics and chronic risk factors, not on acute risk factors and pathway observations (primarily regarding last days of life). For example, the Task Force learned nothing from the current version of the DoDSER regarding observations of recent insomnia or angry outbursts, agitation, expressed feelings of hopelessness, recent reckless behavior, etc. Moreover, in an attempt to standardize data elements, significant other data may be lost. For example, the DoDSER asks whether there was evidence of intent to die, but it does not allow the coder to document what that evidence was if it did exist. Nor is it administered in a standardized manner; data are entered into the DoDSER via a web form submitted by behavioral health providers, primary healthcare providers, or command-appointed representatives. Significant concerns exist regarding the training and qualifications of these varied personnel to enter data consistently with decreased variation in interpretation. Training and discipline are needed to ensure quality entries are made.

Recommendation

Standardize DoDSER surveillance throughout the DoD, including specification of qualifications of surveyor and required training.

Finding: Valid DoDSER analysis of risk and protective epidemiologic factors is hindered by access challenges to the Defense Medical Surveillance System (DMSS).

DISCUSSION: One issue the Task Force identified is that the DoDSER does not allow for valid analyses of risk factors because of restricted access to population data for a comparison matched sample. The Armed Forces Health Surveillance Center (AFHSC) maintains DMSS. A complex and time-intensive process for accessing DMSS data hinders effective DoDSER analysis and interpretation that would help inform prevention programs. Analysis would be facilitated greatly by an agreement to allow fluid and consistent access to DMSS for appropriate surveillance purposes, including the automatic filling of select DoDSER data fields.

The DoDSER lacks dynamic, interview-based, observations of symptoms, behaviors, and communications along the pathway to suicide across the last days of life. Both DoDSER and DMSS are archived historical databases that do not contain this type of qualitative information to inform suicide prevention activities. This additional information will provide a much more robust rich source of data for analysis. The best case study would include a case-control research project based on standardized procedures, inclusive of interviewing family survivors and Service Member peers.

Recommendation

Facilitate consistent and fluid access to DMSS by DoDSER for appropriate surveillance purposes that also allows for automatic filling of select data fields as appropriate. Aggregation of surveillance data reported using the DoDSER is intended to inform suicide prevention efforts across DoD and the Services through centralized offices at both levels, thus access to DMSS is essential.

7.4.2. Standardize Investigations of Suicides and Suicide Attempts to Identify Target Areas for Prevention Policies, Procedures, and Programs

> *Finding:* Currently, investigations are not standardized across DoD or within most of the Services. They are insufficient to inform suicide prevention programs. There is no policy governing the type and method of investigations of suicides or suicide attempts, and valuable information is lost that might prevent future suicides.

DISCUSSION: Investigations of suicides and suicide attempts are inadequate to inform suicide prevention programs. Investigations currently focus on possible criminal activities associated with a death and/or to solve a difficult undetermined cause of death case. The collection of data identified through investigation, which can be aggregated across a large series of cases of military suicides and suicide attempts, is important to preventing future suicides. Investigation results must inform an understanding of common pathways to suicide, notably warning signs (e.g., behaviors, symptoms, other observable signs of distress) associated with, and proximate to, suicidal behavior that surveillance methods are unable to discern. Potential entry points for intervention may be revealed, facilitating development of public health messaging campaigns designed to highlight acute risk factors and points of entry for care. Investigation data informs us about gatekeeper and professional training programs, the dynamics of personal relationships, the command climate, personality nuances, and other environment issues that existed and may have contributed to the suicide. An investigation paints a picture of the dynamics surrounding the time of death.

The psychological autopsy is the current best practice for collecting this sort of data. The psychological autopsy is an extensive and intensive retrospective recreation of a decedent's biography, notably focusing on the last days of life (hence, the pathway toward death). It involves the collection and analysis of a range of available and archived documents regarding the decedent (e.g., medical, psychiatric, legal, criminal, military, and educational records) and in-depth interviews with knowledgeable informants about the decedent (ranging from family members to peers). The result of this data gathering is a vibrant and *dynamic* picture of the life and the death trajectory of the decedent which reveals risks, vulnerabilities and the state of mind at the time of death. When aggregated over a large number of cases and analyzed, common acute risk factors (i.e., warning signs) may be observed, and common points at which interventions might have been instituted are often identified.

DoD could benefit by performing a 2- to 3-year period of gathering baseline data from military suicides using a modified psychological autopsy/root cause analysis (RCA) protocol, systematically and scientifically administered to better define acute risk factors (observable signs, symptoms, and behaviors) and potential points of intervention along observed pathways to suicide, notably in the last days of life. The goals of such an effort would be identification of specific data elements to enhance and mature the current DoDSER; and inform future prevention efforts.

An example of this type of research may be demonstrated in the work of Gray and colleagues (2002), who conducted psychological autopsies on 151 consecutive youth suicides in the State of Utah. In addition to delineating common risk factors (e.g., 89 percent were males; 58 percent used firearms), these researchers documented that almost two-thirds of the decedents had contact with the state juvenile justice system and revealed a direct correlation between the number of felony referrals and increased suicide risk.

When modified by aspects of another post-mortem investigative tool, the RCA, the psychological autopsy (which focuses mainly on the decedent) broadens to include a better understanding of the decedent in relationship to systems with which he or she interacts. The RCA is commonly used in hospital settings to discern whether issues of the hospital environment, staff training, staffing patterns, inter-staff communication, and the like might have played a role in a suicide of a patient while hospitalized. The outcome of this amalgam of the psychological autopsy and the RCA is an enhanced understanding of the reason that the suicide occurred, where it occurred, and the possible causal and proximate relationship between that environment and the individual. The American Association of Suicidology (AAS) currently employs such an amalgam in a causal analysis study of suicides on railroad rights-ofway funded by the Federal Railroad Administration. In the DoD, an amalgam of the psychological autopsy and the RCA would inform as to potentially modifiable military service, healthcare, or other variables that might be linked to suicides among Service Members.

Recommendations

Standardize the suicide investigation process across DoD with the sole focus being suicide prevention. The investigation process should be non-attributional, all-inclusive of the days and weeks preceding a suicide or suicide attempt, and be reported in a redacted form, from the Services to OSD, to maintain confidentiality.

Institute a modified psychological autopsy and root cause analysis protocol with a standardized process of reporting to a centralized office at the Service and OSD-level. The results of modified standardized investigative procedures can be used to refine and modify the DoDSER and improve surveillance methods. A modified investigatory protocol must include a focus on last days of life; development of a pathway to death that enables identification of potential points of intervention; interaction between person and environment; and access to all currently collected surveillance, as well as medical and personnel records.

Place investigative responsibilities in the Safety Division offices of each Service to leverage the expertise, external party team management experience, protected (confidential) approach, and effectiveness of aviation mishap investigations.

Review legal protections and make recommendations to Congress, as necessary, to ensure protected status of investigations.

Finding: Autopsy data that local civilian authorities collect is often unavailable to the Armed Forces Medical Examiner (AFME) and delays a timely manner of death determination.

DISCUSSION: Autopsies are performed to determine the manner and cause of death. The location where a death occurs determines which jurisdiction and who is authorized to conduct the autopsy for that particular death. All deaths, including suspected suicides, occurring within federal jurisdiction are conducted by the Office of the Armed Forces Medical Examiner (AFME), regulated by DoDI 5154.30 (2003). All AFMEs and AFME-appointed examiners in the field are general or forensic pathologists. Most AFMEs have four to six years of post-medical school training and are eligible for board certification. Civilian MEs are physicians with forensic pathology specialty experience and/or credentials. Thus, autopsies that civilian authorities conduct on military members who die by suicide in civilian jurisdictions are performed by personnel with varied levels of education and experience (J. Cantrell, personal communication, 16–17 June 2010).

AFME-conducted psychological autopsies are performed by mental health professionals who have active, unrestricted licenses, who have received specific forensic training to conduct the assessment, and who are authorized to conduct psychological autopsies and to submit reports of findings. Currently, only forensic psychologists and forensic psychiatrists conduct psychological autopsies (R. Malone, personal communication, 16 June 2010).

With few exceptions, AFME performs autopsies on suspected suicide cases occurring on military installations outside the continental United States (CONUS). On military installations within CONUS, AFME performs most, but not all of the autopsies on suspected suicide cases. For suspected suicide cases occurring in the local civilian community, autopsies on deceased active duty military members may be performed by the authorized civilian official in that jurisdiction, or with authorized official permission, the AFME or AFME-affiliated ME may conduct the autopsy. From 1 January 2003 through 31 March 2009, AFME performed 36.1 percent of the autopsies on cases resulting in suicide as the cause of death (AFME Briefing 1, October 2009).

Occasionally, the manner of death is difficult to determine. Inconsistencies in autopsy findings and manner of death determinations may arise when civilian authorities perform the autopsy and the AFME classifies the manner of death as suicide. In these instances, what the civilian medical examiner or coroner determined as manner of death and what the AFME establishes as manner of death may conflict. This conflict may occur in cases of Russian Roulette, when an individual believes the weapon is empty and places it to his or her head and fires it, but the weapon is actually loaded.

Other cases in which determining the manner of death is complicated involve what appear to be intentional automobile accidents. Many civilian medical examiners determine the manner of death in such cases to be accidental, whereas AFME will usually determine the manner of death as suicide.

Occasionally, toxicology will reveal that the decedent was intoxicated by either drugs or alcohol, which may further complicate determining the manner of death. Risk-taking behavior by the decedent poses challenges when classifying the manner of death. Actions involving inherently dangerous behaviors carry a high risk of death and imply "sub-intent" to do self-harm or accept the risk of serious injury or death, and connote an acceptance of possibly fatal outcome. Attempting to determine the decedent's state of mind and intent are extremely difficult.

Classification of such deaths as suicide provides a consistent approach and reflects the most common practice (AFME Briefing, 1 October 2009). Occasionally, the manner of death in a complex case may be classified as "undetermined." This classification is used when the information pointing to one manner of death is no more compelling than one or more other competing manners of death in consideration of all available information. The final arbiter in such cases is the AFME.

In accordance with DoDI 5154.30 (2003), autopsies must be completed within 60 days of receipt at AFME.

Autopsy reports may require up to 6 months for completion because of pending pathology reports, but completion is often delayed pending receipt of information from civilian authorities, which usually go well beyond 6 months.

Problems arise if AFME requires additional information from civilian investigation (criminal or ME) authorities when performing the autopsy in a case where the death occurred outside a military base or federal jurisdiction. This is particularly common in cases that appear to be a straightforward suicide in which the civilian criminal investigation is closed quickly and further information that AFME might need from the civilian criminal authority is gone.

AFME requires a variety of information to complete autopsy reports, some of which is often missing or absent (not required) in civilian autopsy reports. Occasionally, AFME can obtain the information needed from the civilian ME, but in other cases, civilian authorities will not release any information to the AFME without a subpoena. These factors depend entirely on the civilian jurisdiction regulations of the state in which the death occurred. In addition, there is a much higher use of "undetermined" as a manner of death in civilian autopsies.

Data that AFME collects from autopsy cases with the confirmed cause of death as suicide is provided on request directly to the Service Suicide Prevention Program Managers (SPPM). SPPMs work weekly with the AFME directly to ensure accurate accounting of the suicides and consistency of information regarding pending and confirmed suicides.

Because of the consistent, reliable standards that AFIP and AFME employ, autopsies performed by AFME produce high-quality and quantity of data. Autopsies conducted outside the federal authority offer a "mixed bag" of quality and quantity of data captured and obtaining the data can be problematic.

Most Service Members autopsies, with respect to suicide, are done in the civilian community.

Recommendation

Recommend legislation to create procedures that facilitate the timely transfer and sharing of civilian autopsy findings on Service Members (Active Duty, Reserve Component, National Guard) with the Armed Forces Medical Examiner's Office. Evaluate the appropriateness and necessity of access to other civilian findings to improve the tracking of members of the Armed Forces at-risk.

7.4.3 Ensure that All Initiatives and Programs Have a Program Evaluation Component

Finding: The Services do not routinely evaluate their suicide prevention programs to determine their effectiveness in helping to reduce suicidial behaviors

DISCUSSION: The Services should be commended for spending significant time and money developing new initiatives for suicide prevention. In particular, in recent years, they have dramatically increased the pace and quantity of such resources and initiatives. The Task Force, although gratified to see the energy put forth to prevent suicides, found that with few exceptions, the Services do not evaluate these programs to determine whether they affect suicidal behavior or play a meaningful role in a carefully considered strategic approach to suicide prevention. Hence, there is no way of knowing whether such programs should be strengthened, discontinued, or continued in a modified manner. The lack of program evaluation contributes to a lack of knowledge about the effectiveness of any individual initiative and contributes to inefficient use of DoD resources, effort, and time. More importantly, ongoing evidenced-based improvements in suicide prevention programs are not feasible without such program evaluation.

Recommendation

Every suicide prevention program initiated by DoD or the Services must contain a program evaluation component.

7.4.4. Support and Incorporate Ongoing Research to Inform Evidence-Based Suicide Prevention Practices

Finding: Currently, no unified, strategic, and comprehensive DoD plan exists for research in the area of military suicide prevention

DISCUSSION: In recent years, the need for research programs on the topic of military suicide prevention has become more evident. The US Army Research and Materiel Command has taken the initiative to support research in military suicide prevention. In 2009, it organized meetings with civilian and DoD suicide prevention experts to discuss a specific plan for suicide prevention research.

The Army STARRS study, with a 5-year performance period, is recognized as a significant undertaking in better understanding risk and protective factors for military suicide and suicide-related behaviors. The Air Force, in collaboration with the University of Rochester, has made an important contribution to the understanding of community-based military interventions as they relate to the prevention of military suicide based on analyses pertaining to the 11 implemented Air Force suicide prevention initiatives.

Although the Task Force commends these important contributions and the ongoing research (see Appendix H) in the area of military suicide prevention, current research efforts on military suicide prevention need to be enhanced. The Task Force also recognizes that research on military suicide prevention is challenging within the DoD system because of numerous regulatory and administrative issues.

Although the protection of human subjects as research participants is understandably recognized, current structural problems and delays in the DoD Institutional Review Board processing of suicide-related projects is an additional impediment by investigators in moving the objectives of such research forward in an expedited manner.

Recommendation

Create a unified, strategic, and comprehensive DoD plan for research in military suicide prevention: (1) ensuring that the DoD's military suicide prevention research portfolio is thoughtfully planned to cover topics in prevention, intervention, and postvention; and (2) assisting investigators by creating a DoD regulatory and human protections consultation board that is responsible primarily for moving suicide-related research forward in an expedited manner.

> Age: 35
> Rank/MOS: Sergeant First Class/Drill Instructor
> Branch of Service: Army
>
> This outstanding Soldier was one of the few selected to become a Drill Instructor - to train others to become Soldiers. He served his nation superbly for over 15 years.
>
> He also suffered from depression as well as bi-polar disorder for which he sought help. His wife reported that his course was difficult, with ups and downs, and that his condition was compounded by challenges with access to care and ineffective treatments.
>
> He was hospitalized several times, each time being discharged with inconsistent follow up and continuity. His treatment over the years included art therapy as well as numerous medications.
>
> According to his family, the side effects from many of those medications affected him on the job as well as at home – requiring frequent dosage adjustments and medications changes. He attempted suicide several times. Ten days before his twins were born, he attempted suicide for a fourth time and was referred to the unit's chaplain. He wanted more help but the unit was not taking him seriously enough.
>
> After his fourth attempt, "he lost all hope and faith in the system to care for him." The head of psychiatry told his wife they were so overrun with mental illness that they could not possibly accommodate all the soldiers that needed help. He died by hanging on the installation following four suicide attempts.

CONCLUSION

The recent increasing rates of Service Member suicides are alarming and unacceptable. The magnitude of this unfolding crisis reflects more than the deaths by suicide we can count; it is the whole "iceberg" of suicide risk factors—depression, anxiety, PTS, substance abuse, relationship discourse, financial challenges, and legal and disciplinary problems. The Department and the Services are investing heavily in prevention programs and research to address the rising numbers and trends. Service leadership is engaged at every level. The Task Force viewed many of the Service programs as exemplary and the Department has demonstrated enormous concern for its members. There are numerous opportunities to improve the effectiveness of current programs, and above all, achieve unity of effort. Suicide *is* preventable. An immediate, renewed, and strategic focus, with necessary resources, will be required to reverse the current trend.

The Services have been, and continue to be, engaged in a long war highlighted by continuous and sustained operational deployments, and a demanding operations tempo. Although the resilience of the overall force has been remarkable given the demands, the effects on the force are evident, and the wear and tear on people continues to accumulate. Service Members and their families bear the human cost of serving their nation to keep our American way of life, and our liberties and freedoms, secure. They routinely experience extraordinary physical and psychological stressors; frequent, extended, and repetitious separations; disruptions in social connectedness; delays in achieving personal goals in life; and general instability and ambiguity with respect to their environment. Numerous commissions, task forces, and research reports have documented the "hidden wounds of war"—the psychological and emotional injuries that have so affected our military members and their families. Without time to periodically allow Service Members to recover and restore total fitness and balance in every dimension of their lives, the stressors will continue to have a cumulative impact on Service Member well-being that manifests itself in a host of negative behaviors. One of the worst is suicide. Emphasizing total force fitness and Service Member well-being is one approach to protecting Service Members from these negative outcomes and will contribute to mission readiness at the same time.

This report is the culmination of reviews of data, studies and programs; discussions with Service Members, families and care providers; and analyses of site visits, research and expert opinion. In this report, Task Force members presented their consensus findings and recommendations for strengthening the force and preventing suicide in members of the Armed Forces. The Task Force is confident that implementing the recommendations in this report will make a significant difference in the total fitness of the force, the well-being of all Service Members, and the prevention of suicide. Effective action must proceed with a sense of urgency, yet occur in the context of a strategic plan and consistent policy.

This report is a call for more effective action. The opportunity is here. Suicide is preventable.

Appendix A. Section 733 of the National Defense Authorization Act of Fy 2009

Department of Defense Task Force on the Prevention of Suicide By Members of the Armed Forces

a) Requirement to Establish.--The Secretary of Defense shall establish within the Department of Defense a task force to examine matters relating to prevention of suicide by members of the Armed Forces.
b) Composition.—
    1) Members.--The task force shall consist of not more than 14 members appointed by the Secretary of Defense from among individuals described in paragraph (2) who have demonstrated expertise in the area of suicide prevention and response.
    2) Range of members.--The individuals appointed to the task force shall include—
        A. at least one member of each of the Army, Navy, Air Force, and Marine Corps;
        B. a number of persons from outside the Department of Defense equal to the total number of personnel from within the Department of Defense (whether members of the Armed Forces or civilian personnel) who are appointed to the task force;
        C. persons who have experience in—
            I. national suicide prevention policy;
            II. military personnel policy;

III. research in the field of suicide prevention;
IV. clinical care in mental health; or
V. military chaplaincy or pastoral care; and

D. at least one family member of a member of the Armed Forces who has experience working with military families.

3) Individuals appointed outside department of defense.--Individuals appointed to the task force from outside the Department of Defense may include officers or employees of other departments or agencies of the Federal Government, officers or employees of State and local governments, or individuals from the private sector.
4) Deadline for appointment.--All appointments of individuals to the task force shall be made not later than 180 days after the date of the enactment of this Act.
5) Co-chairs of task force.--There shall be two co-chairs of the task force. One of the co-chairs shall be designated by the Secretary of the Defense at the time of appointment from among the Department of Defense personnel appointed to the task force. The other co-chair shall be selected from among the members appointed from outside the Department of Defense by members so appointed.

c) Assessment and Recommendations on Suicide Prevention Policy.--

1) In general.--Not later than 12 months after the date on which all members of the task force have been appointed, the task force shall submit to the Secretary a report containing recommendations regarding a comprehensive policy designed to prevent suicide by members of the Armed Forces.
2) Utilization of other efforts.--In preparing the report the task force shall take into consideration completed and ongoing efforts by the military departments to improve the efficacy of suicide prevention programs.
3) Elements.--The recommendations (including recommendations for legislative or administrative action) shall include measures to address the following:

A. Methods to identify trends and common causal factors in suicides by members of the Armed Forces.
B. Methods to establish or update suicide education and prevention programs conducted by each military department based on identified trends and causal factors.
C. An assessment of current suicide education and prevention programs of each military department.
D. An assessment of suicide incidence by military occupation to include identification of military occupations with a high incidence of suicide.
E. The appropriate type and method of investigation to determine the causes and factors surrounding each suicide by a member of the Armed Forces.
F. The qualifications of the individual appointed to conduct an investigation of a suicide by a member of the Armed Forces.
G. The required information to be determined by an investigation in order to determine the causes and factors surrounding suicides by members of the Armed Forces.
H. The appropriate reporting requirements following an investigation conducted on a suicide by a member of the Armed Forces.

I. The appropriate official or executive agent within the military department and Department of Defense to receive and analyze reports on investigations of suicides by members of the Armed Forces.

J. The appropriate use of the information gathered during investigations of suicides by members of the Armed Forces.

K. Methods for protecting confidentiality of information contained in reports of investigations of suicides by members of the Armed Forces.

D. Administrative Matters.—

VI. Compensation.--Each member of the task force who is a member of the Armed Forces or a civilian officer or employee of the United States shall serve without compensation (other than compensation to which entitled as a member of the Armed Forces or an officer or employee of the United States, as the case may be). Other members of the task force shall be treated for purposes of section 3161 of title 5, United States Code, as having been appointed under subsection (b) of such section.

1) Oversight.--The Under Secretary of Defense for Personnel and Readiness shall oversee the activities of the task force.

2) Administrative support.--The Washington Headquarters Services of the Department of Defense shall provide the task force with personnel, facilities, and other administrative support as necessary for the performance of the duties of the task force.

3) Access to facilities.--The Under Secretary of Defense for Personnel and Readiness shall, in coordination with the Secretaries of the military departments, ensure appropriate access by the task force to military installations and facilities for purposes of the discharge of the duties of the task force.

E. Report.—

1) In general.--The task force shall submit to the Secretary of Defense a report on its activities under this section. The report shall include--

A. a description of the activities of the task force;

B. the assessment and recommendations required by subsection (c); and

C. such other matters relating to the activities of the task force that the task force considers appropriate.

2) Transmittal to congress.--Not later than 90 days after receipt of the report under paragraph (1), the Secretary shall transmit the report to the Committees on Armed Services of the Senate and the House of Representatives. The Secretary may include in the transmittal such comments on the report as the Secretary considers appropriate.

F. Plan Required.--Not later than March 1, 2010, the Secretary of Defense shall develop a plan based on the recommendations of the task force and submit the plan to the congressional defense committees.

G. Termination.--The task force shall terminate 90 days after the date on which the report of the task force is submitted to Congress under subsection (e)(2).

Appendix B. Summarized Responses to NDAA 09 Requirements

The Department of Defense Task Force on the Prevention of Suicide by Members of the Armed Forces was established by Section 733 of the National Defense Authorization Act (NDAA) for Fiscal Year 2009 (TAB B) in response to Congressional concerns about matters relating to the prevention of suicide by members of the Armed Forces. Per that language, the Task Force was required to submit to the Secretary of Defense a report containing "recommendations regarding a comprehensive policy designed to prevent suicide by members of the Armed Forces."

Section 1.1 of this report provides information about where in the report the reader will find the specific Findings and Recommendations that address each element in the Section 733, NDAA 2009 language. This appendix summarizes that information.

1) *Not later than 12 months after the date on which all Task Force members have been appointed, the Task Force shall submit to the Secretary a report containing recommendations regarding a comprehensive policy designed to prevent suicide by members of the Armed Forces.*

Suicide and the prevention of suicide are issues confronting not only the Department of Defense but also the United States and remainder of the world's nations. Preventing suicide is a complex, multi-factorial issue requiring multi-factorial solutions; occasionally, even the most effective prevention strategies or medical interventions will not prevent every tragedy from happening. Some suicidal individuals internalize their psychological pain so deeply that others do not see it, and they become known as suicidal only after the fact. There are others that cannot be reached to prevent their premature deaths, and there are those for whom treatments do not work sufficiently well or fast enough for them to tolerate their distress until they can be helped them. As the World Health Organization (WHO) states, "Not all suicides can be prevented, but a majority can." While recognizing this reality, the Task Force strongly believes the DoD must still work toward the ideal of not one suicide in the Armed Forces. In the same way, while it is known that not all heart attacks will be prevented, work continues toward that end state with education, training, and treatment Work must continue toward the same end in our suicide prevention strategy—one suicide is one too many.

As discussed throughout this report, the US military takes suicide and suicide prevention seriously, and all branches have had active programs for years. In recent years, however, the military has experienced an increasing rise in the number of suicides resulting in a suicide rate that in some branches is now higher than the civilian population. While suicide prevention is complex and research into the most effective strategies also is by nature of the issue complex, there are a large number of approaches common to other public health issues that are "best practices" for which randomized controlled trial evidence of their effectiveness to prevent suicide may not yet exist, but there is every reason to believe that they will and do work. This Task Force set forth to provide recommendations that would reflect the multi-dimensional nature of suicide prevention and would provide a basis of a solid, comprehensive program for preventing suicide in members of the Armed Forces.

A Framework for Suicide Prevention in the Armed Forces: Lessons from Cardiac Prevention and Control Before the 1960s, out-of-hospital episodes of sudden cardiac death stemming from ventricular fibrillation were almost universally fatal; today, however, survival rates are considerably improved, notably in communities where integrated community-wide systems of cardiac care have been implemented. King County, Washington, is an excellent example of a program demonstrating successful outcomes. Its program has been constructed on numerous integrated interventions, including promoting community cardiac wellness, prompt recognition of a cardiac event, early notification of emergency medical personnel, a tiered response system, quality care, strong rehabilitation repatriation, and follow-up, supported by an intensive research program, adequate funding, and community management (Sandal et al., 2003). As an example of a similar approach to suicide prevention within the DoD and the Services is the US Air Force's initially successful suicide prevention program. This program, now an evidence-based practice, similarly was developed and implemented as a general systems approach, requiring leadership involvement and organizational support as its core focus. Any type of general systems approach must be fostered and must include continued program review, correction, and leveling to be and remain successful. (Sanddal, 2003)

The Task Force believes comprehensive suicide prevention requires a public health approach to the issue, approaching the problem from multiple angles. The Task Force identified four major focus areas which it believes constitute a suicide prevention program poised for success. All Service suicide prevention programs must consider initiatives and policies that align under each of these four focus areas to holistically organize their efforts for suicide prevention. Based on current Service programs and identified gaps, the Task Force identified 18 strategies for DoD to adopt to enhance suicide prevention efforts. The four focus areas are as follows: (1) Organization and Leadership; (2) Wellness Enhancement and Training; (3) Access to, and Delivery of, Quality Care; and (4) Surveillance, Investigations and Research. These four form key lines of defense in our fight to eliminate suicide in members of the Armed Forces. (Please see paragraph 5 for additional information.)

The Task Force strongly believes that suicide prevention begins with coherent policy generated from OSD. Therefore, one of the foundational recommendations in this report is an OSD-level office appropriately staffed and resourced for success. Many adaptive adjustments to new requirements within suicide prevention and policy development have occurred at the Service, installation, and command levels but have been notably absent at the DoD level. Strategic planning, one of the most critical aspects of program management, routinely occurs at the DoD level, yet suicide prevention program planning is notably deficient at this level. DoD has no staff dedicated full time in the area of suicide prevention. The absence of a central DoD office on suicide prevention leads to a lack of unity of effort in suicide prevention; as a result of this deficiency, Service programs do not benefit from a department-wide strategic approach to suicide prevention. A DoD-level suicide policy and program management office requires appropriate personnel and resources needed for coordinating and fulfilling the critical strategic planning, data analysis and reporting, program and policy development, and program evaluation requirements currently missing within DoD suicide prevention. (Please see Section 7.1.1 for additional information.)

2) *The Task Force shall take into consideration completed and ongoing efforts by the military departments to improve the efficacy of suicide prevention programs.*

In the course of its data-gathering activities, the Task Force received briefings and reports of the current suicide prevention efforts occurring at a multitude of different levels across the military. At the DoD level, DCoE and the SPARRC provide information related to their roles and ongoing efforts. The Services provided briefings regarding the current status of their suicide prevention programs in addition to the new initiatives under way, including the Army's Task Force on Suicide Prevention, Battlemind Training, Warrior Resilience Training, the Real Warriors Campaign, and the Marines NCO Training. The VA spoke specifically to the role its crisis line provides active duty Service Members. The Army Reserve Component and the National Guard Bureau provided information on their suicide prevention programs and the challenges they face, and a delegation from the Task Force was briefed by the Air Force Reserve Command when they visited Robins Air Force Base. The Task Force also reviewed several successful civilian programs addressing suicide prevention. Finally, during the site visits conducted by the Task Force, Service Members of all ranks were asked about the efficacy of the suicide prevention programs at their base, camps, and installations. All these factors were considered in rendering the Task Force recommendations contained in this report. (See also Sections 1.3 and 1.4 and Appendices D-F for additional details.)

3) *The recommendations (including recommendations for legislative or administrative action) shall include measures to address the following:*

A. *Methods to identify trends and common causal factors in suicides by members of the Armed Forces.*

Currently there is no factor known to be sufficient in and of itself to cause a suicide. Suicides are caused by a confluence of multiple risk factors converging in time. Therefore the term "risk factor" rather than "causal factor" is used in this report.

The DoD and Services currently use data systematically entered into the DoDSER. Information is also gleaned from command investigations, criminal investigations, and psychological autopsies to identify trends and common causal factors of suicides by members of the Armed Forces; however, these processes are not coordinated and lack a central point for collecting, analyzing, and reporting results. The Task Force recommends the previously discussed centralized DoDlevel suicide prevention division collate this data, analyze it, and use such analyses to inform suicide prevention policies, training, and prevention.

The Task Force recommends that for purposes of preventing suicide among Service Members, surveillance data must inform an understanding of common pathways to suicide, notably warning signs including behaviors, symptoms, and other observable signs of distress associated with and proximate to suicidal behavior. This detailed data is routinely acquired by performing a psychological autopsy. When the data is mined, aggregated, and disseminated, potential entry points for intervention are revealed, facilitating the development of public health messaging campaigns designed to highlight acute risk factors and points of entry for care. Surveillance data also informs both gatekeeper and professional training programs and maintains program currency regarding what is known about the population at-risk.

In addition to the aforementioned methods of identifying trends and causal factors of suicide, the Task Force recommends a revised method of investigating suicides. This method, well known to the military, is patterned after the aircraft accident investigation process, specifically the Safety Investigation Board and the risk-cause analysis model. (For more details, see finding Section 7.4.1).

B. *Methods for establishing or updating suicide education and prevention programs conducted by each military department based on identified trends and causal factors.*

Current Service suicide prevention training programs have limited effectiveness resulting from a lack of a strategic approach to skills-based suicide prevention training. The Task Force recommends development of Service-level, comprehensive suicide prevention training strategies developed at the DoD-level suicide prevention division that tailor curricula to the specific knowledge, skills and attitudes required of each sub-population in the military community. Training programs will reflect lessons learned via the comprehensive data analysis performed at the DoD level suicide prevention division. Training programs also will include continuous program evaluation processes to ensure effectiveness. (See Section 7.2.3 for further information, and Element E below.)

C. *An assessment of current suicide education and prevention programs of each military department.*

Each Service is devoting enormous energy and resources toward nearly 900 suicide prevention activities across their 407 military installations worldwide. Although each is addressing many areas in its individual efforts, these efforts should be better coordinated within and across the Services to leverage Service expertise, data analysis, lessons learned, best practices, and the host of other programs. (Please see Sections 7.2.1 and 7.2.3 for more information.)

D. *An assessment of suicide incidence by military occupation to include identification of military occupations with a high incidence of suicide.*

There is insufficient data at present to support identification of military occupations with a high incidence of suicide. At the time of this writing, scientific evidence also does not seem to support a relationship between suicide and military occupation.

The Task Force obtained information related to suicides by career field from each Service. The individual Service numbers are provided in Section 3 of the report. However, the Task Force strongly cautions readers against drawing any conclusions from the data provided. Because of the low rate of suicides in any specific career field, statistically valid rates of suicide in a career field are rare. Less-than-statistically valid data makes comparisons between career fields almost impossible. Complicating the issue further is that career fields come and go over the years, or are merged into, or diverged from, existing career fields. Therefore, the denominator of the rate calculation may vary from year to year, nullifying comparison data. Career fields between the Services also vary, so comparisons at that level are generally not valid. A further complication in some high-interest career fields, such as recruiting and drill instructors, is that the data reflects the duty being performed at the time of the suicide, not the underlying career field of the deceased.

Preliminary evidence provided to the Task Force examined the relationship between career field and suicide and did not find a significant relationship (Bell, 2010). Consistent with previous studies, failed relationships and a mental health diagnosis were identified as primary stressors. Soldiers who view their leadership positively experienced a greater sense of unit cohesion and morale (OMNF-I & OTSG, 2006; OMNF-I & OTSG, 2009). Numerous efforts are underway to continue to understand the role career field may have in relation to suicide and suicide prevention. (Please see Section 6.2 and Appendix G for more information.

E. *The appropriate type and method of investigation to determine the causes and factors surrounding each suicide by a member of the Armed Forces.*

The Task Force reviewed and evaluated a range of investigations currently in place and found that results of these investigations insufficiently informed policy, prevention activities, and/or training programs. Among the various investigatory processes reviewed (e.g., criminal death investigations, command investigations, medical incident investigations), the Task Force found that aircraft accident and safety investigations best informed consequent safety policy and prevention activities. The Task Force regards this model as an example of one that will improve the current standard of suicide investigations.

DoDSER is the investigative procedure currently in use and intended to determine the causes and factors associated with suicides by members of the Armed Forces. The Task Force found that, as currently constructed, the DoDSER insufficiently addresses questions most in need of answer to determine *preventable* causes of suicide, observable "warning signs" observable as near-term risk factors, and potential points of entry along the decedent's pathway toward death that offered points of intervention. The Task Force believes that the DoDSER can be a valuable surveillance tool if modified and enhanced by findings from standardized investigations and psychological autopsies that lead to root cause analyses. (Please see Section 7.4.2)

F. *The qualifications of the individual appointed to conduct an investigation of a suicide by a member of the Armed Forces.*

The Task Force found that the investigation of suicides via the DoDSER was hindered by a lack of standardization of procedures and methodology. Notably, the Task Force found that data entered into the DoDSER was collected by behavioral health providers, primary care providers, or command-appointed representatives. The Task Force has significant concerns regarding the training and qualifications of these varied personnel—hence, the reliability and validity of data derived. The Task Force recommends that standardized procedures be developed for these investigations, including specified qualifications of the surveyor to include education and training in the behavioral sciences and specific to the investigative procedures developed for the DoDSER. The Task Force further found that family members often had valuable and unaddressed observations regarding their loved one's last days and benefited from active involvement in the investigative process regarding their loved one's death. Therefore, the individual appointed to conduct these investigations should be trained to understand the impact of suicide on family members and have a developed level of sensitivity to their needs and reactions during the process of data gathering. To preserve a psychological and behavioral health perspective in the suicide investigation and the specialized psychological analytic skills necessary to conduct a suicide investigation, the Task Force recommends that a cadre of experts from each Service provide personnel to support that aspect of the Service Safety Office suicide investigation, the same way that aviation accidents are investigated by the Service Safety Centers augmented by specially trained personnel in various career fields from across that Service. These experts must be trained as investigators and must be skilled and certified by the DoD to perform psychological autopsies in concert with the investigations as the investigation team deems necessary.

The Task Force recommends placing investigative responsibilities with the Safety Division offices of each Service to leverage the expertise of personnel trained in performing psychological autopsies per the current DoDI 5154.30 (Armed Forces Institute of Pathology Operations). This cadre of expert suicide investigators also must be trained in routine safety investigation processes and protocols as deemed appropriate by the Chief of DoD Suicide Prevention Division. The Task Force recommends that the lead investigator and person responsible for the conduct and report of a suicide investigation administered by the Service Safety Office be a licensed psychological subject matter expert (SME). (See Section 7.4.2).

G. *The required information to be determined by an investigation to determine the causes and factors surrounding suicides by members of the Armed Forces.*

Current suicide investigation and surveillance systems are insufficient to inform prevention programs and require system and policy creation and revision.

The Task Force recommends a privileged investigation process (protective information); similar to the ones conducted in aviation Safety Investigation Boards and psychological autopsy/root cause analysis protocols. Current data collected during suicide investigations should be continued. However, the Task Force recommends that the investigation process be enhanced significantly to include a focus on the decedent's pathway toward death, with a specific focus on last days of life, to better establish identification of potential points of intervention, interactions between person and environment, and observable warning signs that could be referenced in Service public education, gatekeeper, and professional training programs (See section 7.4.1 for additional information).

The Task Force does not recommend a full investigation be accomplished on all suicide attempts.

However, the (properly trained) installation Suicide Program Coordinator should ensure that an accurate DoDSER report is completed and the data forwarded to the OSD Suicide Prevention Division. Information gleaned from suicide attempts also can be used to inform prevention policies and clinical practices and procedures.

H. *The appropriate reporting requirements following an investigation conducted on a suicide by a member of the Armed Forces.*

Suicide investigations will be conducted by a cadre of personnel external to the installation experiencing the event, headed by an officer of the Service's safety office. Once the suicide investigation report is complete, that officer shall outbrief the installation and unit commander and forward the report through Service channels to the new OSD Suicide

Prevention Policy Division. The OSD Suicide Prevention Policy Division should be responsible for reporting standards, data analysis, lessons learned, systems review, and similar tasks that in turn inform future policy and procedural changes (See Sections 7.1.1 and 7.4.2 for additional information).

I. The appropriate official or executive agent within the military department and Department of Defense to receive and analyze reports on investigations of suicides by members of the Armed Forces.

Reports on investigations of suicides by members of the Armed Forces should be distributed to the respective Service suicide prevention offices, the military Assistant Secretaries of Manpower and Reserve Affairs, and to a newly created DoD Suicide Prevention Policy Division. The suicide prevention offices in the military Services and the DoD should be placed organizationally to allow coordination and oversight of policy across the many functional communities involved in suicide prevention. These functional communities include personnel, quality of life, family programs, health and wellness, deployment health, safety, chaplains, and training. Because no existing policy division for suicide prevention exists within OSD today, the Task Force believes that this division should be created directly within the Office of the Under Secretary of Defense for Personnel and Readiness. This division must be staffed and resourced adequately to develop and disseminate suicide prevention policy and procedures to the Services. This policy development must be informed by systematic evaluation of the suicide prevention programs, surveillance of suicidal behaviors, and reports of suicide investigations. The Task Force did not find justification to recommend relocating existing Service suicide prevention offices; however, the Service Chiefs should ensure that ultimate responsibility of the overall suicide prevention program lies with the Service leadership and does not give the impression that suicide prevention has been delegated solely to the Service medical or mental health communities. The Task Force believes that medical care and behavioral healthcare are important aspects of suicide prevention, but an effective suicide prevention program goes well beyond medical and behavioral healthcare. Each office receiving these reports has respective roles of analysis and interpretation for informing improvements in policy and practice (See Section 7.1.1).

J. The appropriate use of the information gathered during investigations of suicides by members of the Armed Forces.

The appropriate use of such information is to prevent further suicides, determine causal factors and trends, inform and guide future policy and prevention efforts, guide DoDSER modifications, inform and guide research efforts, and inform sharing and collaboration efforts with the VA and HHS. The Services should use the data to provide a report to next of kin with standardized data elements, thus allowing all survivors to receive appropriate and consistent information about the death of their Service Member.

Current surveillance systems are insufficient to inform prevention programs and require system and policy creation and revision. The Task Force recommends that legal protections must be reviewed for these proposed investigations and recommendations made to Congress as necessary to ensure protected status of investigations. The aggregation of reports also must inform suicide prevention efforts across the Service and DoD through centralized offices at both levels (See Section 7.4.1 for additional information.

K. *Methods for protecting confidentiality of information contained in reports of investigations of suicides by members of the Armed Forces.*

The Task Force believes that suicide investigations and psychological autopsies should be protected by 10 USC 1102 and a DoDI yet to be developed, similar to DoDI 6055.07 (Accident Investigation, Reporting, and Record Keeping) to protect the information obtained through the newly proposed Suicide Investigation Board process. HIPAA requirements should be reviewed for applicability as the new investigations process is developed.

10 USC 1102. Confidentiality of medical quality assurance records: qualified immunity for participants.

a) *Confidentiality of Records*—Medical quality assurance records created by or for the Department of Defense as part of a medical quality assurance program are confidential and privileged. Such records may not be disclosed to any person or entity, with limited exceptions.

DoDI 6055.07 (Accident Investigation, Reporting, and Record Keeping)

This DoDI covers investigating, reporting, and recordkeeping during accident investigations. Enclosure 2 of this DoDI provides detailed information about privileged safety information.

Health Insurance Portability and Accountability Act (HIPAA)

HIPAA covers any information related to the past, present, or future mental or physical health of individuals, including information about payment for care. To be covered by HIPAA, information must be kept by a covered entity—a healthcare provider, healthcare plan, or healthcare clearinghouse. Combined with some fact that identifies a person (name, address, telephone number, Social Security number) creates "protected health information" or PHI. PHI can be oral, handwritten, or electronic.

APPENDIX C. TASK FORCE MEMBER BIOGRAPHIES

Alan Lee "Lanny" Berman, Ph.D.

Dr. Berman, a Distinguished Adjunct Professor of Psychology at American University in Washington, DC, serves as Executive Director of the American Association of Suicidology and President of the International Association for Suicide Prevention. He also maintains a private practice of psychotherapy and psychological/forensic consultation in Washington. His previous positions include Professor with tenure (1979–1991), Associate Professor (1975–1979), Assistant Professor (1970–1974), and Instructor (1969) in the Department of Psychology at American University, Washington, DC. From 1991–1995, Dr. Berman was Director of the National Center for the Study and Prevention of Suicide at the Washington School of Psychiatry. He received a B.A. from the Johns Hopkins University in 1965 and a

Ph.D. from The Catholic University of America in 1970. Dr. Berman is a consulting editor for *Suicide and Life-Threatening Behavior, Crisis and Archives of Suicide Research.*

He also is a fellow of the American Psychological Association and the International Academy of Suicide Research. Dr. Berman has authored seven books and more that 100 peer-reviewed articles and book chapters in suicidology and suicide prevention. He is the recipient of the Edwin S. Shneidman and Louis I. Dublin awards for his research and career contributions to suicide prevention.

John Bradley, M.D., Colonel

Colonel Bradley is the Chair, Department of Psychiatry, at Walter Reed Army Medical Center and National Naval Medical Center and the Vice Chair, Department of Psychiatry, at Uniformed Services University.

Colonel Bradley received his commission upon completion of advanced ROTC as a Distinguished Military Graduate from the University of Rhode Island. He received his Doctor of Medicine from the Uniformed Services University in 1989.

He then trained in Psychiatry at Letterman Army Medical Center in San Francisco, California. During his career, Colonel Bradley has held various positions in operational and clinical assignments.

He served as the Division Psychiatrist for the 1st Armored Division in Bad Kreuznach, Germany. He subsequently served as Chief of Psychiatry at US Army Hospital, Heidelberg, Germany, deploying to Sarajevo with the Stabilisation Force in Bosnia and Herzegovina (SFOR) and to Bulgaria on a Partnership for Peace mission.

Upon returning to the United States, Colonel Bradley served as Chief of the Inpatient Psychiatry Service and Consultation-Liaison Service at Eisenhower Army Medical Center on Fort Gordon, Georgia.

During this assignment, he also deployed to Egypt to participate in Bright Star 99–00. After completion of the US Army Command and General Staff College, Colonel Bradley then served as Deputy Commander for Clinical Services at the US Army Medical Department Activity (MEDDAC), Fort Meade, Maryland.

Following this appointment, he served as Chief of Outpatient Behavioral Health at Walter Reed Army Medical Center. He deployed to Operation Iraqi Freedom with the 528th Combat Stress Control Detachment, and returned to Walter Reed in 2006 as Chair, Department of Psychiatry. Colonel Bradley's military awards and decorations include the Bronze Star Medal, Meritorious Service Medal (2OLC), Army Commendation Medal, and Polish Multinational Division Service Medal. He also has been honored with the Order of Military Medical Merit.

Colonel Bradley is Board Certified in Psychiatry and holds a medical license in the State of California.

Bonnie Carroll

Ms. Carroll is currently the President of the Tragedy Assistance Program for Survivors (TAPS). TAPS is the national non-profit peer-based veterans' service organization addressing the emotional, psychological, and administrative needs of military survivors, including care for more than 1,000 family members whose loved ones have died by suicide. Ms Carroll also serves as the civilian Co-Chair of the Department of Defense (DoD) Task Force on Suicide Prevention by Members of the Armed Forces. Ms. Carroll is an Army widow and a Reserve Major in the US Air Force. In her civilian career, she has served as Deputy Senior Advisor for Programs, Ministry of Communications, Baghdad, Iraq; Deputy White House Liaison, Department of Veterans Affairs (VA); Deputy Director, Governor's Office, Anchorage, Alaska; and Executive Assistant for Cabinet Affairs, West Wing, The White House. She is a graduate of several Service schools, including the Defense Equal Opportunity Management Institute and USAF Logistics Officer Course. Ms. Carroll holds a B.A. in Public Administration/Political Science from American University in Washington, DC, and completed the JFK School of Government Executive Leadership Program at Harvard University (2003). Her military experience includes service as Chief, HQ USAF Casualty Operations. Ms Carroll also serves on the DoD Military Family Readiness Council, Board of the Association of Death Education and Counseling, VA Advisory Committee on Disability Compensation, and Sesame Street Advisory Board for the national "Talk, Listen, Learn" campaign. She has co-authored several books that address coping with traumatic loss, including *Living with Grief After Sudden Loss*; *Living with Grief, Children and Adolescents*; and *Living with Grief, Who We Are, How We Grieve.*

Robert G. Certain, D.Min.

Reverend Certain is currently a Rector at St. Peter–St. Paul Episcopal Church in Marietta, Georgia. His past positions included St. Margaret's Episcopal Church and School in Palm Desert, California (1998–2007); Priest in Charge, St. Barnabas on the Desert Episcopal Church, Scottsdale, Arizona (1998–2007); Rector, St. Alban's Parish, Harlingen, Texas (1989–1994); Rector, Holy Apostles Parish, Memphis, Tennessee (1985–1989); Rector, Trinity Parish, Yazoo City, Mississippi (1978–1985); Assistant Rector, St. Peter's Parish, Kerrville, Texas (1977–1976); and Assistant Rector, Christ Episcopal Church, South Pittsburg, Tennessee (1974–1976). Reverend Certain's education and professional training began at Emory University, Atlanta, Georgia with a B.A. in 1969, The School of Theology—The University of the South, Sewanee, Tennessee with a Master of Divinity in 1976 and a Doctor of Ministry in 1990. He was ordained a Deacon in 1975 and a Priest in 1976. Reverend Certain also has been published in numerous publications. His most recent published article is "Wartime Sacrifice" for Chaplain Magazine, Spring 2010. Reverend Certain's military career began in 1969 as a US Air Force Navigator/Bombardier. In 1972, during his 100th mission over Vietnam, his aircraft was hit by a surface-to-air missile and then-Captain Certain spent from 1972 to 1973 as a prisoner of war in Hanoi, North Vietnam. His military awards and decorations include the Bronze Star (Valor), Meritorious Service Medal, Prisoner of War Medal, Vietnam Service Medal, Distinguished Flying Cross (Heroism), Purple Heart (1 OLC), Air Medal (4 OLC), Air Force Commendation Medal, and the Republic of Vietnam Cross of Gallantry. Dr. Certain left active duty in 1977 and retired as a Chaplain, United States Air Force Reserves, at the United States Air Force Academy on July 8, 1999.

Jeffory C. Gabrelcik, Chief Master Sergeant

Chief Master Sergeant Gabrelcik currently serves as Chief, Air Force Review Boards, for the Deputy Secretary of the Air Force, Manpower and Reserve Affairs, Air Force Review Boards Agency. In this role, Chief Gabrelcik directly supports the Director of the Air Force Review Boards Agency by advising on matters pertaining to and influencing the health, morale, welfare, and effective utilization of personnel and resources. Chief Gabrelcik also is a participating and voting member on the Secretary of the Air Force Personnel Council. He has more than 22 years of personnel (HR) expertise and responsibility/experience in casualty reporting, casualty notification, and casualty affairs. He has performed duties throughout numerous contingencies as Personnel in Support of Contingency Operations (PERSCO), managing personnel accountability and casualty reporting. Chief Gabrelcik entered the Air Force in 1988 and completed all military education requirements and myriad professional military and civilian education courses. His deployments in support of numerous military and support operations include Iraq, Turkey, Qatar, United Arab Emirates, England, Italy, Germany, Panama, and Kuwait. He was one of the architects of the DoD Physical Disability Board of Review in 2008 and its future sustainment. Chief Gabrelcik is the recipient of many military awards and honors, including the Meritorious Service Medal with three oak leaf clusters, Air Force Commendation Medal, Air Force Achievement Medal with three oak leaf clusters, Joint Meritorious Unit Award, National Defense Service Medal with star, and NATO Medal.

Ronald L. Green, Sergeant Major

Sergeant Major Green currently serves as Senior Enlisted Advisor, Headquarters and Service Battalion, Headquarters, US Marine Corps. He enlisted in the Marine Corps on 27 November 1983 and attended recruit training at Marine Corps Recruit Depot, Parris Island, South Carolina. Upon completion of recruit training, Private First Class (PFC) Green was assigned to Hotel Battery, 3rd Battery, 3rd Battalion, 11th Marines at Camp Pendleton, CA. While assigned as a cannon cocker with Hotel Battery, PFC Green was promoted meritoriously to Lance Corporal in August 1984. In November 1985, Lance Corporal Green was transferred to Delta Battery, 2nd Battalion, 12th Marines, in Okinawa, Japan. He was promoted meritoriously to Corporal in May 1985. In November 1986, Corporal Green rotated back to Camp Pendleton with Delta Battery. Corporal Green was promoted meritoriously to Sergeant in September 1986. Sergeant Green was reassigned to Marine Corps Base Camp Pendleton in 1988 as a tower operator for Southern Impact Area Control (SIAC), also known as "Long Rifle." In January 1990, Sergeant Green was ordered to Drill Instructor Duty at Marine Corps Recruit Depot, Parris Island, SC, where he served as a Drill Instructor and Senior Drill Instructor with Charlie Company and as Drill Master for 1st Battalion. He was promoted meritoriously to Staff Sergeant in July 1992. Staff Sergeant Green was accelerated to the rank of Gunnery Sergeant in 1997 and promoted to First Sergeant in December 2000. In December 2004, First Sergeant Green was selected to the rank of Sergeant Major and transferred to Headquarters Marine Liaison Activity (HMLA–169) in April 2005. In June 2008, Sergeant Major Green transferred to Headquarters Battalion, Headquarters Marine Corps, Henderson Hall, Arlington, VA. Sergeant Major Green's personal awards include the

Meritorious Service Medal, Navy and Marine Corps Commendation Medal with four Gold Stars in Lieu of Fifth Award and the Navy and Marine Corps Achievement Medal with two Gold Stars in Lieu of Third Award.

Marjan Ghahramanlou Holloway, Ph.D.

Dr. Holloway is an Assistant Professor of Medical and Clinical Psychology and an Assistant Professor of Psychiatry at Uniformed Services University of the Health Sciences (USUHS) in Bethesda, Maryland. She is a Licensed Maryland Psychologist and a certified therapist of the Academy of Cognitive Therapy, with a private clinical practice in Chevy Chase, Maryland.

Dr. Holloway received a B.S. in Biology and a B.A. in Psychology with a minor in English Literature in 1994 from the University of California, Irvine.

She received a M.A. in Pre-Clinical Psychology in 1997 from Chapman University and a Ph.D. in 2003 in Clinical Psychology from Fairleigh Dickinson University.

Dr. Holloway completed a clinical internship at Springfield Hospital Center in 2001. She completed her post-doctoral training at the Center for the Treatment and Prevention of Suicide and the Center for Cognitive Therapy at the University of Pennsylvania under the mentorship of Dr. Aaron T. Beck.

Before her current position, she held a Research Associate and Adjunct Lecturer appointment at the University of Pennsylvania. Dr. Holloway has worked on numerous randomized controlled trials with suicidal individuals. As Project Director for an NIMH/CDC funded project, she trained and supervised mental health professionals in the delivery of an outpatient suicide prevention treatment protocol.

Dr. Holloway provides suicide assessment and management trainings for the Center for Deployment Psychology and has served as a supervisor for the Department of Veterans Affairs' Suicide Prevention Coordinators. She is a member of the Department of Defense Suicide Prevention and Risk Reduction Committee and the co-chair of the North Atlantic Treaty Organization (NATO) Human Factors Exploratory Team on international military suicide.

Dr. Holloway is the author of several peer reviewed manuscripts, book chapters, and encyclopedia entries. She has presented at numerous symposia, workshops, clinical roundtables, and national and international conferences.

Dr. Holloway's laboratory at USUHS focuses on programmatic research in suicide prevention for the United States military, with an emphasis on inpatient-based interventions for individuals hospitalized following a suicide attempt.

She is a principal investigator on research supported by the congressionally directed Medical Research Program, the National Alliance for Research on Schizophrenia and Depression, and the Military Operational Medicine Research Program.

David Alan Jobes, Ph.D., ABPP

Dr. Jobes is a Professor of Psychology and Associate Director of Clinical Training at The Catholic University of America in Washington, DC, where he has been since 1987. Dr. Jobes earned his B.A. in Psychology at the University of Colorado, Boulder, CO (1981); his M.A. in General Psychology at American University, Washington, DC (1984); and his Ph.D. in Clinical Psychology at American University, Washington, DC (1988). He completed his clinical internship at the Washington, DC, Veterans Affairs Medical Center. Dr. Jobes is a Board Certified Clinical Psychologist (American Board of Professional Psychology) and is a licensed psychologist in the District of Columbia. He has been an active clinical researcher in suicide risk assessment and treatment. He has published extensively in professional journals and has five books on the topic of clinical suicidology. Dr. Jobes has served as a consultant to the Centers for Disease Control and Prevention, National Institute of Mental Health, Federal Bureau of Investigation, Institute of Medicine of the National Academy of Sciences, Department of Veterans Affairs, and Department of Defense. He is a past President of the American Association of Suicidology. Dr. Jobes also maintains a private clinical and forensic practice at the Washington Psychological Center.

Janet E. Kemp, RN, Ph.D.

Dr. Kemp has 20 years of experience working with veterans and currently serves as National VA Mental Health Director for Suicide Prevention. She is the Chief of the Education, Training, and Dissemination Core at the VISN 2 Center of Excellence (CoE) in Canandaigua, NY, having transferred recently from a similar position at the VISN 19 Mental Illness, Research, and Education Clinical Center. In her CoE role, she is provides patient education concerning suicide awareness and prevention, current assessment and treatment strategies, and new findings in the area of suicide and assists the Center Director in the implementation of Suicide Prevention Programs throughout the VA system. In the National Mental Health Director position, Dr. Kemp directs and advises the suicide prevention coordinators at each local VA and is the national program manager for the VA Suicide Hotline. Dr. Kemp has conducted extensive qualitative research about war experiences and effects. Her current projects include suicide attempt and completion database development as well as studies involving veteran suicide attempt experiences and the experiences of veterans with traumatic brain injuries who have attempted suicide. She received her undergraduate degree in nursing from the State University of New York at Plattsburgh and graduate degrees from the University of Colorado Health Sciences Center in Denver, CO. She has adjunct Assistant Professor appointments at the University of Rochester and the State University of New York at Buffalo. Her recent publications and presentations include work on women veterans' experiences and suicide prevention and risk assessment.

David A. Litts, OD, FAAO

Dr. Litts is a Distinguished Scholar at the Education Development Center and Director, Science and Policy, at the National Suicide Prevention Resource Center (SPRC), a position he has held since 2002. During his tenure at SPRC, Dr. Litts led the development of the Suicide Prevention *Best Practices Registry*, SPRC's very popular curriculum for mental health clinicians, *Assessing and Managing Suicide Risk,* the Emergency Department Poster and Triage Guide, the Suicide Prevention Tool Kit for Rural Primary Care, the SAFE-T Card (an assessment guide for mental health professionals), and multiple SPRC publications, including *After a Suicide: Recommendations for Religious Services and Other Public Memorial Observances*. Dr. Litts also has focused on the launch of the public-private partnership to catalyze the advancement of the National Strategy for Suicide Prevention—the National Action Alliance for Suicide Prevention.

Before his work at SPRC, Dr. Litts was Special Advisor to the US Surgeon General on suicide prevention. He monitored progress on 15 key recommendations in the 1999 "Surgeon General's Call to Action to Prevent Suicide," including completion of the National Strategy for Suicide Prevention. Dr. Litts retired from the United States Air Force in 2003 after 23 years on active duty. Before his retirement, Colonel Litts was the Director, USAF Surgeon General's Operations Group and Executive Director, USAF Suicide Prevention Team at the Office of the Air Force Surgeon General. He was an Adjunct Professor at Pennsylvania College of Optometry from 1987–1988 and at the College of Optometry, Ferris State College from 1981–1983. He received a B.S. in Chemistry in 1976 from Hope College in Holland, Michigan, graduating magna cum laude. He received a Doctor of Optometry in 1980 from the Illinois College of Optometry, graduating magna cum laude and as valedictorian, and he is a Life Fellow with the American Academy of Optometry. Dr. Litts has co-authored several publications and has received the following honors: United States Surgeon General's Exemplary Service Award (2003), US Surgeon General's Exemplary Service Medal (2001), Defense Meritorious Service Medal (1995), Air Force Meritorious Service Medal (1987, 1991, 1993, and 1999), Secretary's Award for Distinguished Service (Department of Health and Human Services, 1999), and Air Force Commendation Medal (1984 and 1998).

Richard T. McKeon, Ph.D., MPH

Dr. McKeon is currently the Acting Branch Chief for the Suicide Prevention Branch in the Center for Mental Health Services in the Substance Abuse and Mental Health Services Administration, Department of Health and Human Services, where he provides support to all branch suicide prevention activities, including the Garrett Lee Smith State/Tribal Youth Suicide Prevention, and Campus Suicide Prevention grant programs, National Suicide Prevention Lifeline, and Suicide Prevention Resource Center. Dr. McKeon received his Ph.D. in Clinical Psychology from the University of Arizona and his Master of Public Health in Health Administration from Columbia University.

He has spent most of his career working in community mental health, including 11 years as director of a psychiatric emergency service and 4 years as Associate Administrator/Clinical Director of a hospital-based community mental health center in Newton, New Jersey. He established the first evidence-based treatment program for chronically suicidal borderline patients in the State of New Jersey, using Dialectical Behavior Therapy.

In 2001, he was awarded an American Psychological Association Congressional Fellowship and worked for United States Senator Paul Wellstone, covering health and mental health policy issues. He spent 5 years on the Board of the American Association of Suicidology as Clinical Division Director.

He also served on the Board of the Division of Clinical Psychology of the American Psychological Association. In 2008, the Secretary of Veterans Affairs appointed him to the Secretary's Blue Ribbon Work Group on Suicide Prevention.

In 2009, the Secretary of Defense appointed him to the Department of Defense Task Force on Suicide Prevention in the Armed Services. He also serves as Co-Chair of the Federal Working Group on Suicide Prevention.

Peter J. Proietto, Master Gunnery Sergeant

Master Gunnery Sergeant Proietto currently serves as Senior Enlisted Advisor, Safety Division, at the Headquarters Marine Corps, a position he has held since December 2008. In this role, he is the Senior Enlisted Advisor to the USMC Suicide Prevention Program to ensure relevancy and impact of the program's prevention message for all Marines. He coordinates command suicide prevention efforts and conducts visits as an adjunct inspector for the HQMC Inspector General. Before this position, Master Gunnery Sergeant Proietto was a Senior Enlisted Advisor to the Task Force National Capital Region (2007–2008); Staff Non-Commission Officer in Charge of Special Programs, Special Operations Branch (2006–2007); and Chief Firearms Instructor (2005– 2006). His military occupational specialties include the following: infantry unit leader/operations chief, scout sniper, combat marksmanship instructor, anti-tank TOW missile gunner, demolitions/assaultman, and Marine rifleman. He has participated in several professional trainings, including Ending Suicide.com Suicide Prevention Training course, Basics of Suicide Prevention Course, High Risk Dignitary Protection Training Course, Basic Field Firearms Officer Course, and Advanced Staff Non-Commissioned Officer Course. Master Gunnery Sergeant Proietto is the recipient of numerous awards and recognitions, including the Bronze Star Medal with Valor Device (2003), Bronze Star Medal (2008), Meritorious Service Medal (2004), Joint Service Commendation Medal (2003), and Marine Corps Commendation Medal (2006).

Philip Volpe, D.O., Major General

Major General Volpe currently serves as the Commanding General of Western Regional Medical Command, United States Army, and Senior Marketing Executive for TRICARE Puget Sound. He also serves as the military Co-Chair of the Department of Defense Task Force on the Prevention of Suicide by Members of the Armed Forces. General Volpe is a Board-Certified Family Medicine Physician. He was commissioned as a Captain in the Medical Corps in 1983, entering the Army through the Health Professions Scholarship Program. He holds a B.S. in Pre-Professional Studies from the University of Notre Dame and a Doctorate in Osteopathic Medicine from the New York College of Osteopathic Medicine. He completed his internship and residency training in family medicine at Tripler Army Medical Center from 1983 to 1986. General Volpe is a Fellow of the American Academy of Family Physicians and a Diplomat of the American Board of Family Medicine. He was selected as the Uniformed Services Family Physician of the Year in 1996 and served as the President, Uniformed Services Academy of Family Physicians from 2003 to 2004. He served in various command and staff positions at every level throughout his career, including more than 10 years in command. General Volpe has participated in various deployments, including Operation JUST CAUSE in Panama (2nd Ranger BN/USSOCOM); Operation HURRICANE ANDREW RELIEF in South Florida (Command Surgeon, 82nd ABN DIV); Operation

RESTORE HOPE in Somalia (Command Surgeon, Task Force Ranger); Operation UPHOLD DEMOCRACY in Haiti (JSOTF Surgeon); Operation CLEAN SWEEP (Hurricane Fran Relief) in North Carolina (Hospital CDR); and numerous classified special operations missions. Among his awards and decorations are the Defense Superior Service Medal, Legion of Merit (4 OLC), Bronze Star Medal, Purple Heart Medal, Defense Meritorious Service Medal, Meritorious Service Medal, Army Commendation Medal with "V" Device, Combat Parachutist Badge, and Combat Medical Badge. General Volpe is a graduate of the Army War College, was inducted into the Order of Military Medical Merit, and was awarded the Surgeon General's "A" Proficiency Designator for Family Medicine.

Aaron Werbel, Ph.D., Commander, Medical Service Corps, US Navy

Commander Werbel currently serves as Behavioral Health Affairs Officer and Suicide Prevention Program Manager at Headquarters, United States Marine Corps, in Quantico, Virginia. He is an Adjunct Assistant Professor in the Department of Clinical and Medical Psychology at the Uniformed Services University of the Health Sciences and a certified trainer of mental health providers in "Assessing and Managing Suicide Risk." Commander Werbel received a B.S., with honors, in psychology from the University of Michigan (1988), an M.A. in Clinical Psychology from Michigan State University (1993), and a Ph.D. in Clinical Psychology from Michigan State University (1997). In 1997, he completed his pre-doctoral clinical internship at the National Naval Medical Center in Bethesda, Maryland. Upon graduation, he became a member of the internship training staff at the National Naval Medical Center in Bethesda, Maryland, where he was assigned as head of behavioral healthcare for the Internal Medicine Department HIV/AIDS clinic. Subsequently, Commander Werbel moved overseas to work as a staff psychologist at the United States Naval Hospital, Naples, Italy. He also served as head of the behavioral healthcare clinic and substance abuse rehabilitation program at the Capodichino Branch Medical Clinic in Naples. Upon his return to the United States, Commander Werbel became a staff psychologist at the Midshipmen Development Center of the United States Naval Academy in Annapolis, Maryland, where he also was the regimental psychologist for plebe training. Commander Werbel is now the Chair of the Federal Executive Partners Working Group on Suicide Prevention and a member of the DoD Suicide Prevention and Risk Reduction Committee and the USMC Combat Operational Stress Control Advisory Board. He is an augment inspector for the USMC Inspector General Inspections Division and Program Manager of the Leaders Guide for Managing Marines in Distress. Commander Werbel is affiliated with several professional organizations, including the International Association for Suicide Prevention (IASP) (Member), IASP Task Force on Defense and Police Forces (Founder and Chair), IASP Postvention Task Force (Member), National Register of Health Service Providers in Psychology (Member), and American Association of Suicidology (Member). He was a member of the 2007 Department of Defense Task Force on Mental Health. He has been an invited speaker at numerous national and international conferences.

Appendix D. Task Force Meetings October 2009–July 2010

Task Force Meeting Falls Church, VA	Date of Meeting 7 August 2009 (Preparatory)
Bethesda, MD	1 October 2009
San Diego, CA	8 October 2009
Bethesda, MD	10 November 2009
Bethesda, MD	14 December 2009 (Preparatory)
Bethesda, MD	15 December 2009
Washington, DC	14 January 2010 (Preparatory)
Washington, DC	15 January 2010
Norfolk, VA—Cancelled	11 February 2010
Norfolk, VA—Cancelled	12 February 2010 (Preparatory)
San Antonio, TX	11 March 2010
San Antonio, TX	12 March 2010 (Preparatory)
Colorado Springs, CO	11 April 2010
Colorado Springs, CO	12 April 2010
Arlington, VA	10 May 2010 (Preparatory)
Arlington, VA	11 May 2010
Arlington, VA	12 May 2010 (Preparatory)
Arlington, VA	13 May 2010 (Preparatory)
Arlington, VA	14 May 2010 (Preparatory)
Reston, VA	9–10 June 2010 (Preparatory)
Washington, DC	22–24 June, 2010 (Preparatory)
Teleconference	6 July 2010 (Preparatory)
Reston, VA	13–15 July 2010 (Preparatory)
Teleconference	27 July 2010 (Preparatory)

APPENDIX E. BRIEFINGS RECEIVED AT TASK FORCE MEETINGS

Month	Meeting Theme/Objective (Open and Preparatory Meetings)	Meeting Date, Location, Speakers, Presentation Titles
August	A. Preparatory: Initial administration and committee requirements	A. Date: 7 August 2009 (Preparatory Meeting) Location: Falls Church, VA
October	A. Open: Service suicide data	A. Date: 1 October 2009 Location: Bethesda, MD Presentations: Service Data Review (SDR): • SDR: Army—Bruce A. Shahbaz, Walter o. Morales • SDR: Navy—Bonnie R. Chavez • SDR: Marine Corps—CDR Werbel • SDR: Air Force—Lt Col Michael Kindt • AFIP—CAPT Joyce Cantrell, CDR Rosemary Carr-Malone, Lynne Oetjen-Gerdes • Suicide Prevention: Valuable Information Learned from Army Surveillance and Research—COL Elspeth Cameron Ritchie, LTC Paul Bliese
	B. Open: Programs/family members	B. Date: 8 October 2009 Location: San Diego, CA Presentations: • DoD Suicide Event Report—Dr. Gahm • TAPS Testimony—TAPS Members • Defense Centers of Excellence: SPARRC Programs—CDR Hawkins
November	A. Open: Organizations/survivors	A. Date: 10 November 2009 Location: Bethesda, MD Service Members: CPT Emily Stehr, Airman First Class Taylor A. Yager, Corporal Kaitlyn M. Scarboro-Vinklarek Presentations: • Army Suicide Prevention Task Force—Brigadier General McGuire • Defense Centers of Excellence—Brigadier General Sutton • Epidemiological and public health perspectives in military suicide research, WRAIR—Dr. Charles Hoge • Behavioral and Social Health Outcomes Programs, USACHPPM—LTC Michael Bell

APPENDIX E. (CONTINUED)

Month	Meeting Theme/Objective (Open and Preparatory Meetings)	Meeting Date, Location, Speakers, Presentation Titles
December	A. Preparatory: Report outline/sub-committees B. Open: Suicide investigations	A. Date: 14 December 2009 (Preparatory Meeting) Location: Bethesda, MD B. Date: 15 December 2009 Location: Bethesda, MD Presentations: • U.S. Army Criminal Investigative Command—COL Eric Belcher and Mr. Guy Surian • U.S. Air Force Office of Special Investigations—Mr. Kevin Poorman • U.S. Navy and Marine Corps Investigations—Mr. Michael Keleher and LCDR Sara Tetreault • Navy/Marine Corps Aviation and Safety Investigations—LCDR Jeffrey Alton and Mr. Kimball Thompson • Air Force Accident and Safety Investigations Boards—Mr. Glenn Parr
January	A. Preparatory: DoD/VA Suicide Prevention Conference discussion B. Open: Investigations/research	A. Date: 14 January 2010 (Preparatory Meeting) Location: District of Columbia B. Date: 15 January 2010 Location: Washington, DC Presentations: • Root Cause Analysis processes—Dr. Geoffrey Rake • AFME Psychological autopsy—CDR Rosemary Malone • Resiliency/Soldier Fitness—COL Carl Castro • MHAT VI—MAJ Jeffrey Thomas • RAND Study—Mr. Rajeev Ramchand • Real Warrior Campaign—Ms. Julie Hughes • Service Member Panel—MAJ Hall
February	A. Open: Research/Reserve and National Guard Programs B. Preparatory: Site visits and working sessions.	A. Date: 11 February 2010 (Cancelled) Location: Norfolk, VA B. Date: 12 February 2010 (Cancelled) Location: Norfolk, VA

Month	Meeting Theme/Objective (Open and Preparatory Meetings)	Meeting Date, Location, Speakers, Presentation Titles
March	A. Open: Programs	A. Date: 11 March 2010 Location: San Antonio, TX Presentations: • Veterans Affairs Briefing—Dr. Janet Kemp • U.S. Army Reserve Component Briefing—Mr. Jose Mojica • Army National Guard Briefing—MAJ(P) Reggie Barnes • Suicide Prevention in Primary Care—Dr. Craig Bryan • Community Health Approach—Col Wayne Talcott • Warrior Resiliency Program—COL Bruce Crow
	B. Preparatory: Site visits and working sessions	B. Date: 12 March 2010 (Preparatory Meeting) Location: San Antonio, TX
April	A. Open: Research/Reserve, U.S. Coast Guard, and National Guard Programs	A. Date: 12 April 2010 Location: Colorado Springs, CO Presentations: • Michigan Buddy to Buddy Support Program—Ms. Marcia Valenstein • US Coast Guard briefing—Mr. John Reibling • VISN 19 Researchers—Peter Gutierrez and Lisa Brenner • Air Force Suicide Investigation Process—Col Lorna Westfall • The Role of Messaging—Linda Langford
	B. Preparatory: site visits and working sessions	B. Date: 13 April 2010 (Preparatory Meeting) Location: Colorado Springs, CO

APPENDIX E. (CONTINUED)

Month	Meeting Theme/Objective (Open and Preparatory Meetings)	Meeting Date, Location, Speakers, Presentation Titles
May	A. Preparatory: Site visits and working sessions	A. Date: 10 May 2010 (Preparatory) Location: Arlington, VA
	B. Open: Final briefings and data gathering	B. Date: 11 May 2010 Location: Arlington, VA Presentations: • New Jersey Veterans Helpline – COL Stephen Abel • Community-based Veterans Centers – Dr. Alphonse Batres • ABHIDE database – Dr. Kenneth Cox • Anti-stigma programs – Dr. Patrick Corrigan
	C. Preparatory: Site visits and working sessions	C. Date: 12 May 2010 (Preparatory Meeting) Location: Arlington, VA
	D. Preparatory: Site visits and working sessions	D. Date: 13 May 2010 (Preparatory Meeting) Location: Arlington, VA
	E. Preparatory: Site visits and working sessions	E. Date: 14 May 2010 (Preparatory Meeting) Location: Arlington, VA
June	A. Preparatory: writing/discussion	A. Date: 9 June 2010 (Preparatory Meeting) Location: Washington, DC
	B. Preparatory: writing/discussion	B. Date: 10 June 2010 (Preparatory Meeting) Location: Washington, DC
	C. Preparatory: writing/discussion	C. Date: 22 June 2010 (Preparatory Meeting) Location: Washington, DC
	D. Preparatory: writing/discussion	D. Date: 23 June 2010 (Preparatory Meeting) Location: Washington, DC
July	A. Preparatory: Review of draft report	A. Date: 6 July 2010 (Preparatory Meeting) Location: Teleconference
	B. Preparatory: Writing/discussion	B. Date: 13 July 2010 (Preparatory Meeting) Location: Reston, VA
	C. Open: Report to DHB	C. Date: 14 July 2010 Location: Bethesda, MD
	D. Preparatory: Writing/discussion	D. Date: 15 July 2010 (Preparatory Meeting) Location: Reston, VA
	E. Preparatory: Review of draft report	E. Date: 27 July 2010 (Preparatory Meeting) Location: Teleconference

APPENDIX F. SITES VISITED BY TASK FORCE DELEGATIONS

Installation Visited Camp Lejeune, NC	Date of Visit 9–10 February 2010	Service Marine Corps
Norfolk Naval Base, VA	9 February 2010	Navy
Portsmouth Naval Hospital, VA	10 February 2010	Navy
Marine Corps Air Station Beaufort, SC	22–23 February 2010	Marine Corps
Naval Submarine Base Kings Bay, GA	22–23 February 2010	Navy
Marine Corps Recruit Depot Parris Island, SC	24–25 February 2010	Marine Corps
Langley Air Force Base, VA	3 March 2010	Air Force
Fort Bliss, TX	9–10 March 2010	Army
Lackland Air Force Base, TX	9–10 March 2010	Air Force
Marine Corps Base Camp Pendleton, CA	22–23 March 2010	Marine Corps
Fort Benning, GA	22–23 March 2010	Army
Naval Base San Diego, CA	24–25 March 2010	Navy
Naval Hospital San Diego, CA	24-25 March 2010	Navy
Warner Robins Air Force Base, GA	25–26 March 2010	Air Force
Peterson Air Force Base, CO	14–15 April 2010	Air Force
Fort Carson, CO	14–15 April 2010	Army
Jacksonville Naval Base, FL	27–28 April 2010	Navy
Fort Riley, KS	28–29 April 2010	Army
Fort Campbell, KY	5–6 May 2010	Army

APPENDIX G. SERVICE SUICIDE DATA BY CAREER FIELD

The Task Force is unable to determine any suicide risk attributable specifically to occupation. There are insufficient data at this time to support identification of military occupations with a high incidence of suicide owing to occupation alone. In addition, at the time of this writing, scientific evidence does not seem to support a relationship between suicide and military occupational specialty.

The Task Force did obtain information related to suicides by career field from each of the Services.

The individual Service statistics are provided here. However, the Task Force strongly cautions readers against drawing any conclusions from the data provided for the following reasons:

- The low rate of suicide in any specific career field makes determining statistically valid rates of suicide in a career field challenging. Less than statistically valid data make comparisons between career fields almost impossible.
- The definition of career fields changes over the years—career fields come and go, or are merged into, or diverged from, existing career fields. Therefore, the denominator of the rate calculation (i.e., the total population in a career field) may vary from year to year, nullifying comparison data.
- Career fields among the Services also vary, so comparisons at that level are generally also not valid.
- Data on some high interest career fields such as recruiting and instructing reflect the data being performed at the time of the suicide, not the underlying career field of the deceased.

Preliminary evidence provided to the Task Force examined the relationship between career field and suicide and did not find a significant relationship (Gahm, 2010). Consistent with previous studies, failed relationships and a mental health diagnosis were identified as primary stressors.

In addition, Soldiers who view their leadership positively experienced a greater sense of unit cohesion and morale (MHAT VI, 2009). Numerous efforts are underway to continue to understand the role an individual's career field may have in relation to suicide and suicide prevention.

Appendix H. International Perspective on Suicide in Military Populations

Appendix H summarizes representative studies published in the last several years.

United Kingdom

Fear and colleagues (2009) examined more than a quarter century of suicides among United Kingdom (UK) Armed Forces personnel and identified statistically fewer suicides than expected when compared with the general UK population. This finding cut across all three services and was true for all age groups, except Army males under 20 years of age. This group had more than 1.5 times the number of deaths expected. Similarly, Kapur and colleagues (2009) examined 224 suicides among those who had left the UK Armed Services between 1996 and 2005 and found no greater rate of suicide than that of the general population. However, the risk of suicide in men aged 24 years and younger was two-to-three times higher than that of the general population and was associated with shorter length of service, lower service rank, and having the least contact with a mental health specialist.

ACTIVE DUTY ARMY SUICIDES BY MILITARY OCCUPATIONAL SPECIALTY CODE 2001-2009

Enlisted MOS	MOS Title	2001	2002	2003	2004	2005	2006	2007	2008	2009	2001-2009	2010*	Average Population* 2010-2009	Average suicide rate** 2001-2009 per 100,000
00Z	Command Sergeant Major					2				1	3		1281	26.0
02D	French Horn Player		1								1		38	292.4
09B	Trainee								1	1	2		168	132.3
11B	Infantryman	5	14	6	8	17	18	22	18	36	144	22	48215	33.2
11C	Indirect Fire Infantryman			1	1				3	2	7		5688	13.7
11H	Heavy Anti-armor Weapons Infantryman		1								1		1986	50.4
11M	Fighting Vehicle Infantryman	2	1	2							5		9689	51.6
11X	Infantry Recruit		2		1						3		974	34.2
11Z	Infantry Senior Sergeant				1			1			2		1440	15.4
12B	Combat Engineer	1		3	1				1		6		9083	22.0
13B	Cannon Crewman		3	5	1	4	4	2	3	2	24	2	10107	26.4
13D	Field Artillery Automated Tactical Systems Specialist			2	1		1	1	1		6		2202	30.3
13E	Cannon Fire Direction Specialist		1								1		517	21.5
13F	Fire Support Specialist			1		1	1	1	1	3	8	2	5489	16.2
13M	Multiple Launch Rocket System Crewmember				1			1			2		2667	8.3
13R	Field Artillery Firefinder Radar Operator							1		1	2		600	37.0
13S	Field Artillery Surveyor						1			1	2		482	59.3
13Z	Field Artillery Senior Sergeant									1	1		686	16.2
14E	Patriot Fire Control Enhanced Operator/Maintainer				1		1				2		1400	15.9
14J	Air Defense C4 and Intelligence Tactical Operations Center Enhanced Operator/Maintainer	1					1				2	2	1583	14.0
14R	Bradley Linebacker Crewmember				1						1		797	13.9
14S	Air and Missile Defense Crewmember	1	1	1			1				4	1	1879	23.7
14T	Patriot Launching Station Enhanced Operator/Maintainer	1							2		3		2442	13.7
14Z	Air Defense Artillery Senior Sergeant									1	1		285	39.0
15B	Aircraft Powerplant Repairer								1		1		561	25.5
15D	Aircraft Powertrain Repairer							1			1		463	30.9
15F	Aircraft Electrician							1			1		436	32.8
15G	Aircraft Structural Repairer							1		1	2		597	47.9
15H	Aircraft Pneumo-hydraulics Repairer						1				1		392	36.4
15J	OH-58D/ARH Armament/Electrical/Avionics Systems Repairer										0	1	812	0.0

Enlisted MOS	MOS Title	2001	2002	2003	2004	2005	2006	2007	2008	2009	2001-2009	2010*	Average Population* 2010-2009	Average suicide rate** 2001-2009 per 100,000
ACTIVE DUTY ARMY SUICIDES BY MILITARY OCCUPATIONAL SPECIALTY CODE 2001-2009														
15K	Aircraft Components Repair Supervisor									1	1		239	69.7
15P	Aviation Operations Specialist					1			1		2	2	1992	14.3
15R	AH-64 Attack Helicopter Repairer								1		1	2	2119	6.7
15S	OH-58D/ARH Helicopter Repairer							1		2	3		832	51.5
15T	UH-60 Helicopter Repairer					1	1	1	1	2	6		3564	24.1
15U	CH-47 Helicopter Repairer					2		1			3		1879	22.8
15W	Unmanned Aerial Vehicle Operator										0	1	871	0.0
15Y	AH-64D Armament/Electrical/Avionic Systems Repairer						1				1		1002	14.3
18B	Special Forces Weapons Sergeant		1		1	1				1	4		992	44.8
18D	Special Forces Medical Sergeant								1		1		824	13.5
18E	Special forces communications Sergeant		1	1					1		3		1035	32.2
18Z	Special forces Senior Sergeant								1		1		1021	10.9
19D	Cavalry Scout	2	2		1	3	3	7	4	6	28	4	9859	31.6
19K	M1 Armor Crewman	3	3	1	3	1	2	4	3	5	25	2	9754	28.5
19Z	Armor Senior Sergeant										0	1	622	0.0
21B	Combat Engineer				1	4	3	2	8	5	23	2	8514	38.6
21C	Bridge Crewmember					1					1		689	20.7
21E	Construction Equipment Operator						2			1	3	1	1672	25.6
21F	Crain Operator					1					1		216	115.7
21K	Plumber										0	1	216	0.0
21N	Horizontal Construction Engineer							1			1		468	30.5
21U	Topographic Analyst								1		1		415	34.4
21W	Carpentry and Masonry Specialist										0	1	1020	0.0
25B	Information Technology Specialist				1		1	1	3	2	8	1	4470	25.6
25C	Radio Operator Maintainer					1					1		1056	13.5
25F	Network Switching Operator							1			1		2640	5.4
25L	Cable systems installer								1	1	2		1759	16.2
25Q	Multichannel Transmission Systems Operator-Maintainer				2			1	2	2	7	2	3815	26.2
25S	Satellite Communication Systems Operator-Maintainer						1		2	1	4		2263	25.3
25U	Signal Support Systems Specialist					2	3	2	3	1	11	1	7842	20.0

Enlisted MOS	MOS Title	2001	2002	2003	2004	2005	2006	2007	2008	2009	2001-2009	2010*	Average Population* 2010-2009	Average suicide rate** 2001-2009 per 100,000
22X	Patriot System Repairer			1							1		187	133.7
31B	Military Policeman			1	3	2	4	7	4	4	25	8	13414	26.6
31C	Radio Operator Maintainer	1									1		1325	18.9
31E	Internment Resettlement Specialist								1	1	2		1153	28.9
31F	Networking Switching Systems Operator-Maintainer	2	1	2							5		4353	28.8
31R	Multichannel Transmission Systems Operator-Maintainer	1									1		6046	4.1
31S	Satellite Communication Systems Operator-Maintainer	2			1						3		2018	37.2
31U	Signal Support Systems Specialist			1	1						2		7172	7.0
31W	Telecommunications Operations Chief		1								1		1609	15.5
33W	Military Intelligence Systems Maintainer/Integrator							1			1		1202	11.9
35D	Air Traffic Controller				1						1		234	85.5
35E	Radio and Communications Equipment Repairer		1								1		1204	16.6
35F	Intelligence Analyst					1			2	1	4		1741	25.5
35H	Common Ground Station Analyst							1			1		254	43.7
35M	Human Intelligence Collector								1		1	1	1023	10.9
35N	Signal Intelligence Analyst									1	1		761	14.6
35P	Crypotologic Linguist							1			1		883	18.9
35T	Avenger Repairman					1					1		516	32.3
35Z	Signal Intelligence Senior Sergeant								1		1		81	137.2
36B	Finance Management Technician										0	2	1081	0.0
42A	Human Resources Specialist			1	2	1	2		4	5	15	2	9860	21.7
42F	Human Resources Information system Management Specialist			1							1		481	29.7
42L	Administrative Specialist			1							1		3185	4.5
42R	Army Bands Person							1			1		1247	13.4
44B	Metal Worker								1		1		906	12.3
44C	Financial Management Technician							1			1		2064	8.1
44E	Machinist			1							1		398	27.9
45B	Small Arms Artillery Repairer							1	1		2		600	37.0
45G	Fire Control Repairer								1		1		335	33.2
45K	Armament Repairer	1									1		862	12.9
51B	Carpentry and Masonry Specialist		1								1		1112	30.0

Table: ACTIVE DUTY ARMY SUICIDES BY MILITARY OCCUPATIONAL SPECIALTY CODE 2001-2009

ACTIVE DUTY ARMY SUICIDES BY MILITARY OCCUPATIONAL SPECIALTY CODE 2001-2009

Enlisted MOS	MOS Title	2001	2002	2003	2004	2005	2006	2007	2008	2009	2001-2009	2010*	Average Population* 2010-2009	Average suicide rate** 2001-2009 per 100,000
51H	Construction Engineering Supervisor				1						1		460	72.5
51R	Interior Electrician				1						1		205	162.6
52C	Utilities Equipment Repairer						1				1		1311	8.5
52D	Power Generation Equipment Repairer		1	1		1	1	1	2		7	2	3342	23.3
54B	Chemical Operations Specialist							1			1		6568	5.1
55B	Ammunition Specialist	1	1		1						3		2844	26.4
55D	Explosive Ordinance Disposal Specialist					1					1		920	27.2
56M	Chaplain Assistant			1					2	2	5		1319	42.1
57E	Laundry and Shower Specialist				1						1		356	140.4
62B	Construction Equipment Repairer			1				2	2		5		1608	34.5
62E	Heavy Construction Equipment Operator			1							1		1570	21.2
62J	General Construction Equipment Operator		1								1		758	44.0
63A	M1 Abrams Systems Maintainer					1			1		2		1278	17.4
63B	Wheeled Vehicle Mechanic	1	4	2	4	6	3	3	3	7	33		14621	25.1
63D	Artillery Mechanic					1			1		2		591	37.6
63H	Track Vehicle Repairer					3			2	2	7		2843	27.4
63J	Quartermaster and Chemical Equipment Repairer							1		1	2		1311	17.0
63M	Bradley Fighting Vehicle Systems Maintainer			1	1	1			1		4		1598	27.8
63S	Heavy-Wheel Vehicle Mechanic	2			1						3		2891	25.9
63W	Wheel Vehicle Repairer	1	1	1	1						4		3249	30.8
63X	Maintenance Supervisor							1			1		1641	8.7
63Z	Mechanical Maintenance Supervisor							1			1		869	12.8
67R	AH-64 Attack Helicopter Repairer	2									2		1979	33.7
67T	UH-60 Helicopter Repairer		1								1		4089	8.2
68A	Biomedical Equipment Specialist								1		1		679	36.8
68D	Operating Room Specialist						1				1		717	19.9
68E	Dental Specialist								1		1		1445	17.3
68J	Medical Logistics Specialist									1	1		1208	20.7
68K	Medical Laboratory Specialist										0	1	873	0.0
68Q	Pharmacy Specialist									1	1		608	41.1

Enlisted MOS	MOS Title	2001	2002	2003	2004	2005	2006	2007	2008	2009	2001-2009	2010*	Average Population* 2010-2009	Average suicide rate** 2001-2009 per 100,000
ACTIVE DUTY ARMY SUICIDES BY MILITARY OCCUPATIONAL SPECIALTY CODE 2001-2009														
68V	Respiratory Specialist							1			1		320	78.1
68W	Health Care Specialist						1	5	9	5	20	2	17483	28.6
71L	Administrative Specialist			1							1		3140	3.5
73C	Finance Specialist	2									2		1793	27.9
73D	Accounting Specialist				1						1		571	43.8
74B	Information Systems Operator-Analyst			1							1		3742	6.7
74D	Chemical, Biological, Radiological and Nuclear Specialist	1			2		3	1	2	5	14	1	6519	30.7
74Z	Information Systems Chief			1							1		165	151.5
75B	Personnel Administration Specialist	1	1	1							3		3343	29.9
75H	Personnel Services Specialist	1	3								4		7383	18.1
76J	Medical Supply Specialist	1									1		1063	94.1
77F	Petroleum Supply Specialist		1	1							2		8556	7.8
77W	Water Treatment Specialist		1								1		905	36.8
79R	Recruiter	1		2		1	3		2		9	1	3116	32.1
88H	Cargo Specialist				1	1				1	3		1830	18.2
88L	Watercraft Engineer							1			1		364	30.5
88M	Motor Transport Operator	1	1	4	2	4	3	2	1	7	25	2	13998	19.8
88N	Transportation Management Coordinator									2	2	1	1980	11.2
88Z	Transportation Senior Sergeant						1				1		275	40.4
89B	Ammunition Specialist					1		3	1	2	7		2643	44.1
89D	Explosive Ordinance Disposal Specialist					1				1	2	1	1399	23.8
91A	MI Abrams system Maintainer						1				1		634	17.5
91B	Wheeled Vehicle Mechanic										0	4	1971	0.0
91C	Utilities Equipment Repairer	1									1		703	15.8
91E	Dental Specialist	1									1		1220	9.1
91H	Track Vehicle Repairer										0	2	230	0.0
91J	Medical Logistics Specialist			1							1		999	11.1
91R	Veterinary Food Inspection Specialist						1				1		773	14.4
91W	Health Care Specialist			1	5	2	5	1			14		11068	14.1
91X	Mental Health Specialist										0	1	764	0.0
92A	Automated Logistics Specialist		1	5	1	1	1	1	3	1	14	3	12409	12.5

ACTIVE DUTY ARMY SUICIDES BY MILITARY OCCUPATIONAL SPECIALTY CODE 2001-2009

Enlisted MOS	MOS Title	2001	2002	2003	2004	2005	2006	2007	2008	2009	2001-2009	2010*	Average Population* 2010-2009	Average suicide rate** 2001-2009 per 100,000
92F	Petroleum Supply Specialist				1	4	1		1	2	9	1	9599	10.4
92G	Food Service Specialist		1	6	1	1	2	4	2	4	21	2	10410	22.4
92M	Mortuary Affairs Specialist									1	1		506	22.0
92R	Parachute Rigger					1					1	1	1799	6.2
92S	Shower/Laundry and Clothing Repair Specialist		1				2				3		1011	33.0
92Y	Unit Supply Specialist		1	1	1	1	1	1	6	1	13	3	13146	11.0
93C	Air Traffic Controller			1							1		1399	23.8
93P	Aviation Operations Specialist	1		1							2		1919	34.7
94D	Air Traffic Control Equipment Repairer									1	1		188	106.4
94F	Computer Directions System Repairer							3			3		1142	52.5
94R	Patriot System Repairer						1				1		412	48.5
94Y	Integrated Family of Test Equipment Operator and Maintainer							1			1		237	84.4
95B	Military Policeman	4	5	2			1				12		14254	28.1
96B	Intelligence Analyst		1				1	1			3		4488	9.5
97B	Counter Intelligence Agent						1				1		1737	8.2
97E	Human Intelligence Collector			1			1	1	1	2	6		1430	59.9
98C	Signals Intelligence Analyst			1	1	1					3		2424	17.7
Grand Total Enlisted		**45**	**61**	**71**	**61**	**80**	**88**	**103**	**124**	**141**	**774**	**92**		
	Average population adjusted based on the number of years the MOS has been in existence. See formula multiplier for number of years.													
Officer Branch		**2001**	**2002**	**2003**	**2004**	**2005**	**2006**	**2007**	**2008**	**2009**	**2001-2009**	**2010***	**Average Population CY2010-2009**	**Average suicide rate 2001-2009 per 100,000**
11	Infantry			2		3		1	1	1	8		5980	14.9
12	Armor	1	3	1	1						6		3417	19.5
13	Field Artillery	1	1		1			1	1	2	7	1	4580	17.0
14	Air Defense				1						1		1882	5.9
15	Aviation		2		1	1	1	2	1	1	9		6430	15.6

ACTIVE DUTY ARMY SUICIDES BY MILITARY OCCUPATIONAL SPECIALTY CODE 2001-2009

Enlisted MOS	MOS Title	2001	2002	2003	2004	2005	2006	2007	2008	2009	2001-2009	2010*	Average Population* 2010-2009	Average suicide rate** 2001-2009 per 100,000
18	Special Forces								1		1		1861	6.0
19	Armor							1		1	2		3438	6.5
21	Engineer			2							2		3331	6.7
25	Signal Corps				1					1	2		3817	5.8
27	Judge Advocate General Corps			2					1		3		1622	20.6
31	Military Police									1	1	1	1832	6.1
35	Military Intelligence	1					1		2	4	8		4606	19.3
37	Psychological Operations								1		1	1	410	27.1
38	Civil Affairs			1					1		2		774	81.1
42	Adjutant General					1	1	1		2	5		1821	30.5
47	USMA Professor								1		1		99	112.2
48	Foreign Area Officer		1					1			2		1081	20.6
53	Information Systems Management	1									1		447	24.9
56	Command and Unit Chaplain							2	1		3		1391	24.0
61	Army Medical Corps		1					2	1	1	5		4251	13.1
64	Veterinary Corps		1				1			1	3		454	73.4
65	Army Medical Specialist Corps						1			2	3		1133	29.4
66	Army Nurse Corps	1									1		3207	3.5
67	Medical Sciences			1			1		1		3		4119	8.1
74	Chemical						1				1		1251	8.9
88	Transportation Corp						1				1		2176	5.1
91	Ordinance					2					2		3120	7.1
92									1	1	2		3303	6.7
Grand Total Officer		**5**	**9**	**9**	**5**	**7**	**8**	**11**	**14**	**18**	**86**			

*The definition of career fields changes over the years—career fields come and go, or are merged into, or diverged from, existing career fields. Therefore, the denominator of the rate calculation (i.e., the total population in a career field) may vary from year to year, nullifying comparison data. Career fields among the Services also vary, so comparisons at that level are generally also not valid. Data on some high interest career fields such as recruiting and instructing reflect the data being performed at the time of the suicide, not the underlying career field of the deceased.

**The low rate of suicide in any specific career field makes determining statistically valid rates of suicide in a career field challenging. Less than statistically valid data make comparisons between career fields almost impossible.

ACTIVE DUTY NAVY SUICIDES BY RATING 2001-2009

RATING	TITLE	2001	2002	2003	2004	2005	2006	2007	2008	2009	TOTAL SUICIDES 2001-2009	SUICIDES 2010 YTD (30 JUN)	AVG POPULATION *	AVG SUICIDE RATE PER 100,00 2001-2009 **
AB (ABH/ABF/ABE)	Aviation Boatswainmate	1	2	2	1	1		3	3		13		10,180	14.19
AC	AirTraffContrlBasc				1	2	1				4		2,609	17.04
AD	Avn MachnstsMateBasic	1	1		2		1	1	2	1	9	1	6,614	15.12
AE	Avn ElctrcnsMateBsc	1	2		1		1			2	7		5,017	15.50
AF	Avn Photogrphrs Mate	1							1		2		115	193.24
AG	Aerogrphr						2				2		1,165	19.07
AM (AM/AME/AMS)	Avn StrMech SftyEqt		3	1	1	2	1		4	2	14	2	9,259	16.80
AO	Avn Ordncmn Basc	1	1	1	2		2	1		2	10		7,706	14.42
AT	Avn ElctrcnsTech Basc	3	2	2	1			3	1	1	13	1	9,289	15.55
AW	Avn AntiSubWarf Opr		1		1	1				1	4		2,940	15.12
AZ	Avn MtcAdmMan Basc					1					1		3,036	3.66
BM	Boatswains Mate						1			2	3	1	6,008	5.55
BU	Builder							1		1	2		2,370	9.38
CM	ConstrctnMech	1		1							2		1,855	11.98
CS	Commissaryman		1	1	1		1	2	1		7		8,234	9.45
CT (CTI/CTO/CTT/CTR/CTM/ EW)	Cryptologc Tech/ ElectrncsWarfTech	1		2	3	2	1	2	1	3	15	1	8,192	20.35
DC	Damage Control	1		2		1		1		1	6		3,228	20.65
EM	Electricians Mate		1			1	2	1	2	2	9		7,649	13.07
EN	Engineman	1		1			3			2	7		5,103	15.24
EO	Ept Oprtr						1				1		2,399	4.63
ET	Electronics Tech	4	1	4	2	4	2	4		1	22		12,022	20.33
FC	Fire Control		1	1			1	1	1	1	6		6,214	10.73
FT	Fire Cntrl Tech		1								1		1,269	8.76
GM (GM/GSM/GSE/TM)	GunnersMate/GasTurbTechMechl/GasTurbSysTech Elctrcl/Torpedoman's Mate	1	2	2			2	3	2	2	14		7,784	19.98
HM	Hospital Corpsman	2	3	4	2	2	1	1	1	2	18	1	23,631	8.46
HT	Hull Mtc Tech		1	2		1			1		5		2,513	22.11
IC	InteriorComElctrcn	1		1							2		2,063	10.77
IS	Intellig Speclt				1						1		2,398	4.63
IT	InfoSysTech (ex-RM)	1	2	1		1		1	1	1	8		10,333	8.60
LN	Legalman					1					1		402	27.64
LS / PC / SK/AK	Storekeeper/Avn Storekeeper		4		6	1		2	2	4	19		9,792	21.56

ACTIVE DUTY NAVY SUICIDES BY RATING 2001-2009														
RATING	TITLE	2001	2002	2003	2004	2005	2006	2007	2008	2009	TOTAL SUICIDES 2001-2009	SUICIDES 2010 YTD (30 JUN)	AVG POPULATION *	AVG SUICIDE RATE PER 100,00 2001-2009 **
MA	Master at Arms			1	1			2	2	3	9	1	9,302	10.75
MM	Machinists Mate	4	2	3	3	3	2	2	5	3	27	1	15,360	10.52
MN	Mineman		1				1				2		759	29.28
MR	Machine Repairman				1						1		702	15.83
MT	Missile Tech	1				2	2				5		1,186	46.84
NC									1		1		1,420	7.82
OS	Ops Specit		1	1	2	2		1			7	1	7,689	10.17
PR	Parachut Riggr					1	1	1			3		1,605	19.67
PS	Persnl Specialist					1	1			1	3		3,925	8.49
QM	Qtrmaster	1									1	1	2,171	5.12
SB (new rate)											0	1	758	0.00
SH	Shp Svcman						2		1		3		2,598	12.83
SO									1		1		1,941	5.72
ST (STG/STS)	Sonar Tech/Sonar Tech Sub	1		1	2	1	2			2	9		4,960	20.16
SW	Steelworker				1						1		846	13.13
Undesignated (AN/SN/FN/CN)		8	5	4	3	2	1		2	2	27	2	22,643	13.25
UT										1	1		1,000	11.11
YN	Yeoman	2	1		1			1	2		7		6,090	12.77
TOTAL		38	39	38	39	33	35	34	37	43	336			
Officer		2	5	6	1	4	3	6	3	2	32	1	53235	6.68
Collegiate										1	1			
1105	GenUnrestr LineOfr				1						1			
1110	SurfWar LineOfr		1	1							2			
1165	SurfWarStu LinOfr	1									1			
1175	LineOfr Trad SubWarf			2		1					3			
1305	Ex-Pilot/-NFOfr		1								1			
1310	Pilot Qualfd Ofr		1					1			2			
1317										1	1			
1320	NFOfr Qualfd		1								1	1		
1390	LineOfr inPilotTra					1					1			
1525	AerospEngrgDuOfr Mtc			1							1			
2100	MedCorps Ofr						1				1			
2300	MedSvcCorps Ofr						1	1			2			
2900	Nurse Corps Ofr		1			1		1			3			
2905	Nurse Corps Ofr			1							1			

ACTIVE DUTY NAVY SUICIDES BY RATING 2001-2009														
RATING	TITLE	2001	2002	2003	2004	2005	2006	2007	2008	2009	TOTAL SUICIDES 2001-2009	SUICIDES 2010 YTD (30 JUN)	AVG POPULATION *	AVG SUICIDE RATE PER 100,00 2001-2009 **
3100	SuppCorps Ofr							1			1			
5100	CivEngCorps Ofr							1			1			
6120	SurfOps LineOfr	1									1			
6180	Electrncs Surf Ofr			1							1			
6420	DProcsg LimDuOfr					1					1			
7181	Electroncs Tech Ofr						1				1			
7491	Security Tech Ofr							1			1			
7321										1	1			

*The definition of career fields changes over the years—career fields come and go, or are merged into, or diverged from, existing career fields. Therefore, the denominator of the rate calculation (i.e., the total population in a career field) may vary from year to year, nullifying comparison data. Career fields among the Services also vary, so comparisons at that level are generally also not valid. Data on some high interest career fields such as recruiting and instructing reflect the data being performed at the time of the suicide, not the underlying career field of the deceased.

**The low rate of suicide in any specific career field makes determining statistically valid rates of suicide in a career field challenging. Less than statistically valid data make comparisons between career fields almost impossible.

AFSC	DUTY TITLE	2001	2002	2003	2004	2005	2006	2007	2008	2009	TOTAL SUICIDES 2001 2009	SUICIDES 2010 YTD (30 JUN)	AVG POPULA TION *	AVG SUICIDE RATE PER 100,000 2001 2009 **
	ACTIVE DUTY AIR FORCE SUICIDES BY AIR FORCE SPECIALTY CODE 2001-2009 END OF FY													
10XXX	Operations Commander												285	0.00
11XXX	Pilot		1				1	2			4		12,007	3.70
12XXX	Combat Systems		1				3			1	5		3,820	14.54
13XX	Space, Missile & C2													
13XXX	Space, Missile & C2												4,949	0.00
14XX	Intelligence													
14XXX	Intelligence			2					1		3		2,880	11.57
15XXX	Weather							1			1		652	17.04
16XXX	Operations Support												1,304	0.00
17XXX	Non-Rated Operations												3005	0.00
1AXXX	Aircrew Operations	3	2	1	3		1	1	2		13		8,669	16.66
1CXXX	Command Control Systems Operations	2	1		2	2	1		1		9		11,732	8.52
1NXXX	Intelligence		1	1	1	3	3	3	2	5	19		11,119	18.99
1PXXX	Aircrew Flight Equipment								1	1	2		2,397	9.27
1SXXX	Safety												366	0.00
1TXXX	Aircrew Protection				1						1		2,289	4.85
1UXXX	Unmanned Aerospace System (UAS)												260	0.00
1WXXX	Weather				1						1		2,442	4.55
20XXX	Logistics Commander												181	0.00
21XXX	Logistics												3,900	0.00
2AXXX	Aerospace Maintenance (Logistics)	4	4	12	11	8	9	7	11	8	74		59,304	13.86
2EXXX	Comm-Elec/Wire Systems Maintenance (Logistics)	1	1	1	1	1	1	3		1	10		11,760	9.45
2FXXX	Fuels (Logistics)	3			1	2		1			7		4,083	19.05
2GXXX	Logistics Plans												740	0.00
2MXXX	Missile Maintenance (Logistics)			1					1		2		2,289	9.71
2PXXX	Precision Measurement (Logistics)	1							1		2		940	23.64
2RXXX	Maintenance Management (Logistics)			1							1		1,613	6.89
2SXXX	Material Management (Logistics)	1		1							2		8,821	2.52
2TXXX	Transportation & Vehicle Mgt (Logistics)		1			1	2			2	6		12,710	5.25

ACTIVE DUTY AIR FORCE SUICIDES BY AIR FORCE SPECIALTY CODE 2001-2009														
		END OF FY												
AFSC	DUTY TITLE	2001	2002	2003	2004	2005	2006	2007	2008	2009	TOTAL SUICIDES 2001-2009	SUICIDES 2010 YTD (30 JUN)	AVG POPULATION *	AVG SUICIDE RATE PER 100,000 2001-2009 **
2WXXX	Munitions & Weapons (Logistics)	2	1	1	6	2	2	2	2		18		15,274	13.09
30XXX	Support Commander												295	0.00
31XXX	Security Forces						1				1		807	13.77
32XXX	Civil Engineering												1,335	0.00
33XXX	Communications Commander							1			1		3,888	2.86
34XXX	Services						1				1		425	26.14
35XXX	Public Affairs												393	0.00
36XXX	Personnel												1235	0.00
37XXX								1			1		910	12.21
38XXX	Force Support/ Manpower												486	0.00
3AXXX	Knowledge Operations Mgt (Support)	1		1	2				1		5		9,259	6.00
3CXXX	Communication-Computer Systems (Support)	1	1	2	2		2		2	3	13		13,124	11.01
3DXXX	Cyberspace Support												28,617	0.00
3EXXX	Civil Engineering	2	2	5	4	1	1	1		2	18		17,968	11.13
3HXXX	Historian												69	0.00
3MXXX	Services		1				2	1			4		4,540	9.79
3NXXX	Public Affairs												2,002	0.00
3PXXX	Security Forces	8	2	2	4	5	3	6	4	9	43		24,206	19.74
3SXXX	Mission Support						1		2		3		8,238	4.05
40XXX	Medical Commander												101	0.00
41XXX	Health Services												1,092	0.00
42XXX	Biomedical Clinicians												1,132	0.00
43XXX	Biomedical Specialists												1,214	0.00
44XXX	Physician								1	1	2		2,065	10.76
45XXX	Surgery												784	0.00
46XXX	Nurse					1					1		3,495	3.18
47XXX	Dental									1	1		923	12.04
48XXX	Aerospace Medicine			1			1				2		593	37.47
4AXXX	Medical	1						1			2		4,785	4.64

ACTIVE DUTY AIR FORCE SUICIDES BY AIR FORCE SPECIALTY CODE 2001-2009														
		END OF FY												
AFSC	DUTY TITLE	2001	2002	2003	2004	2005	2006	2007	2008	2009	TOTAL SUICIDES 2001-2009	SUICIDES 2010 YTD (30 JUN)	AVG POPULATION *	AVG SUICIDE RATE PER 100,000 2001-2009 **
4BXXX	Bioenvironmental Engineering									1	1		902	12.32
4CXXX	Mental Health Service		1				1		1		3		677	49.24
4DXXX	Diet Therapy												381	0.00
4EXXX	Public Health						1						958	0.00
4HXXX	Cardiopulmonary Laboratory												304	0.00
4JXXX	Physical Medicine												329	0.00
4MXXX	Aerospace & Operational Physiology												342	0.00
4NXXX	Aerospace Medical Service & Surgical Service	1				1	1	1		2	6		7,008	0.30
4PXXX	Pharmacy												957	0.00
4RXXX	Diagnostic Imaging												965	0.00
4TXXX	Medical Laboratory			1			1		2		4		1,323	33.59
4VXXX	Ophthalmic												271	0.00
4YXXX	Dental		1						1		2		2,541	8.75
51XXX	Judge Advocate		1					1			2		1,264	17.58
52XXX	Chaplain									1	1		533	20.85
5JXXX	Paralegal			1							1		966	11.50
5RXXX	Chaplain Assistant			1	1		1				3		445	74.91
60XXX	Acquisition												50	0.00
61XXX	Scientific Research & Development								1		1		883	12.58
62XXX	Developmental Engineer				1						1		2,531	4.39
63XXX	Acquisition									1	1		2,556	4.35
64XXX	Contracting												906	0.00
65XXX	Finance												842	0.00
6CXXX	Contracting (Acquisition)												1,256	0.00
6FXXX	Financial (Acquisition)			1		2		1			4		2,963	15.00
71XXX	Special Investigations												376	0.00
7SXXX	Special Investigations												867	0.00
80XXX	Commander												46	0.00
81XXX	Training Commander/Instructor		1								1		958	11.60
82XXX	Academic Program Mgr												147	0.00

AFSC	DUTY TITLE	2001	2002	2003	2004	2005	2006	2007	2008	2009	TOTAL SUICIDES 2001-2009	SUICIDES 2010 YTD (30 JUN)	AVG POPULA-TION *	AVG SUICIDE RATE PER 100,000 2001-2009 **
ACTIVE DUTY AIR FORCE SUICIDES BY AIR FORCE SPECIALTY CODE 2001-2009		END OF FY												
83XXX	Recruiting Service												105	0.00
84XXX	Historian													-
85XXX	USAF Honor Guard												5	0.00
86XXX	Operations Mgmt												152	0.00
87XXX	Inspector General												71	0.00
88XXX	Aide/Protocol												56	0.00
8AXXX	Flight Attendant												148	0.00
8BXXX	Military Training Instructor/Leader												914	0.00
8CXXX	Family Support Center												150	0.00
8DXXX	Linguist Debriefer/Interrogator												41	0.00
8EXXX	Research & Development Craftsman													-
8FXXX	First Sergeant				1				1		2		1,186	18.74
8GXXX	USAF Honor Guard												251	0.00
8HXXX	Special Duty Identifiers												265	0.00
8JXXX	Correctional Custody Supervisor													-
8MXXX	Postal Specialist												623	0.00
8PXXX	Courier/Defense Attache Specialist												209	0.00
8RXXX	Recruiter	1									1		2,441	4.55
8SXXX	Missile Facility Mgr/Sensor Operator									1	1		180	61.73
8TXXX	Professional Military Education Instructor												596	0.00
90XXX	General Officer								1		1		35	317.46
91XXX	Commander/Wing Commander												458	0.00
92XXX	Student								1		1		546	20.35
93XXX	Patient													-
95XXX	Non Extended AD USAFR Academy CAP Liaison Officer													-
96XXX	Unclassified Officer												18	0.00
97XXX	Exec Officer Above Wing Level												245	0.00
9AXXX	Awaiting Retraining/Discharge/ Separation/ Retirement						1				1		303	36.67
9CXXX	CMSgt of the AF												1	0.00

ACTIVE DUTY AIR FORCE SUICIDES BY AIR FORCE SPECIALTY CODE 2001-2009														
		END OF FY												
AFSC	DUTY TITLE	2001	2002	2003	2004	2005	2006	2007	2008	2009	TOTAL SUICIDES 2001-2009	SUICIDES 2010 YTD (30 JUN)	AVG POPULA-TION *	AVG SUICIDE RATE PER 100,000 2001-2009 **
9DXXX	Dormitory Mgr												288	0.00
9EXXX	Command CMSgt												139	0.00
9FXXX	Reporting Identifiers												69	0.00
9GXXX	Airmen Aide									1	1		211	52.66
9JXXX	Prisoner												36	0.00
9LXXX	Interpreter/Translator												54	0.00
9PXXX	Patient												1	0.00
9SXXX	Technical Applications Specialist												448	0.00
9TXXX	Basic Airman/Officer Trainee/Pre-Cadet Assignee	1			2						3		6,070	5.49
9UXXX	Unallotted Airman													-
UNK		2	3	1	2		2				10		1,537	72.29
X1XXX														-
TOTAL		35	26	37	47	29	44	34	40	41	333		347,497	10.65

*The definition of career fields changes over the years—career fields come and go, or are merged into, or diverged from, existing career fields. Therefore, the denominator of the rate calculation (i.e., the total population in a career field) may vary from year to year, nullifying comparison data. Career fields among the Services also vary, so comparisons at that level are generally also not valid. Data on some high interest career fields such as recruiting and instructing reflect the data being performed at the time of the suicide, not the underlying career field of the deceased.

**The low rate of suicide in any specific career field makes determining statistically valid rates of suicide in a career field challenging. Less than statistically valid data make comparisons between career fields almost impossible

USMC SUICIDES BY MILITARY OCCUPATIONAL SPECIALTY CODES 2002 - 2009														
MOS	MOS DESCRIPTION	2001	2002	2003	2004	2005	2006	2007	2008	2009	TOTAL SUICIDES 2001-2009	SUICIDES 2010 YTD (30 JUN)	AVG POPULATION *	AVG SUICIDE RATE PER 100,000 **
0100	Basic Administrative Marine				1						1		424	29
0121	Personnel Clerk (Pmos)							1		2	3		2,593	14
0151	Basic Administrative Clerk						1	1		1	3		3,508	11
0193	Personnel/Administrative Chief					1					1		1,708	7
0200	Basic Intelligence Marine								1		1		347	36
0231	Intelligence Specialist (Pmos)		1								1		1,600	8
0241	Imagery Analysis Specialist								1	1	2		338	74
0300	Basic Infantryman				2		2	1			5		1,742	36
0302	Infantry Officer		1	1							2		2,326	11
0311	Rifleman		3	4	3	4	1	3	7	13	38		21,047	23
0313	Lav Crewman					1					1		1,107	11
0321	Reconnaissance Man (Pmos)									1	1		1,413	9
0331	Machinegunner				1		1	1	2		5		3,721	17
0341	Mortarman			1	1			4	2		8		3,935	25
0351	Infantry Assaultman				2	1				3	6		2,420	31
0352	Antitank Missleman						1	2			3		1,624	23
0369	Infantry Unit Leader		1		2	1	1		2		7		0	
0400	Basic Logistics Marine									1	1		366	34
0402	Logistics Officer						1				1		1,448	9
0411	Maintenance Management Specialist							1			1		1,232	10
0431	Log/Embark Specialist (Pmos)									1	1		1,311	10
0481	Landing Support Specialist					1			1	2	4		1,048	48
0511	Magtf Planning Specialist				1			1			2		354	71
0612	Tactical Switching Operator (Pmos)					1		1			2		1,806	14
0621	Field Radio Operator (Pmos)					1	2	1	2	2	8		5,433	18
0651	Data Systems Technician		1			1	1				3		1,401	27
0659	Data Chief					1					1		557	22
0800	Basic Field Artillery Man		1					1	1		3		485	77
0802	Field Artillery Officer						1				1		814	15
0811	Field Artillery Cannoneer			1	1	1		1		2	6		2,652	28

USMC SUICIDES BY MILITARY OCCUPATIONAL SPECIALTY CODES 2002 - 2009														
MOS	MOS DESCRIPTION	2001	2002	2003	2004	2005	2006	2007	2008	2009	TOTAL SUICIDES 2001-2009	SUICIDES 2010 YTD (30 JUN)	AVG POPULATION *	AVG SUICIDE RATE PER 100,000 **
0844	Field Artillery Fire Control Man			1	1				1		3		737	51
0861	Fire Support Man			1							1		643	19
1300	Basic Engr, Const And Equip Man			1	1						2		658	38
1316	Metal Worker					1		1			2		349	72
1341	Engineer Equipment Mechanic (Pmos)				1						1		1,406	9
1345	Engineer Equipment Operator				1			1			2		1,706	15
1371	Combat Engineer					3			1	1	5		3,457	18
1800	Basic Tank And Aslt Amphib Crewman		2								2		263	95
1812	M1a1 Tank Crewman			1							1		737	17
1833	Aav Crewman (Pmos)								2		2		2,176	11
2100	Basic Ordnance Marine									1	1		452	28
2111	Small Arms Repairer/Technician				1						1		1,578	8
2146	Main Battle Tank Repairer Tech			1							1		526	24
2147	Light Armored Vehicle (Lav) Repair							1			1		568	22
2161	Repair Shop Machinist								1		1		174	72
2171	Electro-Optical Ordnance Repairer				1	1					2		474	53
2300	Basic Ammunition And Eod Marine						1				1		231	54
2311	Ammunition Technician					1				1	2		1,599	16
2621	Spec Comm Signals Coll Opranl (Pmo						1			1	2		773	32
2631	Elint Intercept Operator								1		1		192	65
2651	Special Intel Sys Admin/Comm									2	2		482	52
2671	Middle East Crypt Linguist (Pmos)				1						1		215	58
2844	Ground Comm Org Repairer (Pmos)		1						1	1	3		1,104	34
2846	Ground Radio Intermediate Repairer								1		1		553	23
2847	Telephone Sys/Pers Comp Repairer									1	1		662	19
2862	Electronics Maintenance Tech								1		1		544	25
2881	Tm/Ate Technician			1							1		0	
3002	Ground Supply Officer								1		1		660	19
3010	Ground Supply Operations Officer									1	1		34	368
3043	Supply Admin And Oper Spec (Pmos)		2				1		1		4		4,071	12
3051	Warehouse Clerk (Pmos)						1		1		2		3,023	8
3052	Packaging Specialist (Pmos)								1		1		272	46

MOS	MOS DESCRIPTION	2001	2002	2003	2004	2005	2006	2007	2008	2009	TOTAL SUICIDES 2001-2009	SUICIDES 2010 YTD (30 JUN)	AVG POPULATION *	AVG SUICIDE RATE PER 100,000 **
USMC SUICIDES BY MILITARY OCCUPATIONAL SPECIALTY CODES 2002 2009														
3112	Distribution Mgmt Specialist (Pmos									1	1		0	
3381	Food Service Specialist			1	3	1		1			6		2,541	30
3451	Fiscal/Budget Technician							1			1		399	31
3521	Automotive Maint Technician			1					1	3	5		4,465	14
3531	Motor Vehicle Operator			2	4	1	1	1	1		10		6,531	19
3533	Logistics Vehicle System Operator				1				1	1	3		2,017	19
3537	Motor Transport Operations Chief			1				1			2		1,142	22
4341	Combat Correspondent								1		1		461	27
4402	Judge Advocate			1					1		2		0	
4600	Basic Tsng & Audiovisual Spt Mar									1	1		85	147
4641	Combat Photographer									1	1		162	77
5800	Basic Mil Police & Corrections Mar		1								1		625	20
5811	Military Police		1	2	1	1					5		4,138	15
6046	Aircraft Maint Admin Spec (Pmos)		1			1	1				3		1,201	31
6048	Flight Equipment Technician							1	1		2		939	27
6062	Aircraft Inter Lvl Hydr/Pneu Mech		1								1		310	40
6073	Aircraft Maint Gse Technician									1	1		448	28
6112	Helicopter Mech, Ch-46		1						1		2		404	62
6113	Helicopter Mech, Ch-53						1				1		651	19
6123	Helicopter Power Plants Mech, T-64			1							1		202	62
6152	Helicopter Airframe Mech Ch-46		1								1		317	39
6153	Helicopter Airframe Mech Ch-53						1			2	3		570	66
6156	Tiltrotor Airframe Mechanic							1			1		295	42
6212	Fixed Wing Acft Mech Av-8/Tav-8									1	1		462	27
6217	Fixed Wing Acft Mech F/A-18							1	1		2		668	37
6222	Fixed Wing Acft Power Plants F-402			1							1		127	98
6252	Fixed Wg Asem Av-8/Tav-8 (Pmos)						1				1		359	35
6257	Fixed Wing Airframe Mech F/A-18								1		1		488	26
6300	Basic Avionics Marine (Oma)					1					1		421	30
6324	Aircomm Navelecwpns Systech U/Ah-1				1					1	2		658	38
6337	Acft Electrical Sys Tech F/A-18							1			1		318	39
6412	Aircraft Comm Systems Tech					1					1		176	71

USMC SUICIDES BY MILITARY OCCUPATIONAL SPECIALTY CODES 2002 - 2009														
MOS	MOS DESCRIPTION	2001	2002	2003	2004	2005	2006	2007	2008	2009	TOTAL SUICIDES 2001-2009	SUICIDES 2010 YTD (30 JUN)	AVG POPULATION *	AVG SUICIDE RATE PER 100,000 **
6423	Aviation Electronics Micro-Minatur						1				1		133	94
6432	Acft Electrical/Instrument/Flight							1			1		141	89
6531	Aircraft Ordnance Technician							1			1		1,450	9
6541	Aviation Ordnance Systems Tech					1					1		979	13
6672	Aviation Supp Specialist (Pmos)									1	1		1,807	7
6800	Basic Weather Service Marine						1				1		50	250
7257	Air Traffic Controller		1		1						2		528	47
7562	Pilot Hmh/M/L/A Ch-46				1						1		702	18
7565	Pilot Hmh/M/L/A Ah-1					1					1		508	25
7599	Pilot flight Student						1				1		1,080	12
8011	Basic Marine W/Enl Guarantee								1		1		4,802	3
8041	Colonel Ground (Pmos)									1	1		417	30
9900	General Service Marine			2			1	1			4		1	50,000
9971	Basic Marine W/Enl Guarantee		2	1							3		1	37,500
9999	Sergeant Major/First Sergeant		1		1						2		0	
	Total		23	26	34	28	25	33	42	52	263			

*The definition of career fields changes over the years—career fields come and go, or are merged into, or diverged from, existing career fields. Therefore, the denominator of the rate calculation (i.e., the total population in a career field) may vary from year to year, nullifying comparison data. Career fields among the Services also vary, so comparisons at that level are generally also not valid. Data on some high interest career fields such as recruiting and instructing reflect the data being performed at the time of the suicide, not the underlying career field of the deceased.

**The low rate of suicide in any specific career field makes determining statistically valid rates of suicide in a career field challenging. Less than statistically valid data make comparisons between career fields almost impossible.

ACTIVE DUTY COAST GUARD SUICIDES BY RATING 2001-2009														
ABBRE-VIATION	CG RATINGS ('00-09)	2001	2002	2003	2004	2005	2006	2007	2008	2009	TOTAL SUICIDES 2001-2009	SUICIDES 2010 YTD (30 JUN)	AVG POPULA-TION *	AVG SUICIDE RATE PER 100,00 2001-2009**
AET	Avionics Electrical Technician				1						1		798	13.92
AMT	Aviation Maintenance Technician		1				1				2		1,682	13.21
AST	Aviation Survival Technician										0		332	0.00
AVT	Avionics Technician										0		175	0.00
BM	Boatswain's Mate		1	2	2		1	1	1		8		4,985	17.83
DC	Damage Controlman										0		916	0.00
EM	Electrician's Mate										0		1,110	0.00
ET	Electronics Technician								1		1		1,452	7.65
FS	Food Service Specialist	1		1						1	3		1,233	27.03
FT	Fire Control Technician										0		54	0.00
GM	Gunner's Mate						1	1			2		808	27.50
HS	Health Services Technician							1			1		744	14.93
HSD	Health Services Dental Assistant										0		18	0.00
IS	Intelligence Specialist										0		65	0.00
IT	Information Systems Technician				1						1		513	21.66
IV	Investigator										0		6	0.00
MCPO-CG	Master Chief Petty Officer of the CG										0		1	0.00
ME	Maritime Enforcement Specialist										0		1	0.00
MK	Machinery Technician	1			1						2		4,149	5.36
MST	Marine Science Technician			2							2		994	22.36
MU	Musician										0		50	0.00
OC	Officer Candidates										0		20	0.00
OS	Operations Specialist				1						1		1,481	7.50
PA	Public Affairs Specialist	1									1		86	129.20
PS	Port Security Specialist										0		36	0.00
QM	Quartermaster										0		203	0.00
RD	Radarman										0		84	0.00
SK	Storekeeper	1									1		1,355	8.20
TC	Telecommunications Specialist										0		272	0.00
TT	Telephone Technician										0		59	0.00

ACTIVE DUTY COAST GUARD SUICIDES BY RATING 2001-2009

ABBREVIATION	CG RATINGS ('00-09)	2001	2002	2003	2004	2005	2006	2007	2008	2009	TOTAL SUICIDES 2001-2009	SUICIDES 2010 YTD (30 JUN)	AVG POPULATION *	AVG SUICIDE RATE PER 100,00 2001-2009**
YN	Yeoman		1								1		1,700	6.54
UNK	Rating info not available										0		2	0.00
Non-Rate	Airmen, Firemen, and Seamen	1	2	2	2	1		1			9		6,307	15.86
Officers			1	1		2				3	7		9,706	8.01
CG Acad Cadets													942	0.00

*The definition of career fields changes over the years—career fields come and go, or are merged into, or diverged from, existing career fields. Therefore, the denominator of the rate calculation (i.e., the total population in a career field) may vary from year to year, nullifying comparison data. Career fields among the Services also vary, so comparisons at that level are generally also not valid. Data on some high interest career fields such as recruiting and instructing reflect the data being performed at the time of the suicide, not the underlying career field of the deceased.

**The low rate of suicide in any specific career field makes determining statistically valid rates of suicide in a career field challenging. Less than statistically valid data make comparisons between career fields almost impossible.

Hawton and colleagues (2009) examined armed forces personnel presenting to the hospital for self-harm behavior (low lethality suicide attempts and self-injurious acts) and found that fewer of these patients than those among the general population who self-harmed had evidence of past psychiatric disorders or treatment or prior histories of self-harm. Almost two-thirds (62.7 percent) were under 25 years of age; 62 percent had relationship problems, 43.9 percent had employment problems, and 40.5 percent had misused alcohol.

Canada

Tien and colleagues (2010) conducted a retrospective chart review of all Canadian Forces members who died in the quarter century between 1983 and 2007. Suicide was the third leading cause of death, accounting for 17 percent of all deaths. Belik and colleagues (2009) examined lifetime and current suicide attempts among active duty personnel and found attempts among men and women to be significantly related to sexual and other traumas and a dose-response effect (i.e., the greater the number of traumatic events experienced, the greater the association to attempted suicide).

Scandinavian Peacekeeping Personnel

The suicide rate among former Swedish peacekeeping personnel was found to be lower than that of the general population (Michel, Lundin, & Larsson, 2007) In contrast, a moderately but significantly increased standard mortality ratio for suicide (SMR = 1.4) was found among former Norwegian peacekeepers; however, when adjusted for marital status (peacekeepers had a lower rate of marriage), this SMR was reduced to insignificance (Thoreson, Mehlum, & Moller, 2003) Thoreson and Mehlum (2006) compared 43 suicides with 41 fatal accidents among Norwegian peacekeepers in a psychological autopsy study and found mental health problems to be significantly related to risk for suicide, as was living alone and the breakup of a love relationship.

Israel

Two Israeli studies found suicides to be more common among Israeli Soldiers least expected to be at-risk. Bodner and colleagues (2006) compared 429 suicides with 499 matched Soldiers and found that those who died by suicide had better pre-military psychological adjustment and motivation to serve. Those people who died by suicide and who served in combat, versus those who did not, also had fewer referrals for psychological adjustment, a higher sense of duty, higher scores on an autonomy scale, and fewer unit changes. Apter and colleagues (2008) examined 43 18- to 21-year-old male soldier suicides and 171 consecutive admissions for a range of non-fatal suicidal behaviors and found that completers and near-lethal attempters had higher IQs and medical fitness ratings and were in more demanding assignments than other groups. A psychological autopsy study by Orbach and colleagues of 67 Israeli soldier suicides found that, during the last days of life, those who died by suicide exhibited a split between an emotional state of mind (with emotional deterioration) and relatively stable military functioning.

Although the generalizability of findings from these studies is questionable, one indisputable fact can be derived: suicide (thus its prevention) among armed forces members knows no geographic boundary and is an issue for numerous countries other than the United States. Notably, the International Association for Suicide Prevention (www.iasp.info) recently (2007) established a task force to improve international collaboration to promote the scientific understanding of suicidal behaviors necessary to reduce suicides among military personnel.

Lastly, two reports of military-based suicide prevention programs outside the United States have been published. Rozanov and colleagues (2002) implemented a prevention program in a 10,000 soldier Ukranian Army unit and reported dramatic decreases in suicide rates after, versus before, implementation. Gordona and Milovoje (2007) presented results from their prevention program implemented in the Army of Serbia and Montenegro in 2003, demonstrating a dramatic first year post-implementation decline in rates. Each study suffers from serious methodological flaws, however; thus these findings must be accepted with caution.

APPENDIX I. LISTING OF DOD SUICIDE PREVENTION RESEARCH

The projects listed here are illustrative of current suicide research conducted in DoD and in conjunction with other agencies. The list is by no means all inclusive. The services are conducting or supporting work on multiple efforts to better understand suicides and related factors. Their work involves training assessments, focus groups, and questionnaires that while complying with Integrated Research Board protocols do not constitute formal clinical research per research definitions. In addition, the services are working on a myriad of projects to understand the effectiveness of their suicide prevention programs and training.

Army Study to Assess Risk and Resilience in Service Members (Army STARRS)
Funding: $50,000,000
Sponsor: US Army Medical Research and Materiel Command
Period of Performance: 60 Months

Mr. Bob Ursano of the Uniformed Services University (USUHS) in Bethesda, MD, leads the Army Study to Assess Risk and Resilience in Service Members (Army STARRS) research program. The purpose of this program is to conduct a multi-phase epidemiological study that considers diverse psychosocial and neurobiological risk and protective factors for suicidal behaviors and secondary outcomes to provide evidence-based recommendations for implementation of Army suicide prevention interventions. The data obtained from the ongoing Pre- and Post-Deployment Health Reassessment Program (PDHRP) surveys will be used as secondary outcomes. The approach is a case-controlled survey that will assess Soldiers who made nonfatal attempts and relatives of Soldiers who committed suicide within a psychological autopsy framework. Parallel data will be collected from carefully matched controls. Blood samples and saliva samples also will be collected to allow neurobiological risk and protective factors to be studied. The survey component will include active duty personnel across all phases of Army service. Survey reports will be linked to subsequent ASER records and PDHRP reports to study prospective associations of predictors with suicidal behaviors and secondary outcomes.

A Systematic Review of Air Force Suicide Deaths: Enhancing Suicide Prevention Efforts
Funding: University Intramural Support
Sponsor: Uniformed Services University of the Health Sciences—New Faculty Startup
Period of Performance: 2006—2011

Dr. Marjan Holloway at USUHS leads this study, in collaboration with Dr. David Jobes at Catholic University. The study involves a retrospective psychological autopsy to systematically examine all closed case files of active duty Air Force personnel who died by suicide between 1996 and 2007. 485 variables will be coded by using the Suicide Death Investigation Template organized into six general areas of interest: demographics, military specific information, suicide event, risk factors, protective factors, and helping services utilization. The study aims are as follows: (a) gain an understanding of factors associated with suicide death among AF decedents; (b) compare decedents on several factors, including prior suicide history, alcohol misuse, and helping services utilization; and (c) evaluate in a qualitative analysis the common themes conveyed in suicide notes of decedents and to describe these themes in relation to major theoretical constructs related to suicide behavior. The findings are expected to better inform the Air Force Suicide Prevention Program education, identification, and prevention efforts by providing a more precise description of suicide risk and missed opportunities for prevention.

Antidepressants and the Risk of Self-harm and Unintentional Injury Among Younger Veterans Amount: $656,184
Sponsor: US Army Medical Research and Materiel Command
Period of Performance: 24 Months

Dr. Matthew Miller at Harvard College leads this study. The goals of this project include: (a) to evaluate the association between antidepressant use and risk of suicide, intentional self-harm, and motor vehicle related fatal and non-fatal injuries in a population of veterans aged 50 years and younger; (b) to determine whether a particular class of antidepressants (e.g., Selective Serotonin Uptake Inhibitors) is associated with a disproportionately high risk of fatal and nonfatal motor vehicle injuries compared to other antidepressant classes (e.g., Seratonin Norepinepherine Reuptake Inibitors). The study will use the Department of Veterans Affairs healthcare utilization database linked to cause specific mortality files and appropriate pharmaco-epidemiologic methods to address the aims as well as many of the limitations of prior observational work.

Blister Packaging Medication to Increase Treatment Adherence and Clinical Response: Impact on Suicide-related Morbidity and Mortality
Amount: $1,173, 408
Sponsor: US Army Medical Research and Materiel Command
Period of Performance: 36 Months

Dr. Peter Gutierrez at the VA Medical Center in Denver, CO, leads this research study. This study will determine whether blister packaging medication significantly increases treatment adherence and whether blister packaging significantly decreases intentional self-poisoning behavior. This study will compare blister packaging to dispensing as usual by tracking former psychiatric patients for 12 months post-discharge and obtaining monthly reports (self-report and medical record review) of suicide-related behaviors.

Brief Cognitive Behavioral Therapy for Military Populations
Amount: $1,967, 035
Sponsor: US Army Medical Research and Materiel Command
Period of Performance: 36 Months

David Rudd, Ph.D. from Texas Tech University leads the Brief Cognitive Behavioral Therapy for Military Populations project. This program will examine the effectiveness of Brief Cognitive-Behavior Therapy (B-CBT), a 12-session modification of the previously tested and empirically supported approach to treating suicidality, as a psychotherapeutic treatment of suicidality among military personnel through a randomized clinical trial. The approach for this study will involve 150 participants who will be randomly assigned to one of two conditions: B-CBT (experimental condition) or treatment as usual (control condition-the existing outpatient treatment currently available at Fort Carson, CO). Participants are assessed with a clinician-administered interview and self-report scales obtained during intake at 1, 3, 6, 12, 18, and 24- month intervals.

Brief Intervention to Reduce Suicide Risk in Military Service Members and Veterans
Amount: $2,671, 337
Sponsor: US Army Medical Research and Materiel Command
Period of Performance: 36 Months

The Brief Intervention to Reduce Suicide Risk in Military Service Members and Veterans research project is a collaboration among five institutions: (1) VA VISN 2 Center of Excellence at Canandaigua VAMC (Dr. Diane Currier & Dr. Kerry Knox); (2) Columbia University (Dr. Barbara Stanley); (3) VA VISN 19 Mental Illness Research Education and Clinical Center (MIRECC; Dr. Lisa Brenner); (4) USUHS and Walter Reed Army Medical Center (Dr. Marjan Holloway); and (5) University of Pennsylvania and Philadelphia VAMC (Dr. Gregory Brown). The first aim of the study is to evaluate the efficacy of a safety planning intervention on suicide ideation, suicide-related coping, and attitudes toward help seeking for hospitalized military personnel at high suicide risk. The second aim of the study is to evaluate the effectiveness of a safety planning intervention on suicide attempts, suicide ideation, and attendance in outpatient mental health and substance abuse intervention programs, and suicide-related coping for veterans at high suicide risk in emergency department (ED) settings.

Components of Effective Suicide Prevention in the Air Force
Amount: $2,124,049
Sponsor: NIMH and Air Force Medical Operations Agency/SGHW
Period of Performance: 08/24/2006—05/30/2011

The University of Rochester has conducted ongoing evaluation of the Air Force Suicide Prevention program since its inception in 1997. Dr. Kerry Knox leads this project, which examines the implementation of the program and changes in Service suicide rates. Dr. Knox's ongoing research has resulted in two significant publications. The first, published in 2003, in the British Medical Journal, "Risk of suicide and related adverse outcomes after exposure to a suicide prevention program in the US Air Force: cohort study," found a decrease in suicide rates associated with program implementation. The second, published in May 2010, in the American Journal of Public Health, "The US Air Force Suicide Prevention Program: Implications for Public Health Policy," found the long-term effectiveness of this program depends on extensive implementation and effective monitoring of implementation. Suicides can be reduced through a multilayered, overlapping approach that encompasses key prevention domains and tracks implementation of program activities. The goal of this study is to conduct a prospective, longitudinal study of a sustained suicide prevention program in a dynamic population, the Air Force. This continues research on suicide prevention in the Air Force through the measurement of multiple indicators of four core functional components of program dissemination and implementation. The study models the effects of levels of program dissemination and implementation on rates of suicide and related adverse mental health outcomes. Systematic monitoring of compliance with the Air Force's Suicide Prevention Program allows investigation of the relationship between dissemination, implementation, and positive mental health outcomes for Air Force personnel, with a major focus on the effectiveness of the program resulting in sustained reductions in suicide rates.

Deployment-Related Factors Associated With Suicidal Behaviors
Funding: University Intramural Support
Sponsor: Uniformed Services University of the Health Sciences—New Faculty Startup
Period of Performance: 2009—2010

The purpose of this retrospective de-identified dissertation study, being conducted by Capt Shannon Branlund at USUHS, under the supervision of Dr. Marjan Holloway, is to access existing population-based databases to examine factors that may be associated with suicide behavior in active duty military personnel participating in OIF/OEF operations. The primary aims are to (1) evaluate the relationship between deployment-related factors, psychological risk factors, and suicide ideation, and (2) investigate differences in deployment experience and clinical symptomatology among Service Members who have died by suicide, those who have expressed suicide ideation, and those with no suicide behavior. An additional aim is to examine potential deployment-related mediators in the relationship between suicide ideation and suicide death. The study will use data obtained from deployment-related health assessments, the Defense Medical Surveillance System, and the Air Force and USMC Suicide Prevention Offices. It is hoped that the study findings will contribute to our understanding of the ways deployment-related factors interact to influence suicide behavior among military Service Members following deployment.

Drug-Related Overdoses Among a Military Population
Amount: $282,040
Sponsor: US Army Medical Research and Materiel Command
Period of Performance: 18 Months

Investigator Toby Cooper, PharmD, BCPS, R.Ph. from Darnell Army Medical Center (DAMC) in Fort Hood, TX, leads the Drug-Related Overdoses Among a Military Population research study. The goal of this research is to measure socio-demographic and clinical diagnostic correlates of medication abuse and demographic characteristics of patients, contrasting post-deployed OEF/OIF Soldiers and non-deployed personnel. This study also will determine the factors associated with deployment status among patients with medication overdose. This study is a longitudinal, retrospective epidemiological multivariable approach and regression of OEF/OIF deployment status on socio-demographic and clinical variables.

High-Risk Suicidal Behavior in Veterans—Assessment of Predictors and Efficacy of Dialectical Behavior Therapy (DBT)
Amount: $1,279, 912
Sponsor: US Army Medical Research and Materiel Command
Period of Performance: 36 Months

This research program is led by Dr. Marianne Goodman of the James J. Peters VA Medical Center, Bronx, NY. The overall purpose of this project is to test whether DBT can be applied to veterans irrespective of personality diagnosis. This study aims to accomplish the following: (1) examine the efficacy of a 6-month treatment with standard DBT compared with treatment as usual (TAU) in 120 veterans recently discharged from an acute psychiatric inpatient stay with high risk suicidal behavior; (2) recruit veterans recently discharged from an acute psychiatric inpatient hospitalization and compare 150 veterans with high-risk suicidal behavior to 150 veterans without such behavior in symptom domains focusing on interpersonal functioning and resiliency; and (3) explore the effect of DBT on the candidate intermediate symptoms of interpersonal functioning and resiliency associated with high risk suicidal behavior. The study design is a randomized control trial (RCT) of 150 veterans with high-risk behavior and 150 without high-risk behavior. Participants will receive not only 6 months of TAU versus DBT but also a battery of assessments at months 6, 12, and 18.

Inpatient Post-Admission Cognitive Therapy (PACT) for the Prevention of Suicide Attempts: A Pilot Study
Amount: $60,000
Sponsor: National Alliance for Research on Schizophrenia and Depression
Period of Performance: 24 Months

Dr. Marjan Holloway at USUHS leads this pilot study of Inpatient Post-Admission Cognitive Therapy (PACT) for the Prevention of Suicide Attempts. The pilot trial of an adapted cognitive behavioral intervention titled, Post-Admission Cognitive Therapy (PACT), is expected to show promise in reducing not only the likelihood of post-hospitalization suicide attempt behavior but also the psychological risk factors associated with suicide (e.g., depression, hopelessness, suicide ideation, and post-traumatic symptoms). The proposed design is a randomized controlled pilot trial with blinded outcome assessments. Twenty-four individuals over age 18 who were hospitalized at the Walter Reed Army Medical Center's Inpatient Psychiatry Unit following a suicide attempt will be enrolled in the study. Eligible participants will be assigned randomly to either a PACT condition or a control condition. Both groups will receive enhanced usual care and will participate in a 1-, 2-, and 3-month follow-up. If PACT demonstrates to be clinically feasible, acceptable, and associated with preliminary evidence of improvement in symptoms relative to the control condition, a larger, more adequately powered randomized controlled trial will be proposed to definitively determine the efficacy of PACT.

Optimizing Screening and Risk Assessment for Suicide Risk in the US Military
Amount: $753,159
Sponsor: US Army Medical Research and Materiel Command
Period of Performance: 36 Months

The Optimizing Screening and Risk Assessment for Suicide Risk in the US Military research program is led by Mr. Thomas Joiner of Florida State University in Tallahassee, FL. The aim of this study is to compare promising brief and superior risk factor assessment candidates and determine which tool or combination of tools optimally predicts future suicide-related indices. This study included Army Recruiter Course (ARC) attendees as participants. The approach for this project will utilize innovative research materials that will be integrated into an existing survey and assessment infrastructure.

Pilot Trial of Inpatient Cognitive Therapy for the Prevention of Suicide in Military Personnel with Acute Stress Disorder or Post-Traumatic Stress Disorder
Amount: $457,609
Sponsor: DoD Congressionally Directed Medical Research Program
Period of Performance: 36 Months

The pilot trial of cognitive therapy is led by Dr. Marjan Holloway at USUHS. The broad objective of this research is to effectively utilize a unique window of opportunity during the hospitalization period following a recent suicide attempt to deliver a brief and targeted cognitive behavioral intervention for traumatized individuals with diagnoses of Acute Stress Disorder (ASD) or PTSD. A total of 50 traumatized patients hospitalized at the WRAMC for a recent suicide attempt will be randomly assigned to one of two conditions: (1) Post-Admission Cognitive Therapy + Enhanced Usual Care (PACT+EUC) or (2) Enhanced Usual Care (EUC).

The PACT+EUC condition will consist of six 1-hr individual cognitive therapy sessions administered over 3 days. The EUC condition will consist of the usual care patients receive at an inpatient facility during their hospitalization in addition to assessment services provided by the study.

The primary outcome variable is the number of subsequent suicide attempts. Secondary outcome measures include the severity of depression, hopelessness, suicide ideation, and posttraumatic symptoms. Patients in both conditions will be assessed on the dependent measures at baseline and at 1-, 2-, and 3- month follow-up intervals.

Posttraumatic Stress Disorder, Substance Abuse and Self Harm: Mediating Relationships with Respect to Combat Stress
Amount: $218,000
Sponsor: US Army Medical Research and Materiel Command
Period of Performance: 18 Months

This research program is led by Dr. Valerie Stander from the Naval Health Research Center (NHRC). The aim for this research is to investigate the possibility that the development of PTSD and substance use problems may mediate the effects of combat trauma on suicidality and general self-harm behaviors among Marine Corps and Navy Service members.

The methodology for this research is a multivariate structural equation modeling approach applied to existing Combat Stress and Substance Use survey data, to assess a mediated model of the effects of combat stress on suicidality, self-harm behaviors, and relationships among both demographics and primary research variables.

Process Improvement for the Management of Suicide Risk
Amount: $1,250,000
Sponsor: Warrior Resilience Program (WRP)
Period of Performance: 36 Months

The Process Improvement for the Management of Suicide Risk study is a collaboration between Dr. David Jobes (Catholic University) and the Army WWRP located at Fort Sam Houston, TX. The purpose for this study is to improve procedures for clinically assessing mitigating suicidal risk among patients referred for outpatient behavioral health and among soldiers assigned to the Warrior in Transition Battalion (WTB).

RAND Report
Funding: $525,000
Sponsor: Office of the Secretary of Defense, the Joint Staff and the DoD Intelligence Community
Period of Performance: Completed

The RAND report research project is a collaboration with RAND Health Center for Military Health Policy Research and the Forces and Resources Policy Center of the RAND National Defense Research Institute.

The purpose of this project was to review the current evidence detailing suicide epidemiology in the military and to identify "best-practice" suicide-prevention programs. Additionally, this project described and cataloged suicide-prevention activities within the DoD, across each Service and provided recommendations to ensure that the DoD and each Service has a comprehensive suicide-prevention program. This data was collected via a thorough review of all relevant policies and materials, conducting interviews with individuals knowledgeable of specific suicide prevention activities within the DoD and subject matter experts within the field of suicidology. The report is awaiting final clearance prior to its release to the public.

Texas Youth Suicide Prevention Project
Amount: $840,000
Sponsor: HHS' Substance Abuse and Mental Health Services Administration (SAMHSA)
Period of Performance: 36 Months

The Texas Youth Suicide Prevention Project is a collaboration between the San Antonio Center for HealthCare Services (CHCS), Brooke Army Medical Center Pediatrics (BAMC), and the Warrior Resilience Program (WRP). The project location is BAMC and the Fort Sam Houston schools. The purpose is early detection of military youth (grades 5 -12) at risk for depression or suicide and referral for behavioral health services.

The Association between Suicide and OEF/OIF Deployment History
Amount: $1,961,003
Sponsor: US Army Medical Research and Materiel Command
Period of Performance: 36 Months

The Association between Suicide and OEF/OIF Deployment History research project is led by Dr. Mark Reger from Madigan Army Medical Center. The aim of this study is to compare suicide rates among non-Veterans and Veterans with and without a history of OEF/OIF deployment. Additionally, the project seeks to determine whether active duty and veteran National Guardsmen and Reservists with a history of OEF/OIF deployment are at increased risk of suicide compared to non-Veterans and post-deployed service members/Veterans.

This study will also examine the relationship between suicide rates and rates of deaths of undetermined intent among non-Veterans and Service Members/Veterans with and without a history of OEF/OIF deployment.

The purpose of this study is to develop a database in collaboration with other federal agencies to provide population-based estimates of the rates of suicide among service members from the beginning of OIF/OEF.

Typologies of Air Force Suicides
Funding: University Intramural Support
Sponsor: Uniformed Services University of the Health Sciences—New Faculty Startup
Period of Performance: 2009—2011

The purpose of the current dissertation study, being conducted by First Lieutenant Jeffery Martin, under the supervision of Dr. Marjan Holloway, is to examine existing surveillance data of Air Force suicides to determine whether a useful typological model of suicide could be developed for the Air Force.

The major aims of the current study are as follows: (1) describe the characteristics of Air Force suicides between 1996 and 2006, (2) compare characteristics of Air Force suicides before the onset of OEF with suicides occurring afterward, (3) employ hierarchical cluster analysis to determine the presence of homogeneous subgroups based on demographic and psychosocial characteristics, and (4) evaluate the stability and external validity of these subgroups.

The study will use data obtained from the Suicide Event Surveillance System (SESS), which is a database that the Air Force maintains on active duty suicides. It is hoped that findings from the study will explain potential pathways to military suicide and, through this understanding, will enhance military screening, prevention, and intervention efforts.

APPENDIX J. RECOMMENDED LEVEL OF RESPONSIBILITY TO IMPLEMENT TASK FORCE RECOMMENDATIONS

	Recommendation	Congress	DoD/ OSD	Joint Staff	Service
	Focus Area 1: Organization and Leadership				
Strategic Initiative 1A:	Create, restructure, and resource suicide prevention offices at the OSD, Service, installation, and unit levels to achieve unity of effort.				
Recommendation 1	Build, staff, and resource a central OSD Suicide Prevention Office that can effectively develop, implement, integrate, and evaluate suicide prevention policies, procedures, and surveillance activities.		•		
	This office should reside within the Office of the Under Secretary of Defense for Personnel and Readiness and be granted the coordinating authority that enables strategic suicide prevention oversight from OSD, through the Services, and down to the unit level.				
Recommendation 2	Prioritize resources to adequately staff, fund, and organize the headquarters-level suicide prevention offices, within each Service, to successfully meet all current requirements.				•
Recommendation 3	Services should require full-time civilian suicide prevention coordinators at all installations identified by major commands. Major commands must facilitate the consistent implementation of Service suicide prevention strategy down to the small unit level and installations must ensure appropriate resourcing of this position in order to fully support both DoD suicide prevention policy, and Service policy and programs.				•
Recommendation 4	Sufficiently resource suicide prevention coalitions that strategically integrate installation and major command suicide prevention efforts and informs the Service-level program office. This coalition should also function to coordinate support services through collaboration on overarching social/behavioral risk problems on the installation.				•
Recommendation 5	Require full-time suicide prevention program coordinators at each MTF (or regionalized when covering several non-hospital MTFs) to facilitate the standardized implementation of Service suicide prevention strategy on behalf of the MTF commander and ensure the adherence to standardized policies and practices.		•		•
Recommendation 6	Direct unit-level suicide prevention program officers to facilitate the implementation of Service policies.				•
Strategic Initiative 1B:	Equip and empower leaders (provide them tools) to establish a culture that fostersprevention as well as early recognition and intervention.				
Recommendation 7	Strengthen and reinvigorate the fundamentals of military garrison leadership at the unit level with a focus on supervisor-subordinate interactions and mentoring. Ensure that frontline supervisor training is mandatory, occurs prior to assuming a supervisory role, and includes critical skills building in interpersonal relationships.				•
Recommendation 8	Ensure that professional military education, ranging from basic training to Senior Service				•

Appendix J. (Continued)

	Recommendation	Congress	DoD/ OSD	Joint Staff	Service
	Schools, develops leaders with the interpersonal and leadership skills required to fulfill their leadership and mentoring responsibilities, as well as promotes the wellbeing and total fitness of the Service Members under their charge.				
Recommendation 9	Maintain a sufficiently small front-line supervisor-to-subordinate ratio to ensure the person-centered leadership functions can occur.				•
Recommendation 10	Add validated behavioral risk questions to unit climate surveys to help commanders detect relative elevations in behavioral risk across their military units and respond with appropriate preventive measures. Mandate the use of unit climate and risk surveys annually and upon accepting and relinquishing command.		•		•
Recommendation 11	Develop monthly risk reports from a multitude of sources and services to create a snapshot of the unit and the ability to compare a commander's unit with like units across the				•
	Service and at the installation, while also allowing for the identification of positive and negative trends with reference to risk behaviors by members in that unit.				
Recommendation 12	Disseminate and enforce "zero tolerance" policies that prohibit prejudice, discrimination, and public humiliation towards individuals who are responsibly addressing emotional, psychological, relational, spiritual, and behavioral issues; as well as towards those seeking help to increase their psychological fitness and		•	•	•
	operational readiness. Support these policies by holding leaders and supervisors accountable and by sustained communications campaigns.				
Strategic Initiative 1C:	Develop strategic communications that promote life, normalize "help-seeking behaviors,"and support DoD suicide prevention strategies.				
Recommendation 13	Develop and implement sustainable training programs for PAOs serving Service leaders, senior leaders, and installation commanders in crafting health-promoting messages that support the goals and objectives of the		•		•
	Services' suicide prevention and health promotion programs; avoid counterproductive or dangerous messages whenever making statements or discussing suicide-related information or statistics.				
Recommendation 14	Instruct PAOs to disseminate nationally recognized recommendations for reporting on suicide as they interact with news media on the subject of suicide.		•		•
Recommendation 15	Develop and disseminate communication guidelines to commanders for use in the wake of a local suicide event.		•		•
Strategic Initiative 1D:	Reduce stigma and overcome military cultural and leadership barriers to seeking help.				
Recommendation 16	Develop an aggressive Stigma Reduction Campaign Plan, communications effort, and implement policies to root out stigma and discrimination. Follow scientifically based health communications principles in these campaigns.			•	•

	Recommendation	Congress	DoD/ OSD	Joint Staff	Service
Recommendation 17	Promote values that encourage seeking the assistance of chaplains, healthcare, and behavioral healthcare professionals to enhance spiritual, physical, and psychological fitness.			•	•
Recommendation 18	Develop and implement campaigns to inculcate values and norms aligned with promoting the well-being, connectedness, and psychological and spiritual fitness of Service Members. Use well-planned, multi-year communications campaigns at the DoD and Service levels, employing the best of health communications science as part of that effort.		•		•
Recommendation 19	Target a specific component of the communications campaign to ensure that		•		•
	Service Members who hold security clearances and the mental health providers who see them are aware of policies that exclude reporting certain instances of mental health care on the SF-86.				
Recommendation 20	Adjust manning levels, especially in elite units and certain military occupational specialties, to support developing and maintaining comprehensive fitness by all members.		•		•
Recommendation 21	Infuse curricula for all levels of military specialty training with expectations that even the most effective Service Members will occasionally experience difficulties that require temporary interruptions in their qualifications for full duty. Teach that the responsibility of others in the unit is to support them during those times.				•
Recommendation 22	Discourage and refrain from use of the term "malingering" in association with suicide-related behaviors. Ensure DoD and Service suicide prevention policies and guidelines eliminate using the word "malingering".		•		•
Strategic Initiative 1E:	Standardize Suicide Prevention Policies and Procedures.				
Recommendation 23	Implement DoD and Service guidance for commanders and military recruit instructors that addresses the management of suicide-related behaviors during basic training.		•		•
Recommendation 24	Develop and implement a DoD-wide policy requiring immediate command notification and chain of care (or chain of custody) for individuals who become aware they are being investigated for a criminal or other serious offense, immediately after they confess to a crime, and/or soon after they are arrested and taken into custody.		•		
Recommendation 25	Establish clear DoD, Joint and Service guidance for removal and subsequent re-issue of military weapon and ammunition for Service Members recognized to be at risk for suicide.		•		
	The guidance should emphasize a collaborative, team approach to the decision-making process and specify documentation requirements.				
	Focus Area 2: Wellness Enhancement and Training				
Strategic Initiative 2A:	Enhance well-being, mental fitness, life skills, and resiliency.				

Appendix J. (Continued)

	Recommendation	Congress	DoD/ OSD	Joint Staff	Service
Recommendation 26	Improve access to, and promote utilization of, state-of-the-art training in critical life skills (e.g., financial management, communication, marriage and family relationships, anger management, and conflict resolution).				•
Recommendation 27	Expand the practice of embedding behavioral health providers in operational units. Conduct studies to determine the range of effective staffing ratios for embedded providers.				•
Strategic Initiative 2B:	Reduce stress on the force and on military families.				
Recommendation 28	Balance uniformed end-strength with operational requirements by either increasing military end-strength or decreasing operational commitments.	•	•		
Recommendation 29	Recommendation Provide sufficient, high-quality dwell time for redeploying Service Members in keeping with the most current military health research. Initial post-deployment dwell time should ensure an initial period (of at least several months) in which Service Members can restore their wellbeing, and should not include extended temporary duty (TDY) or extended "gear-up" training for the next deployment.	•	•	•	•
Recommendation 30	Reduce operations tempo and day-to-day work requirements on individuals and units to sustainable levels that support the wellness of Service Members and their families. Create white space in training schedules, especially in post-deployment periods.		•		•
Recommendation 31	Review in-garrison military training requirements with the goal of eliminating and/or combining training, thereby reducing the time burden on units and Service Members.				•
Strategic Initiative 2C:	Transform suicide prevention training of Service Members, leaders, and families to enhance skills.				
Recommendation 32	Develop DoD and Service-level comprehensive suicide prevention training strategies. Develop and disseminate state-of-the-art training curricula addressing the specific knowledge, skills, and attitudes required of each sub-population in the military community. Incorporate industry-standard evaluation practices throughout the development and dissemination phases. Focus efforts on skills-based training.		•		•
Recommendation 33	Target and train families (including parents, siblings, significant others, and next of kin) as a suicide prevention training strategy, and consider it an important part of the chain of care for Service Members. Family members should be educated and trained to recognize the signs of stress and distress, to know whom to call for advice, and to understand how to respond in emergencies.				•
Recommendation 34	Develop strategies to locate and remain in contact with families during every phase of the deployment cycle. Develop and disseminate pre-deployment and reintegration education and training programs germane to suicide prevention for family members.				•

	Recommendation	Congress	DoD/ OSD	Joint Staff	Service
Recommendation 35	Proactively seek opportunities to collaborate with other federal agencies in their efforts to support military families.		•		•
	Focus Area 3: Access to, and Delivery of, Quality Care				
Strategic Initiative 3A:	Ensure available and reliable access to high-quality behavioral healthcare.				
Recommendation 36	Implement policies that optimize access to care for all Service Members which are specifically designed for behavioral health care, and monitor access standards closely for compliance.		•		•
Recommendation 37	Train all caregivers in the governing rules applicable to appropriate and necessary information sharing among providers, outside agencies, and with Service Members' commands.				•
Recommendation 38	Develop interdisciplinary treatment plans for Service Members at risk for suicidal behavior.				•
Recommendation 39	Implement coordination of care plans across longitudinal lines (e.g., permanent change of station, temporary change of station, deployment and redeployment transitions, temporary duty with other units, release from active duty, demobilization, confinement, hospitalization, and extended leave periods).				•
Recommendation 40	Establish multidisciplinary case management teams to ensure the highest quality of coordinated care by the team of commander, clinical provider, and non-clinical care provider.				•
Strategic Initiative 3B:	Leverage and coordinate military community-based services, as well as local civilian community services (especially with respect to the Reserve Component).				
Recommendation 41	Optimize and coordinate community-based services to leverage their capabilities to enhance protective factors for Service Members.				•
Recommendation 42	Promote and utilize coordinated community outreach and awareness activities provided by clinicians and other installation-based care providers to improve access to care and reduce stigma.				•
Recommendation 43	Encourage Service Members to have annual face-to-face "conferences" with chaplains for the purpose of resolving questions of guilt and to obtain referrals to appropriate caregivers for other concerns beyond the chaplain's scope of expertise and experience.				•
Recommendation 44	Develop a comprehensive policy to promote systematic and regular communication among clinical and non-clinical providers.				•
Strategic Initiative 3C:	Leverage and coordinate military community-based services, as well as local civilian community services (especially with respect to the Reserve Component).				
Recommendation 45	Manage care across transition points and monitor Service Members identified as being at- risk for suicide.				•
Recommendation 46	Assess Military OneSource capabilities to ensure a seamless transition of care system is established for suicidal or at-risk Service Members who utilize their services. This transitional care system needs to take into account challenges involving medical documentation, timeline of transition, and maximizing Service Member compliance with the transition plan.				•

Appendix J. (Continued)

	Recommendation	Congress	DoD/ OSD	Joint Staff	Service
Recommendation 47	Develop, evaluate, and more widely disseminate peer-to-peer and other programs that intentionally promote not only connectedness but also risk identification and response among Reserve Component Service Members.		•		•
Recommendation 48	Promote easy access to evidence-based treatments and community support services for post-deployment Reserve Component Service Members.		•		•
Recommendation 49	Ensure all Reserve Component Service Members receive face-to-face behavioral health checks post-deployment/post-demobilization and before being remobilized, with an emphasis on connecting them with professional services during the post-deployment phase.		•		•
Recommendation 50	Provide guidance on how behavioral health providers and commanders should best communicate with each other to promote effective suicide prevention practices for Service Members.		•		•
Recommendation 51	Establish and use interdisciplinary "human factors" type boards (emphasizing topics like physical, social, behavioral, psychological, nutritional, environmental, spiritual, and medical health) on all installations to coordinate suicide prevention care for at-risk Service Members.		•		•
Recommendation 52	Take steps to make "mental fitness" commensurate with "physical fitness" within military culture as a core value of military life. Ensure every Service Member receives a mental fitness assessment and appropriate wellness education as part of his or her periodic heath assessment.				•
Recommendation 53	Integrate behavioral health treatment teams into DoD primary care settings to overcome stigma and increase the likelihood of access to care; as well as to establish an early intervention approach to suicide prevention. Where this is not possible, train primary care providers and their staff in the assessment and management (and triage) of acute suicide risk patients.				•
Recommendation 54	Develop a standard and systematic medical documentation system to identify high-risk patients and track the care provided. Continually review and update the record (documentation).		•		
Recommendation 55	Suicide watch should be used only as a last resort and only until appropriate mental healthcare becomes available. Provide consistent guidance to units for these exceptional instances, as well as "just in time" training (e.g., online training). If units have a suicide prevention coordinator, the management of these rare instances could fall to that individual's responsibility. A suicide watch training program should be developed and similarly instituted.				•
Strategic Initiative 3D:	Standardize effective crisis intervention services and hotlines.				
Recommendation 56	Provide clear direction and consistent messaging regarding the promotion and usage of the National Suicide Prevention Lifeline 1- 800-273-TALK (8255)		•		•

	Recommendation	Congress	DoD/ OSD	Joint Staff	Service
	as a national suicide prevention hotline resource available to all Service Members and their families, as well as the use of local crisis hotlines (or information lines) focusing on specific populations.				
Recommendation 57	Formalize existing interconnectedness of the DCoE Outreach Call Center, National Suicide Prevention Lifeline, and Military OneSource to enable each agency too quickly and effectively route calls to appropriate responders. Ensure ongoing quality review and quality improvement efforts focused on emergency rescue situations, follow-up referrals for callers at-risk, and linkages with community providers of crisis services (e.g., mobile outreach teams).		•		
Recommendation 58	Optimize the availability of suicide hotline services to deployed Service Members using the same National Suicide Prevention Lifeline number to ensure best response capabilities.				•
Strategic Initiative 3E:	Ensure all "helping professionals" are trained in the competencies to deliver evidencebased care for the assessment, management, and treatment of suicide-related behaviors.				
Recommendation 59	Develop clinical practice guidelines to promote the utilization of evidence-based practices for the assessment, management, and treatment of suicide-related behaviors.		•		•
Recommendation 60	Dedicate sufficient behavioral health resources to military health facilities to allow for timely mental health assessment and treatment.		•		•
Recommendation 61	Train all military healthcare providers (including behavioral health providers) and chaplains on evidence-informed suicide risk assessment, management, and treatment planning. Create and provide continuing education tailored to their specialty and area of expertise.				•
Strategic Initiative 3F:	Develop effective postvention programs to support families, Service Members, and unit leaders after a suicide.				
Recommendation 62	Incorporate postvention programs targeted at the decedent's military unit, family and community after a tragedy or loss to reduce the risk of suicide. Postvention efforts must address Service Members affected by a significant loss, especially after a fallen comrade's death in combat or in garrison when the unit is impacted. Unit-level postvention efforts must focus on effective debriefing and prevention when they are impacted by a significant tragedy or loss.			•	•
Recommendation 63	Train first responders, chaplains, casualty notification officers, and family interviewers on how to best respond to suicide and suicide-related events when working with families or next of kin.				•
Recommendation 64	Provide families with comprehensive emotional support following the death of a loved one by suicide. All those affected, including significant others and battle buddies, should have access to resources that will help them cope with traumatic grief, such as the peer-based support organization Tragedy Assistance Program for Survivors (TAPS) and the Department of Veterans Affairs (VA) Vet Centers. These organizations offer free services to all who are grieving, with focused support for suicide loss.			•	•

Appendix J. (Continued)

	Recommendation	Congress	DoD/ OSD	Joint Staff	Service
Recommendation 65	Ensure that Service criminal investigation agencies are staffed appropriately with family advocates trained in communicating with family members whose loved ones might have died by suicide. Maintain effective communication with surviving family members during the investigative process.				•
Recommendation 66	Develop a consistent DoD policy on memorials that encourages remembrance based on how the Service Member lived, rather than the manner of death. Use WHO/IASP guidelines to avoid increasing risk through glamorizing death, and SPRC recommendations for conducting memorial services.		•		
	Focus Area 4: Surveillance, Investigations, and Research				
Strategic Initiative 4A:	Conduct comprehensive surveillance aimed at identifying individuals at-risk and informing prevention efforts.				
Recommendation 67	Structure DoD to implement surveillance efforts in a standardized manner, with a core focus on informing and improving suicide prevention activities. The DoDSER must be matured, expanded, and refocused to fulfill this surveillance role.		•		
Recommendation 68	Standardize DoDSER surveillance throughout the DoD, including specification of qualifications of surveyor and required training.		•		
Recommendation 69	Facilitate consistent and fluid access to DMSS by DoDSER for appropriate surveillance purposes that also allows for automatic filling of select data fields as appropriate. Aggregation of surveillance data reported using the DoDSER is intended to inform suicide prevention efforts across DoD and the Services through centralized offices at both levels, thus access to DMSS is essential.		•		
Strategic Initiative 4B:	Standardize investigations of suicides and suicide attempts to identify target areas for prevention policies, procedure,s and programs				
Recommendation 70	Standardize the suicide investigation process across DoD with the sole focus being suicide prevention. The investigation process should be non-attributional, all-inclusive of the days and weeks preceding a suicide or suicide attempt, and be reported in a redacted form, from the Services to OSD, to maintain confidentiality.		•		
Recommendation 71	Institute a modified psychological autopsy and root cause analysis protocol with a standardized process of reporting to a centralized office at the Service and OSD-level. The results of modified standardized investigative procedures can be used to refine and modify the DoDSER and improve surveillance methods. A modified investigatory protocol must include a focus on last days of life; development of a pathway to death that enables identification of potential points of intervention; interaction between person and environment; and access to all currently collected surveillance, as well as medical and personnel records.		•		•
Recommendation 72	Place investigative responsibilities in the Safety Division offices of each Service to leverage the expertise, external party team management experience, protected (confidential) approach, and effectiveness of		•		

	Recommendation	Congress	DoD/ OSD	Joint Staff	Service
	aviation mishap investigations.				
Recommendation 73	Review legal protections and make recommendations to Congress, as necessary, to ensure protected status of investigations.		•		•
Recommendation 74	Recommend legislation to create procedures that facilitate the timely transfer and sharing of civilian autopsy findings on Service Members (Active Duty, Reserve Component, National Guard) with the Armed Forces Medical				•
	Examiner's Office. Evaluate the appropriateness and necessity of access to other civilian findings to improve the tracking of members of the Armed Forces at-risk.				
Strategic Initiative 4C:	Ensure that all initiatives and programs have a program evaluation component.				
Recommendation 75	Every suicide prevention program initiated by DoD or the Services must contain a program evaluation component.		•		•
Strategic Initiative 4D:	Support and incorporate ongoing research to inform evidence-based suicide prevention practices.				
Recommendation 76	Create a unified, strategic, and comprehensive DoD plan for research in military suicide prevention: (1) ensuring that the DoD's military suicide prevention research portfolio is thoughtfully planned to cover topics in prevention, intervention, and postvention; and (2) assisting investigators by creating a DoD regulatory and human protections consultation board that is responsible primarily for moving suicide-related research forward in an expedited manner.		•		

APPENDIX K. GLOSSARY

Active Duty—full-time duty in the active service of a uniformed service, including active duty training (full-time training duty, annual training duty, and full-time attendance at a school designated as a military service school [e.g., United States Military Academy]).

Armed Forces Health Longitudinal Technology Application (AHLTA)—Department of Defense's (DoD) electronic medical record/information system

Battlemind Training—Army program using resiliency training that assists the Soldiers transitioning from the combat-zone to the "home zone." Warfighting skills and the "battle" frame of reference sustain the soldier in the operational setting. It is critical to transition successfully because effectiveness at home is as important as effectiveness in combat.

Billet—a personnel position or assignment that one person may fill.

Casualty Notification Officer—a specially trained officer and enlisted personnel charged with personally notifying family members about the death of an active duty Service Member. They provide initial guidance and support in assisting families deal with the loss of their military member.

Chain of Command—the succession of commanding officers from a superior to a subordinate through which command is exercised.

Coordinating Authority—a commander or individual who is assigned responsibility for coordinating specific functions or activities involving forces of two or more military departments, two or more point force components, or two or more forces of the same

Service. The commander or individual has authority to compel agreement. If the essential agreement cannot be obtained, the matter is referred to an appointing authority. Coordinating authority is more applicable to planning and similar activities than to operations.

Dependent/Immediate Family—a Service Member's spouse, children who are unmarried and under 21 years of age or who, regardless of age, are physically or mentally incapable of self-support; dependent parents, including step and legally adoptive parents of the Service Member's spouse; and dependent brothers and sisters, including step and legally adoptive brothers and sisters. See also Beneficiary.

Direct Care—health care for active duty and other classes of beneficiaries provided inside the military treatment facility (MTF) system (e.g., care received at National Naval Medical Center Bethesda, Landstuhl Regional Medical Center, health care provided to forces deployed to combatant sites, and other locations overseas).

Family Member(s)—relatives of Service Members who may or may not be beneficiaries. This group may include Service Member parents, step-parents, grandparents, siblings, aunts, uncles, nieces, nephews, and cousins.

Health Care Provider—a broad term encompassing licensed clinical professionals (e.g., physicians, psychologists, advanced practice nurses, licensed clinical social workers). Commonly, health care providers, who have prescription writing privileges, may include trained and licensed professionals such as registered nurses

Individual Medical Readiness (IMR)—a means for assessing an individual Service Member's readiness level against established metrics to determine medical deploy ability in support of contingency operations.

Installation—a grouping of facilities, located in the same vicinity, which supports particular functions. Installations may be elements of a base.

Installation Services—are designed to offer a range services, community resources, and other necessary information unique to Service Members and their families. Each Service has oversight of its respective FSCs. The Army is the US Army Community and Family Support Center (CFSC), the Navy is the Fleet and Family Support Center, the Air Force is referred to as Airmen and Family Readiness Center, and the Marine Corps is referred to as Marine and Family Services.

Marine for Life (M4L)—a program that provides transition assistance to Marines who honorably leave active service and return to civilian life and provide support to injured Marines and their families.

Marine Operational Stress—Surveillance Program (MOSSP)—an integrated progression of deployment cycle-specific educational briefs, health assessments, and leadership tolls designed to prevent, identify early, and manage effectively combat/operational stress injuries at all levels.

Medical Evaluation Board (MEB)—physical and /or mental health problems that are expected to render a Service Member unable to fully perform his/her duties exceeding 90 days require an MEB. A Limited Duty Board is a type of MEB that places a member in a less than full duty status for 6 months. If a Service Member has a condition that is incompatible with military duty or that results in disqualification from worldwide deployment for more than 12 months, he/she will be referred to a Physical Evaluation Board (PEB).

Military Health System—a health system that supports the military mission by fostering, protecting, sustaining, and restoring health.

Military OneSource—a toll-free, 24/7 clearinghouse service that provides information and resources to active duty personnel and their beneficiaries.

Military Treatment Facility (MTF)—a military hospital or clinic on or near a military base.

Network—healthcare services available through TRICARE outside the Direct Care System (e.g., Medical Treatment Facility).

Operational Stress Control and Readiness (OSCAR) Program—a program in which Navy behavioral health personnel are embedded with Marine Corps personnel involved in direct operational combat settings.

Physical Evaluation Board (PEB)—the PEB provides a formal fitness-for-duty and disability determination that may return the Service Member to duty (with or without assignment limitations), place the member on the temporary disabled/retirement list, separate the Service Member from active duty, or medically retire the member. These recommendations are forwarded to a central medical board. The Service Member is permitted to have legal counsel at these hearings and can appeal these recommendations.

Post-Deployment Health Assessment (PDHA)—a mandatory procedure for each Service Member who is redeploying from combatant operations. The PDHA consists of two parts: (1) each returning Service Member must fill out form DD 2796, entitled the PDHA; and (2) the Service Member must have a face-to-face interview with a trained health care provider. This action must be completed within 5 days before or after redeployment. If this is not possible, the member's commander should ensure that it is completed, processed, and filed in the permanent medical record within 30 days of the Service Member's return.

Post-Deployment Health Reassessment (PDHRA)—a mandatory program designed to identify and address health concerns, with a specific emphasis on mental health issues that might have emerged since deployment and redeployment. The PDHRA form (DD 2900), which also is web-based, can be filled out online, provides a second health assessment for the 3 to 6 month period after redeployment. These forms must be reviewed by a healthcare provider, and any follow-up with the Service Member must be undertaken.

Post-Traumatic Stress Disorder (PTSD)—an anxiety disorder that may occur following an experience or witnessing a traumatic event. A traumatic event is a life-threatening event such as military combat, natural disasters, terrorist incidents, serious accidents, or sexual assault in adult or childhood. Most survivors of trauma return to normal given a little time; however, some people will have stress reactions that do not go away on their own or may even worsen over time. These individuals may develop PTSD.

Redeployment—the withdrawal and redistribution of forces; to transfer to another place or job.

Reserve Component—the Army National Guard, Army Reserve, Naval Reserve, Marine Corps Reserve, Air National Guard, Air Force Reserve, Coast Guard Reserve, and Reserve Corps of the United States Public Health Service.

Service Member—a person appointed, enlisted, or inducted into a branch of the military services, including Reserve Components (e.g., National Guard), cadets, or midshipmen of the military service academies.

Stigma—the shame or disgrace attached to something regarded as socially unacceptable.

Traumatic Brain Injury (TBI)—a blow or jolt to the head or a penetrating head injury. The injury may be caused by falls, motor vehicle accidents, assaults, and/or other incidents. Blast and concussive events are a leading cause of TBI for active duty military personnel involved in war zones. TBI can temporarily or permanently impair a person's cognitive skills, interfere with emotional well-being, and diminish physical abilities. Persons with TBI also remain at high risk for developing delayed symptoms.

TRICARE—DoD's healthcare plan for active duty, active duty beneficiaries, retirees, and their beneficiaries.

Veterans Health Information Systems and Technology Architecture (VistA)—the Veterans Health Administration electronic medical information/record system.

APPENDIX L. ACRONYMS

AAS	American Association of Suicidology
AD	Active Duty
AFHSC	Armed Forces Health Surveillance Center
AFI	Air Force Instruction
AFIP	Armed Forces Institute of Pathology
AFME	Armed Forces Medical Examiner
AFPAM	Air Force Pamphlet
AHLTA	Armed Forces Health Longitudinal Technology Application
AR	Army Regulation
ASD(HA)	Assistant Secretary of Defense (Health Affairs)
ASER	Army Suicide Event Reports
ASIST	Applied Suicide Intervention Skills Training
B-CBT	Brief Cognitive-Behavior Therapy
CAIB	Community Action Information Board
CDC	Centers for Disease Control and Prevention
CFSC	Community and Family Support Center
CISM	Critical Incident Stress Management
CNA	Center for Naval Analyses
CNO	Chief of Naval Operations
CoE	Center of Excellence
CONUS	Continental United States
COMDTINST	Commandant Instruction
CSF	Comprehensive Soldier Fitness
DAMC	Darnell Army Medical Center
DARPA	Defense Advanced Research Projects Agency
DCoE	Defense Centers of Excellence
DHB	Defense Health Board (formerly the Armed Forces Epidemiological Board)
DMDC	Department of Defense Manpower Data Center
DMSS	Defense Medical Surveillance System
DoD	Department of Defense
DoDI	Department of the Defense Instruction
DoDSER	Department of Defense Suicide Event Report

DON	Department of the Navy
DONSIR	Department of the Navy Suicide Incident Report
DS3	Disabled Soldier Support System
EAP	Employee Assistance Program
EFPB	Executive Force Preservation Board
EO	Executive Order
FSC	Family Support Center
FY	Fiscal Year
GAO	United States Government Accountability Office
GED	Graduation Equivalency Diploma
GMT	General Military Training
HA	Health Affairs
HIPAA	Health Insurance Portability and Accountability Act
HQMC	Headquarters Marine Corps
IASP	International Association for Suicide Prevention
IDS	Integrated Delivery System
IG	Inspector General
IMR	Individual Medical Readiness
IOM	Institute of Medicine
IPT	Integrated Production Team
ITS	Individual Training Standards
JAG	Judge Advocate General
JTF CapMed	Joint Task Force, National Capital Region Medical
LOD	Line of Duty
M4L	Marine for Life
M&RA	Manpower and Reserve Affairs
MCO	Marine Corps Order
ME	Medical Examiner
MEB	Medical Evaluation Board
MEDDAC	US Army Medical Department Activity
MFLC	Military and Family Life Consultant
MHAT	Mental Health Advisory Team
MOA	Memorandum of Agreement
MOSSP	Marine Operational Stress and Surveillance Program
MIRECC	Mental Illness Research Education and Clinical Center
MTF	Military Treatment Facility
NATO	North Atlantic Treaty Organization
NCO	Non-Commissioned Officer
NDAA	National Defense Authorization Act
NHRC	Naval Health Research Center
NIMH	National Institute of Mental Health
NSSP	National Strategy for Suicide Prevention
OAFME	Office of the Armed Forces Medical Examiner
OCCH	Office of Chief of Chaplains
OEF	Operation Enduring Freedom
OIF	Operation Iraqi Freedom

OMNF-I	Office of the Surgeon Multinational Force Iraq
OPNAV	Office of the Chief of Naval Operations
OPNAVINST	Chief of Naval Operations Instructions
OSC	Operational Stress Control
OSCAR	Operational Stress Control and Readiness
OSD	Office of the Secretary of Defense
OTSG	Office of the Surgeon General
PACT	Post-Admission Cognitive Therapy
PAO	Public Affairs Office
PDHA	Post-Deployment Health Assessment
PDHRA	Post-Deployment Health Re-Assessment
PDHRP	Pre- and Post-Deployment Health Reassessment Program
PEB	Physical Evaluation Board
PERSCO	Personnel in Support of Contingency Operations
PFC	Private First Class
PH	Psychological Health
PRP	Personnel Reliability Program
PTS	Post-Traumatic Stress
PTSD	Post-Traumatic Stress Disorder
QPR	Question, Persuade, Refer
RCA	Root Cause Analysis
ROTC	Reserve Officers' Training Corps
SAMHSA	Substance Abuse and Mental Health Services Administration
SAPRO	Sexual Assault Prevention & Response Office
SECNAVINST	Secretary of the Navy Instruction
SESS	Suicide Event Surveillance System
SF	Standard Form
SFC	Spiritual Fitness Check
SFOR	Stabilization Force in Bosnia and Herzegovina
SIAC	Southern Impact Area Control
SPARRC	Suicide Prevention and Risk Reduction Committee
SPC	Suicide Prevention Coordinator
SPPM	Suicide Prevention Program Manager
SPRC	Suicide Prevention Resource Center
STARRS	Study to Assess Risk and Resilience in Service Members
T2	National Center for Telehealth and Technology
TAU	Treatment As Usual
TAPS	Tragedy Assistance Program for Survivors
TBI	Traumatic Brain Injury
TDY	Temporary Duty
UK	United Kingdom
UMT	Unit Ministry Team
UN	United Nations
US	United States
USA	United States Army
USAF	United States Air Force

USCG	United States Coast Guard
USD (P&R)	Under Secretary of Defense (Personnel & Readiness)
USFOR-A	Office of the Command Surgeon US Forces—Afghanistan
USMC	United States Marine Corps
USN	United States Navy
USUHS	Uniformed Services University of the Health Sciences
VA	Department of Veteran Affairs
VHA	Veterans Health Administration
VistA	Veterans Health Information Systems and Technology Architecture
WHO	World Health Organization

APPENDIX M. REFERENCES

Apter, A., King, R.A., Bleich, A., Fluck, A., Kotler, M., & Kron, S. (2008). Fatal and non-fatal suicidal behavior in Israeli adolescent males. *Archives of Suicide Research, 12(1)*, 20–29.

Beard, J. (2008). DARPA's bio-revolution: An array of program aims to improve the safety, health, and well-being of the military and civilians alike. Retrieved from http://www.darpa.mil/Docs/Biology-biomedical services200807171322092.pdf.

Belik, S.L., Stein, M.B., Asmunson, G.J., & Sareen, J. (2009). Relation between traumatic events and suicide attempts in Canadian military personnel. *Canadian Journal of Psychiatry, 54(2)*, 93–104.

Bell, M. (2009). Behavioral and social health outcomes program update. US Army Public Health Command (Provisional). Presentation to the DoD Task Force on the Prevention of Suicide by Members of the Armed Forces (Bethesda, MD).

Bodner, E., Ben-Artzi, E., & Kaplan, Z. (2006). Soldiers who kill themselves: the contribution of dispositional and situational factors. *Archives of Suicide Research, 10(1)*, 29–43.

Center for Disease Control. (2009.) Suicide and Self-Inflicted Injury. Retrieved from http://www.cdc.gov/nchs/fastats/suicide.htm.

Datel, W.E., Jones, F. D., & Esposito, M.E. (1981). Suicide in United States Army Personnel 1977–1978. *Military Medicine, 146(6)*, 387–392.

Defense Manpower Data Center (2010). US Active Duty Military Deaths – 1980 – 2010. Retrieved from http://siadapp.dmdc.osd.mil/personnel/ CASU ALTY/death Rates.pdf.

Department of Defense Task Force on Mental Health. (2007). An achievable vision: Report of the Department of Defense Task Force on Mental Health. Falls Church, VA: Defense Health Board.

Cialdini, R.B. (2001). The science of persuasion. *Scientific American, 28*, 76–81.

Department of Defense. (2003). *DoDI 5154.30: Armed Forces Institute of Pathology Operations*. Retrieved from http://www.dtic.mil/whs/ directives /corres/pdf/515430p.pdf.

Fear, N.T., Ward, V.R., Harrison, K., Davison, L. Williamson, S., & Blatchley, N.F. (2009). Suicide among male regular UK armed forces personnel, 1984–2007. *Occupational and Environmental Medicine, 66*(7), 438–441.

Felker, B., Hawkins, E., Dobie, D., Gutierrez, J., & McFall, M. (2008). Characteristics of deployed Operation Iraqi freedom military personnel who seek mental health care. *Military Medicine, 173(2),* 155–158.

Gahm, G.A., Reger, M.A., Luxton, D.D., Skopp, N.A., & Lee, J.A. (2009). DoD Suicide Event Report: Calendar Year 2008 Annual Report. National Center for Telehealth & Technology, Defense Centers of Excellence for Psychological Healh & TBI. Presentation to the DoD Task Force on the Prevention of Suicide by Members of the Armed Forces (San Diego, CA).

Gerson, A., & Fox, D. (2006). Malingering. In J.E. Fisher & W.T. O'Donohue (Eds.), *Practitioner Guide to Evidence-based Psychotherapy (pp. 386–395*). Retrieved from http://www.springerlink.com/content/ k42670lp47g 326m4/?p=60a170e835f54d6c8bfa49 de1 59fb605&pi=37.

Gordana, D.J. & Milivoje, P. (2007). Suicide prevention program in the army of Serbia and Montenegro. *Military Medicine, 172*, 551–555.

Gould, M.S., Kalafat, J., Harris Munfkah, J.L., & Kleinman, M. (2007). An evaluation of crisis hotline outcomes. Part 2: Suicidal callers. *Suicide and Life-Threatening Behaviors, 37(3)*, 338– 352. Doi: 10.1521/ suli. 2007.37.3.338.

Government Accountability Office. (1989). *Military personnel: Information on active duty deaths and survivor benefits*. Retrieved from http:// archive.gao.gov/t2pbat13/ 139811. pdf.

Hawkins, J. (January, 2010). SPAARC/VA/Service updates. Presentation at the 2010 DoD/VA Suicide Prevention Conference: Building Strong and Resilient Communities, (Washington D.C.).

Hawton, K., Harriss, L., Casey, D., Simkin, S., Harrison, K., Bray, I., & Blatchley, N. (2009). Self-harm in UK armed forces personnel: descriptive and case-control study of general hospital populations. *British Journal of Psychiatry, 194(3),* 266–272.

Helmkamp, J. C. (1995). Suicides in the military: 1980–1992. *Military Medicine, 160(2*), 45–50.

Hoge, C.W., Castro, C.A., Messer, S.C., McGurk, D., Cotting, D.I., and Koffman, R.L. (2004). Combat Duty in Iraq and Afghanistan, Mental Health Problems, and Barriers to Care. *The New England Journal of Medicine 351(1)*, 13-22.

Hourani, L.L., & Hilton, S.M. (1999). Department of Navy Suicide Incident Report (DONSIR): Preliminary findings January to June 1999. San Diego, CA: Naval Health Research Center.

Hourani, L.L., Hilton, S. M., Kennedy, K., & Jones, D.E. (2000). Department of Navy Suicide Incident Report (DONSIR): Summary of 1999 Findings. San Diego, CA: Naval Health Research Center.

Hourani, L.L., Hilton, S.M., Kennedy, K., & Robbins, D. (2000). Department of Navy Suicide Incident Report (DONSIR): Summary of 1999 to 2000 Findings. San Diego, CA: Naval Health Research Center.

Hourani, L.L., Warrack, G., & Coben, P.A. (1997). A demographic analysis of suicide among US Navy Personnel. San Diego, CA: Naval Health Research Center.

Institute of Medicine. (2010). Returning home from Iraq and Afganistan: Preliminary assessment of readjustment needs of verterns service members and their families. Washington DC: The National Academies Press.

Institute of Medicine. (2006). *Reducing suicide: A national imperative*. Washington DC: The National Academies Press.

Jones, D.E., Kennedy, K.R., Hourani, L., Hawkes, C., Long, M.A., & Robbins, D. (2001).Suicide prevention in the Navy and Marine Corps: Applying the public health model. *Navy Medicine, November-December,* 31–36.

Kapur, N., White, D., Blatchley, N., Bray, I., & Harrison, K. (2009). Suicide after leaving the UK Armed Forces: A cohort study. *PLoS Medicine, 6(3),* e26.

Kerce, E.W. (1995). Quality of life in the US Marine Corps (Rep. No. NPRDC-TR-95-4). San Diego, CA: Navy Personnel Research and Development Center.

Lester, P., Peterson, K., Reeves, J., Knauss, L., Glover, D., Mogil, C., Duan, N., Saltzman, W., Pynoos, R., Wilt, K., & Beardslee, W. (2010). The long war and parental deployment: Effects on military children and at-home spouses. *Journal of the American Academy of Child & Adolescent Psychiatry, 49(4),* 310–320.

Luthar, S.S., Cicchetti, D., Becker, B. (2000). The construct of resilience: A critical evaluation and guidelines for future work. *Child Development, 71(3),* 543–562.

Mansfield, A.J., Kaufman, J.S., Marshall, S.W., Gaynes, B.N., Morrissey, J.P., & Engel, C.C. (2010). Deployment and the use of mental health services among Army wives. *New England Journal of Medicine, 362,* 101–109.

Mauer, R. (2010, February 7). Part 1: Combat deaths—after the war, at home. *Anchorage Daily News,* retrieved from http://www.adn.com /2010/02/06/1128156/combat-deaths.html#ixzz0q TiHVdiR.

Michel, P.O., Lundin, T. & Larsson, G. (2007). Suicide rate among former Swedish peacekeeping personnel. *Military Medicine, 172(3),* 278–282.

Moskos, M.A., Olson, L., Halbern, S.R., & Gray, D. (2005). Utah youth suicide study: Psychological autopsy. *Suicide and Life-Threatening Behaviors, 35(5),* 536-546.

Oetjen-Gerdes, L., Cantrall, J., & Malone, R. (2009). *Armed Forces Medical Examiner—Morality Services Division,* briefing provided to DoD Task Force on Suicide Prevention by Members of the Armed Forces. Unpublished data.

Orbach, I., Gilboa-Schechtman, E., Ofek, H., Lubin, G., Mark, M., Bodner, E., Cohen, D., & King, R. (2007). A chronological perspective on suicide—the last days of life. *Death Studies, 31(10),* 909–932.

Oordt, M., Jobes, D., Rudd, M., Fonseca, V., Russ, C., Stea, J., Campise, R., & Talcott, W. (2005). Development of a clinical guide to enhance care for suicidal patients. *Professional Psychology: Research and Practice. 36,* 208–218.

Oordt, M.S., Jobes, D.A., Fonseca, V.P., & Schmidt, S.M. (2009). Training mental health professionals to assess and manage suicidal behavior: Can provider confidence and practice behaviors be altered? *Suicide and Life-Threatening Behavior, 39,* 21–37.

Reger, M.A., Luxton, D.D., Skopp, N.A., Lee, J.A., & Gahm, G. A. (2009). DoD suicide event report: Calendar year 2008 annual report. National Center for Telehealth & Technology, Defense Centers of Excellence for Psychological Health & TBI, 1-165.

Rozanov, V.V., Mohkhovikov, A.N., & Stiliha, R. (2002). Successful model of suicide prevention in the Ukraine military environment, *Crisis, 23,* 171–177.

Sanddal, N., Sanddal, T., Berman, A.L., & Silverman, M.M. (2003). A general systems approach to suicide prevention: Lessons from cardiac prevention and control. *Suicide and Life-Threatening Behavior, 33*(4), 341–352.

Schoenbaum, M., Heinssen, R., & Pearson, J. (2010). *Opportunities to improve interventions to reduce suicidality: Civilian "Best Practices" for Army consideration.* Unpublished manuscript. National Institute of Mental Health.

Scoville, S.L., Gubata, M.E., Potter, R.N., White, M.J., & Pearse, L.A. (2007). Deaths attributed to suicide among enlisted US Armed Forces recruits. *Military Medicine, 172(10)*, 1024–1031.

Silverman, M.M., Berman, A. L., Sanddal, N. D., O'Connell, P.W., & Joiner, T.W. (2007). Rebuilding the tower of babel: A revised nomenclature for the study of suicide and suicide behaviors, part 2: Suicide-related ideations, communications and behaviors. *Suicide and Life-Threatening Behaviors 37(3)*, 264–277.

Stander, V.A., Hilton, S.M., Kennedy, K.R., & Gaskin, T. (2004). *Department of Navy Suicide Incident Report (DONSIR): Summary of 1999–2002 Findings.* San Diego, CA: Naval Health Research Center.

Stander, V.A., Hilton, S.M., Kennedy, K.R., & Robbins, D.L. (2004). Surveillance of completed suicide in the Department of the Navy. *Military Medicine, 169(4)*, 301–306.

Stander, V.A., Hilton, S.M., Doran, A.P., Gaskin, T., & Thompsen, C.J. (2005). *Department of Navy Suicide Incident Report (DONSIR): Summary of 1999–2003 Findings.* San Diego, CA: Naval Health Research Center.

Stander, V.A., Hilton, S.M., Doran, A.P., Werbel, A.D., & Thomsen, C.J. (2006). *Department of the Navy Suicide Incident Report (DONSIR): Summary of 1999–2004 findings (NHRC Tech. Rep. No. 07-05).* San Diego, CA: Naval Health Research Center.

Substance Abuse and Mental Health Administration, Office of Applies Statistics. (2009). The NSDUH report: Suicidal thoughts and behaviors among adults. Rockville, MD. Retrieved on July 27, 2010 from http://www.oas.samhsa.gov/2k9/165/Suicide.htm.

Suicide Prevention Resource Center. (2004). After a suicide: Recommendations for religious services and other public memorial observances. Newton, MA: Education Development Center, Inc.

Suicide Prevention Resource Center (SPRC). (2010). *SPRC Cohort 5 Orientation Webinar Series: Planning strategic communications campaigns.* Retrieved from www.sprc.org/grantees/webinar/ Communi cationPlanningResourcesHandout.doc.

Tien, H.C., Acharya, S., & Redelmeier, D.A. (2010). Preventing deaths in the Canadian military. *American Journal of Preventive Medicine, 38(3),* 331–339.

Thacker, S.B., & Berkelma, R.L. (1988). Public health surveillance in the United States, *Epidemiologic Reviews, 10*, 164–190.

Thoreson, S., Mehlum, L., & Moller, B. (2003). Suicide in peacekeepers—A cohort study of mortality from suicide in 22,275 Norwegian veterans from international peacekeeping operations. *Social Psychiatry and Psychiatric Epidemiology, 38(11),* 605–610.

Thoreso, S. & Mehlum, L. (2006). Suicide in peacekeepers: Risk factors for suicide versus accidental death. *Suicide and Life-Threatening Behavior, 36(4),* 432–442.

US Army. (2009). Army Health Promotion: Army Regulation 600-63. Retrieved from http://www.army.mil/usapa/epubs/pdf/r600_63.pdf.

US Army Office of the Surgeon General (OTSG). (2009). Operation Iraqi Freedom (OIF) Mental Health Advisory Team (MHAT) Report. Retrieved from http://www.armymedicine.army. mil/reports/mhat/mhat_vi/ MHAT_ VI-OIF_EXSUM. pdf.

US Coast Guard. (2009). Commandant Instruction: Suicide Prevention Program. Retrieved from http://www.uscg.mil/directives/ci/1000-1999/ CI17341A.pdf.

US Department of Defense Defense Center of Excellence for Psychological Health and Traumatic Brain Injury (DCoE) & National Center for Telehealth and Technology. (2009). *Department of Defense Suicide Event Report (DoDSER).* Rosslyn, VA.

US Department of Defense Sexual Assault and Prevention Response (SAPRO). (2010). *Mission and history.* Retrieved http://www.sapr.mil/ index.php/about/mission-and-history

US Department of Health and Human Services, National Institute of Health, and National Cancer Institute. (2005). *Making health communication programs work.* Retrieved from http://www.cancer.gov/PDF/41f04dd8-495a-4444-a258-1334b1d864f7/Pink_Book.pdf.

US Department of Navy. (1999). *SECNAV Instruction 6320.24A: Mental health evaluations of members of the armed forces.* Retrieved from http://www.brooksidepress.org/Products/OperationalMedicine/DATA/operationalmed/Instr uctions/6320_24a.pdf.

US Department of Navy. (1999). Marine Corps Order P1700.27A: Marine Corps Community Services Policy Manual (MCCS Policy Manual). Washington DC.

US Department of Navy. (1999). Marine Corps Order P1700.29: Marine Corps Semper Fit Program Manual (MCCS Policy Manual). Retrieved from http://www.usmc.mil/news/publications/Documents/MCO%20P1700.29.pdf.

US Department of Navy. (2000). MCRP 6-11C: Combat Stress. Retrieved from http://www.au.af.mil/au/awc/awcgate/usmc/mcrp61 1c.pdf.

US Department of Navy. (2001). Marine Corps. Order P1700.24B: Marine Corps personal services manual. Retrieved from http://www.usmc.mil/ news/publications/Documents/MCO%20P1700.24B%20W%20CH%201. pdf.

US Department of Navy. (2003). Marine Corps Order P3040.4E: Marine Corps Casualty Procedures Manual. Retrieved from http://www.usmc.mil/ news/publications/Documents/MCO%20P3040.4E.pdf.

US Department of Navy. (2004). Marine Corps Order 1510.89B: Individual Training Standards System for Marine Corps Common Skills. Retrieved from http://www.usmc.mil/news/publications/Documents/MCO% 2015 10.89B.pdf.

US Public Health Services. (1999). *The Surgeon General's Call to Action to Prevent Suicide.* Washington D.C. Retrieved from http://www. surgeongeneral.gov/library/calltoaction/calltoaction.pdf.

World Health Organization. (2010). *World REPORT on Violence and Health.* Retrieved from http://www.who.int/mental_health/prevention/suicide/ suicideprevent/en/.

In: The Enemy Within
Editors: Jack M. Wright and Gabriel E. Lewis
ISBN: 978-1-62081-316-4

Chapter 2

SUICIDE PREVENTION EFFORTS OF THE VETERANS HEALTH ADMINISTRATION*

Erin Bagalman

SUMMARY

Responsibility for prevention of veteran suicide lies primarily with the Veterans Health Administration (VHA), within the Department of Veterans Affairs (VA). The VHA Strategic Plan for Suicide Prevention is based on a public health framework, which has three major components: (1) surveillance, (2) risk and protective factors, and (3) prevention interventions.

No nationwide surveillance system exists for suicide among all veterans; therefore, the actual incidence of suicide among veterans is not known. Surveillance, or systematic collection of data on completed (i.e., fatal) suicides, is essential to define the scope of the problem (i.e., the suicide rate among veterans), identify characteristics associated with higher or lower risk of suicide, and track changes in the suicide rate over time to evaluate suicide prevention interventions. In the absence of a nationwide surveillance system for veteran suicide, the VHA is attempting to determine the rate of suicide among veterans in two ways, both in collaboration with the Centers for Disease Control and Prevention (CDC).

Information collected in surveillance is used to identify suicide risk factors (i.e., characteristics associated with higher rates of suicide) and protective factors (i.e., characteristics associated with lower rates of suicide). This is essential in order to design interventions that reduce risk factors and/or increase protective factors, thus lowering overall risk of suicide. Risk factors are also helpful in identifying at-risk groups or individuals so that interventions can be delivered to the people who need them most. Within the VHA, this research is supported by the Office of Research and Development; a Center of Excellence in suicide prevention; and a Mental Illness Research, Education, and Clinical Center on suicide prevention.

The intervention cycle includes three stages: design and test interventions, implement interventions, and evaluate interventions. The research components mentioned

* This is an edited, reformatted and augmented version of a Congressional Research Service publication, CRS Report *for Congress* R42340, *from* www.crs.gov, *prepared* for Members and Committees of Congress, *dated* February 3, 2012.

above have roles in small-scale pilot testing and large-scale evaluations of interventions. This report discusses seven areas of VHA suicide prevention interventions: (1) easy access to care, (2) education, (3) screening and treatment, (4) limited access to lethal means, (5) suicide hotline, (6) media restrictions, and (7) suicide prevention coordinators.

This report identifies challenges the VHA faces in each component of suicide prevention and discusses potential issues for Congress. A recurring theme is the need for the VHA to work in concert with other federal, state, and local government agencies; private for-profit and not-forprofit health care providers; veterans, their families, and their communities; and other individuals or organizations that might be able to help. Specific challenges in surveillance include timeliness of data, accurate identification of decedents as veterans, and consistent classification of deaths as suicides. Challenges in risk and protective factors research include a need for more collaboration and dialogue among agencies involved in suicide prevention and across other areas of public health (because suicide has some of the same risk and protective factors as other public health problems). Challenges in VHA suicide prevention interventions also include the need for more collaboration and dialogue, as well as an apparent gap between policy and practice, and misperceptions about mental illness and mental health care.

INTRODUCTION

Congress has attempted to address the problem of suicide among veterans through legislation,[1] and the House and Senate Committees on Veterans' Affairs have conducted oversight hearings, both on prevention of veteran suicide specifically and on veteran mental health more broadly.[2] The actual number or rate of veteran suicides is not known, because no nationwide surveillance system for suicide among all veterans exists, but there is consensus that the number is too high.[3] Responsibility for prevention of veteran suicide lies primarily with the Veterans Health Administration (VHA), within the Department of Veterans Affairs (VA). Such a challenging task, however, demands collaboration with other federal agencies, state and local governments, other organizations, communities, and individuals.

Prevention of suicide can be approached in two ways, which are not mutually exclusive. The public health approach intervenes with populations (e.g., distributing educational materials about mental illness and mental health services), whereas the clinical approach intervenes with individuals (e.g., prescribing antidepressant medication to a person diagnosed with depression). The individual focus of the clinical approach limits its reach to those who access the health care system;[4] clinical interventions are necessary but not sufficient. If the goal is to reach a broader population, the public health approach is considered essential.

The public health approach provides the framework for two suicide prevention strategies that are referenced in this report. The National Strategy for Suicide Prevention[5] involves multiple federal departments, including the VA, Defense (DOD), and Education (ED), as well as several agencies within Health and Human Services (HHS).[6] The VHA Strategic Plan for Suicide Prevention[7] is a compilation of VHA activities related to suicide prevention. While this CRS report focuses on suicide prevention efforts of the VHA, activities of other entities are discussed as they relate to VHA activities.

The textbox briefly discusses eligibility for, enrollment in, and use of VHA services. As noted in the textbox, the majority of veterans do not use VHA services. VHA efforts to increase access to care—and to prevent suicide among veterans who do not use VHA services—are discussed later in this report.

Who Is a Veteran? Eligibility for, Enrollment in, and Use of VA Health Care

The term "veteran" may refer broadly to anyone who has served in the armed forces, including those currently serving. In this report, a veteran is someone who has separated from military service following a period of active duty. Although an individual may return to active duty following separation (a particular issue among National Guard and Reserve members who have been activated), current active duty servicemembers are not the focus of this report.

Three additional points may be made relative to veterans and VA health care services:

- *Eligibility:* Not all veterans are eligible for VA health care services (see http://www.va.gov/healthbenefits); Vet Centers (non-medical facilities that provide readjustment counseling services for veterans and their families) have their own eligibility criteria (see http://www.vetcenter. va.gov/Eligibility.asp).
- *Enrollment:* Not all eligible veterans enroll in VA health care services. The number of enrolled veterans in FY2010 was 8.3 million, which is 36.6% of the estimated veteran population of 22.7 million. As noted above, some veterans are not eligible for VA health care services; others may choose not to enroll for various reasons (e.g., they might have employer-sponsored health insurance or other sources of health care services).
- *Use:* Not all enrolled veterans actually use VA health care services. The number of veterans who received health care services in FY2010 was 5.4 million, which is 65.1% of the 8.3 million enrolled veterans, or 23.8% of the estimated veteran population of 22.7 million. Enrolled veterans may choose not to receive care for various reasons (e.g., they might not perceive a need for health care services).

Sources: Estimated number of veterans is from Department of Veterans Affairs, FY2012 Budget Submission, Summary Volume, Volume 1 of 4, February 2011, pp. 1F-1; numbers of veterans enrolled using services are from Department of Veterans Affairs, FY2012 Budget Submission, Medical Programs and Information Technology Programs, Volume 2 of 4, February 2011, pp. 1A-28. See also CRS Report R42324, "Who is a Veteran?"—Basic Eligibility for Veterans' Benefits, by Christine Scott.

The VHA has received both praise and criticism for its suicide prevention efforts and mental health services more generally. In 2010 the Suicide Prevention Resource Center, funded by the Substance Abuse and Mental Health Services Administration (SAMHSA), in collaboration with the non-profit Suicide Prevention Action Network, published a progress report on the National Strategy for Suicide Prevention; the progress report (hereinafter referred to as *Charting the Future*) praises VHA's suicide prevention practices and recommends disseminating them to the rest of the health care system.[8] *Charting the Future* describes the VHA as "one of the most vibrant forces in the U.S. suicide prevention movement, implementing multiple levels of innovation and state of the art interventions, backed up by a robust evaluation and research capacity."[9] In contrast, some congressional testimony has criticized VHA's suicide prevention efforts for inadequacies, such as barriers to accessing care and lack of evidence-based treatments for those who do access care.[10] A 2011 evaluation of VHA mental health services (not limited to suicide prevention efforts) by the Altarum Institute and RAND Health captures both sides of the argument, finding that VHA mental health care is generally at least as good as that of other health care systems, but that it "often does not meet implicit VA expectations."[11]

This report begins with a brief overview of the public health framework for suicide prevention. The three subsequent parts of the report correspond to the three major components of the public health framework: (1) suicide surveillance, (2) suicide risk factors and protective factors, and (3) suicide prevention interventions. The final section addresses potential issues for Congress.

The importance of collaboration and dialogue is a recurring theme across all components of the VHA's suicide prevention efforts. Surveillance requires collaboration to address timeliness of data, accurate identification of decedents as veterans, and consistent classification of deaths as suicides. Risk and protective factors research requires dialogue among agencies involved in suicide prevention and across other areas of public health (because suicide has some of the same risk and protective factors as other public health problems). Successful prevention interventions also require collaboration. Challenges in prevention interventions include an apparent gap between policy and practice, as well as misperceptions about mental illness and its treatment.

A Public Health Framework for Suicide Prevention

As noted previously, both the National Strategy for Suicide Prevention and the VHA Strategic Plan for Suicide Prevention are based on a public health framework. As illustrated in *Figure 1*, the framework has three major components: (1) surveillance, (2) risk and protective factors, and (3) prevention interventions. Suicide surveillance involves collecting data on completed (i.e., fatal) suicides in order to define the scope of the problem. Data collected in surveillance can be used to identify risk factors (i.e., characteristics associated with higher suicide risk) and protective factors (i.e., characteristics associated with lower suicide risk).

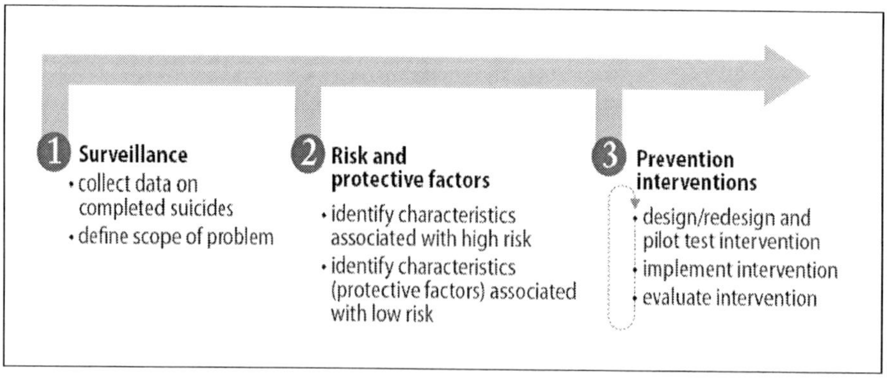

Source: CRS summary of the public health framework described in the National Strategy for Suicide Prevention. U.S. Department of Health and Human Services (HHS), Public Health Service, National Strategy for Suicide Prevention: Goals and Objectives for Action, SMA01-3517, Rockville, MD, 2001, http://store. samhsa.gov/product/ SMA01-3517, pp. 29-40.

Figure 1. A Public Health Framework for Suicide Prevention.

Suicide prevention interventions aim to reduce risk factors and/or enhance protective factors that have been identified; interventions may target high-risk groups or individuals, identified based on known risk factors.

SUICIDE SURVEILLANCE

As noted previously, no nationwide surveillance system exists for suicide among all veterans. Surveillance, or systematic collection of data on completed (i.e., fatal) suicides, is essential for three purposes. First, surveillance defines the scope of the problem, i.e., the suicide rate among veterans. Second, information from surveillance is used to identify characteristics associated with higher or lower risk of suicide. Third, information from surveillance is used to track changes in the suicide rate over time and evaluate suicide prevention interventions. In order to evaluate interventions, suicide surveillance must measure the same thing, in the same way, repeatedly over time.

In the absence of a nationwide surveillance system for veteran suicide, the VHA is attempting to determine the rate of suicide among veterans in two ways, both in collaboration with the Centers for Disease Control and Prevention (CDC). Combining the two methods provides more information about veteran suicide than either method alone, but the combination remains inadequate to the task. For example, one method is limited to enrolled veterans, and the other is limited to fewer than half the states; thus even the combination does not capture all veteran suicides. Also, statistics from both methods have a lag time of years, so that timeliness of data is an ongoing challenge. Each of the two methods is described below, along with its limitations and (where applicable) efforts to overcome those limitations.

Combining VHA Data with the National Death Index (NDI)

The VHA's primary approach to surveillance is illustrated in *Figure 2*. Information about completed (i.e., fatal) suicides is collected in death certificates by state, territorial, and local governments;[12] aggregated into the National Death Index (NDI) by the CDC;[13] and combined with enrollment data by the VHA in order to identify suicides among enrolled veterans.[14]

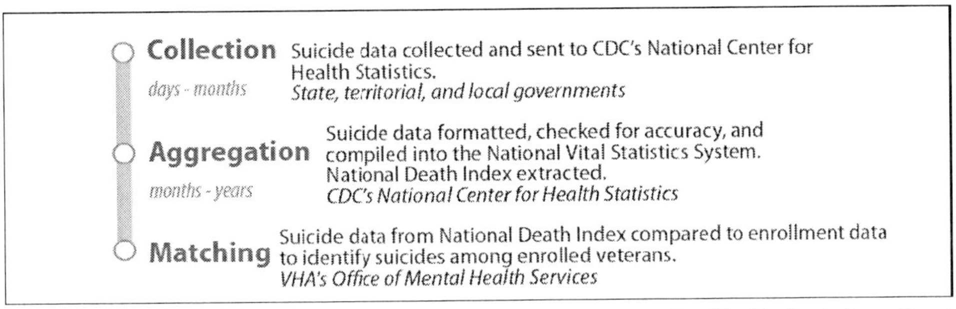

Source: CRS summary of information from CDC, National Center for Health Statistics, About the National Death Index, http://www.cdc.gov/nchs/data_ access /ndi/about_ndi.htm; and from the VHA.

Figure 2. Combining VHA Data with the National Death Index.

This approach is subject to the following limitations:

- The resulting data may not be comparable across jurisdictions.[15]
- The lag between a suicide event and identification of the decedent as an enrolled veteran may be years; this delays the availability of crucial information.
- Suicides among non-enrolled veterans are not captured;[16] this leaves out the majority of veterans.[17]

Accessing the National Violent Death Reporting System (NVDRS)

In an attempt to identify suicides among veterans regardless of enrollment with the VA, the VHA uses the CDC's National Violent Death Reporting System (NVDRS), among other sources of information.18 The NVDRS is a CDC-funded program that enables participating states to supplement death certificates with information from law enforcement agencies, crime laboratories, coroner or medical examiner reports, health providers, and other state and local agencies. Through ongoing active surveillance, NVDRS may increase the likelihood that a death is recognized as a suicide and that a decedent's veteran status is captured (regardless of enrollment with the VHA). The CDC is working to address the limitations of this approach through the following activities:

- Expand the NVDRS to all 50 states, the District of Columbia, and the territories;[19] currently, the NVDRS is in operation in fewer than half the states.[20]
- Increase standardization of data collection and analysis, in order to increase comparability across states.[21]
- Assess the feasibility of linking VHA data directly to state NVDRS programs, thereby eliminating a step in the process and potentially reducing the lag time.[22]
- Link the NVDRS to data from the VHA and the DOD's Suicide Event Report, in order to increase accurate identification of veteran status.[23]

The timeliness of the data is a challenge for the VHA in both methods of surveillance described above. This is a challenge for suicide surveillance nationwide, not limited to suicide surveillance among veterans. Timely reporting of death certificates is identified as a core issue in the 2010 update to the National Strategy for Suicide Prevention.[24]

Suicide Risk Factors and Protective Factors

Identifying characteristics associated with higher rates of suicide (i.e., risk factors) and lower rates of suicide (i.e., protective factors) is essential in order to design effective interventions. Suicide prevention interventions aim to reduce risk factors and/or increase protective factors, thus lowering overall risk of suicide. Knowing what the risk factors are also helps in identifying at-risk groups or individuals so that interventions can be delivered to the people who need them most. Thus the second step in the public health framework for suicide prevention is identification of suicide risk and protective factors using data collected in surveillance. *Table 1* provides examples of risk and protective factors among the general population.

Table 1. Selected Risk and Protective Factors in the General Population

Risk Factors	Protective Factors
Some major physical illnesses, mental disorders, and substance use disorders	Effective clinical care for physical illnesses, mental disorders, and substance use disorders
Barriers to accessing health care	Easy access to a variety of clinical interventions
Stigma associated with help-seeking behavior	Support for help-seeking behavior
Easy access to lethal means (e.g., firearms or poison)	Restricted access to lethal means (e.g., firearms or poison)
Lack of social support and sense of isolation	Strong connections to family and community support
Cultural/religious beliefs that accept suicide	Cultural/religious beliefs that discourage suicide

Source: Examples of risk and protective factors selected from U.S. Department of Health and Human Services (HHS), Public Health Service, National Strategy for Suicide Prevention: Goals and Objectives for Action, SMA01-3517, Rockville, MD, 2001, pp. 35-36, http://store.samhsa.gov/product/SMA01-3517.

Veteran-specific research on suicide risk and protective factors is necessary, because the veteran population differs from the non-veteran population on a variety of characteristics (e.g., gender distribution), some of which may also be associated with suicide risk. The subpopulation of veterans who are enrolled with the VHA may differ from non-enrolled veterans, as well.

The VHA conducts veteran-specific research that builds on research among the general population. Within HHS, both the CDC[25] and the National Institute of Mental Health (NIMH)[26] disseminate research on suicide risk and protective factors within the general population. Also, SAMHSA collects data on suicide attempts and related behavior.[27]

It should be noted that risk factors for attempted suicide may differ from risk factors for completed suicide; for example, women have a higher rate of attempted suicide, but men have a higher rate of completed suicide.[28] Despite a large number of risk and protective factors identified by researchers, it is not yet possible to predict who will attempt or complete suicide.[29] The inability to identify individuals most in need of interventions is one of the reasons a public health approach—with a focus on population-level interventions—is necessary for effective suicide prevention.

Within the VHA, mental health research—including research on suicide risk and protective factors—is supported by two organizational units: the Office of Research and Development (ORD) and the Mental Health Strategic Healthcare Group (MHSHG). In general, the ORD funds intramural research by individual VHA investigators or researchers (including mental health care research).[30]

The MHSHG funds a Center of Excellence (COE) in suicide prevention and a Mental Illness Research, Education, and Clinical Center (MIRECC) on suicide prevention, as well as centers addressing other mental health topics. Examples of research conducted on risk and protective factors by each of these three components—ORD, COE, and MIRECC—are provided below.

The same three research components are also involved in the development and evaluation of suicide prevention interventions.

VHA Office of Research and Development (ORD)

The ORD's Health Services Research and Development Service supports research into suicide risk factors and protective factors.[31]

For example, the VHA conducted a study to identify patient characteristics associated with higher suicide rates among veterans in treatment for depression (a known risk factor in the general population, as well as among veterans).[32]

Another study examined characteristics associated with suicide risk among patients seen in VHA primary care, to help identify factors that primary care providers may be able to use to detect suicide risk.[33] These studies, and others like them, can help the VHA identify veterans at high risk of suicide, so that interventions can be targeted to them.

Center of Excellence (COE)

The COE at Canandaigua, New York, conducts research on suicide risk factors and protective factors, in addition to other suicide prevention activities. Established in August 2007 at the direction of Congress,[34] the COE has the mission of developing and studying evidence-based public health approaches to prevention of veteran suicide, with the goal of reducing morbidity and mortality associated with suicide in the veteran population. In pursuit of its mission, the Epidemiology and Interventions Research Core within the COE collects and analyzes data on suicide risk factors and protective factors (as well as other topics) among both veterans who use VHA services and those who do not.[35]

Mental Illness Research, Education, and Clinical Center (MIRECC)

The MIRECCs, also established at the direction of Congress,[36] conduct research on a range of mental health-related topics, including suicide risk factors and protective factors. Specifically, the MIRECC of the VA Rocky Mountain Network pursues the goal of reducing suicidality in the veteran population, by conducting research on potential contributions of cognitive and neurobiological factors, among other activities.[37]

For example, one study assesses the relationship (if any) between prolonged grief and suicidal ideation.[38] Another study investigates the neurobiology of suicide risk in traumatic brain injury and substance abuse.[39] Other MIRECCs may also conduct research related to suicide, in the course of pursuing their other goals.

SUICIDE PREVENTION INTERVENTIONS

Through effective suicide prevention interventions, people's lives can be saved. Interventions aim to reduce risk factors and/or enhance protective factors, thereby lowering the risk of suicide. They may address entire populations (e.g., all veterans), at-risk subgroups (e.g., veterans diagnosed with PTSD), or high-risk individuals (e.g., veterans with recent suicide attempts).

Suicide prevention interventions are refined in a three-stage cycle. The first stage is to develop and pilot test interventions on a small scale to ensure that they are safe, ethical, feasible, efficacious (i.e., they work under ideal conditions), and effective (i.e., they work under real-world conditions). If interventions are successful in the first stage, the second stage is to implement them on a larger scale. The third stage is to evaluate interventions that have been implemented on a larger scale, to verify their effectiveness and determine for whom they are most effective. The three stages can then be repeated to refine interventions, either to improve their effectiveness or to adjust them for use with a different population (e.g., applying an intervention developed for male veterans to a population of female veterans).

Within the VHA, the same three research components involved in risk and protective factors research are involved in the intervention cycle: ORD,[40] COE,[41] and MIRECC.[42] Because small-scale testing and large-scale evaluation are both integral to suicide prevention interventions, it is worth noting that rigorous research on effectiveness is difficult and lacking for most interventions, both within and outside the VHA.[43]

The rest of this section discusses seven areas of VHA suicide prevention interventions: (1) easy access to care, (2) education, (3) screening and treatment, (4) limited access to lethal means, (5) suicide hotline, (6) media restrictions, and (7) suicide prevention coordinators.

Easy Access to Care

As noted previously, the majority of veterans do not use VHA services. Easy access to care is a protective factor against suicide,[44] and the VHA is making efforts to increase access to care by addressing identified barriers to care, including logistical challenges in scheduling or attending appointments, lack of understanding or awareness of mental health care, stigma associated with mental illness, and concerns about VHA care. In order to address these barriers, the VHA is taking two broad approaches: (1) increasing access to care by offering a broader range of mental health services (e.g., telehealth or off-hours clinics) and (2) providing education about mental illness and mental health care to veterans, their families, health care providers, and others in their communities.[45]

Offering expanded options in mental health services aims to alleviate logistical challenges by making services available in more places at more times.[46] VHA policy requires that new patients requesting or referred for mental health services receive an initial assessment within 24 hours and a full evaluation appointment within 14 days; follow-up appointments for established patients must occur within 30 days.[47] The extent to which these policies are implemented in practice has been questioned in Congressional testimony, news media, and survey responses from both providers and patients.[48]

Educating veterans and others aims to increase understanding of mental health care and mental illness, reduce the associated stigma, and correct misconceptions about VHA care. For example, the VHA incorporates messages intended to reduce stigma into public health and outreach activities.

In addition, the VHA is working to integrate mental health and substance use evaluation and treatment services into other treatment settings, which both increases the convenience and reduces the stigma associated with seeking care.[49] Educational interventions are described in more detail in the next subsection.

Education

The VHA offers suicide prevention education to audiences within VHA facilities and in surrounding communities. VHA requires suicide prevention training for all VHA staff that interact with veterans, plus additional training for health care providers. In the community, the VHA provides education for veterans' families and community "guides."[50] Community guides are trained to recognize individuals who may be at risk of suicide and help them seek treatment. Evidence supports education of guides; however, they must be able to refer individuals to quality mental health services.[51] Thus, access to care and quality of care are essential.

Screening and Treatment

Some types of screening, pharmacotherapy, and psychotherapy are supported by evidence that they reduce the likelihood of suicide.[52]

VHA policy requires screening for a variety of risk factors, including depression, posttraumatic stress disorder (PTSD), problem drinking, traumatic brain injury (TBI), military sexual trauma (MST), and pain; veterans who screen positive must be offered follow-up evaluations and, if appropriate, treatment.[53]

An evaluation of VHA mental health care by the Altarum Institute and RAND Health finds that treatment in the VHA is generally better than in other systems on a variety of measures, but still has room for improvement.[54]

In particular, the evaluation finds that evidence-based treatments (both pharmacotherapy and psychotherapy), while widely available, are not usually provided.[55] Researchers based this finding on a review of medical records, which showed that prescriptions for medication were often not filled for as long as recommended and that psychotherapy, as documented, was often not delivered according to evidence-based guidelines.

Additionally, the evaluation found that assessment is lacking, both at the beginning of treatment and during treatment (to track progress).[56]

Even if a particular treatment is supported by evidence, it will not necessarily be effective for every patient.

The only way to know whether a patient is improving, holding steady, or growing worse is to assess his or her symptoms at intervals.

Limited Access to Lethal Means

The three most common means of completing suicide among the general population are firearms (50%), suffocation (24%), and poisoning (18%).[57] Evidence supports restricting access to lethal means (e.g., firearms, gas, drugs) as a way to reduce suicide rates.[58] The VHA has a gun safety program (as both a child safety initiative and a suicide prevention initiative), which includes distribution of gun safety literature and gun locks. The VHA also encourages demonstration projects and research on blister packaging medications as a way to reduce the incidence of medication overdoses.[59] Means restriction is a promising area still under investigation.[60]

Suicide Hotline

Suicide hotlines are telephone numbers individuals can call for help in crisis situations (e.g., at the moment they are considering suicide). Hotlines are generally toll-free and available around the clock. The Veterans Crisis Line is a joint effort of the VHA and SAMHSA.[61] The main line (1- 800-273-8255) is the National Suicide Prevention Lifeline, operated by SAMHSA.[62] Veterans (or others calling with concerns about veterans) may select option 1 to be directed to the VHA's Veterans Crisis Line, answered by staff at the COE in Canandaigua, New York. Callers may remain anonymous or disclose their identify in order to allow the COE staff to access their VA medical records during the call. Since the Veterans Crisis Line began in 2007, it has received over 500,000 calls, resulting in over 73,000 referrals to Suicide Prevention Coordinators for same-day or next-day service. The Veterans Crisis Line is supplemented by an online chat service (www.VeteransCrisisLine.net/chat) and support via text messaging (text 838255).[63]

The evidence base for suicide hotlines is not sufficient to determine their effectiveness in reducing suicide rates, due to the difficulties inherent in conducting such evaluations.[64] The confidentiality of suicide hotlines renders follow-up with each individual caller impossible. Moreover, national hotlines, such as those operated by SAMHSA and the VHA, serve a large geographic area. A range of other interventions may be in place in localities within the hotline's reach, such that any change in the suicide rate may not be attributable to the hotline.

Media Restrictions

Exposure to a suicide—whether through a personal relationship with the decedent or through media coverage—is a risk factor for suicide.[65] In this way, suicide sometimes seems to act as a contagion, resulting in suicide clusters as one suicide is followed by other imitative suicides. Following a completed suicide, news media may restrict how suicides are reported (e.g., not glamorizing suicide or not reporting the specific means), in an effort to reduce the likelihood of imitative suicides. Evidence has shown that this may reduce suicide at a particular site (e.g., a bridge); however, more evidence is needed to determine whether this approach reduces the overall rate of suicide.[66] The VA monitors depictions of suicide in the media and (working with other federal agencies and partners in academia) encourages both news and entertainment media to depict suicide in a manner that is ethical and responsible.[67]

Suicide Prevention Coordinators

Per department policy, every VA Medical Center has at least one suicide prevention coordinator, whose responsibilities include (among other things) tracking patients who have been identified as at high risk for suicide; the VHA's computerized patient record system enables clinicians to flag high-risk patients, and policy requires that safety plans be developed for them.[68] A safety plan is a written document, developed jointly by a patient and a clinician, that identifies strategies for coping in a crisis (e.g., recognizing warning signs and contacting family members, friends, or mental health providers). Outside the VA, the use of suicide prevention coordinators has not been widely adopted, although some components of the program (e.g., safety plans) are widely used. The suicide prevention coordinator program has been identified as a practice worth emulating by a DOD task force on suicide prevention.[69]

POTENTIAL ISSUES FOR CONGRESS

A recurring theme in recommendations regarding VHA suicide prevention efforts is the need for the VHA to work in concert with other federal, state, and local government agencies; private for-profit and not-for-profit health care providers; veterans, their families, and their communities; and other individuals or organizations that might be able to help. Specific recommendations are organized in the following subsections, according to the public health framework for suicide prevention: surveillance, risk and protective factors, and interventions. Public laws addressing suicide prevention among veterans are described in the Appendix.

Potential Issues in Surveillance

As discussed earlier, three challenges in suicide surveillance are (1) timeliness of data, (2) accurate identification of decedents as veterans, and (3) consistent classification of deaths as suicides. Addressing these three challenges requires the involvement of entities other than VHA.

The Center for a New American Security (CNAS)[70] offers three recommendations related to the timeliness of data. First, CNAS recommends that "Congress should establish reasonable time requirements for states to provide death data to the CDC."[71] It should be noted that states, territories, and cities voluntarily share vital statistics with the CDC. Congress may be able to facilitate or motivate more rapid data sharing by providing resources or incentives.

Second, CNAS recommends ensuring that the CDC's ability to compile national death data expeditiously is not limited by a lack of resources.[72] Third, CNAS recommends that the annual analysis of veteran suicide data be coordinated among VA, DOD, and HHS.[73]

The VHA can identify decedents as veterans only if they are enrolled with the agency.[74] Identification of non-enrolled veterans relies on information gathered in the course of completing the death certificate or on supplemental information gathered as part of the National Violent Death Reporting System. VA researchers conducting a one-time study (not ongoing surveillance) combined information from the National Death Index with information from the DOD's Defense Manpower Data Center (DMDC) to identify suicides among veterans regardless of VA enrollment.[75] Congress may consider whether the DMDC is a source of information that can be used for suicide surveillance among veterans regardless of enrollment.

It is widely believed that inconsistent reporting of suicides across jurisdictions, as well as underreporting of suicides in general, limits the effectiveness of surveillance efforts.[76] Classification of a death as a suicide requires a determination that the death is both self-inflicted and intentional. Determining the decedent's intent is difficult, and coroners or medical examiners may feel pressure not to classify a death as suicide, due to the stigma associated with suicide.

Suicides may be underreported when the manner of death is misclassified as "undetermined" or "accidental" (e.g., poisonings or single-vehicle crashes). Additionally, each jurisdiction (state, territory, or city) has its own requirements for investigating deaths, leading to variability across jurisdictions. Congress may be able to facilitate or motivate more standardization by providing resources or incentives.

Potential Issues in Risk and Protective Factors

Recommendations in the area of risk and protective factors include collaboration and dialogue both among agencies involved in suicide prevention and across other areas of public health. CNAS suggests information sharing between the VA, DOD, and HHS[77] and recommends that the House and Senate Committees on Veterans' Affairs initiate discussions with the House and Senate Armed Services Committees to develop provisions addressing veteran suicide in the National Defense Authorization Act.[78] *Charting the Future* notes that suicide prevention tends to operate in its own silo, even though suicide has some of the same risk and protective factors as other public health problems. It recommends collaboration and dialogue between the suicide prevention effort and other public health efforts, stating, "Strong dialogue will help prevent the field from endlessly recreating wheels and spreading the limited funds too broadly to make a sustainable difference."[79]

Congress may choose to assess whether current levels of collaboration and dialogue are sufficient to ensure rapid dissemination of knowledge and avoid unnecessary duplication of effort. (Note that replication of studies is an integral part of the research process, so a distinction may be made between appropriate and unnecessary duplication of effort.) Congress may mandate, facilitate, or incentivize additional interagency coordination.

Potential Issues in Interventions

Three issues in VHA suicide prevention interventions that have come before Congress during hearings are (1) collaboration and dialogue, as discussed above; (2) an apparent gap between policy and practice; and (3) perceptions about mental illness and mental health care.[80]

If agencies (federal, state, or local) engage in ongoing collaboration and dialogue, sharing evaluations of existing interventions and research into new interventions, they may prevent unnecessary duplication of effort and help build the evidence base more quickly. The recommendations above regarding information sharing and collaboration pertain to intervention research as well.[81] *Charting the Future* advocates fast-tracking all phases of the intervention cycle (designing and pilot testing interventions, implementing interventions, and evaluating interventions), as well as the dissemination of the knowledge gained in each phase.[82] Moreover, congressional testimony has repeatedly called for increased use of non-VA resources, including other federal, state, and local government agencies; private for-profit and not-for-profit health care providers; veterans, their families, and their communities; and other individuals or organizations.[83] The use of non-VA resources might help suicide prevention interventions reach the majority of veterans who do not use VHA services.

A recurring theme in the area of suicide prevention interventions is the apparent gap between policy and practice. Examples of such a gap include the timeliness of mental health appointments and the use of evidence-based treatment. Increasing the timeliness of appointments may require congressional action in the form of additional resources in order to hire more providers, expand office space, or implement technologies such as telemedicine. Other gaps between policy and practice, such as the infrequent use of evidence-based treatment, may be possible for the VHA to address without additional resources; Congress may choose to continue exercising oversight in such areas.

Perceptions about mental illness and mental health care may affect whether veterans make use of treatment available to them. The belief that mental illness is a sign of weakness or something shameful may inhibit individuals or those around them from reaching out. Additionally, the belief that mental health care is not available, not appropriate, or not effective may discourage veterans from seeking care. Both stigma and mistaken beliefs may be reduced through discussions that address the facts of mental illness and mental health care. Thus congressional hearings on suicide, mental illness, or mental health care may have the unintended—but beneficial—consequence of reducing stigma and correcting misunderstandings about treatment.[84]

Appendix. Public Laws Addressing VA Suicide Prevention Efforts

Since Operations Enduring Freedom and Iraqi Freedom began, four public laws have addressed VHA suicide prevention efforts: the Joshua Omvig Veterans Suicide Prevention Act (P.L. 110- 110); the National Defense Authorization Act for Fiscal Year 2008 (P.L. 110-181); the Veterans' Benefits Improvement Act of 2008 (P.L. 110-389); and the Caregivers and Veterans Omnibus Health Services Act of 2010 (P.L. 111-163). Relevant provisions of each are summarized below.

Joshua Omvig Veterans Suicide Prevention Act

The Joshua Omvig Veterans Suicide Prevention Act (P.L. 110-110), enacted in 2007, required the VA Secretary to develop and implement a comprehensive suicide prevention program, and to report to Congress on the program.

The Congressional Budget Office estimated that implementing the Joshua Omvig Veterans Suicide Prevention Act would have "little, if any, cost," because the VA already had implemented or was planning to implement each of the specific requirements.[85]

The textbox below lists the required elements and additional authorized elements of the comprehensive suicide prevention program.

Joshua Omvig Veterans Suicide Prevention Act (P.L. 110-110)

Required elements of the comprehensive suicide prevention program include the following:

- mandatory suicide prevention training for appropriate VA staff and contractors;
- designation of a suicide prevention counselor at each VA medical center;
- outreach and education for veterans and their families to promote mental health;
- mental health assessments of veterans and referrals to appropriate treatment;
- availability of 24-hour mental health care for veterans;
- research on best practices for suicide prevention; and
- research on mental health among veterans with military sexual trauma.

Additional authorized (but not required) elements include the following:

- a 24-hour toll-free hotline staffed by trained mental health personnel;
- peer support counseling; and
- other actions to reduce the incidence of suicide among veterans.

National Defense Authorization Act for Fiscal Year 2008

Section 1611 of the National Defense Authorization Act for Fiscal Year 2008 (P.L. 110-181) directed the VA and DOD Secretaries to jointly develop a comprehensive care and transition policy for servicemembers recovering from serious injuries or illnesses related to their military service.

The law specified that the policy must address (among other things) the training and skills of health care professionals, recovery coordinators, and case managers, to ensure that they are able to detect and report early warning signs of suicidal thoughts or behaviors, along with other behavioral health concerns.

The law further specified that the policy must include tracking the notifications made by recovery care coordinators, medical care case managers, and nonmedical care managers to health care professionals regarding suicidal thoughts or behaviors, along with other behavioral health concerns.

A 2009 Government Accountability Office report indicates that DOD and VA have developed the relevant policies.[86]

Veterans' Benefits Improvement Act of 2008

Section 809 of the Veterans' Benefits Improvement Act of 2008 (P.L. 110-389) grants the VA Secretary authority to advertise in the media for various purposes, including suicide prevention.

Caregivers and Veterans Omnibus Health Services Act of 2010

Section 403 of the Caregivers and Veterans Omnibus Health Services Act of 2010 (P.L. 111-163) requires the VA Secretary to conduct a study to determine the number of veterans who died by suicide between January 1, 1999, and May 5, 2010 (i.e., the date of enactment). As of this writing, the study has not been completed.

End Notes

[1] See the *Appendix* for public laws addressing suicide among veterans.

[2] See, for example, U.S. Congress, Senate Committee on Veterans' Affairs, *VA Mental Health Care: Closing the Gaps*, 112th Cong., 1st sess., July 14, 2011; U.S. Congress, Senate Committee on Veterans' Affairs, *VA Mental Health Care: Addressing Wait Times and Access to Care*, 112th Cong., 1st sess., November 30, 2011; U.S. Congress, House Committee on Veterans' Affairs, Subcommittee on Health, *Understanding and Preventing Veteran Suicide*, 112th Cong., 1st sess., December 2, 2011.

[3] For suicide rates among veterans of Operations Enduring Freedom and Iraqi Freedom (OEF/OIF) using VA health care, and for a discussion of limitations of the data, see CRS Report R41921, *Suicide, PTSD, and Substance Use Among OEF/OIF Veterans Using VA Health Care: Facts and Figures*, by Erin Bagalman.

[4] This report focuses on the public health approach. A full discussion of the clinical approach to suicide prevention is beyond the scope of this report. The pharmacotherapy and psychotherapy mentioned in the "Screening and Treatment" section are examples of the clinical approach.

[5] U.S. Department of Health and Human Services (HHS), Public Health Service, *National Strategy for Suicide Prevention: Goals and Objectives for Action*, SMA01-3517, Rockville, MD, 2001, http://store.samhsa.gov/product/ SMA01-3517; hereinafter referred to as *National Strategy for Suicide Prevention*. The public health framework is described on pp. 29-40.

[6] Federal Working Group on Suicide Prevention, *National Strategy for Suicide Prevention: Compendium of Federal Activities*, 2009, http://www.samhsa.gov/mentalhealth/ NSSP Compendium_v2_March09.pdf. HHS agencies involved in suicide prevention include the Centers for Disease Control and Prevention (CDC), Indian Health Service (IHS), National Institute of Mental Health (NIMH), Substance Abuse and Mental Health Services Administration (SAMHSA), Health Resources and Services Administration (HRSA), Agency for Healthcare Research and Quality (AHRQ), and Administration on Aging (AoA).

[7] Veterans Health Administration, *VHA Strategic Plan for Suicide Prevention: FY 2009–2011*; hereinafter referred to as *VHA Strategic Plan*. The VHA Strategic Plan is based on both public health and clinical approaches; see Element 2.1.

[8] Suicide Prevention Resource Center and Suicide Prevention Action Network (SPAN), Charting the Future of Suicide Prevention: A 2010 Progress Review of the National Strategy and Recommendations for the Decade Ahead, 2010, p. 18, http://www.sprc.org/library/ Charting TheFuture_Fullbook.pdf; hereinafter referred to as Charting the Future.

[9] *Charting the Future*, p. 11.

[10] See, for example, U.S. Congress, Senate Committee on Veterans' Affairs, *VA Mental Health Care: Closing the Gaps*, 112th Cong., 1st sess., July 14, 2011; U.S. Congress, Senate Committee on Veterans' Affairs, *VA Mental Health Care: Addressing Wait Times and Access to Care*, 112th Cong., 1st sess., November 30, 2011; U.S.

Congress, House Committee on Veterans' Affairs, Subcommittee on Health, *Understanding and Preventing Veteran Suicide*, 112th Cong., 1st sess., December 2, 2011.

[11] Katherine E. Watkins and Harold Alan Pincus, *Veterans Health Administration Mental Health Program Evaluation: Capstone Report*, Altarum Institute and RAND Health, 2011, p. 153; hereinafter referred to as *VHA Mental Health Program Evaluation*.

[12] Suicide surveillance relies on information derived from death certificates. Both the legal authority for maintaining registries of deaths and the responsibility for issuing death certificates reside with individual states, territories, and two cities (Washington, DC, and New York, NY).

[13] The National Center for Health Statistics (NCHS) is part of the Centers for Disease Control and Prevention (CDC), within the Department of Health and Human Services (HHS). NCHS works cooperatively with state, territorial, and local jurisdictions to collect information from death certificates in the National Vital Statistics System (NVSS). NCHS extracts information from NVSS to create the National Death Index (NDI), a data set that can be combined with other data sets for research purposes. For more information, see CDC, National Center for Health Statistics, *About the National Death Index*, http://www.cdc.gov/nchs/data_access/ndi/about_ndi.htm.

[14] VHA combines suicide data from the NDI with enrollment records to identify suicides among enrolled veterans. The enrollment file includes veterans receiving benefits from the Veterans Benefits Administration, even if the veterans are not receiving care from VHA.

[15] Researchers at the RAND Corporation summarized variation in suicide statistics across jurisdictions in four domains: (1) how suicides are defined or how ambiguous deaths are classified, (2) qualifications of professionals certifying a death as a suicide, (3) the extent to which possible suicide deaths are investigated, and (4) the quality of data management. Rajeev Ramchand et al., *The War Within: Preventing Suicide in the U.S. Military*, The RAND Corporation, 2011, p. 13, http://www.rand.org; hereinafter referred to as *The War Within*.

[16] The standard death certificate allows officials to indicate if a decedent has ever served in the U.S. Armed Forces; however, this indication captures both veterans and current servicemembers, with no means of distinguishing between the two. Also, the individual responsible for completing the death certificate may not know whether the decedent is a veteran.

[17] See textbox in the Introduction.

[18] *VHA Strategic Plan*, Element 7.1.

[19] HHS, CDC, *Fiscal Year 2012 Justification of Estimates for Appropriation Committees*.

[20] HHS, CDC, *National Violent Death Reporting System*, http://www.cdc.gov/violenc eprevention/nvdrs and http://www.cdc.gov/ncipc/wisqars/NVDRS.

[21] HHS, CDC, *Fiscal Year 2012 Justification of Estimates for Appropriation Committees*.

[22] HHS, CDC, National Center for Injury Prevention and Control, Division of Violence Prevention, *Preventing Suicide: Program Activities Guide*, Atlanta, GA, 2010, http://www. cdc.gov/ViolencePrevention/pub /PreventingSuicide.html.

[23] Ibid.

[24] *Charting the Future*, p. 30.

[25] Centers for Disease Control and Prevention, *Suicide: Risk and Protective Factors*, Atlanta, GA, http://www.cdc.gov/ViolencePrevention/suicide/riskprotectivefactors.html.

[26] HHS, National Institutes of Health (NIH), National Institute of Mental Health, *Publications about Suicide Prevention*, http://www.nimh.nih.gov/health/publications/suicide-prevention-listing.shtml; and National Institute of Mental Health, *Science News about Suicide Prevention*, http://www.nimh.nih.gov/science-news/science-news-aboutsuicide-prevention. shtml.

[27] SAMHSA asks about these topics in the National Survey on Drug Use and Health (NSDUH). See HHS, CDC, *Morbidity and Mortality Weekly Report: Suicidal Thoughts and Behaviors Among Adults ≥ 18 Years—United States, 2008 – 2009*, October 21, 2011, http://www.cdc. gov/mmwr/preview/mmwrhtml/ss6013a1.htm.

[28] HHS, CDC, *Suicide: Facts at a Glance*, 2009, http://www.cdc.gov/violenceprevention /pdf/ suicide-datasheet-a.pdf.

[29] For example, although the single strongest predictor of a completed suicide is a prior suicide attempt, most people who attempt suicide do not subsequently complete suicide, and most people who complete suicides have no history of prior attempts. See *The War Within* and Joel Paris, "Predicting and Preventing Suicide: Do We Know Enough to Do Either?," *Harvard Review of Psychiatry*, vol. 14, no. 5 (2006), pp. 233-240.

[30] The ORD supports research through four research divisions: Biomedical Laboratory Research and Development (BLR&D), Clinical Science Research and Development (CSR&D), Rehabilitation Research and Development (RR&D), and Health Services Research and Development (HSR&D).

[31] A search for "suicide*" at http://www.hsrd.research.va.gov/research/ yields dozens of suicide-related studies conducted within ORD's Health Services Research and Development (HSR&D) Service; some of the resulting studies investigate risk factors and/or protective factors.

[32] VA, VHA, Health Services Research and Development, *Suicide Among Veterans: Using the VA Depression Registry to Inform Care*, Study IIR 04-211, http://www.hsrd.research.va. gov/research/abstracts.cfm?Project_ID=2141695453.

[33] VA, VHA, Health Services Research and Development, *Suicidality: Correlates and Impact on Preference-Weighted Health Status of Veterans in VA Primary Care*, Study SHP 08-160, http://www.hsrd.research.va. gov/research/ abstracts.cfm?Project_ID=2141698711.

[34] U.S. Congress, Committee of Conference, *Making Appropriations for Military Quality of Life Functions of the Department of Defense, Military Construction, the Department of Veterans Affairs, and Related Agencies for the Fiscal Year Ending September 30, 2006, and for Other Purposes*, report to accompany H.R. 2528, 109th Cong., 1st sess., November 18, 2005, H.Rept. 109-305 (Washington: GPO, 2006), p. 39. The committee report directed the VHA "to place more emphasis on psychiatric care of our veterans by designating three centers of excellence to focus on mental health/PTSD needs. These three centers will be established at Waco Medical Center, Texas; San Diego Medical Center, California; and the Canandaigua Medical Center, New York."

[35] VA, VHA, VISN 2 Center of Excellence at Canandaigua, http://www.mirecc.va.gov/ docs/ 2010InfoSheets/ VISN_2_CoE_Canandaigua_Info_Sheet_2010.pdf.

[36] P.L. 104-262, Veterans' Health Care Eligibility Reform Act of 1996, enacted 10/09/1996 (38 U.S.C. § 7320).

[37] VA, VHA, *MIRECC of the VA Rocky Mountain Network (VISN 19 MIRECC)*, http://www. mirecc.va.gov/visn19/ index.asp.

[38] VA, VHA, VISN 19 MIRECC, *Examining Prolonged Grief Disorder and Its Relationship to Self-Directed Violence (SDV) Among Veterans*, http://www.mirecc.va.gov/visn19/ studies/ grief/index.asp.

[39] VA, VHA, VISN 19 MIRECC, *Neurobiology Of Suicide Risk In Traumatic Brain Injury And Substance Abuse*, http://www.mirecc.va.gov/visn19/studies/tbi_sud/index.asp.

[40] One goal of the Mental Health Quality Enhancement Research Initiative (QUERI) within ORD is to "[d]evelop and implement evidence-based suicide prevention strategies." See VA Mental Health QUERI Center, *Strategic Plan*, November 2008, http://www.queri.research. va.gov/about/strategic_plans/mh.pdf#page=21; and VA Mental Health QUERI Center, *Fact Sheet*, June 2011, http://www.queri.research.va.gov /about/ factsheets/mh_ factsheet.pdf.

[41] The COE at Canandaigua evaluates implementation of suicide prevention initiatives.

[42] For example, the MIRECC of the VA Rocky Mountain Network is conducting a pilot program to determine whether providing prescription medication in blister packages (rather than bottles) reduces the likelihood of overdose. Veterans Health Administration, Blister Packaging Medication to Increase Treatment Adherence and Clinical Response: Impact on Suicide-Related Morbidity and Mortality, http://www.mirecc.va.gov/ projects/blisterpack /index.asp.

[43] *The War Within*, p. 13.

[44] Ibid.

[45] U.S. Government Accountability Office, *VA Mental Health: Number of Veterans Receiving Care, Barriers Faced, and Efforts to Increase Access*, GAO-12-12, October 14, 2011, pp. 15-17, http://www.gao .gov/products/GAO-12-12.

[46] Ibid. Examples of expanded options include increasing use of telemental health services and call centers (i.e., telephone counseling), integrating mental health services into primary care settings, increasing the number of mental health staff and mental health clinic hours, and adding more Vet Centers.

[47] VA, VHA, *Uniform Mental Health Services in VA Medical Centers and Clinics*, VHA Handbook 1160.01, September 11, 2008.

[48] U.S. Congress, Senate Committee on Veterans' Affairs, *VA Mental Health Care: Closing the Gaps*, 112th Cong., 1st sess., July 14, 2011; U.S. Congress, Senate Committee on Veterans' Affairs, *VA Mental Health Care: Addressing Wait Times and Access to Care*, 112th Cong., 1st sess., November 30, 2011; Gregg Zoroya and Paul Monies, "Lag in Mental Health Care Found at a Third of VA Hospitals," *USA Today*, November 9, 2011, http://www. usatoday.com/news/ military/story/2011-11-09/veterans-mental-health-care/ 51143216/1; and *VHA Mental Health Program Evaluation*.

[49] *VHA Strategic Plan*, Elements 4.1, 4.2, and 4.3.

[50] *VHA Strategic Plan*, Element 9.1, 9.2, 9.3, and 9.4.

[51] *The War Within*. Outside the VHA, the term "gatekeeper" (rather than "guide") is generally used.

[52] *The War Within*.

[53] *VHA Strategic Plan*, Element 6.2.

[54] *VHA Mental Health Program Evaluation*, p. 153.

[55] *VHA Mental Health Program Evaluation*. For example, among veterans for whom maintenance medication is recommended, less than one-third received the recommended continuous treatment (p. 160). Similarly, among veterans receiving psychotherapy, "most did not include elements of an evidence-based modality" (p. 154).

[56] *VHA Mental Health Program Evaluation*. Less than two-thirds of veterans in a new treatment episode "have a documented assessment of their housing and employment needs" (p. 161). Among veterans with major depressive disorder who were receiving psychotherapy, less than a quarter (23%) "had documentation of an assessment of response to psychotherapy" (p. 155).

[57] Mechanism of injury for suicides among the general U.S. population in CY2007 identified from Centers for Disease Control and Prevention, National Center for Health Statistics. *Compressed Mortality File 1999-2007. CDC WONDER On-line Database, compiled from Compressed Mortality File 1999-2007 Series 20 No. 2M, 2010*, http://wonder.cdc.gov/cmf-icd10.html.

[58] J. John Mann et al., "Suicide Prevention Strategies: A Systematic Review," *Journal of the American Medical Association*, vol. 294, no. 16 (October 26, 2005), pp. 2064-2074.

[59] VHA Strategic Plan, Elements 10.4 and 10.6; and VA, Blister Packaging Medication to Increase Treatment Adherence and Clinical Response: Impact on Suicide-Related Morbidity and Mortality, http://www. mirecc. va.gov/ projects/blisterpack/index.asp.

[60] J. John Mann et al., "Suicide Prevention Strategies: A Systematic Review," *Journal of the American Medical Association*, vol. 294, no. 16 (October 26, 2005), pp. 2064-2074.

[61] *VHA Strategic Plan*, Element 6.10.

[62] Substance Abuse and Mental Health Services Administration, *National Suicide Prevention Lifeline*, http://www.suicidepreventionlifeline.org/.

[63] U.S. Congress, House Committee on Veterans' Affairs, Subcommittee on Health, *Understanding and Preventing Veteran Suicide*, 112th Cong., 1st sess., December 2, 2011, testimony of Jan E. Kemp, RN, Ph.D., National Mental Health Director for Suicide Prevention, Veterans Heath Administration, U.S. Department of Veterans Affairs.

[64] J. John Mann et al., "Suicide Prevention Strategies: A Systematic Review," *Journal of the American Medical Association*, vol. 294, no. 16 (October 26, 2005), pp. 2064-2074.

[65] *National Strategy for Suicide Prevention*, p. 36.

[66] J. John Mann et al., "Suicide Prevention Strategies: A Systematic Review," *Journal of the American Medical Association*, vol. 294, no. 16 (October 26, 2005), pp. 2064-2074.

[67] *VHA Strategic Plan*, Elements 11.1 and 11.2.

[68] VA, Office of Inspector General, *Healthcare Inspection: Evaluation of Suicide Prevention Program Implementation in VHA Facilities, January–June 2009*, Report No. 09-00326-223, Washington, DC, September 22, 2009, http://www.va.gov/oig/54/reports/VAOIG-09-00326-223.pdf; and VA, Office of Inspector General, *Combined Assessment Program Summary Report: Re-Evaluation of Suicide Safety Plan Practices in Veterans Health Administration Facilities*, Report No. 11-01380-128, Washington, DC, March 22, 2011, http://www.va.gov/oig/CAP/ VAOIG-11-01380-128.pdf.

[69] Department of Defense Task Force on the Prevention of Suicide by Members of the Armed Forces, *The Challenge and the Promise: Strengthening the Force, Preventing Suicide, and Saving Lives*, August 2010, pp. 55, 89, http://www.health.mil/dhb/subcommittees-tfpsmaf.cfm; hereinafter referred to as *The Challenge and the Promise*.

[70] CNAS is a 501(c)3 tax-exempt nonprofit organization located in Washington; it describes itself as independent and non-partisan. (http://www.cnas.org/about).

[71] Margaret Harrell and Nancy Berglass, *Losing the Battle: The Challenge of Military Suicide*, Center for a New American Security, Washington, DC, October 2011, p. 9; hereinafter referred to as *Losing the Battle*.

[72] Ibid.

[73] Ibid.

[74] The enrollment file includes veterans receiving benefits from the Veterans Benefits Administration, even if the veterans are not receiving care from VHA.

[75] Han K. Kang and Tim A. Bullman, "Letter: Risk of Suicide Among US Veterans After Returning From the Iraq or Afghanistan War Zones," *Journal of the American Medical Association*, vol. 300, no. 6 (2008), pp. 652-

653. The study was limited to veterans who served in Operations Enduring Freedom and/or Iraqi Freedom and who were separated alive from active duty between October 2001 and December 2005.

[76] See for example Stefan Timmermans, "Suicide determination and the professional authority of medical examiners.," *American Sociological Review*, vol. 70, no. 2 (2005), pp. 311-333; Hugh P. Whitt, "Where did the bodies go? The social construction of suicide data, New York City, 1976-1992," *Sociological Inquiry*, vol. 76, no. 2 (2006), pp. 166- 187; M.J. Breiding and B. Wiersema, "Variability of undetermined manner of death classification in the U.S.," *Injury Prevention*, vol. 12(Suppl II) (2006), pp. ii49-ii54.

[77] *Losing the Battle*, p. 9.

[78] Ibid.

[79] *Charting the Future*, p. 40.

[80] U.S. Congress, Senate Committee on Veterans' Affairs, *VA Mental Health Care: Closing the Gaps*, 112th Cong., 1st sess., July 14, 2011; U.S. Congress, Senate Committee on Veterans' Affairs, *VA Mental Health Care: Addressing Wait Times and Access to Care*, 112th Cong., 1st sess., November 30, 2011; U.S. Congress, House Committee on Veterans' Affairs, Subcommittee on Health, *Understanding and Preventing Veteran Suicide*, 112th Cong., 1st sess., December 2, 2011.

[81] *Losing the Battle*, p. 9; and *Charting the Future*, p. 40.

[82] *Charting the Future*, p. 40.

[83] U.S. Congress, Senate Committee on Veterans' Affairs, *VA Mental Health Care: Addressing Wait Times and Access to Care*, 112th Cong., 1st sess., November 30, 2011; U.S. Congress, House Committee on Veterans' Affairs, Subcommittee on Health, *Understanding and Preventing Veteran Suicide*, 112th Cong., 1st sess., December 2, 2011.

[84] U.S. Congress, Senate Committee on Veterans' Affairs, *VA Mental Health Care: Closing the Gaps*, 112th Cong., 1st sess., July 14, 2011. Senator Murray mentioned stigma in her opening statement, and it was discussed at several points.

[85] U.S. Congressional Budget Office, *Cost Estimate for H.R. 327 Joshua Omvig Veterans Suicide Prevention Act*, March 19, 2007; and U.S. Congressional Budget Office, *Cost Estimate for S.4797 Joshua Omvig Veterans Suicide Prevention Act*, July 10, 2007.

[86] U.S. Government Accountability Office, *Recovering Servicemembers: DOD and VA Have Jointly Developed the Majority of Required Policies but Challenges Remain*, GAO-09-728, July 2009, p. 25.

In: The Enemy Within
Editors: Jack M. Wright and Gabriel E. Lewis

ISBN: 978-1-62081-316-4

Chapter 3

OPENING STATEMENT OF ANN MARIE BUERKLE, CHAIRWOMAN

HOUSE COMMITTEE ON VETERANS AFFAIRS, SUBCOMMITTEE ON HEALTH HEARING ON: UNDERSTANDING AND PREVENTING VETERAN SUICIDE*

12/2/2011

Today we meet to search for answers to the most haunting of questions – what leads an individual who so honorably served our nation, out of helplessness and hopelessness, to take their own life and how can we prevent such a tragedy from happening to one who has bravely worn the uniform and defended our freedom.

Suicide is undoubtedly a complex issue, but it is also a preventable one and I am deeply troubled by its persistent prevalence in our military and veteran communities.

The statistics are sobering – eighteen veterans commit suicide each day with almost a third receiving care from the Department of Veterans Affairs (VA) at the time of their death. Each month, there are 950 veterans being treated by the VA who attempt suicide. The number of military suicides has increased since the start of Operations Enduring Freedom and Iraqi Freedom (OEF/OIF), with data from the Department of Defense (DOD) indicating servicemembers took their lives at an approximate rate of one every 36 hours from 2005 to 2010. We continue to hear tragic stories despite significant increases in recent years in the number of programs and resources devoted to suicide prevention among our service members and veterans.

Today we will hear from VA and DOD that they are making strides in identifying at risk servicemembers and veterans and providing treatment for mental health and other disorders that can lead to suicide.

---

* These remarks were delivered as Opening Statement given on December 2, 2012. Ann Marie Buerkle is Chairwoman, House Committee on Veterans Affairs, Subcommittee on Health.

Yet, no matter how great programs and services are, if they do not connect with those who need them, they do no good at all. VA and DOD continue to struggle with persistent obstacles including data limitations, cultural stigma, access issues, a lack of partnerships with community providers, and outreach that relies on the service member, veteran, or loved one to initiate treatment.

We must do more to reach out to veterans inside and outside of the VA and DOD health care systems to ensure that all those who need it get the help they earned and deserve before time runs out.

Until a family no longer must bear the pain of losing a loved one, we are failing and not enough is being done.

I thank you all for joining us this morning. I now recognize our Ranking Member, Mr. Michaud for any remarks he may have.

In: The Enemy Within
Editors: Jack M. Wright and Gabriel E. Lewis
ISBN: 978-1-62081-316-4

Chapter 4

HOUSE COMMITTEE ON VETERANS AFFAIRS, SUBCOMMITTEE ON HEALTH HEARING ON: UNDERSTANDING AND PREVENTING VETERAN SUICIDE

WITNESS TESTIMONY OF COMMANDER RENÉ A. CAMPOS, USN (RET.), DEPUTY DIRECTOR, GOVERNMENT RELATIONS, MILITARY OFFICERS ASSOCIATION OF AMERICA*

12/2/2011

A decade of war has placed unprecedented demands and stressors on our warriors and their families that will leave scars and unintended consequences for generations to come.

The Departments of Veterans Affairs (VA) and Defense (DoD) have long been faced with the daunting challenge of meeting a significant range of medical and rehabilitation issues. MOAA is particularly concerned about the exponentially growing need to address mental health, behavioral and cognitive conditions, in light of the rising rates of suicides, alcohol and substance use, and a variety of other issues playing out among veterans, servicemembers and their families.

A number of reports support our concerns:

- 2008 VA "Blue Ribbon Work Group on Suicide Prevention in the Veteran Population"
- RAND Health/National Defense Research Institute
    - 2008 "The Invisible Wounds of War"
    - 2011 "The War Within, Preventing Suicide in the U.S. Military"

* These remarks were delivered as Witness Testimony given on December 2, 2012. Commander René A. Campos is USN (Ret.), Deputy Director, Government Relations, Military Officers Association of America.

  - 2011 "Addressing Psychological Health and Traumatic Brain Injury Among Servicemembers and Their Families"
- 2011 Center for a New American Security (CNAS) Report "Losing the Battle: The Challenge of Military Suicide"

The current statistics are disturbing and point to an even greater need to wage an all out battle to end suicide. This will require a sustained national commitment at all levels of government if we are to rid veterans of the psychological and traumatic physical conditions that are threatening their lives and the health and well-being of their families. Sadly these statistics represent the heroes who protect our country and our freedoms:

- 20 percent of suicides in the U.S. are former servicemembers
- One currently serving member died every 36 hours during the period 2005-2010
- 18 veterans die a day—that is one suicide every 80 minutes

Recommendations

MOAA offers three specific recommendations to address current barriers to care:

- Require VA-DoD to establish a single strategy and a joint Suicide Prevention Office that reports directly to the Department Secretaries through the Senior Oversight Committee (SOC).
- Authorize funding to expand VHA mental health capacity and capability in order to improve access and delivery of quality and timely care and information.
- Authorize additional funding to expand outreach and marketing efforts to encourage enrollment of all eligible veterans in VA health care, with special emphasis on Guard and Reserve members, rural veterans, and high-risk populations.

MADAM CHAIRMAN AND DISTINGUISHED MEMBERS OF THE SUBCOMMITTEE, on behalf of the 370,000 members of the Military Officers Association of America (MOAA), I am grateful for the opportunity to present testimony on MOAA's observations concerning the Department of Veterans Affairs' (VA) suicide prevention programs and efforts.

MOAA does not receive any grants or contracts from the federal government.

MOAA thanks the Subcommittee for its interest in this extremely difficult issue and for your leadership in looking out for the health and well-being of our veterans and family members. We also commend the VA for its staunch commitment to enhancing mental and behavioral health programs by working with DoD and other government and non-government entities to help veterans and their families improve their physical and psychological well being.

OVERVIEW OF VA SUICIDE PREVENTION PROGRAMS AND EFFORTS

A number of reports and activities have been published in the last seven years that shine a spotlight on veteran and military suicide and VA's prevention efforts.

In 2008, the RAND Corporation's Center for Military Health Policy Research released a report on "*The Invisible Wounds of War.*" The report highlighted the mental health and cognitive needs of combat veterans, focusing on three wounds: post-traumatic stress disorder (PTSD), depression, and traumatic brain injury (TBI).

The report states that, "Unless treated, PTSD, depression, and TBI can have far-reaching and damaging consequences. Individuals afflicted with these conditions face higher risks for other psychological problems and for attempting suicide...there is a possible link between these conditions and homelessness...the consequences from lack of treatment or under-treatment can have a high economic toll."

RAND made four recommendations that get at these issues:

1) Increase the cadre of providers who are trained and certified to deliver proven (evidence-based) care, so that capacity is adequate for current and future needs.
2) Change policies to encourage more active duty personnel and veterans to seek needed care.
3) Deliver proven, evidence-based care to servicemembers and veterans whenever and wherever services are provided.
4) Invest in research to close information gaps and plan effectively.

Like RAND, our Association believes that restoring veterans to 'full mental health' will be important to reduce long-term economic societal costs.

RAND's *Invisible Wounds of War* was the first study of its kind to estimate that PTSD and depression among servicemembers will cost the nation up to $6.2 billion in the two years after deployment.

The study concludes that investing in proper treatment would provide even larger cost savings—savings that would come from increases in productivity, as well as from reductions in the expected number of suicides.

Additionally, The Journal of Clinical Psychiatry reported that the economic burden of depression to this country was estimated to be $43.7 billion in 1990. By 2000 the cost burden rose to $53.9 billion, which included direct treatment costs, lost earnings due to depression-related suicides, and indirect workplace costs.

In June 2008, the Secretary of the VA convened a *Blue Ribbon Work Group on Suicide Prevention in the Veteran Population*to advise on the research, education and program improvements to the prevention of suicide.

The Work Group consisted of five Executive Branch representatives, two of which were from DoD.

MOAA was encouraged by the Group's findings. According to the report, the Veterans Health Administration (VHA) had a comprehensive strategy in place and a number of promising initiatives and innovations for preventing suicide attempts and completions.

The Group recommended that VHA:

1) Establish an analysis and research plan in collaboration with other federal agencies to resolve conflicting study results in order to ensure that there is a consistent approach to describing the rates of suicide and suicide attempts in veterans.
2) Revise and reevaluate the current policies regarding mandatory suicide screening assessments.
3) Proceed with the planned implementation of the Category II flag (patient is at high risk for suicide), with consideration given to pilot testing the flag in one or more regions before full national implementation.
4) Ensure that suicides and suicide attempts are reported and that procedures are consistent with broader VHA surveillance efforts.
5) Ensure that specific pharmacotherapy recommendations related to suicide or suicide behaviors are evidence-based.
6) Continue to pursue opportunities for outreach to enroll eligible veterans, and to disseminate messages to reduce risk behavior associated with suicide.
7) Ensure confidentiality of health records.
8) Ensure ongoing evaluation of the roles and workloads of the Suicide Prevention Coordinator positions.

This year a Center for a New American Security (CNAS) report entitled, *"Losing the Battle: The Challenge of Military Suicide,"* published some disturbing statistics, noting that suicide among veterans and servicemembers present challenges to the health of America's all-volunteer force. The report addressed the obstacles for confronting suicide. Although most of the 13 recommendations CNAS offered are focused on DoD and the Military Services, most are applicable to VA, such as:

1) Ensuring transfer of mental health information when members relocate
2) Eliminating the cultural stigma associated with mental health care
3) Holding leaders accountable
4) Increasing mental health and behavioral health care professionals, and addressing gaps in programs for drilling Guard and Reserve units
5) Establishing reasonable time requirements for states to provide death data to the Centers for Disease Control (CDC), and that Health and Human Services (HHS) should ensure CDC is resourced sufficiently to expedite the compilation of national death data. VA, DoD and HHS should coordinate annual analysis of veteran suicide data.
6) Sharing of suicide data between VA, DoD and HHS, including discussion with Veterans Affairs and Armed Services Committees to develop a provision to address veteran suicides.

Two other reports were published this year by RAND's Health/National Defense Research Institute and sponsored by the Office of the Secretary of Defense. The first report, *"The War Within, Preventing Suicide in the U.S. Military,"* was intended to enhance the Department's suicide prevention programs and efforts. The second report, *"Addressing Psychological Health and Traumatic Brain Injury Among Servicemembers and Their Families,"* provided DoD a comprehensive catalog of existing programs currently sponsored or funded by the Department to address psychological health and TBI. MOAA believes the recommendations of these two reports are also applicable to VA:

1) Increasing and improving the capacity of the mental health care system to deliver evidence-based care
2) Changing policies to encourage more veterans and servicemembers to seek needed care
3) Delivering evidence-based care in all settings
4) Investing in research to close knowledge gaps and plan effectively
5) Taking advantage of programs' unique capacity for supporting prevention, resilience, early identification of symptoms, and help seeking to meet the psychological health and TBI needs of servicemembers and their families
6) Establishing clear and strategic relationships between programs and existing mental health and TBI care delivery systems
7) Examining existing gaps in routine service delivery that could be filled by programs (formal needs assessment and gap analysis of programs)
8) Reducing barriers faced by programs
9) Evaluating and tracking new and existing programs, and using evidence-based interventions to support program efforts

VHA mental health officials estimate there are approximately 1,600 – 1,800 suicides per year among veterans receiving care in the health system and upwards of 6,400 per year among all veterans. One of the key goals of VA's Mental Health Strategic Plan, implemented in 2004, was to reduce suicide among the veteran population. Out of that plan came a National Suicide Prevention Center of Excellence, a national suicide prevention hotline, a patient record flagging system, and suicide prevention programs in each medical facility.

Speaking at a joint VA-DoD Suicide Prevention Conference last year, VA Secretary Eric Shinseki said every veteran was susceptible to suicide.

"The emotional wounds are no less common than physical injuries; however, they are more difficult to diagnose which adds to the challenge of suicide prevention," said Shinseki. He went on to say that the suicide problem was one of the 'most frustrating' leadership challenges he faces. "Of the 18 veterans who commit suicide each day, five of those veterans are under the care of the VA. Losing five veterans who are in treatment every month, and then not having a shot at the other 13 who for some reason haven't come under our care, means that we have a lot of work to do."

There are a number of predisposing risk factors associated with suicide and mental health disorders that can be diagnosed and treated. Some of these risk factors include:

- PTSD
- Relationship problems
- Financial difficulties
- Substance abuse and addiction
- Ongoing depression
- Social isolation
- Recent illness and/or hospitalization

- Difficulty Sleeping
- Access to firearms

Today, VA has two primary program areas targeting suicide prevention, the National Suicide Prevention Program and the Office of Mental Health Services. Some additional initiatives the Department has implemented include:

- Hiring thousands of additional mental health providers
- Launching a Suicide Prevention Campaign
- Establishing a Veteran's Crisis Line
- Instituting a National Suicide Prevention Coordinator Program
- Directing a suicide prevention safety plan (SPSP) and Practices for high risk patients
- Implementing policy requiring annual depression screening for veterans using VA health care
- Conducting a VA-DoD Suicide Conference
- Establishing a VA-DoD online Suicide Prevention Resource Center

PROGRESS AND CHALLENGES

In conducting our research for this hearing, MOAA was struck by the tremendous level of work that had been done, especially in the last three years. The steadfast determination of the VA Central Office staff and Secretary Shinseki's personal involvement in synchronizing the agency's national suicide prevention efforts is quite visionary.

MOAA gives VA high marks for rebranding its suicide prevention hotline and establishing a National Veterans Crisis Line. Dr. Janet Kemp, VA's National Suicide Prevention Coordinator is to be commended for standing up the suicide hotline, earning her recognition as the 2009 Federal Employee of the Year. The initiative resulted in more than 5,000 immediate rescues. The crisis line is one of the best initiatives according to Dr. Kemp, answering over 450,000 calls and making more than 16,000 life-saving rescues. An anonymous chat service was added to the crisis line and has helped more than 20,000 people.

Additionally, in less than a year VA has expanded agreements from 18 to 48 states to have veteran status on death certificates. Colorado and Illinois have yet to sign an agreement with VA.

Despite these improvements, the VA concedes barriers still exist that challenge its ability to advance suicide prevention to the level needed.

According to a VA Inspector General's "Combined Assessment Program Summary Report: Re-Evaluation of Suicide Prevention Safety Plan Practices in Veterans Health Administration Facilities," released on March 22, 2011, the VA implemented a number of requirements for taking care of patients identified to be at high risk for suicide. One requirement is that there be a written safety plan that should be placed in the medical record, and, that a copy of the plan is given to the patient. The VA IG noted that generally Department's suicide prevention safety plans (SPSP) were comprehensive but the completion of safety plans for all high-risk patients and the timeliness of the plans needed improvement.

In October 2011, The Washington Post published an article titled, *"VA Lacks Resources to Deal with Mental Health, Survey Finds."* The article stated, "Over 70 percent of the survey respondents to a preliminary survey of VA social workers, nurses and doctors think the Department lacks the staff and space to meet the growing numbers of veterans seeking mental health care. More than 37 percent said they are unable to schedule an appointment in their clinic within the mandated 14-day standard."

Senator Patty Murray (D-WA), chairwoman of the Senate Veterans Affairs Committee requested the survey after conducting a hearing this past summer where veterans diagnosed with mental health issues described long waits for treatment in the VA. In a letter to the Department, Senator Murray wrote, "While I understand the Department has concerns that this survey is not comprehensive, after the countless Inspector General and GAO reports, hearings, public laws, conferences, and stories from veterans and clinicians in the field, it is time to act."

MOAA could not agree more. VA and our entire country must address barriers to mental health if we are to win the war on suicide.

Some of the most significant barriers that impede progress are:

- Limitations on mental health capacity and capability, impacting access and quality and timely care (e.g., funding, resources, staffing, hours of operation, infrastructure).
- Lack of total system accountability, oversight, monitoring and evaluation. VA Central Office (VACO) has a comprehensive strategy and policies, but implementation across the health care system is inconsistent and outcomes vary greatly.
- Limitations in data sharing and documentation of information.
- VA and DoD veteran "warrior cultures".
- Limited opportunities for maximizing collaboration, cooperation, and communication to ensure continuity of care and services in a seamless manner.
- Cultural and societal stigma prevents individuals from seeking care.
- Experiences with unprofessional or uncaring VA employees who don't treat veterans with compassion and respect.
- Medical system policies, procedures and logistical challenges make it difficult for veterans and their families to understand and navigate, especially during times of crisis. The VA culture tends to assume because employees understand how VA works, others should know as well.

Some of these barriers are outside of VA's span of control, as noted in the reports mentioned above.

MOAA believes addressing veteran suicides requires an immediate response and a unified strategy coordinated between the VA, DoD and other federal agencies. VA and DoD have had difficulty over the years in keeping up with demand for medical benefits and services from OIF/OEF veterans. As operations start winding down in these theaters we can expect demand to continue for a number decades, and generations to come.

Our country must do all it can to help VA and DoD to ensure our servicemembers have seamless mental health services as they separate or retire from the military—something more than just giving them a web site or toll free number to call when they need help.

Veterans' families, caregivers and children also deserve special attention because of the tremendous burdens they must carry when dealing with the psychological wounds of their loved ones.

Identifying servicemembers who are at high risk and providing them treatment is critical as these individuals will one day be veterans. The sooner we help these individuals; in and out of uniform the better the long-term outcomes will be for veterans, their families and society as a whole.

What Veterans and their Families Tell Us

Veterans and family members we talk to have seen much progress in improving policies and programs at the national level. However, they don't always see these policies and programs implemented or interpreted consistently at all VA medical facilities.

The real tragedy for some veterans who really need help is that they may give up or lose trust in the system. This may be particularly true for severely wounded, ill or injured veterans and their families dealing with the burdens of complex medical conditions.

Here are what veterans and their families told us about their experiences:

PTSD Veteran and Caregiver-Spouse

- The veteran entered the VA system in 2008 as a high-risk patient for suicide and is still at risk today.
- The Caregiver's current issue is addressing the veteran's difficulty sleeping. It took the VA two months to schedule an appointment just to get a fee based referral outside the VA. Now the veteran must wait until May 2012 for VA to do a required sleep study. This Caregiver questions why it takes almost a year for her husband to get the care he needs, especially when VA knows that difficulty sleeping is a risk factor for suicide the veteran has a history of suicidal ideations.
- "I don't trust VA. My Federal Recovery Coordinator (FRC) and I are constantly fighting with people in the VAMC every step of the way. It's like the VA is fighting with itself—why can't they just do what is right? VA is in the business of saving lives and it shouldn't be focused so much on saving money," said the Caregiver.
- Recommendations to improve care:
  - The FRC should have more authority to make things happen in the VA—they are an integral part of the team and likely to have a better understanding of the veteran's mental condition.
  - Access to mental health services
- Veterans with mental health issues should have greater access to fee based services if it takes longer than two weeks to get an appointment.
- Veterans should have more control over their appointments—VA needs to do a better job of accommodating their schedules.

TBI Veteran and Caregiver-Mother

- This severely injured veteran with TBI and a number of physical disabilities had to wait weeks to get the attention of a VA provider from the time of his first thoughts of suicide. It took his mother forcing the issue before VA would see him.
- "The VA tries to treat my son like other patients, but normal protocols don't work. He has half of his brain capacity; he can't talk or communicate normally about how he is thinking or feeling, but he does think and feel, he just can't communicate it the way most people do," she said.
- The Caregiver said, "there were been times the VA medical staff have made comments or their actions hurt her son deeply—one VA provider told her in front of her son that he would never be more than a vegetable." Other providers continue to try pushing her son to institutionalized care because that's what the system normally does for veterans with this level of disability. The veteran's bad experiences at the VA have made it difficult for him to want to do any type of therapy today.
- This Caregiver tries to keep her son as active as possible so he won't get depressed. She says he's lonely and doesn't have any friends so it is easy for him to slip into depression.
- Recommendations to improve care:
    - Family-caregivers for a veteran with severe brain injury need access to services in times of crisis and need the knowledge and tools on how to deal with suicidal ideations. Providers should be open to using alternative therapies or approaches to help veterans with communication challenges. Providers need to be flexible and may need to look outside the VA if services are not available. Providers must do all they can to draw the veteran into the treatment.
    - Veterans should always be treated with compassion and respect—never as though they are on an assembly line.

PTSD/TBI Veteran and Caregiver-Spouse

- The veteran suffers from a number of serious physical conditions as well as PTSD and TBI.
- There have been two incidents of suicidal ideations. The first one was pain related. The second one was in March of this year.
- "When my husband attempted suicide in March the VA doctor told me to take him to the ER. But the ER had no beds and said he may have to wait 24 hours before one was available. They gave me no alternatives. I was scared and no one in the VA did anything to help us or help me know what to do in a situation like this," said the caregiver. She went on to tell us that the typical VA response is to give the patient a machine or medication. "We just want VA to treat us like they care."

Another severely wounded veteran who is an amputee and has TBI told us he was frustrated because his providers seldom talk to him or ask him how he's doing. Their questions and comments are usually directed at his Caregiver-spouse as though he isn't even in the room. He said, "I just want them to know I can and want to contribute to my care—when they don't talk to me it makes me feel like they don't care about me."

According to all these veterans and family members, they are unaware if their veteran's record is flagged or ever has been a flagged as a high-risk patient or if the medical record contains a suicide prevention safety plan.

MOAA Recommendations

MOAA concurs with CNAS and RAND that suicide among veterans and servicemembers challenges the health of our all-volunteer force. CNAS points to some compelling questions for our country to consider:

- If military service becomes associated with suicide, will it be possible to recruit bright and promising young men and women at current rates?
- Will parents and teachers encourage young people to join the military when veterans from their own communities have died from suicide?
- Can an all-volunteer force be viable if veterans come to be seen as broken individuals?
- And how might climbing rates of suicide affect how Americans view active-duty servicemembers and veterans—indeed, how service members and veterans see themselves?

While MOAA supports many of the recommendations and findings in the reports, studies and investigations mentioned above, the sheer volume of recommendations requires prioritizing efforts for improving VA's suicide prevention program. Therefore, MOAA encourages Congress to focus its attention immediately on three specific recommendations which will further enhance VA's suicide prevention efforts as well as help address other systemic issues in its health care system.

MOAA urges:

- *Requiring VA-DoD to establish a single strategy and a joint Suicide Prevention Office that reports directly to the Department Secretaries through the Senior Oversight Committee (SOC).*

A joint office would be responsible for developing, implementing and integrating strategies, policies and procedures, and providing oversight and evaluation of suicide prevention programs and efforts. Congress needs to continue to be VA's and DoD's greatest champion for promoting collaboration, cooperation and communication across and between the two agencies.

A sense of urgency and oversight are needed to address the issue of veteran suicide at all levels of the government. There needs to be a level of commitment similar to that given to wounded warrior issues which came out of the Walter Reed Army Medical Center incident. VA has done a lot to engage with DoD to identify high-risk servicemembers so that a warm hand-off can be made to facilitate continuity of care. But the agency acknowledges a number of challenges still exist because of cultures and the different policies and programs that vary across the DoD and the Military Services.

- *Authorizing funding to expand VHA mental health capacity and capability in order to improve access and delivery of quality and timely care and information.*

Clearly, reports and studies continue to highlight problems with accessing care and shortages in mental health staffing and infrastructure. The VA should invest in staff training, recruiting, and retention programs in order to maintain the highest quality work force and system of care. Caregivers and family members should be provided training, information and tools on how to deal with suicidal ideations and mental health issues.

Congress should fund research to evaluate the efficacy of suicide prevention programs to include a longitudinal study of the economic and societal costs of veteran suicide in this country.

Veterans should have more control over scheduling appointments. theVA must be flexible in delivering care to meet the needs of veterans, including allowing fee based care in emergencies or when wait times exceed two weeks.

- *Authorizing additional funding to expand outreach and marketing efforts to encourage enrollment of all eligible veterans in VA health care, with special emphasis on Guard and Reserve members, rural veterans, and high-risk populations.*

VA recognizes it needs to do a more effective job in working with outside community and faith-based organizations and other government agencies, beyond its current work with veteran and military organizations and other agency partnerships. The VA should reward local medical facilities for expanding their collaborative efforts. A long-term investment in outreach and marketing to improve its image and VA brand is needed to more effectively target these veteran populations.

CONCLUSION

MOAA believes there is a business case to be made for addressing suicide that should consider the impact on national security and the costs to society.

MOAA has no doubt that, with the will and sense of urgency from Congress, the Administration, the DoD/Military Services, and the VA, we can win the war on suicide. Our veterans and military medical systems have eliminated some tremendous barriers with unprecedented results in saving lives on and off the battlefield. We owe these heroes and their families our full commitment to eliminate remaining barriers to mental health care so they can obtain an optimal quality of life.

MOAA is encouraged by the significant progress made by the VA, and we thank the Subcommittee for your leadership and support in helping our nation's veterans and their families.

In: The Enemy Within
Editors: Jack M. Wright and Gabriel E. Lewis

ISBN: 978-1-62081-316-4

Chapter 5

WITNESS TESTIMONY OF TOM TARANTINO, SENIOR LEGISLATIVE ASSOCIATE, IRAQ AND AFGHANISTAN VETERANS OF AMERICA

HOUSE COMMITTEE ON VETERANS AFFAIRS, SUBCOMMITTEE ON HEALTH HEARING ON: UNDERSTANDING AND PREVENTING VETERAN SUICIDE*

12/2/2011

On behalf of Iraq and Afghanistan Veterans of America's 200,000 member veterans and supporters, thank you for inviting me to speak on one of the most pressing issues facing veterans and their families: the staggeringly high rate of suicide among services members and veterans.

My name is Tom Tarantino and I am the Senior Legislative Associate with IAVA. I proudly served 10 years in the Army, beginning my career as an enlisted Reservist, and leaving service as an Active Duty Cavalry Officer. Throughout these 10 years, my single most important duty was to take care of other soldiers. In the military, they teach us to have each other's backs, both on and off the field of battle. And although my uniform is now a suit and tie, I am proud to work with this Congress to continue to have the backs of America's service members and veterans.

Today's hearing on suicide could not have come at a more critical time. The Army recently reported 30 potential suicides among active duty soldiers and non-activated reservists in October, and 25 potential suicides within the same group in September. These are some of the highest numbers we have seen from the Army since it began releasing suicide data in 2009 - and that's just one branch. The Defense Department recently reported that 468 active duty and reserve soldiers, sailors airmen, and Marines committed suicide in 2010. Overall, the

---

* These remarks were delivered as Witness Testimony given on December 2, 2012. Tom Tarantino is Senior Legislative Associate, Iraq and Afghanistan Veterans of America.

Department of Defense tracked 863 suicide attempts. The rate for veterans is likely much higher.

Although we have this limited data about service members, there remains a fundamental gap when it comes to understanding veteran suicide. The VA does not regularly release data on the number of veterans that commit suicide and there is almost no information about veteran suicide among the forty-seven percent of veterans of Operations Enduring Freedom and Iraqi Freedom who never interact with the VA. We therefore only have blurry snapshots of the problem. For example, the VA estimated that in 2009, 6000 veterans committed suicide. It has also said that on average, 950 suicides are attempted each month by veterans who are receiving some type of VA treatment. That's an average of 31 veterans attempting suicide per day. And again, these tragic numbers only capture the limited segment of veterans who interact with the VA.

One of the greatest challenges in understanding and preventing veteran suicide is this lack of full data. If we don't know the entirety of the problem, how can we solve it? Even in this age of information and technology, we still have no way of tracking veterans unless they interact with a social service that happens to ask about their military service. This is unacceptable. To address this problem, we must think outside the box. IAVA recommends collecting this data by expanding existing services like the Center for Disease Control and Preventions' National Violent Death Reporting System. Currently, the CDC collects data on all manner of violent death - including suicide - in 16 states. Veteran status can be reported to the CDC either through the death certificate or by information collected by the medical examiner. By expanding the database to all 50 states, and requiring medical examiners to report veteran status to the CDC, we can get a clearer picture of the problem.

A critical step to understanding how we can stop veteran and service members suicides is to understand that suicide itself is not the whole issue. Suicide is the tragic conclusion of the failure to address the spectrum of challenges returning veterans face. These challenges are not just mental health injuries; they include challenges of finding employment, reintegrating to family and community life, dealing with health care and benefits bureaucracy and many others. Fighting suicide is not just about preventing the act of suicide, it is about providing a "soft and productive landing" for our veterans when they return home.

The conflicts in Iraq and Afghanistan have resulted in a high incidence of mental health injuries among returning service members. According to a RAND study, nearly one third of Iraq and Afghanistan veterans will develop combat-related mental health issues. Many of these cases will go untreated, and if allowed to fester, develop into severe Post Traumatic Stress Disorder.

The problems with Mental Health Care within the VA system have been well-documented over the past few years. The VA reports that 18 veterans in their care commit suicide every day. Wait times for mental health care remain unacceptably high, and there are not enough mental health providers to meet the need.

A recent RAND survey of veterans in New York State revealed that many veterans face difficulty navigating the complex systems of benefits and services available to them. While this survey was specific to New York veterans, the results are indicative of veterans' experiences nationwide. Veterans reported that they do not know how to find the services they need or apply for the benefits they have earned. Even when they are able to find services appropriate for their needs, many vets report frustration in accessing these services. Some veterans report long waiting periods to get an appointment at the VA, while others with frequent appointments have reported having to repeatedly re-tell their stories and experiences to a number of different providers. These delays and lack of continuity certainly cannot help a veteran already suffering from mental health issues. This survey also revealed difficulty in accessing services is not limited to the VA; most respondents could not identify a state agency or non-profit that provided direct mental health services.

We also know that many veterans may not be seeking care because of the stigma attached to mental health injuries. Multiple studies confirm that veterans are concerned about how seeking care could impact their careers, both in and out of the military. Concerns include the effect on their ability to get security clearances and how co-workers and supervisors would perceive them. It is critical that we continue to work to reduce this stigma.

To combat this, IAVA recommends that the VA and DoD partner with experts in the private and nonprofit sector to develop a robust and aggressive outreach campaign. This campaign should focus on directing veterans to services such as Vet Centers, as well as local community and state based services. It should be integrated into local campaigns such as San Francisco's veterans 311 campaign. This campaign should be well-funded and reflect the best practices and expertise of experts in both the mental health and advertising fields. For our part, IAVA has partnered with the Ad Council to launch a public service awareness campaign that is focused on the mental health and invisible injuries facing veterans of Iraq and Afghanistan. Part of this campaign focuses on reducing the stigma of seeking mental health care. We are happy to share our best practices from this campaign to aid in this effort.

TACKLING TRANSITION: PROVIDING A STABLE ENVIRONMENT FOR VETERANS' TRANSITION

Providing a smoother transition from the military to the civilian world is crucial in preventing veteran suicide. Ensuring veterans' access to mental health care is connected to other issues that can contribute to a veterans' sense of stability throughout their transition home. We must tackle the other contributing factors – such as unemployment and homelessness – that could increase the risk for vets who are vulnerable to suicide.

Finding employment is one of the top challenges facing veterans during their transition from military to civilian life. In 2010, the average unemployment rate for OIF/OEF-era veterans was a staggering 11.5%, almost 2 percentage points higher than the national average. This rate is trending even higher so far this year. This leaves veterans wondering where the next pay check will come from, unable to support their families, and unsure of long-term career prospects. Congress wisely addressed this problem recently by passing the VOW to Hire Heroes Act. While this legislation is a critical piece of the puzzle, we must remain vigilant to ensure that the critical programs in the VOW to Hire Heroes Act are implemented.

Some veterans also struggle to find a permanent home. The VA reported that there were more than 13,000 Iraq and Afghanistan veterans homeless in October 2010. Having a place to call home is a foundation upon which to build one's life. Without a home, finding employment, maintaining relationships, and receiving mental health care become more difficult. The number of homeless veterans is already too high. We need to act now to end veteran homelessness. There is no excuse.

Addressing the spectrum of challenges facing veterans during their transition home will go a long way to create a sense of stability for veterans that may be vulnerable to suicide. This is a place you can step up to create a network of support for every veteran as they return home. This robust community of support should be the first line of defense against veteran suicide.

Building a Community of Support

A community of support starts with the families of veterans and service members. These families need to be prepared – and supported – to help smooth the transition of their returning service member. In RAND's study of New York veterans, thirty-five percent of military spouses reported that they struggled to reintegrate the returning service member into day-to-day family life. Families also reported feeling unprepared for the return of the service member; many noted that they did not know what symptoms and behaviors to look for. While there are many resources currently available to assist military families, they are often difficult to navigate and complex to understand. We need to place more emphasis on outreach, education and support for military families so that they in turn can support a returning service member.

The responsibility of support does not lie on our military and veteran families alone. Preventing veteran suicide and easing the transition from military to civilian life is our collective responsibility as a community. Veterans consistently report difficulty relating to their civilian peers. In a particularly poignant example, one RAND respondent stated, "When I'm faced with civilians who don't understand what I've been through, it's really difficult to try [to] get on the same level with them without making [myself] feel pathetic."

His statement tells us two things: (1) we must connect vets to fellow vets that have gone through similar experiences, and (2) we should raise awareness across the civilian community about the experience of these veterans and their families, and the challenges they face reintegrating into the civilian world.

IAVA has been a leader in connecting veterans to their counterparts across the country. One of the signature features of the wars in Iraq and Afghanistan is that less than one percent of Americans have served in either. One of IAVA's top priorities is to connect veterans in local communities and across the country through traditional events and our exclusive Community of Veterans online community. Through IAVA's awareness campaign, in partnership with the Ad Council, we push the message to veterans that they are not alone: there is a community of vets that understands their experiences and has their backs.

But our veterans are not just readjusting to their families or connecting with other veterans. They are coming back to their jobs, using their GI Bill to study at local colleges, and seeking care and services from businesses and providers across the country. We also must focus on extending understanding to spouses and society at large. Teachers and professors should know which of their students are veterans, or the children of veterans or service members. Businesses should invest in the leadership of returning veterans by hiring them. Health care providers must understand the injuries facing these incredible men and women. By promoting awareness, we can ensure that our entire community is able to support our veterans throughout their transition back to civilian life and help stem the tide of veteran suicide.

By accurately measuring the problem, improving access to mental health care, tackling the transition from military to civilian life, and creating a robust community of support for our veterans, we may be able to significantly reduce the number of veterans that attempt and commit suicide each year. Veteran suicide does not have a "silver bullet" solution. But better practices are out there. We don't want to ask ourselves if there was something more we could have done.

Thank you for your time and attention.

In: The Enemy Within
Editors: Jack M. Wright and Gabriel E. Lewis

ISBN: 978-1-62081-316-4

Chapter 6

PREVENTING VETERAN SUICIDE HEARING – ILEM TESTIMONY*

Joy J. Ilem

On behalf of the 1.2 million members of the Disabled American Veterans (DAV), all of whom are wartime disabled veterans, I am pleased to present our views to the Subcommittee on suicide prevention efforts in the Department of Veterans Affairs (VA) and the Department of Defense (DOD).

The increase in suicide among members of the military and veterans, and the innumerable tragic accounts by family members struggling to deal with the aftermath of suicide of a loved one, have raised deep concerns among military leaders, VA health care officials and policy makers, certainly including this Subcommittee. Every suicide by a service member or veteran is tragic, and accentuates the need for every effort to be made at multiple levels to prevent it. Unfortunately, suicide is a complex phenomenon and one that mental health experts have struggled to find solutions and strategies to prevent.

According to researchers, suicide seems to most often occur due to a combination of mental health stresses and societal triggers such as a marital or relationship breakup, a job loss or loss of social status, and is often coupled with overuse of alcohol or other intoxicating substances. The same mindset that can cause a person to take his or her own life is often the mindset that also prevents help-seeking behavior. Sadly, there are no easy fixes or answers to this problem, but according to one expert, "in order to prevent suicides, the complexity of behaviors and drivers of those behaviors need to be understood and addressed…and this requires collecting and analyzing standardized data."[1]

Mental health experts note that emphasis on several critical building blocks for any effective suicide prevention effort would be early intervention and routine mental health screening for all post-deployed military personnel and veterans, along with ready access to robust primary mental health care and specialty treatment programs for post-traumatic stress disorder (PTSD) and substance-use disorder. However, experts also note that having

* This is an edited, reformatted and augmented version of the House Committee on Veterans Affairs, Subcommittee on Health Hearing on: Understanding and Preventing Veteran Suicide, dated February 12, 2011.

sufficient mental health programs and providers is not enough—identifying those at risk for suicide would be vital to prevention. Ongoing research is a critical component to assist in the development of evidenced-based screening and risk assessment measures to accurately identify high risk individuals, and in developing prevention strategies. Likewise, an effective communication strategy to increase awareness about what constitutes mental health, aimed at changing attitudes and behaviors about seeking services for mental health challenges, is another key component to addressing this problem.

According to VA, its basic strategy for suicide prevention requires ready access be made available to veterans for high quality mental health services supplemented by programs designed to help individuals and families engage and participate in care, and to address suicide prevention in the high-risk patients that treatment efforts identify.[2] VA has put in place policies requiring clinicians to conduct routine screenings for depression, PTSD, problem drinking and history of military sexual trauma for all veterans enrolled in VA health care. VA has reported that veterans who screen positive for PTSD are more than four times as likely to indicate suicidal thoughts as veterans without PTSD. For these reasons, if a screening is positive for depression or PTSD, an additional suicide risk assessment is conducted. According to VA, for each veteran identified as at high risk for suicide, a suicide prevention safety plan is developed, components of an enhanced care mental health package are implemented, and the veteran's medical record is flagged so that all providers are alerted to the suicide risk for the veteran.[3]

Every VA medical center is staffed with a suicide prevention coordinator. VA has recently re-branded its suicide hotline into a campaign promoting a broader "Veterans Crisis Hotline," which includes a chat service and a suicide prevention resource center maintained jointly with the DOD on the internet. VA has also been moving forward with programs aimed at reducing stigma and getting veterans to reach out for help. The VA Office of Mental Health Services (OMHS) recently rolled out its new mental health public awareness campaign called *Making the Connection*. This unique campaign is targeted at veterans of all eras of military service, their family members and friends and features personal testimonials from veterans who have struggled with physical injuries and post-deployment mental health challenges following service—and the positive outcomes they have experienced regarding their treatment and personal recovery. The website offers mental health information, resources and support as a way of encouraging veterans to seek help when needed. The goal of the campaign is to reduce stigma in seeking help and to build greater awareness of the numerous resources available to improve the lives of our nation's veterans. DAV appreciates this progress, and we are hopeful the new campaign is successful and improves access and support for needed services for veterans and family members. Despite the implementation of these programs and policies the continuing and troubling suicide rate of veterans still begs the question of what more can be done.

VA estimates that there are approximately 1,600 to 1,800 suicides per year among veterans receiving care within VHA and as many as 6,400 per year among all veterans. This estimate would mean approximately 18 veterans nationally die from suicide per day and five deaths by suicide per day among veterans receiving care in VHA.[4] Additionally, there are 950 suicide attempts per month among veterans receiving care as reported by VHA suicide prevention coordinators (based on data collected from October 1, 2008 through December 31, 2010). In promoting its Veterans Crisis Hotline, VA notes that, as of July 2011, it has received over 400,000 calls, of which over 5,000 were from active duty service members; VA responded to over 16,000 chats and referred over 55,000 veterans to local VA suicide prevention coordinators for same-day or next-day services; over 225,000 calls received were from family members or those concerned about a loved one. Additionally, VA asserts that the Hotline initiated over 15,000 "rescues," and that there have been over 7,000 rescues of actively suicidal veterans as of April 2011.[5],[6]

VA reports that in FY 2010, more than 1.25 million individual veterans were treated in a VA specialty mental health program, medical center, clinic, inpatient setting or residential rehabilitation program. According to VHA guidelines, all new patients requesting or referred for mental health services must receive an evaluation within 24 hours, and undergo a more comprehensive diagnostic and treatment planning evaluation within 14 days. To meet increasing mental health demand, VA has hired over 7,500 full time professional staff since 2005, and during the last three years has trained over 4,000 staff to provide psychotherapies with the strongest evidence for successful outcome for PTSD, depression and other conditions.[7] Unfortunately, despite the significant increase in resources provided by Congress in recent years for veterans' mental health care and VA's efforts to increase staff and implement and improve its primary and specialized mental health programs, we often hear from veterans that are experiencing difficulty gaining access to the mental health treatment they need at a crisis point. We agree with the Congressional Research Service that VA's internal policy requiring providers to make initial assessments with 24 hours, and to begin treatments within 14 days for requested mental health care, is probably not being carried out uniformly and universally.[8] For these reasons, DAV has recently initiated an informal mental health survey of up to 15,000 veterans focused on access to VA mental health services and the quality of care they are receiving. Although informal, it is our hope that the results of this survey, publicized through our DAV social media sites to all veterans, will provide a snapshot of veterans' experiences, their perceptions of access to VA mental health services, and their satisfaction levels with the treatments and programs that VA offers.

A comparable but much smaller query of VA mental health professionals was conducted at the request of Senate Committee on Veterans' Affairs following a July 2011 hearing that examined the gaps in VA mental health care. The resulting August 2011 report, a very small sample due to the quick turnaround time requested, queried 319 general outpatient mental health providers for each facility within five Veterans Integrated Service Networks (VISNs); and 272 responded. Alarming, although not surprising based on the feedback DAV has been receiving, over 70 percent of the respondents reported that their facilities had insufficient mental health staff resources to meet veterans' demands for care, and almost 70 percent indicated that their sites had shortages in physical space to accommodate mental health services. Nearly 40 percent reported they cannot schedule an appointment in their own clinics for a new patient within 14 days, and 46 percent reported that lack of off-hour appointment times was a barrier to care. Over 50 percent reported that growth in patient workloads contributed to mental health staffing shortages, and more than 26 percent noted that the demand for Compensation and Pension examinations diverted clinicians from providing direct care.

Based on the results of this VA internal survey and continuing reports from veterans themselves, it appears that despite the significant progress—specifically an increase in mental health programs and resources, and the number of mental health staff hired by VA in recent years—significant gaps still plague VA's efforts in mental health care. The impact of these gaps may fall greatest on our newest war veterans, many of whom are in need of urgent services.

In the active duty ranks, the Department of Defense (DOD) has also been coordinating data collection systems, mental health programs and research studies in an effort to reduce stigma in seeking mental health care and to prevent suicides in the active duty force. Some measureable progress can be seen in the suicide rate among the services, but overall the numbers still remain troubling. DOD acknowledges that providing mental health support to active duty troops is critical in suicide prevention. Likewise, its experts also confirm that effective, accessible, and supportive clinical care for mental, physical, and substance-use disorders are protective factors in preventing suicides. For these reasons, DOD reports it has updated its policies regarding early detection and intervention for combat and operational stress reactions in the deployment theaters. In 2007, the Department initiated a surveillance system to capture suicide data from the Services in a more central and standardized way. In addition to this effort, DOD reports that the Department and VA have a developed a partnership to improve mental health access and care to service members, veterans and their families. For the past 10 months, DOD and VA have been collaborating and implementing a DOD/VA joint strategy consisting of 28 strategic actions with specific milestones and outputs. DOD has also partnered with VA in hosting an annual suicide prevention conference that provides an opportunity for the departments to share information and strengthen the provider network across the two health care systems.[9]

On this very note, DAV is disappointed to report that Section 401 of Public Law 111-163 has not been implemented 18 months after enactment. This measure requires VA to amend its regulations to enable current members of the armed forces who served on active duty in Operations Enduring or Iraqi Freedom eligible for the readjustment counseling that VA currently provides to veterans under title 38, United States Code, section 1721A. We understand this authority is still in the proposed rulemaking stage; however, we have heard this document was recently forwarded to DOD for required joint concurrence. Thus, even though Congress acted, these military personnel cannot avail themselves of a service that their peers in the veteran population have reported to be very effective in dealing with their readjustment needs. Because stigma and confidentiality still remain a significant barrier for many active duty personnel needing mental health care post- deployment, we ask VA and DOD to expedite this mandate so the Readjustment Counseling Service can open its doors to those on active duty who qualify for the counseling benefit. Again, early intervention has been found to be a key to avoiding long-term mental health conditions and other negative outcomes related to untreated post-deployment readjustment issues. VA's Vet Center Readjustment Counseling Service Program (a non-medical model) and the more recently established Justice Program/Veterans Courts have been very popular among veterans with a focus on peer to peer outreach and treatment versus incarceration respectively. VA estimates it will have approximately 300 Vet Centers operational by the end of 2011, along with 70 mobile Vet Centers for veterans living in rural communities.[10] We believe these resources would be of great benefit to active duty service members who need readjustment counseling but may not receive it due to bureaucratic delay.

DOD tasked the RAND Corporation to evaluate information about military suicides, identify the agreed upon elements that should be part of a state-of-the-art suicide prevention strategy, and recommend ways to make sure the programs and policies provided by each military service reflect the best practices. This request culminated in a February 2011 report from RAND, *"The War Within: Preventing Suicide in the U.S. Military,"* which concluded that people with substance-use disorders and heavy alcohol users face an increased risk for suicide, along with persons with traumatic brain injury or head trauma, those suffering from hopelessness or experiencing certain life events such as relationship problems. Additionally, it was found that availability of firearms correlates positively with suicide. RAND researchers reviewed a wide range of prevention programs but found that while promising practices exist, much still remains unknown about what constitutes a best practice. Based on available literature and discussions with experts, RAND indicated that a comprehensive suicide prevention program should include the following six practices:

- Raise awareness and promote self-care;
- Identify those at high risk;
- Facilitate access to quality care;
- Provide quality care;
- Restrict access to lethal means; and
- Respond appropriately.

RAND made a series of 14 recommendations in its report and noted research suggests that suicide can be prevented. Recommendations include: the establishment of proper tracking and data systems; research; the delivery of high-quality care for those with behavioral health problems and those who are at imminent risk for suicide; proper communication to ensure potential at-risk population is informed and aware of the advantages of using behavioral health care; determining the adequate number of behavioral health specialists needed; and mandate training on evidence-based or state-of-the-art treatment for mental health care providers.

In October 2011, the Government Accountability Office (GAO) issued a report titled, *VA Mental Health: Number of Veterans Receiving Care, Barriers Faced, and Efforts to Increase Access,* covering veterans who used VA from FY 2006 through FY 2010. According to the report, approximately 2.1 million unique veterans received mental health care from VA during this period. Although the number steadily increased due primarily to growth in OEF/OIF/OND veterans seeking care, GAO noted that veterans of other eras still represent the vast majority of those receiving mental health services within VA. In 2010 alone, 12 percent (139,167) of veterans who received mental health care from VA served in our current conflicts, but 88 percent (1,064,363) were veterans of earlier military service eras. GAO noted that services for the OEF/OIF/OND group had caused growth of two percent per year in VA's total mental health caseload since 2006.

Key barriers identified in the GAO report that hinder veterans from seeking mental health care included: stigma, lack of understanding or awareness of mental health care, logistical challenges to accessing care, and concerns that VA's care is primarily for older veterans. GAO found that stigma is also a factor that may discourage veterans from accessing mental health care—especially those who have concerns that their careers could be negatively affected if employers found out that they were receiving mental health treatment. VA indicates it is aware of these barriers and continues to implement efforts to increase veterans' access to mental health care, including its integration of mental health services into primary care.

Clearly, ten years of war have taken a toll on the mental health of American military forces. Combat stress, PTSD and other combat- or stress-related mental health conditions are prevalent among veterans who have deployed to war environments in Iraq and Afghanistan. Regrettably, as was learned from our experiences in other wars, especially the Vietnam conflict, psychological reactions to combat exposure are common. Experts note that if not readily addressed, such problems can easily compound and become chronic. Over the long term, the costs mount due to impact on personal, family, emotional, medical, and financial damage to those who have honorably served our nation. Delays in addressing these problems can culminate in self-destructive circumstances, including substance-use disorders, incarceration, and suicide attempts. Increased access to mental health services for many of our returning war veterans is a pressing need, particularly in early intervention services for substance-use disorders and provision of evidence-based care for those with PTSD, depression, and other consequences of combat exposure.

Unique aspects of deployments to Iraq and Afghanistan, including the frequency and intensity of exposure to combat, guerilla warfare in urban environments, and the risks of suffering or witnessing violence, are strongly associated with a risk of chronic PTSD. Applying lessons learned from earlier wars, VA anticipated such risks and mounted earnest efforts for early identification and treatment of behavioral health problems experienced by returning veterans. VA instituted system-wide mental health screenings, expanded mental health staffing, integrated mental health into primary health care, added new counseling and clinical sites, and conducted wide-scale training on evidence-based psychotherapies. VA also has intensified its research programs in mental health. However, critical gaps remain today, and the mental health toll of this war is likely to grow over time for those who have deployed more than once, do not seek or receive needed services, or face increased stressors in their personal lives following deployment.[11]

Testimony by RAND, other researchers, and VA has addressed the physical and mental health impact of these wars based on the unique nature of the wars, particular wartime risks and multiple military deployments for many service members. The current plethora of data to date on our newest generation of war veterans related to increased rates of PTSD, depression, substance-use disorders, high risk-taking behaviors, and traumatic brain injury are well known—but despite all the information available, Dr. Charles W. Hoge, a leading researcher on the mental health toll of the conflicts in Afghanistan and Iraq, observes that VA is not reaching large numbers of returning veterans, and high percentages of veterans who do seek care drop out of treatment. In a recent analysis, Hoge wrote,"...veterans remain reluctant to seek care, with half of those in need not utilizing mental health services. Among veterans who begin PTSD treatment with psychotherapy or medication, a high percentage drop out...with only 50% of veterans seeking care and a 40% recovery rate, current strategies will effectively reach no more than 20% of all veterans needing PTSD treatment."[12]

DAV agrees with Dr. Hoge's view that VA must develop a strategy of expanding the reach of treatment, to include greater engagement of veterans, understanding the reasons for veterans' negative perceptions of mental health care, and "meeting veterans where they are."[13]

VA attempts to meet the needs of wartime veterans with post-deployment mental health challenges through two parallel treatment models: a nationwide network of medical centers and outpatient clinics that offer a more traditional medical and psychiatric approach with recent integration of mental health into primary care; and, community-based storefront Vet

Centers that use a non-medical psychological model to provide readjustment counseling and related services to combat veterans and to their immediate families. In some locations, the two programs work together closely; in others, there is only limited coordination. Veterans are free to choose one model over the other or a combination of both services. However, the differences in approach may help explain why some veterans do not pursue VA treatment, and why those who do often discontinue it. While DAV strongly supports the Vet Center program, we also believe VA must maintain a robust mental health system as a part of VA medical care. Both programs are critical to veterans struggling with chronic mental illnesses and especially to new veterans who are in need of readjustment services.

New veterans generally report having had positive experiences with Vet Centers and their staffs, a high percentage of whom are themselves combat veterans and who convey an understanding and acceptance of combat veterans' problems. While these centers do not provide mental health services in the traditional sense, their strengths tend to fill the gaps reported by younger veterans regarding mental health care in VA medical centers and primary care clinics.

Dr. Hoge echoes several of these points in urging what amounts to a call for a more veteran-centric approach to treating PTSD and other war-related conditions:

Improving evidence-based treatments...must be paired with education in military cultural competency to help clinicians foster rapport and continued engagement with professional warriors...Matching evidence-based components of therapy to patient preferences and reinforcing narrative processes and social connections through peer-to-peer programs are encouraged. Family members, who have their own unique perspectives, are essential participants in the veteran's healing process and also need their own support.[14]

Since the beginning of the conflicts in Iraq and Afghanistan, VA has faced a number of daunting challenges in providing care to a new generation of war veterans—particularly in post-deployment readjustment and in mental health. Initially, the needs and expectations of OEF/OIF/OND veterans and their families proved to be different from those of veterans who had typically been under VA care. We believe new veterans and their families want the DOD and VA to transform their approaches to post-deployment mental health services, and to stress family-centered treatment rather than focus solely on individual veterans—a paradigm shift for VA. Over its history, VA has concentrated primarily on the single veteran patient to the exclusion of family in almost all cases. But this new generation of veterans is younger, technologically savvy, and demands improved access to information via the Internet, access to state-of-the-art prosthetic items, expertise in trauma care, and advanced rehabilitation methods. They also expect support for their family caregivers and better transition and collaboration between DOD and VA in policies for family caregivers. Likewise, Congress, advocacy groups, and community stakeholders, including groups in the private sector offering specialized services, have been very active in pressing for change in how VA relates to community providers and how it furnishes care in its mental health and rehabilitative services.

Last year, the VA OMHS introduced a public health model for VA to meet the mental health needs of OEF/OIF/OND veterans with the precept that most war veterans will not develop chronic mental illness if VA concentrates on early intervention, de-stigmatization, use of effective mental health models, and makes greater outreach efforts. The goal of VA's strategy is to promote healthy outcomes and strengthen families, with a focus on resilience and recovery. This initiative requires VA to evolve from its more traditional medical model to an approach that would be less reliant on establishing a diagnosis and developing a treatment plan, and more on helping veterans and their families regain or retain an overall balance in their physical, social and mental well-being despite the stresses of military deployments. Most important, the strategy calls for VA to reach out to veterans in their communities, adjust its message, make access easier and on these veterans' terms, and reformat programs and services to meet the needs of veterans and their families, rather than expecting veterans to fit into VA's traditional array of available services.[15]

In preparing for this hearing, DAV observed that DOD and VA clearly have made concerted efforts to address the challenges each Department faces in meeting the mental health needs of post-deployment active duty personnel and wartime veterans. Also, both agencies are populated with dedicated mental health experts, researchers and policymakers who continue to develop solutions to prevent suicide and the less devastating but still serious emotional and behavioral consequences of exposures to war. However, despite both Departments' obvious efforts and progress, much more needs to be accomplished to fulfill the nation's commitments to veterans who are challenged by serious and chronic mental illnesses, and those needing post-deployment mental health readjustment services. Based on studies noted earlier in this statement, it appears DOD may have less difficulty collecting data to analyze the need for policy changes simply because DOD maintains access to data on the active duty population including pertinent demographic information, recorded facts on wartime and other hardship deployments, marital status, health information and personal stressors. However, DOD is burdened by a number of barriers unique to the military services that prevent military personnel from coming forward for help. The fear of being perceived as "weak;" worry over losing rank; being identified as unreliable in stressful or hazardous situations; and anxiety about being discharged in disgrace – all these fears contribute to a reticence in military service personnel who are struggling, from revealing their feelings to others or to seek help inside their command structure. DOD leaders have publicly acknowledged these types of cultural obstacles do in fact exist and that DOD is still working to address them systemically.

On the other hand, VA is challenged with access to veterans' data for those who have not come to VHA for care. Because veterans are private citizens, and privacy of medical and personal information is the governing law, VA is at a distinct disadvantage in gaining extensive data on mental health status, suicide rates and other relevant information about the general veteran population. However, based on clinical and research experience with enrolled veterans, what VA does know can be very beneficial for all veterans. Experts note that timely, early intervention services can improve veterans' overall quality of life, address substance-use problems, prevent chronic illness, promote recovery, and minimize the long-term disabling effects of undetected and untreated mental health problems. We encourage VA to build on that knowledge and to be more transparent in dealing with the daunting challenges it faces in overcoming the existing gaps in its mental health programs and in the crucial need to address suicide, which has become so pressing. DAV believes VA is moving in an appropriate direction but needs to know more by learning directly from veterans trying to access the VA system (as well as those who don't) to better understand their unique needs and desires for treatment and services. Listening to veterans' feedback is essential to creating a system that meets them where they are, works for them, and is effective in achieving the recovery they seek.

As a final thought, we recommend the Subcommittee review VA's implementation of sections 102-105 of the Veterans' Mental Health and Other Care Improvements Act of 2008,

Public Law 110-387, a measure DAV strongly supported as a part of our Stand Up For Veterans initiative. These requirements, if implemented faithfully by VA, would go a long way toward addressing many of the lingering issues discussed in this testimony today. Also, we recommend a close review by your professional staff of our discussion in the FY 2012 *Independent Budget* (IB) on the topics of mental health and transition needs of OEF/OIF/OND veterans, as well as the new discussion of those subjects in the upcoming IB for FY 2013.

Madam Chairwoman and Members of the Subcommittee, this concludes my testimony on behalf of DAV. I would be pleased to respond to your questions.

[1] The Hon. Jonathan Woodson, M.D., Asst. Secretary of Defense for Health Affairs, U.S. Department of Defense, Testimony before the United States House of Representatives Committee on Armed Services, Hearing on "Current Status of Suicide Prevention Programs in the Military." (September 9, 2011).

[2] Department of Veterans Affairs, Fact Sheet: VA Suicide Prevention Program, Facts about Veteran Suicide. (April 2011)

[3] Antonette Zeiss, Ph.D., Acting Deputy Patient Care Services Officer for Mental Health, Veterans Health Administration, U.S. Department of Veterans Affairs, Testimony before the United States House of Representatives Committee on Veterans' Affairs, Hearing on "Mental Health: Bridging the Gap Between Care and Compensation for Veterans." (June 14, 2011).

[4] John D. Daigh, Jr., M.D., Assistant Inspector General for Health Care Inspections, Office of Inspector General, U.S. Department of Veterans Affairs, Testimony before the United States Senate Committee on Veterans' Affairs, Hearing on "VA Mental Health Care: Closing the Gaps." (July 14, 2011).

[5] Antonette Zeiss, Ph.D., Acting Deputy Patient Care Services Officer for Mental Health, Veterans Health Administration, U.S. Department of Veterans Affairs, Testimony before the United States House of Representatives Committee on Veterans' Affairs, Hearing on "Mental Health: Bridging the Gap Between Care and Compensation for Veterans." (June 14, 2011).

[6] Department of Veterans Affairs, Fact Sheet: VA Suicide Prevention Program, Facts about Veteran Suicide. (April 2011)

[7] Antonette Zeiss, Ph.D., Acting Deputy Patient Care Services Officer for Mental Health, Veterans Health Administration, U.S. Department of Veterans Affairs, Testimony before the United States House of Representatives Committee on Veterans' Affairs, Hearing on "Mental Health: Bridging the Gap Between Care and Compensation for Veterans." (June 14, 2011).

[8] Suicide, PTSD, and Substance Use Among OEF/OIF Veterans Using VA Health Care: Facts and Figures, Congressional Research Service, July 18, 2011

[9] The Hon. Jonathan Woodson, M.D., Asst. Secretary of Defense for Health Affairs, U.S. Department of Defense, Testimony before the United States House of Representatives Committee on Armed Services, Hearing on "Current Status of Suicide Prevention Programs in the Military." (September 9, 2011).

[10] Antonette Zeiss, Ph.D., Acting Deputy Patient Care Services Officer for Mental Health, Veterans Health Administration, U.S. Department of Veterans Affairs, Testimony before the United States House of Representatives Committee on Veterans' Affairs,

Hearing on "Mental Health: Bridging the Gap Between Care and Compensation for Veterans." (June 14, 2011).

[11] Brett T. Litz, National Center for Post-Traumatic Stress Disorder, Department of Veterans Affairs, "The Unique Circumstances and Mental Health Impact of the Wars in Afghanistan and Iraq," A National Center for PTSD Fact Sheet (January 2007). http://www.nami.org/ Content/Microsites191/NAMI_Oklahoma/Home178/Veterans3/Veterans_Articles/5uniquecircumstancesIraq-Afghanistanwar.pdf

[12] Charles W. Hoge, MD, "*Interventions for War-Related Posttraumatic Stress Disorder: Meeting Veterans Where They Are*," JAMA, 306(5): (August 3, 2011) 548.

[13] Ibid.

[14] Hoge, "Meeting Veterans Where They Are," 551.

[15] Harold Kudler, VA/DOD/State and Community Partnerships: Practical Lessons on Implementing a Public Health Model to Meet the Needs of OEF/OIF Veterans and Their Families, VA Course on Implementing a Public Health Model for Meeting the Mental Health Needs of Veterans, PowerPoint presentation (Baltimore, MD, July 28, 2010).

In: The Enemy Within
Editors: Jack M. Wright and Gabriel E. Lewis
ISBN: 978-1-62081-316-4

Chapter 7

PREVENTING VETERAN SUICIDE HEARING – HARRELL TESTIMONY*

Margaret C. Harrell

Madame Chairwoman Buerkle, Ranking Member Michaud, and members of the Subcommittee: Thank you for the privilege of testifying today. It is an honor to be here. Military suicide, that of both service members and veterans, is a tragedy that affects more than the individual. Each suicide devastates a family, a unit, and a community. There are also implications beyond the local.

Military suicide is a national security issue. George Washington said, "The willingness with which our young people are likely to serve in any war, no matter how justified, shall be directly proportional to how they perceive the Veterans of earlier wars were treated and appreciated by their nation." If Washington was correct, suicide among service members and veterans threatens the health of the all-volunteer force. Mentors and role models, including parents, teachers and, importantly, veterans, play a critical role in the enlistment decisions of young men and women. We should realize that these mentors and role models will not steer youth toward the military if they perceive damage to service members or a failure to address the mental health care needs of those who have served their country.

While the topic at hand is suicide prevention among veterans, I urge the committee to recognize the importance of considering both veteran and service member suicide. This recommendation is based upon more than the recognition of suicide as a tragic outcome; it is based upon the pragmatic recognition that we can only be sure that improvements have been made when the frequency of suicide decreases amongst both of these populations. There is, for example, a possibility that a decrease in the frequency and number of suicides among service members could represent only expeditious out-processing of service members struggling with mental health wounds of war. Likewise, a decrease in veteran suicide, once we have greater visibility of these outcomes, could reflect the shifting of suicides to the time

---

* This is an edited, reformatted and augmented version of the House Committee on Veterans Affairs, Subcommittee on Health Hearing on: Understanding and Preventing Veteran Suicide, dated February 12, 2011.

prior to military discharge. Only the joint consideration of both service member and veteran outcomes will highlight reasons for increased concern or will identify success.

There does not currently exist a systematic combined analysis of service member and veteran suicide. Neither the Department of Defense (DOD) nor the Department of Veterans Affairs (VA) fully consider or analyze suicide in one another's population. Given the potential implications of veteran suicide for the all-volunteer force, both the VA and the DOD should seek to understand which veterans, and how many veterans, are dying by suicide. In particular, we should recognize that veterans who left the service only shortly before they killed themselves may have suffered from unaddressed mental health wounds incurred while in service to their nation.

This testimony derives from a CNAS policy brief, *Losing the Battle: The Challenge of Military Suicide*, which discussed the stark numbers of the veterans and service members who die by suicide every day. The policy brief also identified obstacles to improvement and made recommendations to address these obstacles. This testimony focuses upon the recommendations most applicable to the veteran community.

It is important to note that the U.S. military and veteran population cannot avoid the stark reality of suicide entirely. Service members and veterans reflect the broader American public, which not only suffers from suicide, but also stigmatizes mental health care. Further, some service members enter military service with mental health challenges and we should not conclude that serving in the military caused these suicides.

This testimony also notes that leaders in the services and the VA deserve recognition for their actions to reduce the rate of suicide among service members and veterans. Senior military leaders have exerted considerable effort in recent years to acknowledge and confront the challenge of suicide. The VA and each of the military services have emphasized the development of suicide prevention programs, education about the risk of suicide and the most effective ways to prevent it. The DOD suicide prevention programs, with slogans such as "Never Leave a Marine Behind" and "Never Let Your Buddy Fight Alone," resonate with service members by being service-specific and embedded in their service cultures. The services ensure that the necessary tools, such as hotlines, are readily available. The VA's Veterans Crisis Line is especially important in this regard. In its first three years, the hotline received more than 144,000 calls involving veterans and saved more than 7,000 actively suicidal veterans.[1] Challenges remain nonetheless.

SERVICE MEMBER AND VETERAN SUICIDE

From 2005 to 2010, service members took their own lives at a rate of approximately one every 36 hours.[2] While suicides in the Air Force, Navy and Coast Guard have been relatively stable and lower than those of the ground forces, U.S. Army suicides have climbed steadily since 2004. The Army reported a record-high number of suicides in July 2011 with the deaths of 33 active and reserve component service members reported as suicides. Suicides in the Marine Corps increased steadily from 2006 to 2009, dipping slightly in 2010.

The VA estimates that a veteran dies by suicide every 80 minutes,[3] but is impossible, given the paucity of current data, to determine the suicide rate among veterans with any accuracy or to understand which veterans are dying.

THE RELATIONSHIP BETWEEN MILITARY SERVICE AND SUICIDE

Although the number of military suicides has increased since the start of the wars in Afghanistan and Iraq, the prevailing wisdom has been that suicides are not linked directly to deployment.[4] However, recent analysis of Army data demonstrates that soldiers who deploy are more likely to die by suicide.[5] Data have long indicated definitive links between suicide and injuries suffered during deployment. Individuals with traumatic brain injury (TBI), for instance, are 1.5 times more likely than healthy individuals to die from suicide.[6] Additional factors that heighten risk include chronic pain and post-traumatic stress disorder (PTSD) symptoms such as depression, anxiety, sleep deprivation, substance abuse and difficulties with anger management.[7] These factors are also widely associated with deployment experience in Afghanistan and Iraq.

Some psychiatric experts argue that there is an indirect relationship between suicide and military service during wartime. In the psychiatric field, one school of thought, known as the interpersonal psychological theory of suicide, suggests that the following three "protective" factors preclude an individual from killing oneself: belongingness, usefulness and an aversion to pain or death.[8] Any one of these protective factors normally is sufficient to prevent suicide. Traditionally, military service has had a protective quality: Military service members have been less likely to die by suicide than civilians. It appears now, however, that the nature of military service – especially during wartime – may weaken all three protective factors.[9] The cohesion and camaraderie of a military unit can induce intense feelings of belonging for many service members. Time away from the unit, however, may result in a reduced or thwarted sense of belonging, as individuals no longer have the daily support of their units and feel separate and different from civilians. This is especially true for Guardsmen, Reservists, and for veterans.

The responsibility inherent in military service, the importance of tasks assigned to relatively junior personnel and the high level of interaction among unit members establish the importance and usefulness of each unit member, particularly in an operational environment. In contrast, the experience of living in a garrison environment (for active component personnel) or returning to a civilian job (for Guardsmen, Reservists and veterans) or, worse, unemployment, can introduce feelings of uselessness. Individual accounts of military suicide both in the media and in interviews with us echo this sentiment. Over and over, these accounts show that individuals withdrew, felt disconnected from their units and their families, and perceived themselves as a burden.

The third protective factor – an aversion to pain or death – is especially important in considering military suicide, because military service is one of the few experiences that can override this factor. Repeated exposure to military training as well as to violence, aggression and death dulls one's fear of death and increases tolerance for pain.[10] Thus, the very experience of being in the military erodes this protective factor, even for service members who have not deployed or experienced combat, in part because service members experience pain and discomfort from the beginning of their training.[11] By removing some of the protective factors of suicide, therefore, military service, especially during wartime, may predispose an individual toward suicide.

Challenges and Recommendations

There are obstacles to addressing suicide that should be resolved. Some of these obstacles are especially difficult to eliminate. Many of the recommendations we have made pertain specifically to service member suicide, for two reasons. First, we know more about service member suicide than about suicide amongst veterans. The lack of understanding about suicide among veterans reduces the likelihood of actionable recommendations. Second, reducing the challenges to mental health among service members should also improve the mental health of recently discharged veterans.

Challenge I

Americans lack a complete accounting of veteran suicide. The estimation of veteran suicides is extrapolated from extremely limited data. Specifically, states provide death data to the Centers for Disease Control (CDC) for inclusion in the National Death Index, but only 16 U.S. states indicate veteran status in their data.[12] The number of veteran suicides from the remaining 34 states is extrapolated to estimate the overall number of veteran suicides.[13] Further, the current numbers are extrapolated from three year-old data.

An effort is underway to match the Social Security numbers in the national death data with DOD files to identify veterans included in the data. This effort provides the capability to analyze the data and characterize the veteran victims of suicide. It will thus be possible to quantify veteran suicide and contribute an understanding of the number of suicides among Post-9/11 veterans, as compared with veterans of earlier generations. This analysis could also permit an understanding of whether veterans kill themselves soon after leaving the military.

Recommendation

Given the potential implications of veteran suicide for the all-volunteer force, the DOD should seek to understand which veterans, and how many veterans, are dying by suicide. In particular, the DOD, as well as the VA and the country at-large, should recognize that many veterans who left the service only shortly before they killed themselves may have suffered from unaddressed mental health wounds incurred while in service to their nation. Congress should establish reasonable time requirements for states to provide death data to the CDC, and the Department of Health and Human Services (HHS) should ensure that the CDC is resourced sufficiently to expedite compilation of national death data. The DOD, the VA and HHS should coordinate efforts to analyze veteran suicide data and should conduct these analyses annually.

Challenge II

As service members return home from deployment, they complete a post-deployment health assessment (PDHA). As part of this assessment, they are asked questions about their physical and mental health, such as, "Did you encounter dead bodies or see people killed or wounded during this deployment?" and "During this deployment, did you ever feel that you were in great danger of being killed?" There are also self-evaluative questions, such as, "Are you currently interested in receiving information or assistance for a stress, emotional or alcohol concern?" While we do not question the contents of the assessment, its administration has been problematic.

A 2008 study found that when Army soldiers completed an anonymous survey, reported rates of depression, PTSD, suicidal thoughts and interest in receiving care were two to four times higher as compared to the PDHA. Likewise, our interviews with veterans uncovered numerous accounts of returning service members whose unit leaders advised them to fabricate answers. Individuals across all services have been told, "If you answer yes to any of those questions, you are not going home to your family tomorrow." This may be factually correct, but it neglects to inform service members of the implications of answering untruthfully – namely, that they will have difficulty receiving treatment or compensation for mental health problems that appear after their service. As an improvement, the 2010 National Defense Authorization Act requires trained medical or behavioral health professionals to conduct the PDHA evaluations individually and face-to-face, in the hope that service members will respond honestly to a trained health professional.[14]

Recommendation

Unit leaders should encourage members to complete the PDHA truthfully and should underscore that an honest answer will allow them to link any future mental health problems requiring treatment to their military service. This is especially important for veterans, as the PDHA informs decisions regarding their eligibility for mental health care after they separate from service.

Challenge III

There is a national shortage of mental health care and behavioral health care professionals, a factor linked to higher rates of suicide. According to the VA, suicide rates decreased by 3.6 deaths per 100,000 in seven regions[15] where staff numbers increased to levels recommended in the 2008 Veterans Health Administration Handbook.[16] Sixteen regions are still not manned to these levels, however. Additionally, for the Army, only 80 percent of the psychiatrist and 88 percent of the social worker and behavioral health nurse positions are filled. With respect to psychologists, 93 percent of positions are filled.[17] Military hospital commanders have temporary authority to hire psychologists and social workers and behavioral health nurses on an as-needed basis, but a shortage of care providers precludes them from easily filling that gap. This shortage is a national issue, which affects the availability of care providers for the DOD and the VA. It also affects veterans' families, who seek treatment from the civilian health care system to cope with the strain of reintegration.

Recommendation

Congress should permanently establish expedited or direct hire authority allowing military hospitals to hire behavioral health care providers. Congress should require the VA to establish deadlines by which all twenty-three VHA regions will be manned to the recommended levels of behavioral health care providers. Additionally, and especially in the meantime, the VA should increase their use of existing public-private partnerships to provide mental health care, to the extent that such partnerships would expedite evidence-based care to veterans.

Challenge IV

Permanent change of station (PCS) moves are a feature of military life. Individuals also often relocate their families as they leave the military. However, because professional organizations license mental health care providers on a state-by-state basis, a geographical move across state lines can preclude continued care from the same provider. When a care provider and a veteran, service member or family member invest in developing a care relationship, and that relationship is severed by a move, patients are often reluctant to begin treatment anew.

Recommendation

Congress should establish a federal pre-emption of state licensing such that mental health care can be provided across state lines for those instances in which military service members or family members have an established pre-existing care relationship.

Challenge V

The programs and services designed to understand and reduce service member and veteran suicide should complement one another and gain both efficiency and effectiveness from interacting synergistically. Obtaining veteran suicide data and understanding the circumstances surrounding individuals who die by suicide depends on the states and the HHS, as well as on the participation of the VA and the DOD.[18] Within DOD, the military services and components do not regularly and consistently share information. Information should also be shared between the House Armed Services Committee (HASC) and the Senate Armed Services Committee (SASC), who interact primarily with DOD and the Senate Committee on Veteran Affairs and the House Veterans Affairs Committee, who interact primarily with the VA..

Recommendation

The DOD, the VA and HHS should share data and information pertaining to suicide. The military services' leaders should meet regularly to discuss issues and approaches pertaining to suicide, and to share lessons learned. The Senate Committee on Veterans Affairs and the House Veterans Affairs Committee should embrace the opportunity to work with the SASC and HASC, with the intent of developing provisions for the NDAA to address the problem of veteran suicide.

Challenge VI

The health and survival of service members hinges on the removal of the stigma associated with mental health care. This stigma exists in both military and civilian culture. In the military, it prevents many service members from seeking help to address mental health care issues; 43 percent of soldiers, sailors, airmen and Marines who took their own lives in 2010 did not seek help from military treatment facilities in the month before their deaths.[19] The percentage of service members seeking help has improved – from 40 percent in 2008 and 36 percent in 2009 to 57 percent in 2010 – but the stigmatization of mental health care remains an issue.[20] Military leaders recognize the importance of removing this stigma. Indeed, recently retired Chairman of the Joint Chiefs of Staff Admiral Mike Mullen identified the stigma of PTSD as the greatest challenge confronting troops returning from war in Iraq and Afghanistan,[21] and other DOD leaders at the highest levels have urged service members to seek mental health care as needed. Nevertheless, the stigma persists.

This culture is unlikely to change quickly. Leaders have not provided sufficient guidance about how to remove the stigma associated with depression and suicidal thoughts, and they have not consistently disciplined service members who belittle or ridicule members with mental health issues.[22] Removing the stigma for PTSD, an invisible injury, will be especially difficult, given that some service members do not even consider TBI, which is physically evident and recognizable, a "real injury."[23] Yet the stigma must be removed to address and treat PTSD and TBI, both of which are linked to suicide. The effect of military culture will also inform and bear upon the perspectives and behavior of veterans even after they leave the military service.

Recommendation

Military leaders must eliminate the stigma associated with mental health care and hold unit leaders accountable for instances in which individuals are ridiculed for seeking treatment.

Challenge VII

Misuse of prescription medication is another obstacle to addressing the problem of military suicide. Approximately 14 percent of the Army population is currently prescribed an opiate.[24] Forty-five percent of accidental or undetermined Army deaths from 2006 to 2009 were caused by drug or alcohol toxicity,[25] and 29 percent of Army suicides between 2005 and 2010 included drug or alcohol use.[26]

Data collected from civilian populations indicate that adults aged 18-34 are the most likely to have attempted drug-related suicides,[27] and that 58.9 percent of drug-related suicide attempts resulting in visits to an emergency room involve psychotherapeutic drugs.[28] Another 36 percent of emergency room visits for suicide attempts involve pain medications.[29] If we anticipate similar rates among military service members, it is important to address the excess prescription medicine among military service members. Yet, there is no opportunity to do so. When military doctors prescribe an alternative medication or dosage from what a service member was previously prescribed, there is no request made for the service member to return the remainder of his or her prior medication. Instead, military doctors dispense additional medications, because only law enforcement personnel can conduct "take-back" programs for medications. On January 26, 2011, the Army Vice Chief of Staff requested that the Drug Enforcement Administration (DEA) permit the Army's military treatment facilities and pharmacies to accept excess prescription medicine for disposal.[30] The request was denied.

Recommendation

The DEA should grant the DOD authority to accept and destroy excess prescription medication from military service members. Given this authority, the Office of the Army Surgeon General should initiate an effort with the Navy, Air Force and Coast Guard surgeon generals to develop policies and practices regarding how best to account for, and regain possession of, excess prescription medications. Such a drug take-back program will be targeted to the military services, but could also help ensure that service members do not transition out of the military with surplus prescription medications.

Challenge VIII

The DOD approach to suicide prevention depends heavily on what experts refer to as "gatekeeper strategies." The Army, for example, asserts that "[t]here is no other aspect of [its suicide prevention] that is more important for preventing negative outcomes than the vigilance of the individual commander, supervisor, Soldier, law enforcement agent or program/service provider. Leaders, supervisors, and 'Buddies' represent the first level for surveillance of high risk behavior."[31] Although medical and academic experts identify gatekeeper approaches as one of the most promising strategies,[32] the limitations of this approach are notable for the Guard and Reserve, where there are long monthly gaps between drill periods when leaders and peers do not have the opportunity to watch for warning signs. Yet studies indicate that even the smallest amount of contact can reduce the risk of suicide.[33] These findings suggest that even postcards or text messages from unit leaders between drill weekends can help prevent suicides.

Recommendation

The DOD should address weaknesses in gatekeeper-based programs for drilling Guard and Reserve units. Specifically, Guard and Reserve units should develop a leadership communication plan that addresses the stresses on units and details the frequency and method (written, electronic or telephone) by which small unit leaders should remain in contact with their subordinates. Leaders should pay closer attention to this communication following a deployment. Such communication could especially help save the lives of our country's "affiliated veterans," those who periodically return to uniform, either for drill or mobilization and deployment.

Challenge IX

Assessing which suicide prevention strategies are effective requires systematic efforts to understand military suicide. Yet these efforts are thwarted by the existence of too many programs. Suicide prevention programs in the National Guard are a decentralized multitude that the Adjutant General (TAG) of each state and U.S. territory initiates and manages. This grassroots solution is inefficient given that, while some states had more suicides than others, overall the Army National Guard averages slightly more than one suicide per state annually. Although the individual programs may use evidence-based approaches, it will be difficult to demonstrate which suicide prevention programs are effective with the military community or efficacious in reducing suicide, because the small numbers do not support rigorous analysis. Even more important, these programs risk reduction or elimination due to dwindling state resources. This is the case of Minnesota, where there exists both the highest number of National Guard suicides, and also dwindling resources to address their problem.[34]

Recommendation

The National Guard should reduce the number of unique suicide prevention programs, and consider adoption of a systemwide, centrally funded, prevention approach.

CONCLUSION

Addressing suicide among service members and veterans is integral to the fitness and sustainability of the all-volunteer force. It will take a collaborative effort by DOD, VA, federal and state legislatures, and communities to curb suicide among those who have served the United States. The military must take better care of its own. Although a goal of no suicides is unachievable, the increasing number of suicides is unacceptable. Additionally, although the benefits and services available from the VHA will likely remain the best system of care for veterans, the DOD has moral responsibility to acknowledge and understand former service members.

The CNAS policy brief, from which my comments are extracted, is entitled *Losing the Battle: The Challenge of Military Suicide*. America is currently losing its battle against suicide by veterans and service members. As more troops return from deployment, the risk will only grow. To honor those who have served and to protect the future health of the all-volunteer force, America must renew its commitment to its service members and veterans. The time has come to fight this threat more effectively and with greater urgency. Thank you for addressing your attention to this critically important battle.

End Notes

[1] Text refers to period from July 2007 to March 2010. Department of Veterans Affairs, Fact Sheet: VHA Suicide Prevention Program, Facts About Veteran Suicide.

[2] Department of Defense, "The Challenge and the Promise: Strengthening the Force, Preventing Suicide, and Saving Lives," Final Report of the DOD Task Force on Prevention of Suicide by Members of the Armed Forces (August 2010), provides data through 2009. The 2010 data are from the Department of Defense, *Department of Defense Suicide Event Report*, Calendar Year 2010 Annual Report (September 2011).

[3] Department of Veterans Affairs, Fact Sheet: VHA Suicide Prevention Program, Facts About Veteran Suicide (March 2010).

[4] This relationship has not been evident in prior analyses and is not evident in suicide data from the Navy, Air Force, Marine Corps or Coast Guard.

[5] Sandra A. Black et al., "Prevalence and Risk Factors Associated with Suicides of Army Soldiers 2001-2009," *Military Psychology* 23 no. 4 (July 2011), 433-451.

[6] Department of Veterans Affairs, Memorandum from Deputy Under Secretary for Health for Operations and Management, "Recent VHA Findings Regarding TBI History and Suicide Risk" (October 29, 2009) Department of Veterans Affairs, Memorandum from Deputy Under Secretary for Health for Operations and Management, "Recent VHA Findings Regarding TBI History and Suicide Risk" (October 29, 2009).

[7] Sandra A. Black et al., "Prevalence and Risk Factors Associated with Suicides of Army Soldiers 2001-2009," 442; and E. C. Harris and B. Barraclough, "Suicide as an Outcome for Mental Disorders: A Meta-analysis," *British Journal of Psychiatry* 170 no. 3 (March 1997), 205-228.

[8] Thomas Joiner, *Why People Die by Suicide* (Cambridge, MA: Harvard University Press, 2007).

[9] See the discussion of these effects in Edward A. Selby et al., "Overcoming the Fear of Lethal Injury: Evaluating Suicidal Behavior in the Military through the Lens of the Interpersonal-Psychological Theory of Suicide," *Clinical Psychology Review* 30 no. 3 (April 2010), 298-307.

[10] Craig J. Bryan et al., "Challenges and Considerations for Managing Suicide Risk in Combat Zones," *Military Medicine* 175 no. 10 (October 2010), 713-718; and Edward A. Selby et al., "Overcoming the Fear of Lethal Injury."

[11] C. J. Bryan et al., "A Preliminary Test of the Interpersonal-Psychological Theory of Suicide Behavior in a Military Sample," *Personality and Individual Differences* 48 no. 3 (February 2010), 347-350.

[12] The states are Alaska, Colorado, Georgia, Kentucky, Maryland, Massachusetts, New Jersey, New Mexico, North Carolina, Oklahoma, Oregon, Rhode Island, South Carolina, Utah, Virginia and Wisconsin.

[13] Even if all states indicate veteran status, suicides will still be underreported because of the vulnerability of civilian death data to the social stigma of suicide.

[14] The National Defense Authorization Act for FY 2010, Public Law 111-84, sec. 70.

[15] The Veteran Health Administration (VHA) is a subordinate organization to the Department of Veterans Affairs. The VHA is divided into 23 regions called Veterans Integrated Service Networks.

[16] Department of Veterans Affairs, Veterans Health Administration Handbook 1160.01 (September 11, 2008)

[17] Army personnel numbers are as of July 2011, from communication with Army Medical Command representative (September 29, 2011).

[18] The CDC is subordinate to the HHS.

[19] Fifty-seven percent of DOD suicides were seen at a military treatment facility in the month prior to their deaths. Department of Defense, *Department of Defense Suicide Event Report*, Calendar Year 2010 Annual Report (September 2011), 23.

[20] Department of Defense, *Department of Defense Suicide Event Report*, Calendar Year 2009 Annual Report (2010), 29; and Department of Defense, *Department of Defense Suicide Event Report*, Calendar Year 2008 Annual Report (2010), 26.

[21] Stephanie Gaskell, "Stigma of Posttraumatic Stress Disorder Is Greatest Challenge of Returning Troops: Mullen," *Daily News* (April 19, 2010).

[22] See, for example, the following news article for a publicized account of such ridicule: http://www.q13fox.com/news/kcpq-suicide-rate-spiking-at-jointbaselewismcchord-20110817,0,1023250.story.

[23] The authors interviewed veterans who did not mention their own TBI in response to the question, "Were you physically wounded during deployment?" When interviewees mentioned TBI in subsequent conversations, they would typically explain that their initial answer only included "real injuries.

[24] U.S. Army, *Health Promotion Risk Reduction Suicide Prevention Report* (August 2010), 45. Also, the Army estimates that 30,401 soldiers would test positive for a medical review officer–reviewable drug, with 3,925 representing illicit use. Ibid., 44.

[25] Ibid., 4.

[26] Ibid., 43.

[27] 2004 data, as reported by Substance Abuse and Mental Health Services Administration, *The OAS Report: Suicidal Thoughts, Suicide Attempts, Major Depressive Episode & Substance Use among Adults* 34 (2006), 5, http://www.oas.samhsa.gov/2k6/suicide/suicide.pdf, as of September 9, 2011.

[28] Substance Abuse and Mental Health Services Administration, *The OAS Report: Suicidal Thoughts, Suicide Attempts, Major Depressive Episode & Substance Use among Adults*, 6.

[29] Substance Abuse and Mental Health Services Administration, *The OAS Report: Suicidal Thoughts, Suicide Attempts, Major Depressive Episode & Substance Use among Adults*, 6.

[30] Peter W. Chiarelli, Vice Chief of Staff, U.S. Army, letter to Joseph T. Rannazzisi, Deputy Assistant Administrator, Drug Enforcement Administration, Office of Diversion Control (January 26, 2011).

[31] U.S. Army, *Health Promotion Risk Reduction Suicide Prevention Report*, 46.

[32] Mann et al., "Suicide Prevention Strategies: A Systematic Review."

[33] Alexandra Fleischmann et al., "Effectiveness of Brief Intervention and Contact for Suicide Attempters: A Randomized Controlled Trial in Five Countries," *Bulletin of the World Health Organization* 86 no. 9 (September 2008), 703-709.

[34] Mark Brunswick, "Anti-Suicide Program for Military Runs Low: Shortfall Comes as Minnesota Guard Fights High Suicide Rates," *Star Tribune*, October 2, 2011.

In: The Enemy Within
Editors: Jack M. Wright and Gabriel E. Lewis
ISBN: 978-1-62081-316-4

Chapter 8

PREVENTING VETERAN SUICIDE HEARING – WATKINS TESTIMONY*

Katherine E. Watkins

SUICIDE PREVENTION EFFORTS AND BEHAVIORAL HEALTH TREATMENT IN THE VETERANS HEALTH ADMINISTRATION[a]

Chairman Buerkle, Representative Michaud, and distinguished members of the Committee, thank you for inviting me to testify today. It is an honor and pleasure to be here. In this testimony, I will briefly summarize the evidence that mental illness has a strong association with suicide and that providing high-quality behavioral health treatment can reduce the risk of both attempted and completed suicide. Then I will describe the results of a recent study of the quality of behavioral health care provided by the Veterans Health Administration (VHA) to veterans with mental illness and substance use disorders and discuss the implications of this study's findings for suicide prevention. I will conclude by proposing specific steps which VHA could take to improve the quality of care provided to veterans with mental illness and substance use disorders--steps which, if taken, could further reduce suicide risk among our nation's veterans.

While suicide remains a rare event that is difficult to predict, studying the characteristics of individuals who attempt and complete suicide allows us to identify common risk factors and thus direct efforts toward prevention. Research studies have shown that over 90 percent of suicide victims have a diagnosable mental illness.[1-5] In the veteran population, depressive disorders, post-traumatic stress disorder (PTSD), bipolar I disorder and drug and

* This is an edited, reformatted and augmented version of the House Committee on Veterans Affairs, Subcommittee on Health, Hearing on: Understanding and Preventing Veteran Suicide, dated February 12, 2011.

[a] The opinions and conclusions expressed in this testimony are the author's alone and should not be interpreted as representing those of RAND or any of the sponsors of its research. This product is part of the RAND Corporation testimony series. RAND testimonies record testimony presented by RAND associates to federal, state, or local legislative committees; government-appointed commissions and panels; and private review and oversight bodies. The RAND Corporation is a nonprofit institution that helps improve policy and decision making through research and analysis. RAND's publications do not necessarily reflect the opinions of its research clients and sponsors.

alcohol disorders are risk factors for both attempted and completed suicide.[6-10] In one study, among veterans being treated at a VA hospital after a suicide attempt, a review of their medical records indicated that 31.8 percent had a diagnosed alcohol disorder, 21.8 percent had a drug use disorder, 21.2 percent had a psychotic disorder, and 18.5 percent had a depressive disorder.[10] Another study of veterans who completed suicide showed that bipolar disorder posed the greatest estimated risk of suicide among men, and substance use disorders posed the greatest risk among women.[11] While most individuals with mental illness do not complete suicide, the strong association between mental disorders and suicide suggests that among those with vulnerability to suicide, untreated or worsening mental disorders may be causally related to suicide. Examples of vulnerability include a genetic predisposition to suicide and hopelessness.[12-15]

Identification and treatment of mental disorders is important because appropriate treatment for mental disorders may reduce the risk of suicide. Most of the data supporting this assertion come from cross-sectional studies which show an association between treatment and reduced risk. Among veterans who received a new diagnosis of depression, suicide attempt rates were lower among patients being appropriately treated with antidepressants than among those who were not.[16,17] Among individuals with bipolar disorder, continued treatment with mood-stabilizing drugs is associated with a decreased rate of completed suicide compared to brief or interrupted treatment with these medications, and the rate of suicide decreases consistently with the number of additional prescriptions.[18] Lithium and clozapine, two important pharmacotherapies for mental disorders, may have specific suicide-prevention qualities.[19,20] There are no studies of whether appropriate treatment for PTSD or for substance use disorders reduces suicide risk, although intoxication can exacerbate impulsivity and hopelessness, and many suicide attempts occur in the context of substance use.[6] This is an area where further research is needed. A recent RAND review of suicide prevention efforts in the US military concluded that the strongest empirical evidence for preventing suicide involved providing high-quality mental health treatment.[21]

The majority of individuals who die by suicide have contact with either a primary care or mental health provider in the year prior to the suicide, and nearly half have contact in the month before suicide.[22] In one study of veterans who had contact with VA treatment services and who completed suicide, all were outpatients at the time of death, 60 percent were hospitalized for psychiatric reasons in the year before death and 83 percent of those who were hospitalized completed suicide within two months of hospital discharge.6 In another study of 968 veterans who completed suicide in the community, 22 percent had received health care in the VA system in the year prior to death; of these, 58 percent had not seen a mental health professional.[23] These studies suggest that there are opportunities for health care providers to intervene, provide appropriate care, and possibly prevent suicide.

In 2005, the VA commissioned RAND and the Altarum Institute to conduct a comprehensive evaluation of the VA.'s mental health and substance use treatment system.[24-26] The results reported below describe care provided in fiscal years (FY) 2007 and 2008. We do not have data on whether the quality of care has changed since then.

In FY 2008 there were 906,394 veterans receiving care at the VHA for one or more of the following diagnoses: schizophrenia, bipolar I disorder, PTSD, major depressive disorder, and substance use disorders. Although they represented approximately 3.8 percent of the estimated number of all living veterans and 16.5 percent of all veterans who used VHA services in FY 2008, they accounted for 34.4 percent of all VHA costs. Approximately half had either multiple mental health conditions or a co-existing physical condition. The majority of utilization and costs were for the treatment of physical health conditions.

To evaluate quality of care, the research team developed 88 performance indicators,[27] or measures of the quality of care. We used indicators to assess the degree to which recommended care was delivered and to identify gaps in quality. Some indicators applied only to a single diagnosis, such as antidepressant use in major depression, and some applied across diagnoses, such as assessment for suicide ideation. Where there was sufficient sample size, we evaluated performance by Veterans Integrated Service Network (VISN), age, gender, rural/urban residence and Operation Enduring Freedom/Operation Iraqi Freedom (OEF/OIF) status.

Below I discuss study findings as they may relate to suicide prevention. Results are reported as VHA national averages. VISN level performance was estimated to identify average VISN performance and to test whether each VISN was significantly above or below the average VISN performance. A list of VISN number and region is provided at the end of the document (see Table 1). Evidence-based treatments are treatments that have been demonstrated through research to be effective.

Evidence-Based Treatment for Major Depression

Among veterans with major depression, treatment with antidepressants is associated with decreased suicide risk. Almost half (48 percent) of veterans beginning a new treatment episode for major depression filled prescriptions for a 12-week supply of antidepressant medication; 20 percent did not fill any prescription for antidepressants during the appropriate timeframe. There was a 20 percentage point difference between the highest and lowest performing VISNs for this performance indicator. Six VISNs (9, 15, 19, 20, 22 and 23) performed significantly better than the VISN average. Another seven VISNs (3, 5, 7, 8, 12, 16 and 18) performed significantly below the VISN average. Those veterans least likely to have the requisite 12-week supply were younger, rural, and had served in OEF/OIF. While some veterans may not want antidepressants, the observed variation of 20 percentage points across VISNs suggests that care can, and should, improve in those VISNs with lower rates.

To minimize the likelihood of relapse, antidepressants need to be continued for 4 to 9 months. However, only 31.2 percent of veterans in a new episode of treatment for major depression filled prescriptions for a 6-month supply of antidepressant medication; and 17.1 percent filled no prescriptions for antidepressant medication. The remaining 51.3 percent of veterans filled a prescription, but for less than a 6-month supply. While some veterans may choose to terminate treatment prematurely, research suggests that clinical interventions such as telephone outreach can improve medication adherence[28] and outcomes. Adherence means using the medication as prescribed.

Among all study veterans who were beginning a new episode of treatment, only 38.3 percent received at least one psychotherapy visit. Among those with major depression who were receiving psychotherapy, 30.9 percent received psychotherapy that had elements of cognitive behavioral therapy, an evidence-based treatment for major depression. For those veterans receiving psychotherapy, increasing the delivery of evidence-based psychotherapy could improve outcomes and decrease suicide risk.

Evidence-Based Treatment for Bipolar I Disorder

Continuous treatment with a mood stabilizer medication is the mainstay of treatment for bipolar I disorder and is associated with a decreased rate of completed suicide.[18,29,30] Thirty-two percent of veterans with bipolar I disorder received continuous treatment with a mood stabilizer, 81.2 percent received intermittent treatment and 18.8 percent did not receive any treatment with a mood stabilizer. The difference between the highest and lowest performing VISNS was 12.1 percentage points. Seven VISNS (1, 6, 11, 15, 19, 20) had proportions that were higher than the average VISN and an equal number of VISNS (3, 5, 8, 12, 16, 18 and 21) had proportions that were lower. Eight percent of veterans with bipolar 1 disorder received inappropriate treatment of an antidepressant without use of a mood stabilizer, a practice associated with higher levels of suicidal behavior.[29] Veterans over age 65 or under age 35, and OEF/OIF veterans were at greatest risk for not receiving appropriate care.

Research suggests that use of lithium as a mood stabilizer may have specific suicide-prevention properties. However the therapeutic range within which the beneficial effects of lithium outweighs its toxic effects is quite narrow, and there is substantial clinical consensus that lithium levels should be monitored. Among patients with bipolar I disorder who were beginning treatment with lithium, (N=2,562 out of a total number of 65,090 with bipolar 1 disorder and 14,285 veterans in a new treatment episode), 51.6 percent received lithium drug level monitoring in a timely manner.

Evidence-Based Treatment for PTSD

Although PTSD increases suicide risk, it is unknown whether treatment for PTSD reduces suicide risk. This is an important area for further research. We found that 20 percent of veterans with PTSD who were receiving psychotherapy had documentation that at least one psychotherapy visit contained elements consistent with cognitive behavioral therapy, an evidence-based treatment for PTSD. Significantly fewer veterans at one VISN (VISN 10) had documentation of any visits with elements of cognitive behavioral therapy. Among veterans not receiving psychotherapy who were beginning a new episode of treatment for PTSD, 26 percent received an adequate trial of selective serotonin reuptake inhibitors, a class of antidepressants.

Evidence-Based Treatment for Schizophrenia

Continuous treatment with antipsychotic medication is critical for preventing relapse and rehospitalization[31] among patients with schizophrenia. Approximately 37 percent of veterans in the schizophrenia diagnostic cohort received continuous treatment with an antipsychotic medication. Over 80 percent filled at least one prescription for an antipsychotic medication and 18.1 percent did not receive any antipsychotic medication. There was significant variation across VISNs, with the percentage difference between the highest and lowest performing VISN being almost 20 percentage points. Seven VISNs (1, 10, 11, 15, 19,

20, and 23) significantly exceed the VISN average; an equal number of VISNs (3, 5, 7, 8, 16, 18, and 22) had 12-month supply fill rates significantly lower than the VISN average.

EVIDENCE-BASED TREATMENT FOR DRUG AND ALCOHOL DISORDERS

Numerous clinical trials have proven brief interventions to be effective for individuals with alcohol abuse. In our study, fifty-nine percent of veterans with alcohol abuse or dependence had documentation that they received a brief intervention for their alcohol use, 35 percent had a documented referral to mental health specialty care, and 5 percent were already in specialty care. Overall, 71 percent had documentation of appropriate care. VISN 9 had a significantly lower proportion of veterans with documentation of appropriate care. There is substantial empirical support for pharmacotherapy for individuals with alcohol dependence. For veterans beginning treatment for alcohol dependence, 6 percent received pharmacotherapy.

ASSESSMENT FOR SUICIDE IDEATION AND EMPLOYMENT AND HOUSING PROBLEMS

Identification of and attention to psychosocial stressors are key components of high-quality psychiatric care and may also decrease suicide risk. In cross-sectional studies, psychosocial stressors such as unemployment are associated with attempted and completed suicide.[9,32-39] Among the mentally ill, homelessness is also associated with suicide. In a study of 7,224 homeless individuals with mental illness, rates of lifetime suicide attempts were above 50 percent; 26.9 percent of the sample had a suicide attempt that resulted in a medical hospitalization.[35] While it is unknown whether interventions to decrease unemployment and homelessness would decrease suicide risk, attention to these issues is a critical part of quality mental health care. Identifying whether clinical interventions to address homelessness and unemployment among the mentally ill reduce risk is an important area for further study.

The mental health assessment of a new patient should include an evaluation of suicide ideation and the patient's psychosocial support system.[40,41] We found that 82 percent of veterans in the study were assessed for suicide ideation. Three VISNs (4, 6 and 7) had significantly higher proportions of documentation of suicide ideation assessment, and two VISNs (2 and 19) had significantly lower proportions. Among veterans with identified suicide ideation, 96.4 percent had documentation of appropriate follow-up.

Assessment of psychosocial needs includes finding out whether the patient had an acceptable physical shelter and whether or not the patient had purposeful daily activity. Among study veterans beginning a new episode of treatment, 60 percent had documentation of an assessment of housing needs, 62 percent had documentation of an assessment of employment needs, and 44 percent had documentation of both assessments. Compared to the average VISN, VISN 10 had a significantly greater proportion of veterans who had documentation of both assessments (57.9 percent) and VISN 18 had a significantly lower proportion (31.8 percent). This variation across VISNs (26 percentage points) was the largest for any indicator. More veterans with a documented need were offered housing services (81 percent) than were offered employment services (28 percent).

SUPPORTED EMPLOYMENT AND SOCIAL SKILLS TRAINING

Certain evidence-based forms of psychosocial rehabilitation, such as social skills training, increase the capacity of individuals with severe mental illness to live independently. Among veterans with schizophrenia who received any psychosocial treatment, 16 percent had documented receipt of social skills training. Supported employment is a type of intervention that helps individuals with severe mental illness get and maintain employment, and has a robust evidence base. Among veterans with bipolar disorder, schizophrenia or major depression with psychosis, 1.9 percent used supported employment during the study period. While there was variation across VISNS, no VISN was higher than 3 percent.

Summary and Recommendations

In general, the quality of care provided by the VHA is as good as or better than public or privately-funded care, and of note, most veterans with mental illness are being assessed for suicide and receiving appropriate follow-up. However, in other areas, the quality of care does not meet implicit VA expectations, and there is significant room for improvement. The best evidence to date regarding suicide prevention supports providing quality mental health care. Therefore our recommendations address how the VHA might improve the quality of care for veterans with mental illness and substance use disorders, which may decrease suicide risk.

Increase Proportion of Veterans Who Receive Recommended Length of Pharmacotherapy

More than half of study veterans who began medication treatment did not receive the recommended length of treatment, and more than two-thirds of those on maintenance treatment were non-adherent. This is important because adherence to medication improves outcomes and decreases suicide risk.

Clinical registries are tools that individual clinicians and administrators can access in real time, without technical assistance, and use to systematically monitor symptoms and improve adherence. Clinical registries are not the same as the registries the VA currently has for psychosis and depression. The use of clinical registries is an area with strong potential for quality improvement, since they can be used to track individuals with a specified set of health conditions over time in order to assess how a patient is responding to treatment and whether they are missing appointments or medication refills.

Recommended Strategies: We recommend that the VHA take the following steps:

1. Investigate the basis for low rates of medication adherence among the veteran population, with an emphasis on strategies to improve continuity.
2. Conduct an environmental scan to identify best practices related to clinical registries, with a particular focus on mental-health-specific implementation.
3. Procure or develop a clinical registry module for the VA.'s medical records system that minimizes the need for additional data entry and maintains ease of use and high-level tracking of evidence-based care.
4. Provide training in, and establish formal expectations for, use of registries.

Increase Proportion of Veterans with Documented Assessment of Housing and Employment Needs and Establish Responsibility for Housing and Employment Services

Less than two-thirds of veterans with one of the five mental illnesses studied have a documented assessment of their housing and employment needs. Housing and employment policies lack sufficient detail to identify whether the Veterans Health Administration or the Veterans Benefits Administration is responsible for services.

Recommended Strategies: Two actions are recommended:

1. Develop a standardized documentation template for assessment of psychosocial needs.[42]
2. Clarify what constitutes need for housing and employment services, and clearly define the role of the VHA and the Veterans Benefits Administration with regard to work and housing.

Establish Formal Expectations for Quality Measures

For most mental health treatments, there are no agreed-upon benchmarks to distinguish between levels of performance. Without articulated benchmarks, it is not possible to come to definitive judgments about quality or to judge whether the VA is meeting performance expectations.

Recommended Strategies: We recommend the following actions:

1. The VA should use a combination of empirical evidence on current performance, expert opinion, and performance data from comparable systems to set target benchmarks. At minimum, this benchmark should be the performance of the best-performing VISN.

2. Performance expectations should include a specific definition of the evidence-based treatment and what counts as meeting the benchmark.

Implement Standardized, Individualized Treatment Planning Documents

Treatment plans are incomplete and difficult to locate. In some cases they may not exist. There is no standardized way of documenting patient participation in treatment decisions.

Recommended Strategies: Two actions are recommended:

1. Implement and require the use of standardized, individualized treatment-planning documents that may be linked to problems most often associated with a particular diagnosis, services being offered, and the patient's goals for recovery. The VHA Office of Mental Health Services has recently purchased treatment-planning software but dissemination has been held up because of lack of personnel to integrate the software with the current electronic health record.
2. Incorporate the capacity for patients to comment on and document their participation in treatment planning.

Prioritize Efforts to Make Patient's Entire Health Record Accessible through a Common Portal, Both across and within VISNs

Some VISNs have an electronic health record system that allows any provider within the VISN to access the patient's chart in real time. Other VISNs do not have this capability and it is difficult to access health records across VISNs. This difficulty can potentially impair the quality of care veterans receive if they move or receive treatment in multiple locations.

Recommended Strategy:

1. Prioritize efforts to make patients.' entire health records accessible through a common portal to allow unfettered access and input by all clinicians caring for them across medical centers and VISNS in real time. The VA should direct the Office of Information Technology to ensure that clinicians can access patient data, regardless of where the patient receives care.

Develop and Disseminate National Standards for Evidence-Based Treatments

It is important that treatments be delivered with fidelity, or as they were designed to be delivered. Evidence-based treatments for which the VHA Office of Mental Health Services has disseminated written national standards appear to be implemented with more fidelity than treatments for which the VHA has not disseminated national standards. Specifying what is expected when a particular evidence-based treatment is delivered is an important first step in ensuring treatment fidelity and effectiveness.

Recommended Strategies:

1. Develop and disseminate national implementation standards for evidence-based treatments.
2. Use results from the extensive research conducted by VA implementation-science researchers to address the gaps identified by the evaluation. The VA is unique in that it

has a number of health-services research and development programs, as well as quality-improvement programs. Better communication between VA researchers and VA clinical services could help make use of VA expertise in this area.

Conduct Additional Research Using the Linked Data Set Developed by the Evaluation

Despite the comprehensiveness of our evaluation, a great deal more could be learned. We observed significant variations in performance across every characteristic we examined, sometimes by more than 25 percentage points. Understanding the cause of these variations could allow the VHA to develop strategies to help lower-performing VISNS improve. Knowledge of which practices and quality-improvement strategies are associated with the greatest increases in quality (outcomes) per unit cost could help the VA become more efficient.

Some priority areas for further research suggested by our results are below.

1. What is the basis for variations in care that we observed? To what extent are they a function of poor documentation rather than variation in performance?
2. What can be learned from high-performing or low-performing sites?
3. What are the costs associated with quality improvement?
4. How can high quality be achieved in the most cost-efficient manner?

We do not know how suicide can be prevented, but the best evidence to date supports providing quality mental health care. The VA has substantial capacity to deliver mental health and substance use treatment to veterans with mental illness, and it outperformed the private sector on most quality indicators, which most likely demonstrates the significant advantages that accrue from an organized, nationwide system of care. Nonetheless, the VA is falling short of its own implicit expectations for providing the highest quality of care for our nation.'s veterans. Our study revealed ways in which the VA could build upon its current system of care with marginal effort to improve quality and potentially prevent suicides.

Thank you again for the opportunity to testify today and to share the results of the research. Additional information about our study findings related and recommendations can be found at: http://www.rand.org/pubs/technical_ reports/TR956.html

Table 1. Total FY 2008 VA Mental Health Program Evaluation Veterans, by VISN

VISNF	VISN Name
1	New England Health Care System
2	VA Health Care Network Upstate New York
3	VA New York/New Jersey Health Care System
4	VA Stars and Stripes Health Care Network
5	VA Capitol Health Care Network
6	Mid-Atlantic Health Care Network
7	VA Southeast Network
8	Florida/Puerto Rico Sunshine Health Care Network
9	VA Mid-South Health Care Network
10	VA Health Care System of Ohio
11	Veterans in Partnership Network
12	VA Great Lakes Health Care Network
15	VA Heartland Network
16	South Central VA Health Care Network
17	VA Heart of Texas Health Care Network
18	VA Southwest Health Care Network
19	VA Rocky Mountain Network
20	VA Northwest Network
21	VA Sierra Pacific Network
22	VA Desert Pacific Health Care Network
23	VA Midwest Health Care Network

REFERENCES

[1] Cavanagh, JT; Carson, AJ; Sharpe, M; Lawrie, SM. Psychological autopsy studies of suicide: A systematic review. *Psychological Medicine*. 2003; 33(3), 395-405.

[2] Harris, EC; Barraclough, B. Suicide as an outcome for mental disorders. A meta-analysis. *The British Journal of Psychiatry*. Mar 1997; 170, 205-228.

[3] Wilcox, HC; Conner, KR; Caine, ED. Association of alcohol and drug use disorders and completed suicide: An empirical review of cohort studies. *Drug and Alcohol Dependence*. 2004; 76, Suppl: S11-19.

[4] Mann, JJ. A current perspective of suicide and attempted suicide. *Annals of Internal Medicine*. Feb 19 2002; 136(4), 302-311.

[5] National Institute of Mental Health. Suicide in the U.S.: Statistics and prevention. 2010; http://www.nimh.nih.gov/health/publications/suicide-in-the-us-statistics-and-prevention/index.shtml.

[6] Kleespies, PM; AhnAllen, CG; Knight, JA; Presskreischer, B; Barrs, KL; Boyd, BL; Dennis, JP. A study of self-injurious and suicidal behavior in a veteran population. *Psychological Services*. 2011; 8(3), 236-250.

[7] Brenner, LA; Betthauser, LM; Homaifar, BY; Villarreal, E; Harwood, JE; Staves, PJ; Huggins, JA. Posttraumatic stress disorder, traumatic brain injury, and suicide attempt

history among veterans receiving mental health services. *Suicide and Life-Threatening Behavior.* Aug 2011; 41(4), 416-423.

[8] Guerra, VS; Calhoun, PS. Examining the relation between posttraumatic stress disorder and suicidal ideation in an OEF/OIF veteran sample. *Journal of Anxiety Disorders.* Jan 2011; 25(1),12-18.

[9] Lemaire, CM; Graham, DP. Factors associated with suicidal ideation in OEF/OIF veterans. *Journal of Affective Disorders.* 2011;130(1-2), 231-238.

[10] Weiner, J; Richmond, TS; Conigliaro, J; Wiebe, DJ. Military veteran mortality following a survived suicide attempt. *BMC Public Health.* 2011;11, 374.

[11] Ilgen, MA; Bohnert, AS; Ignacio, RV; McCarthy, JF; Valenstein, MM; Kim, HM; Blow, FC. Psychiatric diagnoses and risk of suicide in veterans. *Archives of General Psychiatry.* Nov 2010;67(11), 1152-1158.

[12] Brent, DA; Mann, JJ. Family genetic studies, suicide, and suicidal behavior. *American Journal of Medical Genetics Part C Seminars in Medical Genetics.* Feb 15 2005;133C(1), 13-24.

[13] Courtet, P; Guillaume, S; Malafosse, A; Jollant, F. Genes, suicide and decisions. *European Psychiatry.* Jun 2010; 25(5), 294-296.

[14] McMillan, D; Gilbody, S; Beresford, E; Neilly, L. Can we predict suicide and non-fatal self-harm with the Beck Hopelessness Scale? A meta-analysis. *Psychological Medicine.* 2007; 37(6), 769-778.

[15] Tsai, SJ; Hong, CJ; Liou, YJ. Recent molecular genetic studies and methodological issues in suicide research. *Progress in Neuro-Psychopharmacology and Biological Psychiatry.* 2011; 35(4), 809-817.

[16] Gibbons, RD; Amatya, AK; Brown, CH; Hur, K; Marcus, SM; Bhaumik, DK; Mann, JJ. Post-approval drug safety surveillance. *Annual Review of Public Health.* 2010; 31, 419-437.

[17] Gibbons, RD; Brown, CH; Hur, K; Marcus, SM; Bhaumik, DK; Erkens, JA; Herings, RM; Mann, JJ. Early evidence on the effects of regulators' suicidality warnings on SSRI prescriptions and suicide in children and adolescents. *American Journal of Psychiatry.* 2007; 164(9), 1356-1363.

[18] Sondergard, L; Lopez, AG; Andersen, PK; Kessing, LV. Mood-stabilizing pharmacological treatment in bipolar disorders and risk of suicide. *Bipolar Disordorders.* 2008; 10(1), 87-94.

[19] Cipriani, A; Pretty, H; Hawton, K; Geddes, JR. Lithium in the prevention of suicidal behavior and all-cause mortality in patients with mood disorders: A systematic review of randomized trials. *American Journal of Psychiatry.* 2005; 162(10), 1805-1819.

[20] Meltzer, HY; Bobo, WV. Pharmacological management of suicide risk in schizophrenia. In: Tatarelli R, Pompili M, Girardi P, eds. *Suicide in schizophrenia.* Hauppauge, NY: Nova Biomedical Books; 2007: 275-302.

[21] Ramchand, R; Acosta, J; Burns, RM; Jaycox, LH; Pernin, CG. The war within: Preventing suicide in the U.S. military. *Santa Monica, CA: RAND Corporation*;2011.
Luoma, JB; Martin, CE; Pearson, JL. Contact with mental health and primary care providers before suicide: a review of the evidence. *American Journal of Psychiatry.* Jun 2002; 159(6), 909-916.

[22] Basham, C; Denneson, LM; Millet, L; Shen, X; Duckart, J; Dobscha, SK. Characteristics and VA health care utilization of U.S. Veterans who completed suicide

in Oregon between 2000 and 2005. *Suicide and Life-Threatening Behavior*. Jun 2011; 41(3), 287-296.

[23] Watkins, KE; Keyser, DJ; Smith, B; Mannle, TE; Kivlahan, DR; Paddock, SM; Mattox, T; Horvitz-Lennon, M; Pincus, HA. Transforming mental healthcare in the Veterans Health Administration: A model for measuring performance to improve access, quality, and outcomes. *Journal for Healthcare Quality*. Nov-Dec 2010; 32(6), 33-42; quiz 42-33. PMCJournal-In Process.

[24] Watkins, KE; Pincus, HA; Paddock, S; Smith, B; Woodroffe, A; Farmer, C; Sorbero, ME; Horvitz-Lennon, M; Mannle, T; Jr.; Hepner, KA; Solomon, J; Call, C. Care for veterans with mental and substance use disorders: good performance, but room to improve on many measures. *Health Affairs*. Nov 2011; 30(11), 2194-2203.

[25] Watkins, KE; Smith, B; Paddock, SM; Mannie, TE; Woodroffe, A; Solomon, J; Sorbero, M; Farmer, C; Hepner, KA; Adamson, D; Forrest, L; Call, C; Pincus, HA. Program evaluation of VHA mental health services: Capstone report (Contract # GS 10 F-0261K). *Alexandria, VA: Altarum Institute and RAND-University of Pittsburgh Health Institute* 2010.

[26] Watkins, KE; Horvitz-Lennon, M; Caldarone, LB; Shugarman, LR; Smith, B; Mannle, TE; Kivlahan, DR; Pincus, HA. Developing medical record-based performance indicators to measure the quality of mental healthcare. *Journal for Healthcare Quality*. 2011; 33(1), 4967. PMID 21199073.

[27] Haynes, RB; Ackloo, E; Sahota, N; McDonald, HP; Yao, X. Interventions for enhancing medication adherence. *Cochrane Database of Systematic Reviews*. 2008(2), CD000011.

[28] Rihmer, Z. Pharmacological prevention of suicide in bipolar patients --a realizable target. *Journal of Affective Disorders*. Nov 2007; 103(1-3), 1-3.

[29] Yerevanian, BI; Koek, RJ; Mintz, J; Akiskal, HS. Bipolar pharmacotherapy and suicidal behavior Part 2. The impact of antidepressants. *Journal of Affective Disorders*. Nov 2007; 103(1-3), 13-21.

[30] Kane, JM. Review of treatments that can ameliorate nonadherence in patients with schizophrenia. *The Journal of Clinical Psychiatry*. 2006; 67 Suppl 5: 9-14.

[31] Blakely, TA; Collings, SC; Atkinson, J. Unemployment and suicide. Evidence for a causal association? *Journal of Epidemiology and Community Health*. Aug 2003; 57(8), 594-600.

[32] Mäki, N; Martikainen, P. A register-based study on excess suicide mortality among unemployed men and women during different levels of unemployment in Finland. *Journal of Epidemiology and Community Health*. 2010. http://jech.bmj.com/content/early/2010/10/21/jech.2009. 105908.long.

[33] Prigerson, HG; Desai, RA; Liu-Mares, W; Rosenheck, RA. Suicidal ideation and suicide attempts in homeless mentally ill persons: age-specific risks of substance abuse. *Social Psychiatry and Psychiatric Epidemiology*. Apr 2003; 38(4), 213-219.

[34] Desai, RA; Liu-Mares, W; Dausey, DJ; Rosenheck, RA. Suicidal ideation and suicide attempts in a sample of homeless people with mental illness. *Journal of Nervous and Mental Disease*. 2003; 191(6), 365-371.

[35] Eynan, R; Langley, J; Tolomiczenko, G; Rhodes, AE; Links, P; Wasylenki, D; Goering, P. The association between homelessness and suicidal ideation and behaviors: Results

of a cross-sectional survey. *Suicide and Life-Threatening Behavior.* 2002; 32(4), 418-427.

[36] Sundararaman, R; Panangala, SV; Lister, SA. Suicide prevention among veterans. Washington, DC: Congressional Research Services;2008.

[37] Fitzpatrick, KM; Irwin, J; Lagory, M; Ritchey, F. Just thinking about it: Social capital and suicide ideation among homeless persons. *Journal of Health Psychology.* 2007; 12(5), 750-760.

[38] Mäkinen, IH; Wasserman, D. Labour market, work environment and suicide. *Oxford Textbook of Suicidology and Suicide Prevention.* New York, NY: Oxford University Press; 2009.

[39] American Psychiatric Association. Practice Guidelines for the Treatment of Psychiatric Disorders Compendium. Washington, D.C.: American Psychiatric Association; 2006.

[40] Veterans Administration, Department of Defense. Management of persons with psychoses. Washington DC: Veterans Health Administration, Department of Veterans Affairs, and Health Affairs, Department of Defense; 2004.

[41] First, MB; Pincus, HA; Schoenbaum, M. Issues for DSM-V: adding problem codes to facilitate assessment of quality of care. *American Journal of Psychiatry.* 2009; 166(1), 1113.

In: The Enemy Within
Editors: Jack M. Wright and Gabriel E. Lewis

ISBN: 978-1-62081-316-4

Chapter 9

PREVENTING VETERAN SUICIDE HEARING – KEMP TESTIMONY*

Jan E. Kemp

Chairwoman Buerkle, Ranking Member Michaud, and members of the Subcommittee: Thank you for the opportunity to appear before you today to discuss the Department of Veterans Affairs' (VA) efforts to reduce suicide among America's Veterans. I am accompanied today by Antonette Zeiss, Ph.D., Chief Consultant for Mental Health, VHA. My testimony today will cover four areas: first, recent data on suicidality in Veterans and VA's Suicide Prevention Program; second, VA's Veterans Crisis Line and Veterans Chat (an online resource); third, VA's outreach and informational awareness efforts to reduce suicide among Veterans; and finally, VA's impact on reducing suicide among high risk Veterans.

Let me begin by saying how very important this issue is to VA and all of us in the VA health community. We believe even one suicide among our Servicemembers or Veterans is one too many. According to the recently released "Charting the Future of Suicide Prevention: A 2010 Progress Review of the National Strategy and Recommendations for the Decade Ahead" prepared by the Suicide Prevention Resource Center and Suicide Prevention Action Network, the Veterans Health Administration (VHA) has "developed a comprehensive strategy to address suicides and suicidal behavior that includes a number of initiatives and innovations that hold great promise for preventing suicide attempts and completions." The Review was developed by the Suicide Prevention Resource Center (a national suicide prevention education organization),with funding from the Department of Health and Human Services (HHS) Substance Abuse and Mental Health Services Administration (SAMHSA) for the National Action Alliance for Suicide Prevention. The Action Alliance is the public-private partnership advancing the National Strategy for Suicide Prevention and was launched in September 2010. The Review cites VA as becoming one of the most vibrant forces in the U.S. suicide prevention movement, implementing multiple levels of innovative and state-of-the-art interventions, backed up by a robust research capacity. We have initiated several

* This is an edited, reformatted and augmented version of the House Committee on Veterans Affairs, Subcommittee on Health, Hearing on: Understanding and Preventing Veteran Suicide, dated February 12, 2011.

programs that put VA in the forefront of suicide prevention for the nation. Chief among these are:

- Establishment of a national Crisis Line, Chat Service, and texting option, including a major advertising campaign to provide the Crisis Line phone number and Web site to all Veterans and their families;
- Placement of Suicide Prevention Coordinators (SPC) at all VA medical centers;
- Development of an enhanced package of care for high risk Veterans;
- Expansion of mental health services;
- Integration of primary care and mental health services; and
- Creation of a new "Make the Connection" campaign to help make it easier to seek mental health assistance.

I will discuss these initiatives in detail later in my testimony.

VA's Suicide Prevention Program

In response to the urgent need for suicide prevention efforts, VA has significantly expanded its suicide prevention program since 2005, when it initiated the Mental Health Strategic Plan and the Mental Health Initiative Funding. In 2006, VA provided training on evidence-based interventions for suicide and provided funding to begin integrating mental health care into primary care settings and expanding services at community-based outpatient clinics (CBOC) for treatment of mental health conditions such as post-traumatic stress disorder (PTSD), and substance use disorders (SUD). In 2007, VA began providing specific funding and training for each facility to have a designated SPC; it also held the first Annual Suicide Awareness and Prevention Day and opened the Veterans Crisis Line (then referred to as the National Veterans Suicide Prevention Hotline) in partnership with SAMHSA.

VA also established access standards that require prompt evaluation of new patients (those who have not been seen in a mental health clinic in the last 24 months) with mental health concerns. New patients are contacted by a clinician competent to evaluate the urgency of the Veteran's mental health needs within 24 hours of their first referral. If it is determined that the Veteran has an urgent care need, appropriate arrangements (e.g., an immediate admission) are made. If the need is not urgent, the patient must be seen for a full mental health diagnostic evaluation and development and initiation of an appropriate treatment plan within 14 days. VA accomplishes its access standards more than 95 percent of the time. In 2007, VA initiated system-wide suicide assessments for those Veterans screening positive for PTSD and depression in primary care; instituted training for Operation S.A.V.E. (which trains non-clinicians to recognize the SIGNS of suicidal thinking, to ASK Veterans questions about suicidal thoughts, to VALIDATE the Veteran's experience, and to ENCOURAGE the Veteran to seek treatment); and required SPCs to begin tracking and reporting suicidal behavior. In addition, VA added more SPCs in its larger medical centers and CBOCs, doubling the number of dedicated suicide prevention staff in the field. By 2008, VA had re-established a monitor for mental health follow-up after patients were discharged from inpatient mental health units, developed an on-line clinical suicide risk training program, and held a fourth regional conference on evidence-based interventions for suicide.

VA also added the development of an enhanced package of care for high risk patients. Evidence clearly demonstrates that once a person has manifested suicidal behavior, he or she is more likely to try it again. As a result, VA also has put in place sensitive procedures to enhance care for Veterans who are known to be at high risk for suicide. Whenever Veterans are identified as surviving an attempt or are otherwise identified as being at high risk, they are placed on the facility high-risk list and their chart is flagged such that local providers are alerted to the suicide risk for these Veterans. In addition, the SPC will contact the Veteran's primary care and mental health provider to ensure that all components of an enhanced care mental health package are implemented. These include a review of the current care plan, addition of possible treatment elements known to reduce suicide risk, ongoing monitoring and specific processes of follow-up for missed appointments, individualized discussion about means reduction, identification of a family member or friend with the Veteran's consent (either to be involved in care or to be contacted, if necessary), and collaborative development with the Veteran of a written safety plan to be included in the medical record and provided to the Veteran. In addition, pursuant to VA policy, SPCs are responsible for, among other things, training of all VA staff who have contact with patients, including clerks, schedulers, and those who are in telephone contact with Veterans, so they know how to get immediate help when Veterans express any suicide plan or intent.

The enhanced care package also includes mandates for follow-up after the high risk designation and safety planning. In 2009, VA launched the Veterans Chat Service to create an online presence for the Veterans Crisis Line.. VA developed and disseminated training programs for safety planning and has continued to monitor all of these efforts and implement facility-specific strategies over the past few years. VA has also released new training programs concerning issues in specific populations, such as geriatrics and women.

VA has augmented the original SPC placement at every facility and large CBOCs with additional suicide prevention team staff, and these staff members are an important component of our mental health staffing. The SPCs ensure local planning and coordination of mental health care and support Veterans who are at high risk for suicide, provide education and training for VA staff, do outreach in the community to educate Veterans and health care groups about suicide risk and VA care, and provide direct clinical care for Veterans at increased risk for suicide. One of the main mechanisms to access enhanced care provided to high risk patients is through the Veterans Crisis Line, and the linkages between the Crisis Line and the local SPCs. For example, when a Veteran, in crisis, calls the Crisis Line, he or she is provided a referral for immediate care, a high risk flag is placed on the chart and the Veteran is provided high risk services. The Crisis Line staff follows up to assure that this care is provided.

VA cannot accomplish this mission alone; instead, it works in close collaboration with other local and Federal partners, including SAMHSA in the Department of Health and Human Services (HHS), and brings together the diverse resources within VA, including individual facilities such as the Center of Excellence in Canandaigua, New York and a Mental Illness Research and Education Clinical Center in Veterans Integrated Service Network (VISN) 19 (Denver, CO). We also work closely with community agencies across the country. The DoD and VA are working together on a number of issues and the VA is a member of the DoD Suicide Prevention and Risk Reduction Workgroup. The DoD/VA Nomenclature and Data

Working Group is moving toward common definitions of fatal and non-fatal suicide events, and working toward a joint data base to better capture the impact of suicide on the military community as a whole.

During fiscal year (FY) 2011, VA's SPCs reported 16,976 suicide attempts among patients and non-patients, 779 of which were fatal (4.5 percent). One of the premises of the VA suicide prevention program is that we can make a difference in Veterans who have attempted suicide and are known to be at high risk. The percentage of those who died from suicide (and reported by VA's Suicide Prevention Coordinators) with a report of previous suicide attempts decreased from 31 percent in FY 2009 to 27 percent in FY 2010 and FY 2011. This suggests that the strategy of implementing the enhanced care package with our high risk patients has been effective.

It is not possible to determine if the reported cases are representative of suicidality in VA's patient population, but we do know that suicidality can be both an acute and a chronic condition. Those who survive attempts are at high risk for reattempting and dying from suicide within a year, so it is essential that we engage survivors in intensified treatment to prevent further suicides. It is precisely because of this concern that VA has initiated the post-discharge follow-up for patients leaving its inpatient mental health units. The data reported above include self-reporting of previous suicide attempts that have not been validated by VA, and all estimates are based on events reported in the SPC database and may not represent the complete number of suicide attempts among Veterans. Also, the records of suicide attempts for 136 Veterans were incomplete and omitted from this analysis.

VA's Vet Centers also fulfill a critical role in reducing the risk of Veteran suicide. Vet Centers promote access to care by helping Veterans and families overcome barriers that impede them from utilizing other benefits or services. Vet Centers remain a unique and proven component of care by providing an alternate door for combat Veterans not ready to access the VA health care system. There are currently 296 Vet Centers operating with four more scheduled to open by the end of 2011. This will bring the total to 300 Vet Centers across the country and in surrounding territories (the U.S. Virgin Islands, Puerto Rico, Guam, and American Samoa). Thirty-nine (39) of these Vet Centers are currently located in rural or highly rural areas. In addition, seventy (70) Mobile Vet Centers provide early access to returning combat Veterans through outreach to a variety of military and community events, including demobilization activities.

Crisis Line and Veterans Chat Service

VHA's Crisis Line started in July 2007, and the Veterans Chat Service was started in July 2009. To date the Crisis Line has:

- Received over 500,000 calls;
- Initiated over 18,000 rescues;
- Referred over 73,000 Veterans to local VA SPCs, for same day or next day services;
- Answered calls from over 6,700 Active Duty Servicemembers;
- Responded to over 31,000 chats; and

- Initiated a pilot program that uses text messaging that is reaching a new group of Veterans who are much more likely to use text messaging than to call.

The Crisis Line has 20 active phone lines and is staffed with mental health professionals and support staff to provide services 24 hours, 7 days a week, 365 days a year. After receiving a call from a Veteran, Servicemember or family member, the responder conducts a phone interview to assess the Veteran's emotional, functional, and psychological condition. The responder then determines the level of the call, namely whether it is emergent, urgent, routine, or informational.

Calls requiring emergency services necessitate keeping the caller (or the person about whom the caller is concerned) safe; urgent care requires same day services at a local VA facility; and routine calls require a consultation by the local SPC. Consults occur if a Veteran consents to a consultation or if emergency services are required; these consults are simply alerts to the SPC and do not mean the Veteran is suicidal. Even if the Veteran is already engaged in treatment, a consultation can be done to alert the SPC to changes in the Veteran's circumstances or to other needs he or she may have.

The online version of the Crisis Line, the Veterans Chat Service, enables Veterans, family members and friends to chat anonymously with a trained VA counselor. If the counselor determines there is an emergent need, the counselor can take immediate steps to transfer the visitor to the Hotline, where further counseling and referral services can be provided and crisis intervention steps can be taken. Veterans Crisis Line and Chat Service are intended to reach out to all Veterans, whether they are enrolled in VA health care or not.

OUTREACH AND AWARENESS OF VA'S SUICIDE PREVENTION EFFORTS

This past year, VA looked hard at its plan to communicate to Veterans and their families the highlights of the Suicide Prevention program as well as those of the Crisis Line and Chat Service. VA and SAMHSA continue to work together to ensure all Americans in emotional distress or suicidal crisis have a single confidential number (1-800-273-8255) to call for help. After much deliberation and consultation with Veterans and users, VA determined that to reach more Veterans and to relay the message that treatment works, it would strategically rebrand the national Veterans Suicide Prevention Hotline An important component of this comprehensive effort involved a new name: *Veterans Crisis Line*, which establishes a unique identity for this critical service. Research informed VA's decision to rebrand the service as a crisis line, thus lowering the threshold from "suicide" to "crisis" for Veterans, Servicemembers, and their families to encourage them to make that critical first call for help. The rebranding is an integrated national outreach effort to increase awareness and use of the Veterans Crisis Line and confidential online chat service, support and promote broader VA suicide prevention efforts, and promote help-seeking behaviors among Veterans at risk of suicide and other mental health problems. The new messaging reinforces the confidentiality of the Veterans Crisis Line for Veterans, Servicemembers, and their families, who may be the first to realize a Veteran is in crisis. Messaging efforts also involve all Service branch representatives to provide messages and "looks" to materials that are Servicemember specific.

As discussed previously, VA's SPCs do a tremendous amount of work to raise awareness about warning signs associated with suicide and the availability of treatment and support. For example, in a typical month, VA's SPCs provide approximately 700 informational and outreach programs in their local communities. As a result, VA identifies approximately 1,500 high risk Veterans a month and adds them to the High Risk List. Between 90 and 95 percent of these Veterans complete safety plans and are involved in the enhanced care package.

In addition to these measures, VA has been aggressively advertising this information and improving outreach to Veterans and family members alike. Suicide prevention outreach needs to use carefully tailored and targeted messaging. Unlike outreach for many other health issues which rely on underscoring the prevalence of the problem, outreach for suicide prevention that emphasizes rising suicide rates among Veterans runs the risk of normalizing suicidal behaviors, helping to convince Veterans in crisis that considering suicide is a normal or even expected response to their challenges—and possibly leading to an increase in suicide attempts. Through our messaging efforts, VA provides effective and safe outreach that focuses on affirming Veterans' strength and resilience and reinforcing help-seeking behavior.

In recent years, VA has supported a series of public education campaigns designed to increase awareness of crisis resources and promote seeking help among Veterans experiencing distress. VA has evaluated each of these campaigns in an effort to understand the impact of public education efforts on calls to crisis services and attitudes related to crisis service use. In a series of studies, VA evaluated the impact of implementation of the Veterans Crisis Line on total call volume to VA and non-VA crisis services, comparisons of call volume in campaign implementation and control communities, and associations between exposure to public education campaign media and willingness to use crisis services when experiencing distress. Results from these assessments have demonstrated strong relationships between implementation of the Veterans Crisis Line and increased use of VA and non-VA toll-free crisis services, significantly increased call volume in communities where concentrated public education campaigns have been implemented, and an increased willingness to use crisis services following exposure to public education media. Together, results from these studies provide consistent evidence of the impact of public education campaigns on awareness and use of crisis services. VA is continuing to assess the impact of public education campaigns for both the Veterans Crisis Line and the Make the Connection campaign in a series of studies designed to measure the impact of repeated exposure to media material among high risk and general populations and the efficacy of media messages tailored to individual histories. A total of four Public Service Announcements have been released and widely distributed. VA spends approximately $4.5 million on this public awareness campaign annually.

VA's Impact on Reducing Suicide

On the macro level, one way to evaluate the impact of VA mental health care and VA's suicide prevention program is to evaluate suicide rates. However, before addressing this issue, it is important to consider who accesses VA health care. For this, it is useful to refer to findings on those Veterans returning from Afghanistan and Iraq who participated in the Post-Deployment Health Re-Assessment (PDHRA) program administered by DoD. Between

February 2008 and September 2009, approximately 119,000 returning Veterans completed PDHRA assessments using the most recent version of DoD's PDHRA form. Of the more than 101,000 who screened negative for Post-Traumatic Stress Disorder (PTSD), 43,681 (43 percent) came to VA for health care services. Among 17,853 who screened positive for PTSD, 12,674 (71 percent) came to VA for health care services. These findings demonstrate that Veterans screening positive for PTSD were substantially more likely to come to VA for care. Findings about depression were similar. Both sets of findings support earlier evidence that those Veterans who come to VA are those who are more likely to need care and to be at higher risk for suicide. The increased risk factor for suicide among those who came to VA is often referred to as a case mix difference. We have just received the 2009 death data from the National Death Index and have begun to look at these numbers in relationship to Veterans who receive care in VA. We are encouraged by these data, which indicate that there is no increase in rates among VA users despite national increases, especially in middle-aged men. We believe that this indicates that our strategies are having an effect. There are some overall positive indicators that include:

- Suicide rates among Veterans who use VA health care have decreased since 2001.
- There is a decrease in suicide rates among Veterans under 30 who use VA health care relative to Veterans who do not use VA services, in those states that report through the National Violent Death Reporting System (NVDRS).
- There is a recent decrease in rates in men aged 40-59 receiving care from VA relative to rates of men of this age in America as a whole.

Specific information obtained from the 2009 data, for Veterans who use VA health care, includes:

- In FY 2009, the suicide rate per 100,000 person-years among all VA health care users was 35.9, as compared to 36.6 in FY 2008. Among males, it was 38.3, versus 38.7 in FY 2008. Among females, it was 12.8, versus 15.0 in FY 2008.
- In FY 2009, there were 22 suicides among male Operation Enduring Freedom/Operation Iraqi Freedom (OEF/OIF) Veterans age 18-24. The suicide rate in this group was 47.1 per 100,000. By comparison, in FY 2008, there were 32 suicides and a rate of 75.4 per 100,000.
- In FY 2009, the suicide rate among individuals with mental health or substance use disorder diagnoses was 56.4 per 100,000, as compared to 23.5 among patients without these diagnoses. The resulting rate ratio was 2.4. This continues a steady trend of reducing rate ratios observed since FY 2001, when the rate among patients with mental health or substance use disorder diagnoses was 78.0 as compare to 24.7 among patients without these diagnoses (rate ratio of 3.2)

VA's Ongoing Research to Identify Risk Factors for Suicide Prevention and Treatment

VA's research portfolio includes studies focused on identifying risk factors for suicide, prevention, and treatment. Risk factors being studied include co-morbid disorders, medications, and behaviors. A few specific examples include:

- In one study, VA researchers seek to determine the prevalence of suicide ideation, plans, and attempts resulting in medical treatment among Veterans currently enrolled in VA's health care system. The researchers will also collect data on a limited number of established risk factors and characteristics unique to military service that can be used to understand correlates of non-fatal suicidal behaviors.
- A VA Suicide and Self-Harm Classification System and Clinical Tool is being evaluated to determine the feasibility for implementation in diverse VA treatment settings and to assess its impact on health care system processes pertaining to the assessment and management of suicide risk.
- The VISN 2 Center of Excellence, in Canandaigua, NY, in collaboration with the National Center for Homelessness among Veterans, is conducting a study of risk factors for suicide among Veterans with a history of homelessness or housing instability. Characteristics of service utilization, the independent effect of homelessness, and differences in risk associated with psychiatric diagnoses are being studied through the use of homeless intake assessments, non-fatal suicide event data, and data obtained from the National Death Index.
- VA researchers are determining the role of a brain chemical called serotonin in suicide and seek to discover whether alterations in levels of this chemical impact suicide.
- The Suicide Assessment and Follow-up Engagement: Veteran Emergency Treatment Project (SAFE VET) is a clinical demonstration project that focuses on providing a brief intervention and follow-up for suicidal Veterans who present to the Emergency Department and Urgent Care Services and who do not require hospitalization. This study also permits us to longitudinally follow risk factors in Veterans identified as being at moderate risk for suicide.
- Motivational Interviewing to Prevent Suicide in High Risk Veterans is a study to test the efficacy of an adaptation of Motivational Interviewing to Address Suicidal Ideation (MI-SI) on the severity of suicidal ideation in psychiatrically hospitalized Veterans at high risk for suicide. The researchers also are examining the impact of MI-SI on risk factors for suicide in Veterans, such as treatment engagement and psychiatric symptoms.
- Many completed studies addressing suicide epidemiology have been published by VA investigators, providing important information related to risk factors.
- VA is also doing extensive work in traumatic brain injury (TBI), including how Veterans with a TBI may be at risk for mental health issues and suicide. Our work in TBI will also give us a broader knowledge about suicide in general.

Conclusion

Madam Chairwoman, as my testimony demonstrates, VA's efforts to provide comprehensive suicide prevention services are comprehensive and continuously improving. Since our suicide prevention effort began in 2005 we have revisited it often to make sure it continues to meet our Veterans' needs, made adjustments when necessary, and will continue to do so as new research helps us uncover new ways to prevent these tragedies. It is clear our mission will not be fully achieved until every Veteran contemplating suicide is able to secure the services he or she needs. The Department appreciates Congressional support of our work in this area. I am prepared to answer your questions.

INDEX

A

B

C

D

E

F

G

H

I

J

N

O

P

S

T

U

V

W

Y